Ruth Dunnell $3850

S0-BYW-175 1989

LORDSHIP AND INHERITANCE IN
EARLY MEDIEVAL JAPAN

JEFFREY P. MASS

Lordship and Inheritance in Early Medieval Japan

A STUDY OF THE KAMAKURA
SŌRYŌ SYSTEM

Stanford University Press, Stanford, California   1989

Stanford University Press
Stanford, California
© 1989 by the Board of Trustees of the
Leland Stanford Junior University
Printed in the United States of America

CIP data are at the end of the book

The photograph on the dust jacket is from *Kamakura bushi*
(vol. 6 of the *Nihon rekishi* series; Tokyo, 1966), p. 22,
and appears by permission of the
Sekai Bunka Publishing Company.

For Rosa

ACKNOWLEDGMENTS

This is the fourth volume of a projected five dealing with warrior government and warrior institutions in Japan's Kamakura age (1180–1333). In the first three volumes, I examined the emergence of the regime itself (the Kamakura Bakufu), its vassal officers in the field (*shugo* and *jitō*), its interaction with the traditional Court-centered polity in Kyoto, and its primary role as a peacemaker and judicial authority, among other related subjects. However, I devoted only limited attention to the rank-and-file warrior houses that made up the Bakufu's constituency. In the present study I will therefore examine the social and economic milieu in which these provincial families operated. As we shall see, the primary determinant of the shape of the warrior family and of intrafamilial relations was property and the patterns of its transmission. The focus of this book will be on property and inheritance in Japan's early medieval age.

I am grateful to various people for their assistance at different stages of this project. My primary debt is to my graduate students, with whom I regularly discussed inheritance issues and with whom I often debated translation problems. The students, now young scholars, who deserve special mention are Bruce Batten, Andrew Goble, and Tom Keirstead. Additionally, I was given valuable assistance by four other students, Karl Friday, Leo Hanami, Joan Piggott, and Hitomi Tonomura. The most unstinting colleague support came from Peter Arnesen, now unhappily lost to our field. In Japan, Seno Seiichirō and Takeuchi Rizō were always generous with their time, as was Kanai Madoka. In England, James McMullen deserves special mention for urging me to complete the manuscript. He said he wanted to read the book. Finally, I must thank the various Japan Centers here and abroad that invited me to speak on my favorite subject and whose members then tested me on my understanding of it.

Financial assistance for the project began with a Guggenheim Fellowship, was continued by grants from the SSRC and Pew Foundation, and ended with support from the Association for Asian Studies (travel grant) and from Stanford University's Japan Fund. To all of these institutions, and to Oxford University, which has given me a new home every year, I am extremely grateful. Finally, I must thank Norris Pope of Stanford University Press for not running for cover at the prospect of doing another one of my books.

J.P.M.

CONTENTS

AUTHOR'S NOTE

The 150 documents translated in this book are cited in the notes by number, date, and type (e.g., Document 55: 1237/8/25 Fujiwara Iekado yuzurijō). At the end of the Documents section I have appended a Chronological Index of Documents Translated, and a list of Document Collections Represented in the Translations. Document collections cited as sources appear in the Bibliography under the name of the volume (or article) in which the collection is published, rather than under the name of their compiler/editor. By contrast, secondary sources are listed in the Bibliography by author.

The following abbreviations are used in the notes to both text and documents:

AK   *Azuma kagami*
DKR   *The Development of Kamakura Rule, 1180–1250*
DNK   *Dai Nihon komonjo*
DNS   *Dai Nihon Shiryō*
HI   *Heian ibun*
KB   *The Kamakura Bakufu: A Study in Documents*
KBSS   *Kamakura bakufu saikyojō shū*
KI   *Kamakura ibun*
WG   *Warrior Government in Early Medieval Japan: A Study of the Kamakura Bakufu, Shugo, and Jitō*

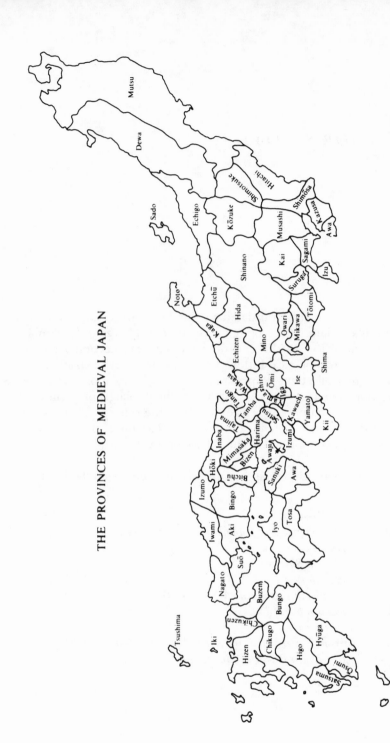

THE PROVINCES OF MEDIEVAL JAPAN

LORDSHIP AND INHERITANCE IN
EARLY MEDIEVAL JAPAN

INTRODUCTION

The appearance of the Kamakura Bakufu in the 1180s marked an important stage in the maturation of the provincial warrior aristocracy in Japan. The Bakufu's emergence meant a shift in the center of gravity away from the Court and absentee estate-holding to a warrior class now seeking to wield authority in its own right. In my earlier studies I noted that the most energetic of these fighting families were concerned with improving their conditions vis-à-vis the civil and religious proprietors (*ryōke*) on whose estates (*shōen*) they served as Kamakura-appointed managers (*jitō*). But the gradual success they registered in this one area neither rested on nor produced much in the way of internal house solidarity. In fact, intrafamily strife among warriors was as much a part of the Kamakura story as was interclass tension. Belying the well-known subordination of self to house so commonly attributed to the Japanese people as a whole, warrior families in the Kamakura age proved remarkably fragile. The balance that was sought (but never more than impermanently struck) between competing house members represents a key link in the institutional chain that shaped Japan's early medieval experience.

The world in which the warriors found themselves was naturally a product of Japan's earlier history. A statist conception of authority had originated in the seventh and eighth centuries when the top rank of society, seeking to escape prior weaknesses, adopted new institutions of land control and central and local administration, mirroring the Chinese system of imperial government. What gave the experiment its coherence were coordinate rank and title hierarchies embracing all officialdom and centered in the new imperial capital of Nara (710–84). During the succeeding Heian period (794–1185) this elaborately conceived bureaucratic scheme began to unravel, but the basic top-to-bottom ordering of society remained intact. Central officials converted themselves into an estate-owning aristocracy, and provincial types, now armed, became the country's land managers and policemen. By the middle of the twelfth century a distinct warrior class had come to dominate the local scene but as yet enjoyed no major share in the national governance of Japan.

During the 1160s and 1170s the leader of one of the country's two great warrior clans, Taira Kiyomori, forced his way into the ruling clique within the capital. However, he was hard pressed to develop new institutions of rule and ended by alienating both his courtier associates and his erstwhile warrior comrades. In 1180, Minamoto Yoritomo, the head of the other great warrior clan, recognized the vulnerability of the Taira-dominated central polity and gathered about himself fighting families wishing to force a change. Setting up headquarters in the eastern village of Kamakura, Yoritomo declared war (the historic Genpei, or Minamoto-Taira, conflict of 1180–85), and out of the ensuing breakdown of order created Japan's first warrior government, the Kamakura Bakufu.[1]

Establishment of the Bakufu, however, did not mean the end of civil rule in Kyoto. Yoritomo's objectives remained limited, paralleling the limitations on his power. The Genpei conflict unleashed a wave of warrior lawlessness locally, obliging the Minamoto chieftain to retain the Court-centered system of authority as a counterweight to military men run amok. There thus evolved the distinctive dyarchy that best describes government in Kamakura times. The Bakufu would take responsibility for protecting and restraining its own vassal-followers, but would guarantee to the Court its historic position atop the land system. In practice, this meant deploying a limited network of constables and stewards (*shugo* and *jitō*) throughout the country, but keeping in place the civil monopoly of estate ownership, as well as the preexisting networks of capital-appointed provincial and estate functionaries.[2]

From the beginning the compromise proved to be fragile, since the men and interests of Kamakura and of Kyoto were now in a sense standing parallel to one another. Yet the equilibrium held for the most part, largely because of Kamakura's willingness to police its own men and because of the remarkably sophisticated institutions of jus-

[1] For the Taira, the rise of warriors, the Genpei War, and the founding of the Bakufu, see *WG*, chaps. 1–4.

[2] For the "dual polity," *shugo*, and *jitō*, see *WG*, chaps. 5–8.

tice that became the centerpiece of its governance.[3] A gradual tilt in favor of the warriors occurred during the thirteenth century, though the trend remained strictly controlled. The fighting men who had gone to war in the 1180s to improve their situations locally were thus only partly successful. With rights in land, rather than lordships over it, they had to take special care to husband and distribute their property. It was within this milieu that Kamakura's vassals (*gokenin*) became prone to seemingly endless family disputes. This is the story that we will take up in the pages that follow.

In all societies there are complex variables that influence how kin relate to one another. Perhaps the most important are the ways in which the principles and practices of family organization and asset transmission intersect. In Japan's Kamakura age, the warrior houses needed to identify ways to perpetuate their existence yet also provide life-supporting shares for individual members. Tensions might develop here, since the disposition of property could either bind or divide a house: the splitting of assets determined to a large extent how people were split. Conditions were further complicated by the absence of uniform rules regarding such matters. Strategy alternated with whim, progeny remained congenitally insecure, and family fortunes often rose and fell on the basis of noninstitutional factors. The thirteenth century may have been a time of unprecedented opportunity for many warrior houses, but few such families seemed able to organize themselves for maximum efficiency.

Standing above all this was the Kamakura Bakufu, whose principal aim was to forestall instability by promoting a view that the past should determine the future. The problem was that economic necessity often required breaking free from the constraints of family and the status quo. To combat this situation the Bakufu adopted policies that were themselves sometimes at odds. For example, whereas it encouraged the authority of house heads vis-à-vis the junior generation, it largely discouraged such power in regard to a head's own collaterals. This was a natural concomitant of partible inheritance, which was standard among warriors at the time: siblings received shares from their parents, which needed to be protected from grasping head-designates. Kamakura was thus obliged to make its tribunals available as family courts and to uphold sibling interests without hopelessly undermining the collective. The Bakufu, at any rate, was intimately involved with the present and future of its followers. It

[3] Kamakura justice is treated in detail in *DKR*, chaps. 3–6.

granted and validated their *jitō* rights and attempted to make sure
that these would not be abused. It also exercised an exclusive right of
certification for the wills and other releases that determined their succession. This latter authority is one that will concern us deeply as we
proceed to examine the progress of warrior houses during the Kamakura age.

For our purposes, the context within which these family and property relationships operated might be called the "inheritance system."[4]
In my earlier volumes I noted the abundance of documents dealing
with *jitō* and *shugo* and with Kamakura's judicial authority. Inheritance materials constitute the other major category of warrior house /
Bakufu records, though the sources often overlap. Since all *jitō* wrote
wills or other conveyances, many became involved in legal disputes
within their own families that Kamakura was called on to untangle.
These two activities—the passage of property and its legal defense—
generated literally a flood of documents, thousands of which survive today.

The number of releases (pre- and post-obit) is probably what is
most impressive. It indicates a belief in the efficacy of written instruments, a level of literacy in the provinces sufficient to nourish that
belief, and a conception of such documents as being both binding
and essential. Because of the long tradition of partible inheritance,
the deathbed wish was considered inadequate, since memories might
simply diverge along self-serving lines. In Europe, wills were commonly used to alienate property to the church, but in Japan the use of
testaments stayed mostly within the family and developed naturally
with hardening concepts of private property and with a growing obligation to parcel what was owned among descendants. As we shall see,
the separation of instruments in Japan for the transfer of property to
kin and non-kin was not absolute at first, though by mid-Kamakura
times devise and alienation were recognized as very different.

As we shall also observe, property concerns dictated to a considerable extent the size and character of the effective family unit—and
kept it as small as possible. Lineal, not lateral, inheritance was always
preferred, which meant that cousins and uncles belonged to their own

[4] Few studies in English have touched on inheritance practices in premodern Japan.
See McCullough, "Japanese Marriage Institutions in the Heian Period"; Kanda, "Methods of Land Transfer in Medieval Japan"; Steenstrup, *Hōjō Shigetoki (1198–1261) and
His Role in the History of Political and Ethical Ideas in Japan*, chap. 2; Wakita, "Marriage
and Property in Premodern Japan from the Perspective of Women's History"; and Arnesen, "The Struggle for Lordship in Late Heian Japan: The Case of Aki."

families before they did to some larger purposeful collective. It follows from this that parents controlled inheritances, though they did so—typical of the age—as individuals. Mothers and fathers independently inherited, possessed, and disposed of their own landed property.

The comparison with Europe is valuable for another reason. Historians of the West regularly remind us of the variation not only between countries but even between adjacent communities. This has little parallel in Japan, where it is possible to speak at least guardedly of countrywide patterns. If there is any distinction to be made it is between the capital and the countryside, that is, between the higher aristocracy and provincial types. What differences did exist locally were only qualifiedly institutional in nature, either idiosyncratic by family or a product of highly individual circumstances.

The point regarding uniformity is an important one, since the practices we discover do not seem to originate with a single region of Japan, i.e., the eastern provinces, which spawned the Kamakura Bakufu. This helps to explain why the Minamoto movement of the 1180s was able to draw in supporters from around the country: many of these houses were organized around similar principles and faced many of the same problems. It was because of their constitutional similarity—whatever their historical differences—that the Bakufu was successful in uniting them by identifying common denominators of concern.[5] At the same time, it suggests that the patterns of family organization and inheritance that we recognize as characteristic of Kamakura times were themselves at least partly inherited. If we are to understand Japan's provincial elite under the Kamakura system, in other words, we need to go back and examine them at an earlier stage under the Heian state. Our study begins, therefore, in the pre-Kamakura era and concerns itself with the patterns of property transference that became one of the cornerstones of the later system.

[5] Typical of the view that medieval inheritance practices in Japan derived from the eastern region known as the Kantō is Murakami, "*Ie* Society as a Pattern of Civilization." For a critique of this position, see Hall, "Reflections on Murakami Yasusuke's '*Ie* Society as a Pattern of Civilization,'" p. 52.

PART ONE

CHAPTER 1

THE HEIAN LEGACY

We do not know how families were organized or how they transmitted property in the era before writing was introduced into Japan. Nevertheless, historians have offered a variety of hypotheses on these subjects, most emphasizing a communal system of possession and/or matrilineal descent patterns. The possibility of a matriarchy in pre-seventh-century Japan is perhaps the hub of this debate.[1] Whatever the case, women were not inferior to men in matters involving property—a condition that might have continued if not for revolutionary changes within the polity. Late in the seventh century, the state apparatus came to be overlaid with an elaborate bureaucracy on the model of that of the Chinese T'ang Empire. Its counterpart in the social sphere was a new patriarchal orientation that attempted to prescribe both the organization of the family and its accompanying succession system.

We know a considerable amount about these efforts from a series of codes promulgated at the time.[2] Not only was public authority minutely prescribed and defined, but much that we would call private was circumscribed under a rigid set of new regulations. For example, a strict formula was dictated for the distribution of house assets to heirs, and an equally strict order of precedence was imposed in the absence of an eldest son. According to the Taihō Code of 702, the residence, servants, and slaves were to go to the eldest son, with half the other mov-

---

An earlier version of this chapter appeared in the *Journal of Japanese Studies* 9, no. 1 (1983), pp. 67–95.

[1] See Wakita, "Marriage and Property," pp. 77–80.

[2] See, e.g., Miller, *Japan's First Bureaucracy: A Study of Eighth Century Government*.

ables going to him and the other half divided equally among his
brothers; daughters were to receive nothing. Similarly, in the event of
the eldest son's premature death, his inheritance was to fall to his own
eldest son, or, in the absence of the latter, to the original heir's younger
brother, then the original heir's second son, and so on down the
line.[3] What we encounter, therefore, are inheritance and succession
formulae whose very complexity—as in other aspects of the Taihō
program—made strict observance of the law largely unattainable.

This does not mean that the codal system failed to make positive
contributions. Under the previous Yamato kingdom, succession disputes had been endemic by virtue of the very absence of guidelines
that could be considered binding. When the codes established that eldest sons were to be made principal heirs, this helped impede much
of that earlier squabbling, since younger sons and brothers were now
aware that they were outside the main line of succession. The Taihō
Code made this explicit in law. But the principle might not have taken
hold had not experience and practicality dictated it. The classic illustration of this relates to the well-known Jinshin War of 672. This unusually severe bloodletting was precipitated by an imperial succession
dispute between a prince and his uncle, both of whom wished to be
emperor. Though the uncle, Tenmu, emerged victorious, fraternal
succession, which may have been common beforehand, was now at
least in part discredited.[4] Practice and principle were fortuitously
coming together.

A second contribution of the codal system derived from the stipulated percentage shares for certain house members. It seems possible
that the Taihō Code was reinforcing here a nonformulaic partible inheritance tradition already in existence. But the Taihō regulation, because it followed Chinese norms, disproportionately favored the principal heir and also excluded women. When the Yōrō Code superseded
its Taihō predecessor later in the eighth century, the new code brought
the regulation into closer accord with preferred Japanese practice.
Henceforth the principal heir would take control of all private chattel,
but residences, movables, and whatever land was held were to be di-

[3] This was the regulation for the highest nobility. See Fukuo Takeichirō, *Nihon kazoku
shi seido gaisetsu*, pp. 62–64.

[4] Hurst, "An Emperor Who Ruled as Well as Reigned: Temmu Tennō," pp. 26–27.
In fact, save for the principle of patrilineal descent, imperial successions never became
subject to a consistent formula; brothers in certain circumstances continued to succeed
one another. See Ronald P. Toby, "Why Leave Nara?" Fraternal succession became
much less frequent in provincial society.

vided on a $2:2:1:\frac{1}{2}$ basis among the heir, his mother, his brothers, and his sisters.[5] In this manner the earlier inequities were partially redressed, daughters were restored to the inheritance pool, and the partible principle that would remain the standard until almost the end of Kamakura times was legitimized. Similarly, with the partible principle now fully established in law, its excess baggage—the original percentage shares—could simply drop away, another victim of codal impracticability. At all events, the clear legacy of the codes' tampering in this area was lineal primogeniture in the matter of house succession, and divided inheritance in the matter of property. It was this kind of balance between corporate and individual needs that became the mainstay of the family system as a whole.

The codes were equally comprehensive and restrictive in other areas affecting the family—for instance, marriage and adoption. In other words, it was state business to prescribe norms regarding what to do in the event not only of an excess of heirs, but also of a dearth of heirs. The heirless man had the choice of adding wives or children or both. But once he made a decision to adopt, he was obliged to satisfy regulations regarding his relationship to the potential adoptee, the conditions of the adoption, etc.[6] And thus, once again, the presence of a legal mechanism to ensure continuity of the family paved the way for the much freer practices of Heian times. Before very long daughters as well as sons were being adopted, often from different clans.[7]

Strictly speaking, inheritance is the transmission of property at death,[8] and this is how the imperial codes envisioned it. But by also prescribing a sharing of assets by progeny, the codes promoted the potential for competition among siblings, which in turn led to the practice of premortem dispositions, and eventually to written conveyances. Sometimes these dispositions involved transmissions of the moment, but in other instances they were promises to pay, which also lent themselves to the emergence of instruments that might be a substitute for memory. The result was to cause all present and potential property owners to become increasingly mindful of their legacies. Inheritance strategy—which became a high art during the Kamakura period—was already a skill to be reckoned with by mid-Heian times. The inspiration for this naturally came from within the central aris-

---

[5] Fukuo Takeichirō, p. 65.
[6] *Ibid.*, pp. 59–61.
[7] *Ibid.*, p. 62.
[8] Goody, "Inheritance, Property, and Women," p. 14.

tocracy, though by the tenth century "estate-planning" techniques
were spreading into the countryside. It is this local dimension of property and inheritance that will be our principal concern in this book.[9]

The question of how provincial land and office first became pri-
vatized is one centering on the conversion of original allotment fields
and (especially) newly opened paddies into transmittable local tenures.[10] In the present treatment, our inquiry must be limited to issues
relating specifically to the conveyance of property, in particular the
following: (1) Who inherited and who released? (2) What was inherited and when? (3) What were the dominant modes and problems of
inheritance? (4) What was the role of higher authority? If we shed
light on some of these questions in their Heian phase, it should be
easier to understand the practices and principles of medieval times.

As early as the tenth century we find the first vehicles of property
transmission, called *shobunjō*. These documents, issued by a donor to a
recipient, included the specifications of the land in question, the fact
(and sometimes the history) of its ownership, the extent (sometimes)
of its fiscal obligations, and (often) a signature from higher authority
signifying the validity of the transmission. An example will illustrate
how this might work. In 996, a man, by his own admission now old,
transferred two parcels of paddy in Shima Province to a niece whom
he had adopted in the absence of true children. For one parcel he
appended a governor's *kugen* (the standard deed acknowledging a
holder's ownership), though for the other he admitted loss of the
kugen through theft. The lands in question had originally been obtained by purchase, and the appropriate sale deeds were also appended. Signatures of agents of the temple to which dues were owed
appear at the end of the document.[11]

What this conveyance reveals is the distance already traveled from
the heyday of the Nara codes. Governors were now recognizing pri-

[9] It needs to be observed that a large group of landholders was neither strictly local
nor central. These were middle-level officials with duties in or affecting the provinces.
Some in this category (or their descendants) became indigenized, whereas others did
not; often we cannot tell which. The survey that follows will try to get around this problem by concentrating on subproprietorships. By definition, these would not have been
held by the ranking elite at the center, even though some of the releases transmitting
them were likely written in Kyoto.

[10] On this subject, see Kiley, "Property and Political Authority in Early Medieval
Japan," chap. 2. Also useful on various aspects of "private land" (*shiryō*) is Uwayokote
Masataka, "Shiryō no tokushitsu."

[11] *Kōmyōji komonjo*, 996/11/3 Ifukube Toshimitsu jiden shobunjō an, *HI*, 2: 504–5,
doc. 362. On *kugen*, see Kanda, "Methods of Land Transfer."

vate tenures, which could be freely bought and sold; females were receiving inheritances and were also being adopted; and central landowning institutions were validating such transactions in exchange for the promise of regular revenues. It is clear from other releases of the tenth century that "hereditary lands" were being conveyed as discretion dictated,[12] a condition that gave impetus to the competitive instincts of heirs and that showed the need for central and provincial arbitration. Ironically, the freedom to convey property contributed directly to the emergence of judicial organs as a substitute for the nonarbitrary codes.

An incident from 971 shows "inheritance justice" already at work. In that year a district head (*gunji*) of Iga Province became involved in a dispute between a woman and her brothers. The woman claimed to have received a conveyance from her father, duly countersigned by her brothers, but, she argued, one of the brothers had infringed upon her land share. The *gunji* agreed with the petition and transmitted his own deposition on the woman's behalf to the proprietor of the estate in question.[13] In this instance, then, what was essentially a family dispute made its way up the ladder of authority, to be settled by an absentee landlord.

Early in the eleventh century we find the appearance of a second instrument of release, the *yuzurijō*. Eventually, this documentary form would become the standard vehicle of inheritance, though *shobunjō* continued to be used. In fact, the two were closely related, as indicated by a document of 1022 in which the term *shobun* appears in the opening while *yuzurijō* appears at the end.[14] Were these then identical? Though some scholars have apparently believed so,[15] others have sought to distinguish them along temporal lines. Thus *shobunjō* are seen as dispositions of the moment, whereas *yuzurijō* emerge as bequests at death. Unfortunately, the record itself tends to undermine this kind of distinction. Since the overwhelming majority of *shobunjō*

[12] E.g., *Tōji hyakugō monjo*, 997/2/28 sō Kaishū shobunjō, *HI*, 2: 505, doc. 364. Fewer than ten such releases survive in all, but various other documents from the tenth century refer to conveyances being made.

[13] *Tōnan'in monjo*, 971/5/22 Iga-no-kuni Abe gunji ge an, *HI*, 2: 440, doc. 299.

[14] *Dai Tōkyū kinen bunko shozō monjo*, 1022/4/26 sō Nōin denchi shobunjō, *HI*, 9: 3509, doc. 4605.

[15] Aida Nirō, for example, refers to the earliest surviving *shobunjō*—a document of 909 (*HI*, 1: 307, doc. 202)—as a *yuzurijō* in one volume and as a *shobunjō* in a companion volume: *Nihon no komonjo*, 1: 894, 2: 533. Satō Shin'ichi simply equates the two document types: *Komonjogaku nyūmon*, p. 252.

were transmissions to donors' children, they had the function—as well as the appearance—of being either pre- or post-obit releases. *Yuzurijō* operated similarly. Yet it is possible to identify a working distinction here. From beginning to end *shobunjō* conveyed land in the form of acreage. *Yuzurijō* did that too—but also came to transmit the landed officerships known as *shiki*. The numbers are revealing here. Of the total of 132 surviving *yuzurijō*, 27 conveyed *shiki*. Of the total of 89 *shobunjō*, not one transmitted a *shiki*.[16] It is also of note that the frequency ratio between these two vehicles gradually came to favor *yuzurijō*. By Kamakura times—clearly the dominant epoch of the *shiki* system—this document type was the nearly exclusive instrument of inheritance.

In 1028, we discover our earliest pure *yuzurijō*, which, as is often the case for emerging forms, is unusual. In it we note the passage of a salt farm to an adopted son (*yōshi*) by four persons, evidently brothers, who had owned the area jointly (*ai tomo ni*). The collective possession implied here was in fact something less than that since individual shares were specified and were being combined to make up a whole. The rationale for the adoption was quite normal—the absence of children—though the collective endeavor was not: four childless brothers were adopting a son and making him their joint heir.[17]

This early conveyance is of interest for a second reason. Its opening phrase *yuzuri-atau* appears on at least a few releases that are not wills, i.e., on sale deeds (*baiken*) and on land commendation documents (*kishinjō*). This suggests that, at this early juncture, the character of a transfer depended on the terms, not the form, of the passage. Though the *yuzurijō* conveying the salt farm was a will, in other cases this was not so—for example, a 1055 vehicle in which the recipient, no relation to the donor, was charged a "release fee" (*yuzuri-ryō*).[18] By the Kamakura period classes of documents were in closer accord with more "modern" types of transactions. But such distinctions would take time to develop.

Records of the eleventh century and beyond are plentiful enough

[16] The *shiki* / non-*shiki* distinction derives from a review of the entire corpus of surviving documents in the *Heian ibun* series. Suzuki Kunihiro (whose totals these are) confirms this conclusion but offers few examples and does not present an inventory in "Zaichi ryōshusei no keisei zokuen genri ni tsuite," pp. 9–12.

[17] *Nagahiro monjo*, 1028/2/13 Ōnakatomi Moriyasu tō enden yuzurijō an, *Ōita ken shiryō*, 3: 27, doc. 1.

[18] *Kyōto daigaku shozō Tōdaiji monjo*, 1055/9/20 Ki Tomoshige denchi yuzurijō, *HI*, 3: 856, doc. 730.

to show that rights of alienation were bound up with the status of individual parcels. Once a unit came to be certified as "owned," it became freely transferable. This made "long possession" superfluous: a title deed—not some ancestral connection—was the simple requirement for heritable ownership. A major consequence of this was the extraordinary movement that now became possible for individual land parcels. People could deal in real estate merely by transferring paper. The proof for this is nowhere more striking than in a sequence that began in 1056. During that year the well-known poet Fujiwara Sanetō deeded various holdings in Iga Province to a nephew, Nobuyoshi, whom he made his adopted son. Sixteen years later Nobuyoshi transferred the inheritance to his wife, Tōma-no-uji, in recognition of their "long years of marriage" (*nenrai fusai no gi*). Two years later, Tōma-no-uji sold two parcels of the land in question to the abbot of Yakushiji Temple, who in turn received a validation of this transaction from the Iga Province governor. The governor added a directive to the local cultivators in which he advised them to obey the orders of the abbot on what were now his "heritable holdings" (*denryō*).[19]

In the foregoing example, then, ownership not only changed hands three times in a twenty-year period; it also changed direction three times. The legacy of Sanetō went first to a nephew, next to the nephew's spouse, and finally (though only in part) to an unrelated priest. Of interest to us is the wife's inheritance and her obvious freedom to alienate her bequest. A survey of Heian-period documents indicates that husband-to-wife transfers were in fact not isolated occurrences. For example, during one eight-year span near the end of the Heian period, we find releases from husbands in no fewer than five cases. The first refers to a long-standing marriage (*nenrai fusai*), the second simply to a marriage (*fusai*), the third to a wife (*tsuma*), and the fourth to a mother's lengthy relationship with children (*nenrai kodomo no haha*). All four transfers involved conveyances made in perpetuity, with no suggestion of entails for the junior generation.[20] The fifth case—a deed

[19] *Tōnan'in monjo*, 1056/2/23 Fujiwara Sanetō shoryō yuzurijō an, *Iga-no-kuni Kuroda-no-shō shiryō*, 1: 55–59, doc. 50; *ibid.*, 1072/int.7/3 Fujiwara Nobuyoshi shobunjō an, 1: 74–75, doc. 68; *ibid.*, 1074/7/6 Tōma-no-uji shoryō baiken, 1: 75–76, doc. 69 (the governor's validation is appended); and *ibid.*, 1075/2/26 Iga kokushi chōsen an, 1: 76–77, doc. 71.

[20] *Kasuga jinja monjo*, 1156/11/24 Gangōji goshi Eikaku yuzurijō, *HI*, 6: 2355, doc. 2859; *Nejime monjo*, 1148/5/9 saki no Ōsumi no jō denpata yuzurijō, *HI*, 6: 2219–20, doc. 2646; *Kōmyōji komonjo*, 1153/10/12 Kōgō Wakasue enden shobunjō an, *HI*, 6: 2322, doc. 2789; *Tōdaiji monjo*, 1152/3/20 sō Hangi yuzurijō, *HI*, 6: 2292, doc. 2755.

of sale for property inherited by a widow—makes explicit a wife's freedom to alienate such legacies.[21]

What are we to make of this? In his study of Heian marriage practices McCullough has correctly observed that marriages were easily formed and easily broken, that polygamy was common, and that husbands and wives regularly lived apart or lived with the wife's family. Yet despite these clear obstacles to intimate, lasting relationships, it is obvious that gratitude and affection did at times induce husbands to bestow property on their wives. The phrase *nenrai fusai*, which might appear in wills as the justification for such bequests,[22] anticipates the Kamakura age when wives regularly inherited from their husbands.

The reverse, however, was rare. We find almost no instances of wives leaving property to their husbands, even though women (through their parents) were inheritors of land. A major reason for this is that widows were more common than widowers, though the bias obviously ran deeper than that. In the only clear-cut case of a conveyance to a husband, the wife's rationale began with the absence of children: only after noting this condition did she refer to a *nenrai fusai*.[23] By contrast, a husband who was also a father might favor a wife in addition to children.

It follows from the foregoing that there was little concept of community property issuing from a marriage. No land fell to the survivor unless explicitly devised,[24] and no releases bore both a mother's and a father's signature. The single exception I have found, a joint release to a daughter, appears to have been an immediate transfer.[25] Thus,

[21] *Tōji hyakugō monjo*, 1153/10 Sakanoue-no-uji baiken, *HI*, 6: 2322, doc. 2790.

[22] There are variations, e.g., *enyū no fusai taru ni yori*, in which *en* means "relation" or "bond," and *yū* is the character for "friend" or "companion." See *Kyōto daigaku shozō Tōdaiji monjo*, 1180/6/18 sō Sōken denpata shobunjō, *HI*, 8: 2997–98, doc. 3916. Such examples seem to date mostly from the twelfth century.

[23] *Kyōto daigaku shozō Tōdaiji monjo*, 1163/1/22 Shinamochi Nakako denchi yuzurijō, *HI*, 7: 2587, doc. 3240.

[24] A notable exception (which cannot be explained) appears in a document of 1118: a widower inherited his wife's unbequeathed property—and then proceeded to sell it. See *Tenri toshokan shozō monjo*, 1118/2/17 Sami Sukechika denchi baiken, *HI*, 5: 1679–80, doc. 1884. Much more typical was an incident of 1080 in which an imperial agency was called on to settle a dispute involving a widower's seizure of lands deeded by his late wife to a grandson. The widower's second wife was similarly accused of incursions. *Yasaka jinja monjo*, 1080/9/3 kebiishi-chō kudashibumi, *HI*, 3: 1180, doc. 1179. The grandson was confirmed in his inheritance. Suzuki Kunihiro, pp. 22–23, also makes the point about the absence of community property.

[25] *Chō komon-fu*, 1118/11/3 sō Ryōken fusai rensho shobunjō an, *HI*, 10: 3859, doc. 4974.

property was received independently by each of the partners and also disposed of that way. Whether it might be managed by the husband during the course of the marriage is a different issue—and one subject to considerable debate.[26] But even if property was so managed, one would need to prove deceit—as opposed to mere convenience— to make the case for some basic inequality. Joint management, like a merging of incomes, might just as easily have implied cooperation as something more sinister.

It follows, then, that it was only in the event of children that assets—by way of separate releases—might actually be combined.[27] At the same time, with the emphasis so clearly on independent possession, no well-developed concept of dowry appeared, if by dowry we mean a marriage portion consisting of property. A bridegroom might expect to receive his wardrobe, residence, and a father-in-law to promote his career.[28] But no land would change hands—at the point of the marriage or later. Brides did of course bring property into their marriages, but these were their own lands—daughters' shares, not wives'.

In fact, women were daughters and sisters before they were wives, mothers, and widows. There is no doubt that the Heian Japanese adhered to the sound principle that preference in inheritance be given to close women before distant males.[29] This meant that a father or mother would normally bequeath to a daughter before a brother, nephew, or grandson.[30] Moreover, daughters who inherited from fathers or mothers regularly received these legacies free of encumbrances. Much as in the case of wives who inherited, they were free to do with the legacies as they pleased. Thus in one instance an eldest daughter (*chakujo*) sold the inheritance she received from her father and even got her mother, now widowed, to cosign the deed of sale.[31]

---

[26] Ishii Ryōsuke has argued vigorously in favor of such male management authority; see "Chūsei kon'in hō." See also Wakita, "Marriage and Property," pp. 81–82. For a different opinion, see Endō Motoo, *Josei shi nōto.*

[27] E.g., in Kamakura times, Document 108: 1273/10/5 sō Kakujitsu yuzurijō an. Actual examples are hard to find, though.

[28] McCullough, pp. 118–27.

[29] For this principle, see Goody, *Production and Reproduction*, p. 93.

[30] There are numerous examples of daughters inheriting property: for an example from a father (with cosignatures by the eldest and second sons), see *Tōdaiji monjo*, 1151/1/29 Tachibana Seishu denchi shobunjō, *HI*, 6: 2276, doc. 2717; for an example from a mother, see *Daitokuji monjo*, 1156/12/3 Fujiwara-no-uji yuzurijō an, *HI*, 6: 2356– 57, doc. 2862.

[31] *Kujō ke monjo*, 1173/6/2 Minamoto Yoshimori no chakujo baiken, *HI*, 10: 173, supp. doc. 119.

Or in another, an inheriting daughter deeded the property to her own adopted daughter.[32]

Despite the advantageous position of women in their familial roles, it remains true that they could not hold government office. Moreover, whereas courtier women could at least possess proprietorships or custodianships over estates,[33] their provincial counterparts normally held no landed *shiki* whatever. These were both serious handicaps, since it meant that women could neither be appointed to nor inherit office; they were able to buy land or to have it released to them, but they could not enjoy the most prestigious and lucrative sources of wealth. At the same time, women were commonly referred to in documents as someone's wife or (especially) daughter, though their surnames were never those of their husbands.[34] It was their brothers who received the best inheritances—generally even from their mothers. Thus, whereas women could become great landowners, their political power was limited. As we shall see, much of this changed when the women of Kamakura were appointed to *shiki*, inherited them, and released them to their daughters. Yet there is no Heian precedent for this—a problem we shall return to presently.

Beyond the disposition of *shiki* to sons, there are other ways to show how males were the preferred vehicle for property exchanges. In the first place, there are decidedly more releases to sons than to daughters. But also, the critical ownership deeds (*kugen*) went to a son when land was parceled to several children. In fact, secondary wills and sale deeds regularly stated that original proof records could not be appended since a larger expanse of land was involved; property could be divided, but earlier validations could not. For example, in 1151 a father's release to his eldest daughter made the point directly—and substituted the signatures of his two eldest sons for the deeds that could not be included.[35] At any rate, siblings of both genders inherited

---

[32] *Tōdaiji monjo*, 1172/3 ama Myōren shobunjō, *HI*, 7: 2804, doc. 3601. The term "nenrai yōshi," meaning "long-time adoptee," appears here.

[33] For a female custodianship, see, e.g., *Ninnaji monjo*, 1134/int.12/15 Taikenmon-in-no-chō kudashibumi, *HI*, 5: 1956, doc. 2310.

[34] Women received given names from their parents and commonly adopted Buddhist names in their old age or widowhoods; for the first, see n. 23 above, for the second, n. 32. Perhaps their most frequent designation, however, was by the family of their origin, e.g., "Fujiwara-no-uji," in n. 30. Even husbands regularly denoted their wives this way: see, e.g., a husband's reference to "Ise-no-uji" in *Kōmyōji komonjo*, 1153/10/12 Kōgō Wakasue enden shobunjō an, *HI*, 6: 2322, doc. 2789.

[35] *Tōdaiji monjo*, 1151/1/29 Tachibana Seishu denchi shobunjō, *HI*, 6: 2276, doc. 2717. See below for a discussion of sibling cosignatures.

from both parents—but sons were given preference in the transfer of holdings whose integrity was critical to the line. This was especially the case when "titled" inheritances—*shiki*—were involved, as we shall see in greater detail later.

Before concluding our brief survey of women and property in the eleventh and twelfth centuries, it will be useful to address one further issue: the extent to which a woman's elder brother(s) maintained an interest in her holdings. In other words, were daughters granted inter vivos endowments, which would lapse upon their deaths and be restored to the main line? Phrased differently, were there life bequests, which were non-alienable, of the type that became so common in the Kamakura period? Though some scholars have apparently thought so, arguing that the absence of the phrase "in perpetuity" implied but a limited grant,[36] this is obviously incorrect. Not only are there a substantial number of releases to women made "in perpetuity,"[37] but there are no examples whatever of the reverse—transfers to daughters containing explicit reversion clauses.[38] Evidently the problem of too many heirs supported by too little property was not so critical that inheritances without encumbrances needed to be limited to sons.

It almost goes without saying, therefore, that entails excluding women are not seen at all, and that entails dictating the direction of female inheritances are few and not very ambitious. For example, in a conveyance of 1173 a woman referred to the last words (*yuigon*) of someone deceased (presumably her father) as she proceeded to name one of her legatees.[39] In another inheritance of nine years later, a woman was advised by her father not to go beyond her siblings (*kyōdai*) should she decide to dispose of her bequest by sale.[40] But this

[36] E.g., Ishii Ryōsuke, "Chūsei kon'in hō."

[37] See, e.g., the four releases by husbands cited in n. 20 above.

[38] There do exist, however, at least two releases to males in which female shares are promised. In the first, the promise was to a grandson, with the female unidentified; *Matano monjo*, 1051/2/25 sō Ryūen yuzurijō, *HI*, 3: 822, doc. 688. In the second, it is the recipient, not the donor, who promises the share of a female after her death, to a male. This appears in an addendum to the main document: *Kuhara bunko shozō monjo*, 1143/6/28 Jūyo denchi haibunjō, *HI*, 6: 2106, doc. 2516. (A later document identifies the male as the recipient's son: *Tōdaiji monjo*, 1160/2/7 Tōdaiji jōza Enson shobunjō, *HI*, 7: 2485–86, doc. 3048.) Both examples concern priestly bequests.

[39] *Tōdaiji monjo*, 1173/6/12 Ōe Sanko denpata shobunjō, *HI*, 7: 2820, doc. 3629. The legatee's relationship is not specified.

[40] *Katsuodera monjo*, 1182/6/11 sō Kakugi denchi ate-okonaijō an, *Minoo shishi, shiryō hen*, 1: 21, doc. 25. For an actual sale to a sibling, see *Ōhashi monjo*, 1073/11/12 sō Keiroku baiken, *HI*, 3: 1115, doc. 1095.

is the extent of it. Certainly there is nothing approaching the naming of grandsons and the barring of granddaughters that we encounter in the Kamakura age. And there is nothing to indicate that entails of whatever kind were considered binding either by legatees themselves or by responsible higher authorities.

The sternest check on a donee's freedom of action was undoubtedly his own parents, who, while still living, could expect obedience and filial behavior under threat of disinheritance (*gizetsu*). In the Kamakura period, such action could occur at any time, that is, before or after property had been promised, transferred, or validated. In the Heian age, rescinding an inheritance was not permitted under imperial or aristocratic (*kuge*) law,[41] though a few cases can be found near the end of the era.[42] In one complicated example of 1177, only the third son of five children was considered guileless by his father and was made sole heir. The eldest son, who had previously been entrusted with certain rice proceeds, was accused of being scheming and deceitful, was disinherited in 1175, and died a year later. Moreover, the second son and two daughters were similarly considered insolent, prompting their father to deny a "parent-child bond" (*oyako-kei*) with them. Only the third son was properly respectful, and he was therefore to be recognized as heir (*chakunan*) and to receive the hereditary house documents and accompanying inheritance.[43] In a second instance, a formal declaration of disinheritance (*gizetsujō*) was issued; and in a final case disinheritance was threatened for any future unfiliality (*fukō*).[44]

Bad blood between parents and children is condemned by all societies but nowhere more vehemently than in Japan. Because of the severity of the consequences and the disesteem in which such behavior was held, overt disobedience toward parents was probably transmuted in most instances into rivalry among siblings. To forestall such trouble, parents adopted a variety of techniques, among them the requiring of cosignatures on releases by those children not named in

[41] Haga Norihiko, *Sōryōsei*, p. 78.

[42] Before the mid-twelfth century the term *gizetsu* appears in only one surviving document—a record of 988; *Kujō ke hon-Engi shiki ura monjo*, 988/int.5/17 bō toijō, *HI*, 2: 468, doc. 327. The matter involved a lawsuit pitting children against a mother who had remarried and her husband.

[43] *Tōji hyakugō monjo*, 1177/11/28 Taira Suketō denpata shobunjō, an, *HI*, 8: 2922–23, doc. 3812.

[44] *Yōmei bunko Hyōhanki ura monjo*, 1164/6 Koremune Tadayuki gizetsujō, *HI*, 7: 2609–10, doc. 3286; *Tōdaiji shozō mondōshō ura monjo*, 1178/4/26 Fujiwara bō yuzurijō an, *HI*, 8: 2937–38, doc. 3826.

particular conveyances. Of dozens of possible examples, perhaps the most revealing is a sequence of three deeds dated the same day by the same donor. The first, from a mother to her first son, bears her signature plus the first son's; the second, to the second son, bears her signature plus the first son's; and the third, to the third son, bears her signature plus those of the first two sons.[45] In other words, the older progeny were obliged to give acknowledgment to a mother's release to those younger than themselves, clearly a form of pledge on their part not to interfere with those holdings in future. The opposite formula was equally common, i.e., a conveyance to an eldest son bearing the signatures of younger siblings, in effect a recognition by them of their older brother's position as primary heir.[46] In between there are diverse combinations of signatures,[47] revealing an obvious belief in the potential efficacy of such written assurances. The identical procedure was followed in the case of sale deeds: the seller obliged his children to cosign such documents as a way of having them renounce all future claim to the lands in question.[48]

Property owners attempted other forms of exhortation in an effort to guarantee peace among heirs. For example, the three sons of a local landholder in Kyushu's Satsuma Province were exhorted to be "of one mind" (*ichimi dōshin*) in administering (*ryōsaku*) the shares stipulated for them by their father.[49] A second father in Kyushu substituted

---

[45] *Tōdaiji monjo*, 1158/12/24 Fujiwara Nakako yuzurijō, *HI*, 6: 2440–41, docs. 2965, 2966, 2964. Or see a similar sequence of two *shobunjō* bearing complementary signatures: *Tōkyō daigaku shozō Tōdaiji monjo*, 1068/11/25 Sakanoue-no-uji shobunjō, *HI*, 3: 1055–56, doc. 1028; and *Sekido bunko shozō Tōdaiji monjo*, 1068/11/25 Sakanoue-no-uji shobunjō, *HI*, 3: 1056, doc. 1029. Same-day conveyances, though common in the Kamakura period, are rare during Heian times.

[46] For example, *Tōji hyakugō monjo*, 1160/10/5 Taira Moritō shobunjō, *HI*, 7: 2508, doc. 3108, which contains the signatures of the father-donor and his third and fourth sons. (The whereabouts of the second son are not specified; perhaps he was deceased.) Or again, *Hayashi Kōin shi shozō monjo*, 1167/2/10 sō Nōin denchi shobunjō, *HI*, 7: 2693, doc. 3415, which bears the signatures of the father-donor, his second son, his eldest daughter (*chakujo*), and another daughter. In both instances, the complement of hereditary documents, a symbol of primacy, was conveyed.

[47] For example, a deed to an eldest daughter signed by the father-donor, the eldest son, and the second son: *Tōdaiji monjo*, 1151/1/29 Tachibana Seishu denchi shobunjō, *HI*, 6: 2276, doc. 2717.

[48] There are dozens of examples, e.g., a *baiken* signed by the seller and her eldest son and daughter: *Tōdaiji monjo*, 1170/12/25 Tachibana Aneko baiken, *HI*, 7: 2771, doc. 4562.

[49] *Hishijima monjo*, 1172/12/8 nyūdō Sainen yuzurijō an, *HI*, 7: 2813, doc. 3612. Or see *Tōkyō daigaku shozō Tōdaiji monjo*, 1068/11/25 Sakanoue-no-uji shobunjō, *HI*, 3: 1055–56, doc. 1028, in which the mother-donor admonishes her children (*kyōdai*) not to be remiss in regard to each other's land shares.

action for words. In a letter of release to his third son, he stated that he was transmitting the latter's share now in order to block future disputes. Then in a follow-up document several weeks later, he included the actual boundaries of the parcels being transferred and obliged the recipient's elder brother to cosign that conveyance.[50] In fact, this raises the question of how common it was for donors to consummate transfers of property before their own deaths. The documents of the Heian and Kamakura periods are exasperatingly vague on this point, though we do know that premortem transmissions were common, sometimes as precautionary measures to avert friction, but sometimes for other reasons as well. In one instance of the latter, a woman transferred some property to her grandson, who proceeded to sell it to another relative, perhaps his aunt, on the very same day![51] In another case, a daughter took the allotment she had received from her mother, got the mother to arrange a sale to a third party, and then had the mother cosign the resulting sale deed.[52] Early bequests to extravagant or needy offspring are of course hardly unique to Japan.

At any rate, despite the best efforts of parents, family quarreling could not always be avoided. The problem was much more severe in Kamakura times, but the final century of the Heian age clearly had its own fair share of inheritance disputes. The character of these quarrels—and the outlets for their resolution—will tell us much about the two periods.

The disputes themselves revolved around promises allegedly made by parents but not kept, multiple releases that were supposedly contradictory, and accusations of infringement by senior—or same-generation—relatives. The first type was especially common when parents died intestate, inasmuch as there was no way of ascertaining the "will" of the deceased. In some instances, property was equitably divided among survivors,[53] but in other cases secondary heirs felt shortchanged. In one such episode a second son argued that the verbal promise of his parents to grant inheritances to younger children

---

[50] *Isshi monjo*, 1102/8/29 Hizen-no-kuni Uno mikuriya kengyō Genkyū yuzurijō an, *HI*, 4: 1439, doc. 1496; *ibid.*, 1102/9/23 Genkyū shobunjō an, *HI*, 4: 1440–41, doc. 1500.

[51] *Kuhara bunko shozō monjo*, 1129/4/14 Yamanobe Nakako shobunjō, *HI*, 5: 1841, doc. 2132.

[52] *Futamigō monjo*, 1136/7/28 Ōnakatomi bō denchi baiken, *HI*, 5: 1989, doc. 2347.

[53] For example, between two sons and a daughter, with the relevant documents going to the eldest son: referred to in *Yokota Ken'ichirō shi shozō monjo*, 1125/7/25 sō bō baiken, *HI*, 5: 1773–74, doc. 2050. Or between two sons: *Kawakamiyama komonjo*, 1173/2/14 Kiyohara Kanehira shichiji sarijō an, *HI*, 7: 2816, doc. 3619.

was ignored by the eldest, who took over everything and then deeded the full estate to his own adopted son. Apparently, however, at least the prospect of a small parcel had been held out to the new heir's aggrieved uncle, which led to a lawsuit, a failure to obtain satisfaction, and then to a second lawsuit.[54] In this instance, then, the absence of a testament from a parent led to a takeover by the senior heir and the retention of the property in question by a representative of his line.

Conflicting testaments would become an endless source of trouble during the Kamakura age, though even earlier we are able to find disputes that hang on this issue. Sometimes it was the false claim of holding a contrary release that was used to justify an unlawful incursion; the rightful owner would be obliged to petition for a validation of his inheritance.[55] But in other cases multiple deeds did actually exist. Thus in 1153 a suit was lodged containing the following argument: that the late father, a man in his eighties, had issued a conveyance to the petitioner in 1152, but that a year earlier he had issued another to a different son involving the same inheritance. According to the plaintiff, the later testament should clearly prevail.[56] This notion of later dispensations superseding earlier ones was naturally bound up with a property owner's growing freedom of discretion. By mid-Kamakura times, the principle of the "later deed" had became one of the pillars of Bakufu justice.

The final type of dispute—instances of unlawful occupancy by siblings or other relatives—occurred after property transfers had already taken place. Persons left dissatisfied by their shares attempted to seize what they felt had been improperly denied them. A classic instance came in 1150, when a younger brother and sister moved against their elder brother's inheritance from their mother, leading to a lawsuit, an investigation, and an affirmation of the original allotment. Thirty-odd years later the winner of that suit referred to it as he proceeded to deed his estate to his own eldest son.[57]

One of the striking things about almost all of these cases is that they involved more than just parcels of land; they involved *shiki*. In this pre-Kamakura era *shiki* were still considered officerships and as such were subject to the jurisdiction of investing authorities. Moreover, un-

[54] *Kōyasan Hōjuin monjo*, 1166/3 sō Tankei ge, *HI*, 10: 163–64, supp. doc. 107.

[55] See *Yoshida Ren shi shozō monjo*, 1145/7/9 Toba in-no-chō kudashibumi, *HI*, 6: 2160–61, doc. 2558.

[56] *Chidori ke monjo*, 1153/4/8 Nakatomi Yūchō ge, *HI*, 10: 140, supp. doc. 78.

[57] *Takeo jinja monjo*, 1183/12/15 Hizen-no-kuni Takeo sha Fujiwara Sadakado yuzurijō, *HI*, 8: 3109, doc. 4121.

like land, which was locally owned and easily parceled among heirs, *shiki* were impartible as well as being the primary means of central-to-local prestige distribution. The impartibility of *shiki* may, in fact, necessitate a refinement of a view originally fostered by Asakawa Kan'ichi and never questioned thereafter: that the most distinctive quality of *shiki* was their "infinite divisibility."[58] As we have known for a long time, new *shiki* could be created out of old—in particular, proprietary and estate managerial posts (*ryōke* and *gesu* or *azukari dokoro shiki*) in place of subdistrict headships (*gōshi shiki*) that were part of the provincial system. The transaction that effected this transformation of public land to private estate was the act of commendation (*kishin*). But this exchange of status, leading to new titles, was not the same as the parceling of a *shiki* by dividing it into parts. Not until Kamakura times would the practice be initiated of chopping a *shiki* into pieces and rendering it, ultimately, into little more than heritable income shares.

At any rate, during the Heian period, two of the most distinctive qualities of *shiki*—their unitary nature and their higher prestige than land—helped set in motion an important development. Gradually, succession to house headship became interwoven with succession to titled property, and a mechanism emphasizing appointment to *shiki* came to be replaced by a two-stage procedure of conveyance and confirmation. Under this arrangement, the identity of the next holder would be left to the discretion of the present occupant, but the authority to certify that choice rested with the governor or estate proprietor concerned. In effect, ownership of *shiki* was becoming local and hereditary but remained subject to judicial review.

It is important to recognize that this was actually a protection for both releasing and confirming interests. By means of a *yuzurijō*, a father might now ensure an inheritance—on his terms. For certifying authorities there were the benefits of regular income and irregular but ongoing involvement with the successions of local families. In practice, as we shall see, almost all *shiki* and family headships were conveyed to eldest sons. This was the course of least resistance, both locally and centrally. Yet the principle of parental discretion, combined with the vagaries of birth and personality, virtually assured that some transfers would not go smoothly. Family histories reflect this—and make it incumbent upon us to trace the inheritance sequences of individual houses. As will become clear, the shape of the Heian family unit over time was defined above all by property concerns.

[58] Asakawa reiterated this idea in almost everything he wrote, and the notion became a fixture, accepted—unquestioningly—by Sansom, Reischauer, and others.

As a matter of standard practice, property in the Heian era was transmitted lineally. There are relatively few instances of lateral transfers, and most of the examples we do find are for minor parcels, not *shiki*.[59] Moreover, when *shiki* were transferred laterally the likelihood was strong that the donor was a priest and probably unmarried.[60] At any rate, faced with the choice of deeding to a sibling or to an adopted child, the overwhelming majority of adults would certainly have preferred the latter. In part, this is explained by the extraordinary ease of adoption outside one's family;[61] but even within, a sibling's offspring rather than the sibling himself would likely have been chosen. The nephew concerned would then have been named the current holder's adopted son.[62]

This preoccupation with lineal continuity, so far removed from the ancient proclivity toward fraternal succession, is seen in other contexts as well. For example, the many releases that contain multiple signatures ought not to be interpreted as expressing some collective sibling interest in land. The signatures are likely to belong to persons of the junior generation and be for the purpose of clarifying individual possessions. A view current among some historians that these countersignatures represent a clear sign of clan cooperation is simply not borne out by the context in which these names were added; if not quite coerced, the signatures were far from being voluntary.[63] At any rate, parent-to-child transfers were the primary objective of in-family land conveyance. Inasmuch as one's brothers and sisters were potential or actual rivals, clannishness in property matters was thereby impeded.

[59] For a typical land portion to a younger brother, see *Sonkeikaku shozō monjo*, 1124/12/12 Yamamura Norifusa shobunjō an, *HI*, 5: 1761, doc. 2025.

[60] See. e.g., *Gangōji monjo*, 1156/11/21 sō Tankei shiryō yuzurijō, *HI*, 6: 2354, doc. 2857.

[61] In 1128, for example, a certain Taira Masayori was in his seventies but had no children. A man identified only as Shichirō was made the object of a "parent-child" (*oyako*) relationship and received Masayori's deed for a shrine in Mimasaka Province and for a subdistrict (*gō*) in Aki. The only stipulation was that Shichirō take possession after his benefactor's death. Three years later the provincial headquarters of Mimasaka, noting Masayori's death, validated the inheritance to "a man named Shichirō." See *Ninnaji monjo*, 1128/12 Taira Masayori yuzurijō, *HI*, 10: 3864–65, doc. 4980; and *ibid.*, 1131/9/15 Mimasaka-no-kuni rusudokoro kudashibumi, *HI*, 10: 3867, doc. 4984.

[62] See, e.g., *Tōnan'in monjo*, 1056/2/23 Fujiwara Sanetō shoryō yuzurijō an, *HI*, 3: 870–73, doc. 763; or *Ichiki monjo*, 1146/8/10 Taira Tsunetane kishinjō, *HI*, 6: 2187–88, doc. 2586. Murakami Yasusuke has stated that brothers were "often adopted," but I find little evidence of this; see his "*Ie* Society as a Pattern of Civilization," p. 303.

[63] Toyoda Takeshi, for example, has seen these signatures as representing clan solidarity; *Bushidan to sonraku*, pp. 163–65.

On the other hand, considerations of a nonmaterial nature did work to bind rather than divide. Ceremonial and religious functions, for example, inhered in clan headship, and component lineages did see themselves as belonging to some larger association. Yet the authority of clan heads did not extend very far. Not only were such persons totally uninvolved in the disposition of wealth other than their own, but the resolution of a kinsman's property disputes was normally outside their purview. As we have noted, the latter prerogative was exercised by tenurial—not familial—authorities, in other words, by governors and estate owners. To use Kiley's terminology, authority was organized "factionally" across social and physical space, not, as Hall has suggested, through the prism of the family.[64]

It is no accident, therefore, that clans—and even branches of clans—have seemed elusive to historians. In fact, it is a distortion of reality to attempt to trace them: they were mere aggregates of heterogeneous and usually noninteracting units and were not in any sense the sums of their separate parts. Yoritomo would come to recognize this as he failed to attract to his standard numerous Minamoto lineages; he opted instead to enroll willing Taira houses and to divide and subdivide any collective that wished to support him on that basis. At any rate, the smallest units were the most effective ones, common clan names being almost meaningless.[65]

If it is useless to approach the family "horizontally," it is altogether essential that we attempt to trace individual lines vertically over time. The secondary heirs and minor branches must be allowed to disappear as we seek to follow main inheriting lines as they approach the Kamakura age. Not surprisingly, we are able to achieve even this modest goal for only a handful of houses in the eleventh and twelfth centuries—unlike the thirteenth century, when some dozens of families might be similarly analyzed. But the cases available to us are from different sections of the country and tend to be for houses that ended with a common status as Kamakura vassals. What follows then are brief profiles of four of these: the Fujiwara of Aki, Kuri of Iwami, Kusakabe of Hyūga, and Chiba of Shimōsa.

The Fujiwara story is significant as a case study of a prominent

[64] Kiley, "Estate and Property in the Late Heian Period"; Hall, *Government and Local Power in Japan, 500–1700*, chap. 4.

[65] Cameron Hurst has made this point in reference to "the Fujiwara"; see *Insei: Abdicated Sovereigns in the Politics of Late Heian Japan, 1086–1185*, chap. 2. Suzuki has elected to stress the cooperative nature of Heian-period families ("Zaichi ryōshusei," pp. 20–22) but admits that this is controversial. I believe the evidence points mostly in the other direction.

The accompanying pages, 26 and 42, contain corrections of typographical errors appearing in the original pages.

heart of the Lord of Higashiyama—the paintings, the pottery, and all those precious things called *karamomo*—passed through the hands of merchants engaged in the Ming trade before they reached Yoshimasa. In the process, these objects enriched the lives and entered the culture of the townspeople. Yoshimasa's indispensable arbiters of taste, the men who judged and professionally appraised his imported art objects and who defined the elegant disciplines of tea and of flower arrangement, were most often of low birth, like Ikenobō Senkei and Murata Jukō. Such men in turn brought these arts to the city populace, transfusing them into the cultural and social lifeblood of Kyoto.[13] In this way the townspeople gained an appreciation of the artistic elements of Higashiyama culture, a process which made possible the birth of an autogenous urban culture.

But the townspeople approached the arts quite differently from the way the aristocracy did. Theirs was not the world of political or social prestige but rather of profit and practicality. The splendors of Muromachi were related intimately with the increasing economic power of the moneylenders. The new aesthetic pastimes developed chiefly as appurtenances of daily life and were nurtured by human requirements. Painting developed within the framework of *fusuma-e* (the *fusuma* is a room divider); ceramics were appreciated in the form of daily implements, of teabowls and of flower vases. Art was esteemed for its utility; at the very least, it ceased being idealized and became something possessed of an extremely practical design.

This tendency to put high value on utility had its political parallel in the manifestation of *tokusei*, or "virtuous rule." The original meaning of the phrase derives from the Confucian ideal of benevolent rule, the universal norm of politics. In the usage current from the end of the Kamakura period, the idea of tokusei assumed a very particular meaning. After the Einin Tokusei Edict (1297), *toku* for "virtue" and *toku* for "profit" were interchangeable, so that "virtuous rule" may be understood as "profitable rule." The Einin Edict, which had the highly utilitarian effect of wiping out debts, was meant to succor the Kamakura shogunate's housemen who had fallen into severe financial straits in the aftermath of the Mongol invasions. The Ashikaga shogunate's tokusei were of a somewhat different sort and were used either to help bakufu finances or to pacify peasant confederations (*do-ikki*). When the populace demanded remissions, the shogunate responded by passing tokusei edicts. Eventually the shogunate became parasitically attached to this "profitable rule" by way of scheming for profits. Yoshimasa alone ordered tokusei some thirteen times. That

13. See Hayashiya Tatsusaburō, *Kabuki izen* (Tokyo, 1954), in *Iwanami shinsho*, 184: 127–144; also idem, *Kyōto* (Tokyo, 1967), pp. 166–169. On the arts of the "Ami," see also "Kinsei no taidō," in *Koten bunka no sōzō* (Tokyo, 1959), pp. 291–295.

ment of bakufu organization which these scholars describe helps immensely to explain the political history of the time. As a result of their work we can see how, under the first five shoguns, there was a parallel effort to build up both the feudal and the monarchal organs of administrative control. The post of deputy shogun (*kanrei*) takes on new significance when the kanrei is seen not only as the prime officer (and hence prime supporter) of the shogun but also as the mediator between the shugo and the tendency toward despotism shown by such shoguns as Yoshimitsu and Yoshinori. It is noteworthy that the Ashikaga shogunate reached the zenith of its power at a time when the allegiance of the shugo was given as much to the idea of the balance of power, as symbolized by the shogun's council of senior vassals, as to the shogun himself. Yoshinori's attempts to enhance shogunal power by the use of a personal bureaucracy ended predictably in his assassination by one of his own senior vassals. The Ashikaga shogunate never achieved an administration capable of governing the entire nation. It could not in the end do more than serve as a symbol of legitimacy for what can be called the "shugo system," in other words for the collectivity of shugo who competed for power in the provinces.

In the final analysis, then, an understanding of the power structure of the Ashikaga shogunate must involve a fourth line of inquiry, namely, a study of the relationships between shogun and shugo and between shugo and the provinces. The subject has been explored in several of its parts, as in the essay by Professor Kawai. But it has yet to be described in its national totality. As Kawai points out, the nature of shogun-shugo relations was not uniform throughout the Ashikaga period. The early period of adjustment through warfare to an uneasy balance of power was succeeded by the era of Yoshimitsu when the shugo of all provinces except those in the Kantō and Kyushu built their residences in Kyoto. In this way they participated in a sort of early version of *sankin-kōtai*, the system whereby the Tokugawa shoguns obliged their vassals to reside in Edo in alternate years. This was also the time of the successful functioning of the system of kanrei rotation and the periodic holding of shugo councils (*yoriai*) for policy decisions. It was as much the effort of the shogun to dominate this balance of power as it was the growth of independent shugo ambitions that destroyed the Muromachi political system. By the time of the Ōnin War, when the shugo-shogun alliance had begun to come apart, a new stage in the relationship of bakufu to shugo had been reached; but at the same time the nature of the shugo themselves had begun to change. By this time the full force of the changes in the countryside which gave rise to new and more locally entrenched regional lords had begun to be felt. As explained by Professor Miyagawa, the chigyō system of landholding now

landholding family that seems to have prospered for more than a century but then fell upon hard times.[66] Successful as public officers (*zaichōkanjin*) within the non-*shōen* land sector, the family floundered shortly after its attempt to enhance its security within the *shōen* system of immunities. Our information on this house begins with a body of documents dating back to 1031, which, if authentic, reveals one of the earliest inheritance sequences now traceable.[67] In 1031, a certain Mita *gō* along with another holding were transmitted by Fujiwara Morinaka to his son Morimitsu. The accompanying deeds were appended to the conveyance, and Morimitsu was instructed to petition the governor, when the latter came down to Aki, to authorize an official appointment.[68] Two things are apparent from this document: that the rights to Mita *gō* were considered heritable although requiring validation, and that a procedure already existed for this kind of transaction. How long the Fujiwara had been in Mita is unknown, although Morinaka's official title of *daijō*, affixed to his conveyance, identifies him as a *zaichōkanjin* member of the governor's regular local staff.

Though the governor's validation is not extant, we can presume there was no trouble about it, since seventeen years later Morimitsu deeded the inheritance to his son Moriyori and took it upon himself to apply to the governor for certification. It is this petition that survives (the release does not), and in an addendum to it the governor recorded his approval.[69] It is noteworthy here that the appeal and the approval shared the same piece of paper, and it is this pattern that is repeated for the next two generations. In each instance (1057 and 1068) the holder's eldest son (*chakunan*) was made heir, though in the second document the petition allowed that the legatee was still a child.[70] Five years later, presumably when the latter reached man-

---

[66] The story is interesting also because of its recounting in new perspective by Peter Arnesen in "The Struggle for Lordship in Late Heian Japan." His version, based on an assumption that certain key documents are forgeries, differs markedly from my own. I am grateful to him for pointing out a few minor errors in my account.

[67] Though branded as forgeries by Arnesen, these documents would still be very old—from about 1139—and would thus represent an entirely credible version of how things happened. The documents would have been intended to persuade contemporaries, but instead (as Arnesen would see it) they have persuaded (fooled) historians.

[68] *Itsukushima jinja monjo*, 1031/6/3 Fujiwara Morinaka yuzurijō, *Hiroshima kenshi, kodai-chūsei shiryōhen*, 3: 157, doc. 1. All subsequent citations are to the same volume, which, incidentally, offers no hint that these documents might not be authentic.

[69] *Ibid.*, 1048/7/2 Takada gunji Fujiwara Morimitsu ge, 3: 157–58, doc. 2. As indicated therein, Morimitsu was now district chief (*gunji*) of the region of which Mita *gō* was a part.

[70] *Ibid.*, 1057/3/10 Takada gunji Fujiwara Moriyori ge, 3: 158–59, doc. 3; *ibid.*, 1068/3/10 Takada gunji Fujiwara Moritō ge, 3: 159, doc. 4.

hood, a special governor's edict was issued appointing him (Yorikata) to the headship (gōshi shiki) of Mita gō.[71]

At this point, the Fujiwara began to expand territorially, and in 1078 a governor's decree appointed Yorikata to a second gōshi shiki in the region. A month later Yorikata conveyed both gō to his heir, Yorinari.[72] Interestingly, however, Yorikata had evidently not retired, since in 1083 the imperial chancellery (daijōkan) authorized his appointment as district magistrate (tairyō),[73] and in 1096 the governor validated his release to his son.[74] The following year this heir (Yorinari) was appointed to two additional gōshi posts in the district,[75] a development paralleling the family's acquisition by purchase of acreage in the region.[76] The Fujiwara were clearly advancing their interests on several fronts.

In 1098, the imperial chancellery confirmed Yorinari's tairyō status, as it had done fifteen years earlier for his father, and three weeks later Yorinari petitioned the governor for validation of his conveyance to the next house head, Naritaka.[77] It is clear from subsequent records that Yorinari did not in fact relinquish a father's control of the family fortunes, and for good reason, because clear signs of trouble had already appeared. Though we lack details, a dispute had arisen between Yorinari and a younger brother, which led to the 1098 confirmation by the Imperial Court of Yorinari's status as tairyō, and then to a reconfirmation eleven years later.[78] More ominous was the fact that

[71] Ibid., 1072/9/10 Aki kokufu, 3: 160, doc. 5.

[72] Ibid., 1078/9/2 Aki kokushi chōsen, 3: 3–4, doc. 2; and ibid., 1078/10/3 Fujiwara Yorikata yuzurijō, 3: 4, doc. 3.

[73] Ibid., 1083/6/7 daijōkanpu, 3: 5, doc. 4. Gunji posts at this time were designated as "greater" or "lesser" offices—tairyō or shōryō.

[74] Ibid., 1096/6 Aki kokushi chōsen, 3: 7, doc. 7. Technically the release was for the family's gunji title.

[75] Ibid., 1097/3/5 Aki kokushi chōsen, 3: 8, doc. 9. In 1096, Yorinari was granted authority in two other gō as well, making a total of six; ibid., 1196/12/26 Aki kokushi chōsen, 3: 7–8, doc. 8.

[76] In 1095, Yorinari had requested a governor's validation of his ownership of 320 chō (1 chō = 2.94 acres) distributed throughout all seven of Takada District's gō; this was approved. Ibid., 1095/8/15 Takada gunji Fujiwara Yorinari ge, 3: 166–67, doc. 14. References to such acquisitions by purchase go back to 1057 (see n. 70), and actual sale documents do survive (to Fujiwara Yorikata in Nosaka monjo, 1076/2/10 Ōshi Sadayuki baiken, 3: 431–32, doc. 4; and to Fujiwara Yorinari in Koji ruien shoshū monjo, 1098/3/28 Tachibana Yoritoki baiken an, 3: 1522, doc. 5).

[77] Itsukushima jinja monjo, 1098/2/20 daijōkanpu, 3: 9, doc. 10; ibid., 1098/3/10 Takada gunji Fujiwara Yorinari ge, 3: 160–61, doc. 6.

[78] The references to the dispute appear in ibid., 1139/6 Fujiwara Naritaka kishinjō, 3: 1467–71, doc. 1. For the reconfirmation, see ibid., 1109/4/30 daijōkanpu, 3: 9, doc. 11.

Yorinari's heir, Naritaka, was not formally invested in the family's *gōshi shiki* beyond the original two titles.[79] The Fujiwara were in fact under pressure from several quarters. At all events, in 1139 Naritaka took the fateful step of commending his private holdings in these two *gō* to a Kyoto aristocrat, expressing the wish that a *shōen* might be established, "following the recent practice of this and other provinces," and also noting his expectation that he and his heirs might be granted a hereditary managership (*gesu shiki*). The recipient of this endowment was a certain Nakahara Moronaga whose family, according to the commendation statement, had been served by Naritaka's forebears.[80] Unfortunately, we do not know what precipitated this extraordinary event in 1139, though we do know that Naritaka's hopes went unrealized. No *shōen* was created until 1154, no *gesu shiki* evolved, and during the same generation the Fujiwara lost most of their influence in Aki Province.

What went wrong? The documents grow murky at this point, though scattered references suggest that Naritaka conveyed copies (*anmon*) of his original deeds to an adopted heir, Yorinobu,[81] and that Yorinobu later released the inheritance (in 1167) to the priest-administrator of Itsukushima Shrine.[82] In other words, the patronage of Nakahara was now recognized as a failure, and the Fujiwara heir was evidently seeking a substitute. But this plan too went awry, since the shrine priest in question was Saeki Kagehiro, the well-known vassal stalwart of Taira Kiyomori, now ascendant in the capital. The Fujiwara's holdings became Itsukushima Shrine lands, and within several more years Kagehiro became *jitō* of the areas in question.[83] It is at this point that the Fujiwara disappear from view, but only in the wake of a final failed effort on their behalf. In the move that led ultimately to the establish-

[79] A reference to this appears in *ibid.*, 1139/6 Fujiwara Naritaka kishinjō, 3: 1467–71, doc. 1.

[80] The nature of this service is not specified, though Naritaka's ancestor, Morimitsu, is mentioned as a former service person (*tsukaibito*). Perhaps some earlier Nakahara had served as provincial governor.

[81] The reference to document copies (the originals were conveyed to Nakahara in about 1144) appears in *Nosaka monjo*, ca. 1151 Takada gun Kazehaya gō nikki an, 3: 687, doc. 77; that to Yorinobu's inheritance in 1151 appears in *Itsukushima jinja monjo*, undated Takada gun Mita-Kazehaya ryō gō daidai chakunan nikki, 3: 126, doc. 82; and that to Yorinobu's status as an adopted son appears in *ibid.*, 1167/6/15 Minamoto Yorinobu yuzurijō, 3: 176–77, doc. 17.

[82] *Itsukushima jinja monjo*, 1167/6/15 Minamoto Yorinobu yuzurijō, 3: 176–77, doc. 17.

[83] For the *jitō* aspects of the story and details on the Saeki as Taira vassals, see *WG*, pp. 108–11.

ment of Saeki's *jitō* authority, Nakahara Narinaga (heir of Nakahara Moronaga, the Kyoto aristocrat who was the original 1139 commendee) added his own commendation to Kagehiro in hopes of receiving a hereditary custodianship (*azukari dokoro shiki*) for himself, and a hereditary *gesu shiki* for the descendants of the Fujiwara.[84] However, nothing came of this effort, save to provide Kagehiro with the documentation and releases he needed to justify his investiture as *jitō*.[85] In 1182, Kagehiro was even able to deed these "hereditary private lands" (*sōden shiryō*) to his own first son, Kagenobu.[86]

And thus the story of the Aki Fujiwara comes to a close, though a few additional details do seem warranted. During a critical ten-year period (1146–56) the governor of Aki Province had been none other than Taira Kiyomori before his rise in the capital. In view of the role played by previous governors in confirming the lands and offices of the Fujiwara, Taira resistance may have been instrumental in thwarting the aims of the original commendation. By the same token, the follow-up commendees, the Saeki, were emerging at this time as Kiyomori's leading vassals in Aki. Naritaka's conveyance to an adopted son, whose identity is otherwise unknown, is also of interest here, since the commendation document of 1139 was in fact cosigned by the husband of an eldest daughter (*chakujo*). This suggests that the Fujiwara had fallen upon bad luck at this point in the matter of heirship: for more than a hundred years the only names appearing in their documents were those of eldest sons; now, however, in the troubled circumstances of the 1140s, Naritaka was apparently unwilling to deed to a daughter. Instead, he went outside his own family.

A further point concerns language and terminology. Though the documents of 1139 and 1167 strike us as vehicles of commendation, the term *kishin* ("commendation") nowhere appears: instead, the words *yuzuri-watashi* and *yuzuri-atau* are used, respectively. Here, then, is a further indication that *yuzurijō* were conveyances to be employed both inside and outside the family, and either before or after death. In most instances they were releases for the clear benefit of progeny. But they could also, in hybrid form, be used for other purposes. Not until the Kamakura age would the distinction between en-

---

[84] *Itsukushima jinja monjo*, 1174/10 Nakahara Narinaga kishinjō, 3: 248–49, doc. 43.

[85] His appointment by the governor came in 1176; *ibid.*, 1176/7 Aki kokushi chōsen an, 3: 252, doc. 46. Arnesen believes this document to be a forgery. Kagehiro's investiture, he argues, did not come until 1180; Arnesen, "The Struggle for Lordship."

[86] *Itsukushima jinja monjo*, 1182/3 Saeki Kagehiro yuzurijō an, 3: 253–54, doc. 48.

dowment and bequest (*kishin* and *yuzuri*) come to rest on relatedness to a donee.[87]

That the Fujiwara's displacement as hereditary officers (*zaichōkan-jin*) probably caused them to lose their opportunity to become *gokenin* is apparent from the many provincial houses that survived—and were enrolled as vassals.[88] An example of this is the Kuri house of Iwami Province, whose story in outline we now turn to. The Kuri were contemporaries of the Fujiwara and first appear in our documents as appointees to a *gōshi* title in 1063.[89] Twenty-one years later Masamune, the incumbent, deeded his office to his son, who, for his part, immediately petitioned the governor for reappointment, citing his father's release. To bolster his case the appellant, Norifusa, noted his family's ancestral possession of the *shiki* in question and stated that his father's old age now made it difficult for him to discharge his duties. When the governor affixed his seal to this petition, the father's retirement was made official and Norifusa succeeded him as chief of Kuri *gō*.[90]

The next document in the sequence is dated 42 years later and is an announcement by the governor of the next Kuri heir's hereditary possession of what are now three *gō*. The edict itself was addressed to the Iwami provincial headquarters (*rusudokoro*), which suggests that it was a follow-up to a release and a petition for certification, neither of which is extant. It was, in effect, a public disclosure of the governor's approval of the new holder, strengthened by references within the edict to noninvolvement by any other person and to a guaranteed heritability by the heir's lineal successors.[91]

Perhaps there was already some hint of trouble to induce this unusual assurance: it was the type of security that governors rarely

---

[87] Most scholars would view the transactions of 1139 and 1167 as commendations—such is the fixed nature of the distinction between in-family and out-family donation. But this is a product of Kamakura experience and has only limited applicability for earlier times.

[88] It seems altogether possible that remnants of the family, bearing different surnames, did become Kamakura vassals at some point. But the family did not enter the Kamakura age either triumphantly or intact.

[89] *Kuri monjo*, 1063/11/3 Iwami kokushi chōsen, *Iwami Kuri monjo no kenkyū*, p. 31, doc. 1. In the mid-eleventh century the family was still known by its ancestral clan name of Kiyowara. This parallels the experience of the Aki "Fujiwara." Had the latter survived, they might later have come to be known as the Takada or Mita.

[90] *Ibid.*, 1084/9/10 Kiyowara Masamune yuzurijō, p. 32, doc. 2; *ibid.*, 1084/9/15 Kiyowara Norifusa ge, p. 33, doc. 3.

[91] *Ibid.*, 1126/6/19 Iwami kokushi chōsen, p. 34, doc. 4.

promised so explicitly and that caused houses like the Aki Fujiwara to
seek out private patronage. At all events, the final Heian document in
the sequence reveals an actual challenge. In 1169, the governor was
called on to adjudicate a claim brought by the next Kuri head alleging
incursion on his holdings by an ambitious neighbor. The suit was upheld and—true to the earlier promise—the Kuri's possession was reaffirmed as hereditary.[92]

At this point—and all the way to the Nanbokuchō era of the fourteenth century—documentation ceases, but the family's genealogy
makes clear that the Heian scion just referred to became a Kamakura
jitō—over a total of four *gō*. His two sons, moreover, divided that
inheritance, another typical development: both lines became *jitō-
gokenin.*[93] And thus the progress of the Kuri from one *gō* to four,
which had taken more than a century, was not upset, as in the case of
the Fujiwara, by a failure of support from higher authorities. Without
an intervening commendation stage, the Kuri entered the Kamakura
period with their inheritance intact, only to divide that legacy (and
themselves) by their own unhindered decision.

The story of the Kusakabe of Hyūga Province in Kyushu ends similarly, with the family dividing and becoming separate vassals of the
newly formed Bakufu. But in this instance substantial infighting lay
behind this development. In other words, if the Aki Fujiwara appear
only once to have experienced severe sibling rivalry, and if the Iwami
Kuri's only visible enemy was a covetous neighbor, the Hyūga Kusakabe show the kind of internal disputation that would become almost
endemic in Kamakura times. Events began peaceably enough with a
governor's appointment of Kusakabe Naosada to the "resident governorship" (*zaikokushi shiki*) of Hyūga in 1123.[94] This was followed nine
years later by his son Naomori's assignment to the same post, under
the rationale that Naosada had become aged and could not carry out
his duties. What is noteworthy in this (besides the reference to an im-
pending retirement) is the absence of any mention of a father's conveyance: the transfer appears to have been made at the discretion of
the governor, who, quoting from a Dazaifu edict, noted the instruction

[92] *Ibid.*, 1169/10 Iwami Kokushi chōsen, p. 36, doc. 6.

[93] *Kuri ke keizu*, p. 97, doc. 57.

[94] *Kusakabe keizu shoshū monjo*, 1123/1/25 Hyūga kokushi chōsen, in Nishioka Toranosuke, *Shōen shi no kenkyū*, vol. 2, p. 437. Naosada bore the title of *gon no suke*—provisional vice governor—suggesting obvious status as a *zaichōkanjin*. He was now accorded
a kind of chief operating authority—the *zaikokushi* post—at the local level.

that someone of merit be chosen to succeed Naosada.[95] It was not until seventeen years later that the first release by a holder was issued— from Naomori to his heir, Morihira, and involving the resident gover- norship plus certain private lands.[96]

That the zaikokushi post was now considered heritable and subject to the holder's choice of successor is made strikingly clear by something that is found to this point only infrequently: Morihira was his father's second son, even though the first son was still very much alive. In fact, the conveyance itself includes the term chakushi—hitherto virtually synonymous with chakunan, "eldest son"—in a context that anticipates Kamakura practice. It can be interpreted here in the sense of "prin- cipal heir," the only possible translation when a chakushi is not an el- dest son. The significance of this lies in the potentially greater empha- sis it could accord to house headship, no longer a matter simply of birth but of choice. As we shall see, the eldest son was not being for- mally disinherited; he was merely passed over for headship of the Kusakabe house. But this decision—involving avoidance of the prac- tice of primogeniture—portended an enhanced significance in being named principal heir. At any rate, the governor approved it and ap- pointed Morihira as zaikokushi.[97]

The elder brother, despite receiving his own inheritance of gunji and gōshi posts, eventually chose to challenge Morihira, who for his own part had also received additional titles.[98] The case was heard in 1175 and led to Morihira's being reconfirmed by the governor.[99] It was, in effect, a reappointment of the ranking provincial officer—and a reinforcement of a father's freedom to select who that incumbent might be. Yet the story has a curious ending in that Morihira, himself childless, adopted a nephew of unknown parentage and deeded the zaikokushi inheritance to him.[100] This was in the 1180s, and as the house genealogy makes clear, Morihira had become a Kamakura jitō, and his nephew fell heir to that status as well. But just as this was hap-

[95] Ibid., 1132/10 Hyūga kokushi chōsen, 2: 438. The Dazaifu was the imperial head- quarters in Kyushu.

[96] Ibid., 1149/3/10 Kusakabe Naomori yuzurijō, 2: 438.

[97] Ibid., 1149/7 Hyūga kokushi chōsen, 2: 438.

[98] The information on additional holdings by the two brothers appears in ibid., 2: 439.

[99] Ibid., 1175/4 Hyūga kokushi chōsen, 2: 439.

[100] Ibid., 1187/2/10 Kusakabe Morihira yuzurijō, 2: 439. It is only clear that the adoptee here (renamed Sanemori) was not a son of Morihira's elder brother; ibid., 2: 439.

pening Morihira's elder brother and his line were also becoming
Kamakura vassals—even as the quarreling continued unabated between them.[101] In this way, the new regime—as it did in so many
other cases—embraced collateral lines and inherited the responsibility, hitherto held by diverse authorities, of serving as ultimate local
peacemakers.

Collateral lines play a major part in our final case study, that of the
well-known Chiba family of Shimōsa.[102] In eastern Japan, home of the
future Bakufu, a long-entrenched *zaichōkanjin* house, claiming descent from the Taira, divided itself into two branches, the Kazusa and
the Chiba, early in the twelfth century. Subsequently, a district headship, hereditary with the Chiba branch, was released to the Kazusa—
but for good purpose. Using his connections, the Kazusa chief, Tsune-
toki, gained immunities for the area in question—and then returned
the headship to the Chiba by adopting his brother's son. This transfer
to a nephew, which occurred in 1124, was approved by the governor.[103] Six years later the nephew took steps of his own—now familiar
to us—to bolster his line's possession. In 1130, he commended his
most important holdings to Ise Shrine, receiving a *gesu shiki* stipulated
as hereditary with his successors, and in 1135 he deeded that inheritance to his own son. At this point, Ise Shrine should logically have
confirmed that transfer, just as the governor's office had done in previous generations. Instead, there followed a series of bizarre developments that had the Chiba head dispossessed by a new governor in
1136, dispossessed again by the head of the Minamoto in 1143 (with
the connivance, significantly, of the Kazusa heir, i.e., his own cousin),[104]
and dispossessed a final time by a local magnate in 1161.[105] The up-
shot of this was that it would not be until Kamakura times that one of
the east's most distinguished houses would succeed even in reacquir-
ing its own homelands.

The episode's significance for us lies in the dependence of even the
most prestigious local families on the patronage and support of higher
public authorities (governors or *shōen* owners), of which the exclusive

---

[101] *Ibid.*, 2: 439.

[102] For further details, see *WG*, chap. 2.

[103] All the information appearing here (and up to 1146) is drawn from a single document: *Ichiki monjo*, 1146/8/10 Taira (Chiba) Tsunetane kishinjō, in *Ichikawa shishi, kodai-
chūsei shiryō*, p. 366, doc. 7.

[104] In other words, the 1124 adopter's natural son bore a grievance that must have
increased when the inheritance was denied him—now for a second time.

[105] For the 1161 development, along with other details, see *Ichiki monjo*, pp. 367–71,
docs. 8–12.

monopoly of probate was one major dimension.[106] Before 1130, the Chiba's hereditary titles were only as secure as the family's continued support by provincial governors, whereas after 1130 that condition should have improved but did not. The Chiba's hereditary rights were in this sense vulnerable, suggesting that holdings in the form of *shiki* might involve risk as well as reward.

In other ways, too, *shiki* inheritances, such as those we have seen in our four case studies, remained constricted. Partitioning was not practiced (thereby limiting, for better or worse, the discretionary rights of donors), and releases to other than eldest sons were decidedly rare. Moreover, *shiki* holding remained predicated on a hierarchical form of reciprocity: both the investor and the investee participated in a dyadic arrangement in which each side came to possess unequal formal titles. The junior partner was thus, as in the case of both the Chiba and the Fujiwara, potentially at a disadvantage. A further point was the impersonal nature of these bondings. One of the distinctive features of the Heian-period *shiki* system was the absence of informal grants and validations. No untitled person, whatever his military prowess, could grant or confirm an office. Similarly, no titled person in the provinces could probate a will except as an agent of some centrally entrenched superior.[107] This meant that prestigious fighting men might provide physical security against neighbors, but not its tenurial counterpart; their role in the latter capacity was limited to a middleman's function defined by positions within hierarchies that they did not dominate. The weakness of the Chiba and Fujiwara, then, was that the very *shiki* which provided them their local wealth and influence bound them to a status that, without central support, they could not preserve. Only with the coming of the Kamakura Bakufu would families such as the Chiba move in the direction of greater independence.

None of this is intended to suggest that local houses were bereft of leverage in seeking to secure their futures. For example, since adop-

---

[106] My argument, then, takes the most extreme exception to one of the principal points put forward by Professor Murakami. Writing in the *Journal of Japanese Studies*, he has stated: "Each proto-ie provided almost all of the necessary functions for itself, including jurisdiction. . . . [E]ach proto-ie's head in Tōgoku [eastern Japan] had all rights of jurisdiction within his organization, and no higher authority, such as the court nobles, could supersede or interfere with this authority." (Murakami, "Ie Society," p. 311.)

[107] E.g., a confirmation by the custodian of Ōi Estate; *Tōnan'in monjo*, 1183/8 Ōi-no-shō azukari dokoro kudashibumi, *Gifu kenshi, kodai-chūsei shiryō hen*, 3: 506–7, doc. 139. In previous generations the confirmations were issued directly by the proprietor.

tion was so easy, no formalized mechanism of escheat developed in which certifying authorities required forfeiture in the absence of male descendants. An eldest son (as we saw for the Fujiwara and Kusakabe) could almost be created on demand. Similarly, the caution with which the Heian Japanese viewed dowry and jointure mitigated against seepage to a spouse's family. In none of our case studies was either of these an issue.[108] At the same time, safeguards were employed in the transfer of property to offspring. In their Heian context these safeguards took the form of cosignatures on releases, land shares to younger children, and *shiki* reserved for eldest sons. The integrity of the lineage was the first priority here and was expressed implicitly in the distinction between *shiki* and other forms of wealth. Only later, when intrafamily discord had become more severe, was everything divided, including *shiki*. But to offset this more advanced concept of partible inheritance, house headship was increasingly emphasized.

At any rate, the legacy bestowed by the Heian period on the Kamakura age was obviously considerable. The inheritance practices that came to dominate in the thirteenth century represented a hybrid of both old and new. But institutional change was unmistakably more gradual during the earlier epoch. By contrast, the Kamakura age experienced a fairly dramatic series of changes that affected both houses and property. As we shall see, the story of the maturing warrior class is closely bound up with the evolving condition of family headship as it was influenced by the dispersal of assets. Let us turn now to the inheritances of warriors in the first third of the Kamakura age.

[108] Jointure was property granted to a married couple; hence a joint tenancy.

CHAPTER 2

FAMILY AND INHERITANCE UNDER THE EARLY BAKUFU

Minamoto Yoritomo had been in exile for twenty years when he decided in 1180 to challenge the Taira. As the eldest among his brothers and as the head of the militarized branch of the Minamoto, he saw himself as the logical leader. Yet the basis for his challenge, an imperial call to arms, did not specify him as commander. Moreover, the prince who issued the call was seeking defeat of the Taira for his own reasons. Passed over for emperor in favor of the maternal grandson of Kiyomori, he was embroiled in a succession dispute with his own family. The prince's plea for support was thus not for the purpose of reviving Minamoto fortunes—even less of championing Yoritomo himself. His appeal therefore galvanized—but also divided—the leading members of the Minamoto clan. Long after Yoritomo had defeated the Taira, he would be seeking to solidify his own headship, which could only be lost to a close relative.

Condemned by generations of historians as paranoid, Yoritomo in fact had well-grounded fears. Just as his own father had challenged his father and also been the object of bitter Minamoto jealousies, so Yoritomo would be challenged at different times by uncles, cousins, and brothers.[1] Phrased differently, the cleavages within the Minamoto clan closely paralleled those in many other central and provincial houses. Component units might coexist and even cooperate during times of stability; but alliances based on kinship remained fragile, even close to their centers. At any rate, when Yoritomo mounted his rebellion in 1180, he encountered kin who were accustomed to remaining at arm's length.

[1] For the travails of Yoritomo's father, see *WG*, pp. 39–46; for Yoritomo's troubles with relatives, *WG*, pp. 66–67, 72–74, 84–85, 143–48.

This kind of loose organization, exemplified by his own clan, was an obstacle to Yoritomo as he set about the task of building his lordship. Not only could he not tolerate any overt disobedience, but he would have to curtail the autonomy of his relatives. Well-known offshoots like the Satake, Shida, and Ashikaga were thus obliged to submit to him unqualifiedly or else face immediate attack. By requiring a greater integration than in the past, Yoritomo was underscoring the inherent weakness of kinship ties. By contrast, his posture toward non-relatives could be gentler; it could even allow less, rather than more, cohesion if that is what potential followers wanted. In fact, in the midst of a war in which the Taira and Minamoto banners were used as pretexts for private battles, numerous houses simply broke apart.[2] A major result was a permanent change in the composition of an untold number of fighting families.

Yoritomo had to deal with all these conditions. In some cases this meant watching a composite house cease to exist; coequal branches would then have to be recognized in its place. In other cases, the pre-war hierarchy of lineages might emerge from the conflict in an altered state. Yoritomo would have to decide how to acknowledge this combination. Where superior and inferior were clearly visible, he could recognize a dominant lineage and seek to foster unity around it. In fact, this pattern—known as the *sōryō* pattern—has been cited by scholars as Yoritomo's main solution here.[3] But actually there were too many fragments seeking autonomy from close kin for any single policy to work. As just noted, a reabsorption into larger kinship units (*ichizoku*, for convenience henceforth referred to by the somewhat awkward term "kindreds") was what many warriors thought they were opposing when they joined the Minamoto in the first place.

It follows then that the Taira-Minamoto war was scarcely the way most participants saw it.[4] This is borne out by the infrequency of major battles even as conditions locally became disordered. As such, the 1185 defeat of the Taira was almost incidental to the restoration of true peace. The problem was one of ending the disharmony among

---

[2] In this sense the Genpei War needs to be viewed as a countrywide series of small civil wars; *WG*, chap. 3.

[3] For the view that Yoritomo adopted the *sōryōsei* (house chieftainship system), see, e.g., Satō Shin'ichi, "Bakufuron," pp. 14–16.

[4] This is basically the view—a true Genpei War—presented in the Kamakura regime's own later account of itself, the *Azuma kagami*. It is also the view of Shinoda, *The Founding of the Kamakura Shogunate, 1180–85*, and Sansom, *A History of Japan to 1334*, chaps. 12–15.

kin and neighbors, and stemming the tide of lawlessness against property. Yoritomo sought his solution in the *jitō shiki*, estate stewardships that could be distributed to his followers. But to proceed with the construction of a network of these officers, he would need to confront the tangle of provincial families. Determining who was and was not a member of which house, and deciding how these different units should be structured and recognized, became a major preoccupation of the postwar period.

During the war itself, field commanders had been obliged to enroll new men mostly on an ad hoc basis. The inclination was strong to take at face value statements about families offered by the recruits themselves. There would be time later on to sort things out. The commanders thus made lists of names, called *kyōmyō*, which were sent back to Kamakura and made the basis of provincial rolls.[5] Since the lists included only the names of individuals, Kamakura's task must have been a formidable one as it sought to reconcile names with families, families with kindreds, and kindreds with other kindreds in view of the duplication of surnames. In the postwar period conflicting claims must have been bewildering. These claims would have dealt with the histories and shapes of families and family interests, the partisanship of component units, and the proper accounting of things for the present and into the future.

It is obvious that Yoritomo had no choice but to proceed slowly and to admit and redress mistakes as he made them. To assist him in this he began to distribute *jitō* titles at the end of 1185. These awards made recipients beholden to Kamakura and also allowed Kamakura to test its *jitō*, in a sense, on the job. Awardees were obliged to discharge estate-managerial functions on behalf of traditional proprietors. There thus occurred numerous cancellations, reassignments, and new appointments.[6] At the same time, these adjustments provided a context, controlled by Kamakura, within which the internal dynamics of houses might emerge. Challenges and other petitions by relatives would af-

---

[5] The clearest example is for Sanuki Province in Shikoku where, in 1184, the names of fourteen men who had offered their loyal service to the Minamoto were included in a *kyōmyō*; *AK* 1184/9/19. Some months later Yoritomo directed that a comprehensive list be prepared for all of western Japan; *AK* 1185/5/8. At the same time, *kyōmyō* were used for an opposite purpose—to convey the names of lawless, captured, dead, and disloyal persons; see, e.g., *AK* 1184/1/27, 1185/4/4, 1185/4/15; and *KB*, docs. 2 and 3: 1184/5/24 Minamoto Yoshitsune kudashibumi an, 1185/3/13 Minamoto Yoritomo kudashibumi an.

[6] See, e.g., *WG*, pp. 123–32; and *KB*, doc. 30: 1186/9/5 Minamoto Yoritomo kudashibumi.

ford Yoritomo new insights about the men who were seeking membership in his band. It is noteworthy that the label *gokenin* ("vassal"),
linked traditionally to 1180, was no factor as yet. The formulation of
this important category did not come until the early 1190s and belongs to a later, rationalizing phase of the Bakufu's construction, not
to the initial enrollment phase being discussed here. To a very considerable degree, then, the Bakufu's *jitō* network provided a partial scaf-
folding for its later *gokenin* system, rather than the reverse.[7]

A follow-up stage in this winnowing (and learning) process came in
1189. This was the occasion of the Bakufu's military campaign in the
north against the Ōshū Fujiwara.[8] The recruitment for this effort cast
a very wide net, which makes it clear that Kamakura had not proceeded very far in rationalizing and defining its vassalage. On the
basis of which warriors answered the call to arms, and on the basis of
the composition of their followings, Kamakura was able to advance
the process of distinguishing leaders from subordinates and of measuring loyalty, merit, and influence. As a result, new men were added
while others were dropped, though unfortunately the record is thin
on specifics.[9] Certainly there was no large-scale round of new *jitō* appointments and no immediate capping of the vassalage.

The final stage would not begin until 1192, when the Bakufu took
its most important steps toward clarifying its collective identity. In
that year it began appointing provincial officers called *shugo*,[10] whose
task it was to compile registers of warriors who warranted permanent
designation as vassals. These lists were different from the earlier *kyōmyō*, since a decade, and ongoing reorganizations, had intervened.[11]
Though only a handful of these compilations survive, they were
probably prepared, one by one, during the half dozen or so years fol-

[7] For a reevaluation of the *gokenin* phenomenon, see Mass, "The Early Bakufu and
Feudalism," pp. 131–35.

[8] *WG*, pp. 144–51.

[9] See, e.g., Document 59: 1239/11/5 Kantō gechijō an, for a reference to a post-Ōshū
award having been made. Also, *KB*, doc. 37: 1192/2/28 Minamoto Yoritomo kudashibumi utsushi, for a termination and replacement on the basis of performance in the
Ōshū Campaign.

[10] There is some dispute about precisely when the first *shugo* were appointed; see
WG, pp. 93–102, 203–10; and Mass, "The Early Bakufu and Feudalism," pp. 133–34.

[11] This is the surmise, for example, of Prof. Tanaka in reference to Sanuki Province
(see n. 5 above). He observes, however, that since the 1190s register is not extant, we are
forced to rely on the earlier list. See Tanaka Minoru, "Sanuki no kuni jitō gokenin ni
tsuite," pp. 369–71.

lowing 1192.[12] An accompanying step was the invention of the label *gokenin* for all who appeared on the lists. With the institutionalization of this category, the warrior class was divided into *gokenin* and *higokenin* (non-vassals), both of whom may earlier have been "Minamoto." And thus, by the end of Yoritomo's lifetime (1199), Kamakura had at last set the boundaries for its own formal membership.

In practice this proved scarcely enough. Since the names of individuals were included on the registers, families per se were not enrolled. Neither were they defined or delimited. In effect, the Bakufu had added its imprimatur to the intrahouse authority of the persons whose names did appear; but it was leaving to them and their kinsmen to cohere or to divide in future. From beginning to end the latter course was always more normal.

As already indicated, kin of the same generation tended to resist subordination to collaterals, a condition exacerbated by the Genpei War. For example, the Edo and Kasai, of different surnames but with a common great-grandfather, were initially acknowledged by Yoritomo as representing a single kindred. The union failed, however, and ultimately had to be dissolved. The two heads were recognized as separate *gokenin*.[13] The case of the Kawagoe and Hatakeyama is similar. In 1180, Kawagoe Shigeyori accepted subordination to his kinsman, Hatakeyama Shigetada, though he quickly moved to achieve independent status.[14] In the next generation the second and third sons of Shigeyori, each a vassal in his own right, joined a Bakufu unit in pursuit of Shigetada, who had now been accused of treachery.[15]

Stories like these can be duplicated readily in many parts of the country. In Kyushu, for example, Yoritomo accepted into vassalage numerous relatives from the Matsuura clan;[16] in Western Honshu, he

---

[12] The six we know of are Tanba (1192), Wakasa (1196), Tajima (1197), Satsuma (1197), Ōsumi (1198), and Izumi (indeterminate); see Tanaka Minoru, "Kamakura shoki no seiji katei—Kenkyū nenkan o chūshin ni shite," p. 24, for the citations. A useful discussion appears in Seno Seiichirō, "Hizen no kuni ni okeru Kamakura gokenin," pp. 30–33.

[13] *AK* 1180/9/29; *WG*, pp. 150–51 (for the Kasai); *Edo shi kankei monjo shū*, p. 1 (for the Edo).

[14] *AK* 1180/8/26, 1180/10/4, 1182/1/28, 1182/8/12, 1184/1/20, 1184/9/14, 1185/11/12, 1187/10/5.

[15] *AK* 1205/6/22. For Shigeyori's sons, *AK* 1219/1/27, 1221/6/18, 1226/4/10, 1228/7/23, 1232/12/23.

[16] For details, see Seno Seiichirō, "Chinzei ni okeru tō—Matsuura tō no baai," pp. 66–72. The trunk line head of the Matsuura was thus in exactly the same situation as the branch chiefs.

did the same for three sons who originated the Masuda, Misumi, and Shufu families;[17] and in the Kanto, he recognized three brothers as heads of the Oyama, Naganuma, and Yūki houses.[18] Yet at the same time, Yoritomo ordered the branches of another kindred, the Miura, to obey their clan chieftain—even as he acknowledged their autonomy.[19] The new status of vassal, distributed to multiple persons within families, bore witness to a society only loosely cemented by blood ties.

Parallel to these compositional changes within families was an unprecedented shifting of property rights. Men who were treacherous or lawless regularly had their land rights redirected to those the regime wished to pacify and/or honor. These rewards were granted as *jitō shiki*, mostly to easterners. Simultaneously, Yoritomo made confirmatory grants, which were *jitō* rewards, *in situ*, over land rights already held. Logically, the recipients of both types of titles, but especially the second, ought to have felt more secure. *Shiki*, mostly hereditary earlier, should have been automatically heritable under Yoritomo.

Yet this is not at all what we encounter. During the first generation we find no *jitō* testaments to children, and no explicit validations of holder-initiated transfers. The exchanges that did take place occurred at the behest of Yoritomo. Does this mean then that the lord of Kamakura did not intend these newly elite titles to be hereditary?

The absence of both wills and confirmations of wills has apparently not been noticed before. Yoritomo did on occasion assign rights to survivors—at times under unlikely circumstances.[20] But this was not in response to wills. In this sense, *jitō* awards were only conditional grants; they represent another in a long list of authoritarian policies attributable to the Kamakura chieftain. Having allowed kin groupings

[17] See Kobayashi Hiroshi, "Iwami no kuni Masuda shi no ryōshusei ni tsuite," pp. 132–33. In the next generation there was a further proliferation of surnames.

[18] These were the sons of Oyama (Fujiwara) Masamitsu: Oyama Tomomasa, Naganuma Munemasa, and Yūki Tomomitsu. The names of all three fill the early pages of *AK*. For Tomomasa's will, see Document 41: 1230/2/20 Oyama Tomomasa yuzurijō.

[19] For the admonition, see *AK* 1193/1/20; yet collaterals were being granted *jitō* rights, e.g., a pair of *jitō shiki* to a nephew of the kindred head, Yoshizumi. See *KB*, doc. 12: 1192/10/21 shōgun ke mandokoro kudashibumi, and *Nakajō ke monjo*, 1192/10/21 shōgun ke mandokoro kudashibumi, *KI*, 2: 51, doc. 630. At this juncture the nephew was called Taira Munezane; less than a generation later he was called Wada Munezane when his bequest to his own nephew, Takai Shigemochi, was confirmed by the Bakufu; Document 12: 1205/2/22 Kantō gechijō. The Miura were rapidly proliferating.

[20] See n. 26 and n. 49 below.

to divide mostly by their own dictates, Yoritomo cut back on that freedom by controlling the flow of their *jitō* titles. At any rate, *jitō* recipients did not attempt to turn their awards into alienable, private property. Not until after the founder's death would the initiative for *jitō* transmissions pass permanently to their holders.

This abridgement by Yoritomo of the hereditary principle needs to be understood in its broadest context. The fate of non-*jitō* titles during the war might be considered germane. In general, holders who experienced risk either commended their property to a new protector or else appealed to one already in place.[21] Yet heritability was not affected, a condition made clear in two ways. First, sale deeds, involving the transfer of rights to non-kin, were unchanged in both number and content.[22] And second, though settlements upon relatives may have been cut back, their range was entirely normal—from a father's release of land to a daughter, to a mother's release of land to a son, to the expected passage of a *shiki* to a male holder's eldest son.[23] At the end of the conflict the frequency of wills was at any rate restored to earlier numbers, and heritability was once again made explicit.[24] Only *jitō* posts represented an exception here. The hand of Yoritomo seems unmistakable.

During the latter's rulership, then, were vassal holdings simply non-transferable? Though wills were not submitted to him,[25] he did at

[21] For a commendation, see *Jingoji monjo*, 1182/7/8 Fujiwara Sadayoshi kishinjō, *HI*, 8: 3067, doc. 4036. For an appeal (of ravagings "in the wake of the Kantō uprising"), along with the response, see *Matsuo jinja monjo*, 1181/9/16 kan senshi, *HI*, 8: 3049, doc. 4005.

[22] About three dozen sale deeds survive from the period of the Genpei War. Typical is one in which the seller noted that his father bought the property a year earlier and transferred it to his son, who, by reason of need, is now reselling it; *Kōmyōji komonjo*, 1181/2 hatake-chi baiken, *HI*, 8: 3030, doc. 3981. The format of these deeds is identical to that of the pre- and postwar era; see, e.g., Documents 53–54: 1237/7/13 Minamoto no ujime baiken an, 1237/8/6 Fujiwara no ujime baiken an.

[23] In sequence, *Tōdaiji monjo*, 1183/2/6 Takebe Narikuni denchi shobunjō, *HI*, 8: 3079, doc. 4067; *Tōdaiji monjo*, 1183/2/19 Fujii Nakako denchi shobunjō, *HI*, 8: 3080, doc. 4069; *Takeo jinja monjo*, 1183/12/15 Takeo sha Fujiwara Sadakado yuzurijō, *HI*, 8: 3109, doc. 4121.

[24] Typical is a courtier's approval of a father-to-son bequest of a custodianship; Document 5: 1187/10/5 udaijin ke mandokoro kudashibumi. For the promise of heritability for a newly established custodianship, see *KB*, doc. 57: 1186/10/16 Hachijōin-no-chō kudashibumi.

[25] I know of only a single exception, which involved non-*jitō* rights: in 1186, Yuasa Muneshige of Kii Province had his conveyance of property rights to children confirmed by Yoritomo; *Sakiyama monjo*, 1186/5/7 Minamoto Yoritomo kudashibumi an, *KI*, 1: 66,

times reassign *jitō* titles, occasionally to a holder's survivors.[26] In other words, petitions by heirs, rather than wills by their fathers, were apparently acceptable, which meant that *jitō* titles were *renewable*, if not yet heritable. Under Yoritomo, then, *jitō shiki* were life awards that the lord might choose to extend. They had not yet become family property.

In fact, the Kamakura lord distributed *jitō* posts to anyone, warrior or non-warrior, male or female, whom he might wish to reward.[27] Of particular note were awards to women, a development wholly without precedent. Hitherto, provincial *shiki* were denied to women; but now, almost casually, they were made available to them—another of Yoritomo's innovations. To cite only the best-known example, his own former wet nurse (who was also the widow and mother of vassals of the Oyama house) was granted an edict of investiture.[28] Commenting on this incident, the *Azuma kagami* noted the lady's "unusual merit in spite of her being a woman."[29] The subject of women's property rights is one we shall return to presently.

In summary, then, Yoritomo's contribution to inheritance practices had both forward- and backward-looking aspects. He converted provincial women into full *shiki* holders; but he refused to countenance the heredification of the *jitō* title. He allowed families to divide and subdivide as they saw fit, and he fully supported the proliferation of new surnames; but he failed to create an environment in which vassals could plan confidently for the future. On balance, Yoritomo did not make a lasting imprint on Japan's inheritance system. Ironically, his immediate successors, less valued by historians, did exactly that.

---

doc. 99. Moreover, in 1191, Kumagaya Naozane issued a will to his fourth son that may have involved a *jitō* portion; Document 7: 1191/3/1 Kumagaya Naozane yuzurijō; and *AK* 1182/6/5, citing a purported investiture of 1182/5/30. But there is no confirmation extant. Finally, what appears from a fragment to be a confirmation of a *jitō* release is actually an initial appointment over homelands in response to a warrior's petition; *Kōzuma monjo*, 1186/5/6 Minamoto Yoritomo kudashibumi an, *KI*, 1: 66, doc. 98; and *ibid.*, 1186/6/27 dazaifu kudashibumi an, *KI*, 1: 82, doc. 119.

[26] See, e.g., a reassignment to a mother after her son was dispossessed, and a further reassignment to the son's widow after he was executed; *AK* 1185/11/12, 1187/10/5. The most explicit example of a son's being confirmed in the holdings of his father is *Iriki Honda monjo*, 1193/9/4 shōgun ke mandokoro kudashibumi an, *KI*, 2: 86, doc. 683. No *jitō shiki* are referred to and there is no mention of a father's release document. See the reference to these same events in *DKR*, doc. 55: 1203/12/28 Hōjō Tokimasa kudashibumi an.

[27] See *WG*, pp. 171–72, for examples.

[28] *Minagawa monjo*, 1187/12/1 Minamoto Yoritomo kudashibumi, *KI*, 1: 172, doc. 287.

[29] *AK* 1187/12/1.

The death of Yoritomo (1199) was followed by a period of unrest within the Bakufu. Conspiracies, real and imagined, dominated political events, leading to the ouster of key families and the bumpy rise of the Hōjō.[30] But with the founder now gone, there was little to prevent *jitō* posts from finally becoming heritable. This did not happen instantly in 1199, but it was the regular condition by 1205.

Though we are not able to trace the process exactly, we are able to note several important steps. In 1199/11, for example, a person who had received a *jitō* post in 1193 petitioned the Bakufu for approval of its passage to his son. When Kamakura agreed, it was taking an action for which there is no known Yoritomo-era precedent.[31] Several months later we see an elaboration. In early 1200, the Bakufu approved the passage of a religious title to a petitioner's son, whereupon the petitioner issued a *yuzurijō*.[32] In both cases a petition by a would-be donor was the first step, followed (at least in the second case) by a conveyance. It was a reversal of the traditional practice of transmission followed by confirmation, but it represented an advance nonetheless.

During the next several years the Bakufu improved its judicial capabilities, which drew it ever more deeply into inheritance questions. In 1202, it announced that compromises based on equity would be the guide for resolving such disputes,[33] and immediately it became embroiled in a number of them. Few, however, proved easily tractable.[34] In fact, Kamakura's own actions often contributed to the trouble. In 1203, for instance, it responded to the death of a *jitō* by replacing him with someone unrelated. However, it offered to review the matter in case there was a challenger. The case dissolved into a judicial quagmire.[35]

But still there were no transfers of *jitō shiki* by will, at least none for which evidence survives. An example of 1201 has been mislabeled

---

[30] See Varley, "The Hōjō Family and Succession to Power," pp. 143–54; and *DKR*, pp. 70–80.

[31] *AK* 1193/11/12; 1199/11/8. The original grant specified a *jitō shiki* though the later confirmation did not.

[32] *Daigoji monjo*, 1200/int.2/29 Kantō migyōsho an, *KI*, 2: 385, doc. 1121; *ibid.*, 1200/3/27 Kigen yuzurijō, *KI*, 2: 388, doc. 1127. The original appointment by Yoritomo occurred in 1185; *ibid.*, 1185/12/30 Minamoto Yoritomo buninjō an, *KI*, 1: 14, doc. 32.

[33] *AK* 1202/5/2. For other judicial advances during these years, see *DKR*, chap. 3.

[34] For example, *Kōzuma monjo*, 1203/4/10 Kantō migyōsho, *KI*, 3: 89, doc. 1354, and its continuation up to 1212: *DKR*, doc. 65: 1212/12/13 shōgun ke mandokoro kudashibumi an. Also, beginning in 1202, the references in *DKR*, doc. 57: 1205/4/25 Kantō gechijō.

[35] *Nejime monjo*, 1203/7/3 Kantō kudashibumi an, *KI*, 3: 94, doc. 1367. For the continuation, see *DKR*, doc. 60: 1206/2/29 Hōjō Yoshitoki hōsho.

(and therefore misinterpreted) by Takeuchi.[36] The earliest authentic case dates from 1204,[37] and within a year the Bakufu was approving these quite routinely. In hindsight, the development seems inevitable since the release and confirmation procedure had long been so normal for other *shiki*.[38] Also, the first generation of *jitō* was now aging, and it was easier for holders to determine their successors than for the Bakufu, normally ignorant of local conditions, to do so. Nor was it sensible to continue accepting petitions by heirs, who might be in competition with one another; testaments by donors were a much more efficient substitute. Finally, the economic base of the vassalage needed to be regularized. Ironically, *jitō* dismissals, which increased momentarily, were a natural part of the process.[39] But greater permanency, like academic tenure, required decisions in both directions.

The years 1204–5 were eventful ones, then, for the vassalage. But they were also portentous for the Bakufu. In 1205, Hōjō Tokimasa, Yoritomo's father-in-law and de facto Kamakura ruler, was ousted by a conspiracy led by his own children. A broader rulership made up of warriors and non-warriors now followed.[40] One result, as we have seen, was the rapid heredification of the *jitō* title. For its part, Kamakura reserved to itself a right of exclusive probate. *Jitō* thus joined the host of other offices that had succumbed to privatization, a condition made "official" when Kamakura announced in 1206 that no at-

[36] See *KI*, 3: 31, doc. 1234, which is labeled "*jitō bō yuzurijō an.*" In fact, the document bears two signatures, and it is the other one (not that of a *jitō*, which appears in second place anyway) that belongs to the donor; see *Kikuōji monjo*, 1201/7/20 suke Jirō yuzurijō an, *Zōtei Kano komonjo*, p. 39, doc. 60; and *ibid.*, 1171/2 Nakahara Yorisada yuzurijō an, *ibid.*, p. 30, doc. 44. The second signatory, one "*jitō shami,*" is unknown, but is possibly the area's dominant local authority; his signature would thus have been an acknowledgment, not a release.

[37] *Ōi monjo*, 1204/12/26 jitō Ki Saneharu yuzurijō an, *KI*, 3: 219–20, doc. 1511. Unfortunately, this document is only a fragment and the term "*jitō shiki*" does not appear. Yet it clearly was a *yuzurijō* conveying property in Musashi Province, and it is signed "*jitō.*" Moreover, a Bakufu confirmation of it, also a fragment, survives from 1212. For a photograph of both documents plus a discussion (though not of this point), see *Ōta ku komonjo, chūsei hen*, pp. 55–56.

[38] During this same period, e.g., *Tōdaiji monjo*, 1201/3/5 Tōdaiji kudashibumi an, *KI*, 3: 4, doc. 1188 (for a confirmation of a father-to-son devise of a *gesu shiki*); and *Sonkeikaku shozō monjo*, 1204/3 bō kudashibumi, *KI*, 3: 133, doc. 1443 (also for a *gesu shiki*).

[39] These are listed and discussed in *DKR*, p. 80, n. 77.

[40] Tokimasa had ruled almost single-handedly from the ouster of Yoriie, the second shogun, in 1203, to his own ouster, by his son and daughter Yoshitoki and Masako, in 1205. See Varley, "The Hōjō Family and Succession to Power," pp. 146–54; Mass, "The Early Bakufu and Feudalism," pp. 128–30; and *DKR*, pp. 70–71, 75–80.

tainders would occur for land rights awarded by Yoritomo except for the very gravest of crimes.[41] This was interpreted to mean that testaments by *jitō* would be approved pro forma.[42] Hitherto safeguarded from the tamperings of estate owners, *jitō* were now made secure from interference by the Bakufu.[43]

In an unexpected (though scarcely illogical) development, external security worked to exacerbate internal rivalries. With the solidification of disposable land rights, cleavages within families sharpened and property disputes multiplied. The period before 1221 saw a general upsurge in suits of this kind, which were inevitably judged by Kamakura.[44] In fact, this was only one dimension of a now rapidly changing situation. *Jitō*, secure in the knowledge that their conveyances would be approved, became more capricious in their decisions. Spitefulness increased, division schemes abounded, and minds were constantly changing. Indeed, as we shall see, *jitō* were writing and rewriting wills and thoroughly intimidating their children.

What were the specific changes that accompanied heredification? For one thing, the almost formulaic selection of an eldest son as successor now gave way to an often fierce competition among siblings. Nothing reflects this better than the rising incidence of disinheritance. A practice still infrequent in late Heian times, disinheritance became common soon after. A non-*jitō* case of 1200 is illustrative. In that year a father inflicted a double indignity on his eldest son: he announced that he was being bypassed, and he forced him to acknowledge this in writing by countersigning the will earmarked for his younger brother. This unfortunate son spent the next forty years disputing with his brothers and nephews over the inheritance that might have been his.[45]

[41] *AK* 1206/1/27.

[42] For a sampling of these confirmations, see Documents 12–15: 1205/2/22 Kantō gechijō (the earliest surviving example), 1208/3/13 Kantō kudashibumi an, 1212/10/27 shōgun ke mandokoro kudashibumi, and 1215/3/23 shōgun ke mandokoro kudashibumi an. Also, *KB*, doc. 103: 1208/int.4/27 Kantō kudashibumi; and *DKR*, p. 225, n. 6, for a reference to a bequest of 1210, and a confirmation of 1217.

[43] The safeguarding of *jitō* from proprietors took the form, of course, of the Bakufu's claiming exclusive authority over appointments and dismissals; *WG*, chap. 5.

[44] E.g., Document 18: 1209/7/28 shōgun ke mandokoro kudashibumi an; Document 20: 1220/12/10 Kantō gechijō. Also, *DKR*, doc. 58: 1205/5/23 Kantō gechijō; *DKR*, doc. 62: 1206/7/14 Kantō kudashibumi; *DKR*, doc. 66: 1213/11/30 Kantō gechijō an; *DKR*, doc. 68: 1217/1/22 dazaifu shugosho kudashibumi an.

[45] Documents 9–10, 61: 1186/4/29 Fujiwara Yukifusa yuzurijō, 1200/int.2 Fujiwara Yukiakira yuzurijō an, 1241/8/22 Kantō gechijō. The land units being transferred here were not *jitō shiki*, though the family was (or would become) *gokenin*.

A second example (involving a *jitō shiki*) shows an opposite result. In 1208, an 80-year-old father, who had earlier divided his property between two sons, now changed his mind. The eldest son was bequeathed the inheritance owing to outrages committed by the son of the other son, i.e., the donor's grandson. In this case, then, it was a second son who was disinherited.[46] Obviously, a *jitō* holder, in the freer environment after 1205, not only could disinherit a child in advance of releasing his title, but he could oblige that child, even after conveyance, to retrocede it. This practice, too, became standard.

A third practice with origins dating from this period is the partitioning of *jitō shiki*. Earlier we noted that, during the Heian era, land was divisible but *shiki* were not. A donor was free to settle property on a variety of heirs, but his *shiki*, the core element of any portfolio, was invariably transferred intact. A *shiki* may have been heritable, in other words, but it was not partible. In the case of *jitō shiki*, heredification was delayed by a generation, as we have seen. Yet just as these titles were becoming hereditary they also became subject to parceling: in 1209, the Bakufu referred to a "one-half *jitō shiki*," a concept not previously articulated.

The circumstances here are of interest. A parent-donor had divided a village, for which he held a *jitō* post, between two sons. One son encroached on the other, prompting a petition and a Bakufu judgment. The judgment acknowledged the divided *shiki*.[47] In other words, the donor had divided the village, but the Bakufu had divided its *shiki*. In future, the initiative would be reversed: donors would do the dividing, creating new *jitō* titles out of old. As a result, the Bakufu would lose control over the shape (and shaping) of its own network.

A fourth new practice, already referred to, received its first stimulus from Yoritomo. This was the proliferation—after 1205—of women *jitō*. Women, in fact, came to hold these titles by four major routes. First, they might simply be appointed—as occurred in 1220 to a woman of Izu Province. What makes this case interesting is that the woman had a brother, who served as her deputy (*jitōdai*).[48] A second, more common route was the assignment of titles previously held by a

[46] Document 17: 1208/7 Jinkaku yuzurijō an. The events of 1208, in fact, represent only a minor episode in what is perhaps the classic early Kamakura-era inheritance dispute—the Ojika Island case. For an accounting of its judicial aspects, see *DKR*, pp. 95–101.

[47] Document 18: 1209/7/28 shōgun ke mandokoro kudashibumi an.

[48] Document 37: 1228/3/30 Kantō gechijō. Nor should we think that women never became deputies; see Document 51: 1237/3/13 Hōjō Yasutoki kudashibumi.

woman's husband. Remarkably, at least some of these cases followed treachery by those husbands against the Bakufu.[49] More logical and normal were assignments to widows whose husbands had died, not treacherously, but loyally in battle.[50] A variation involved intestate cases—husbands who had died before writing their wills.[51] The final two routes were the most common of all: women who inherited *jitō* titles from a parent or spouse; and women who were invested with an executor's authority to follow the death of their husband.[52]

As a result of these reforms, women of the warrior elite reached the acme of their power and influence. As we shall see, this development proved only ephemeral; it was in decline by the late thirteenth century. But for several generations, unmarried women and women as widows had the potential to dominate their families. The widow of Yoritomo, Hōjō Masako, is only the most famous example.[53] At any rate, the origins of this phenomenon, so central to the history of the family, clearly bear closer scrutiny.

The rise of women to full *shiki*-holding status seems related to a secondary development. This was the appearance of "life-tenure" inheritances, expressed by the term *ichigo* ("generation"). From property releases made in perpetuity—the practice in Heian times—there now emerged property releases encumbered by entails. In other words, at almost the same moment that women became *jitō*, some (but not all) of them lost the power to bequeath. Opposition to mothers by children (especially by sons) was a major factor here. Thus, whereas not all transmissions would *need* to be limited, the machinery for making them so had to exist. The effect was to convert women into two types of *jitō* holders—permanent and impermanent, with the power to determine a succession as the critical difference between them. Full possessions included the right to convey *shiki* in wills; limited possessions implied little more than a trust. It seems unlikely that the unfettered type could have become so quickly entrenched without the emergence of its more limited counterpart.

[49] E.g., the case of Kajiwara Kagetaka (a conspirator son of the infamous Kagetoki), and the case of Hatakeyama Shigetada; *AK* 1200/6/29, 1210/5/14.

[50] E.g., *DKR*, doc. 13: 1221/7/24 Kantō gechijō.

[51] Four documents from the mid-Kamakura period show the full range of possible dispositions here: Documents 80–83: 1257/7/6 Kantō gechijō, 1259/12/23 Kantō gechijō, 1265/12/27 Kantō gechijō an, 1272/10/29 Kantō gechijō. In the period before 1221 (though not for a *jitō shiki*), see Document 19: 1218/4/28 goke Ōe yuzurijō.

[52] See Chapter 3 for details.

[53] See Butler, "Woman of Power Behind the Kamakura Bakufu."

We can actually trace this development by looking at the changes in usage and context of the term *ichigo*. Near the end of the Heian period the word appeared for the first time in property records. The "lifetime" referred to was that of the present or future holder, but there was no particular link with women and no connotation of property held in trust.[54] The transition to the new usage came in the 1190s. For example, in a release of 1191, a priest of the Daigoji named two legatees in sequence, both his own disciples. After the death of the first, the inheritance was to go to the second.[55] The term *ichigo* was used to facilitate an entail. In a second example, the rebuilder of Tōdaiji, Shunjōbō Chōgen, issued his testament, dealing with a number of *shōen*. For an estate whose custodianship was held by a widow, Chōgen enjoined her to pass it to her eldest daughter, who in turn was to pass it to her eldest son. Both transfers were to follow the lifetime (*ichigo*) of a female holder, with the ultimate object a male.[56]

Though Chōgen requested the backing of Yoritomo, his dispositions had not in fact been made to vassals. The same was true of a priest's release of 1200, though here the venue was the Kantō for lands that had been granted by Kamakura. The conditions of the release are pertinent: a transfer was made to a son, but a portion was held back for his mother. In other words, the widow of the donor would receive a life bequest, transmittable upon her death to the main heir.[57]

It was at this juncture that *jitō shiki* became heritable, and women were naturally included here. In 1210, for example, a first-generation *jitō* conveyed his title to his daughter.[58] Five years later, the Bakufu confirmed a bequest of three such titles to a wife.[59] Daughters and wives were thus becoming *jitō* by inheritance. Also in 1210 the Bakufu acknowledged the right of a widow to adopt an heir and to bequeath her *jitō* office to him.[60] Even before that date, women were defending their property in Bakufu tribunals against external challengers.[61]

At the same time, however, problems over the division of assets

[54] There are at least ten documents (beginning in 1128) that contain the word *ichigo*. *HI*, 6, docs. 2516, 2939, 3041, 3046; *HI*, 7, doc. 3761; *HI*, 8, docs. 3817, 3830, 4036, 4171; *HI*, 10, doc. 4980.

[55] *Daigoji monjo*, 1191/4/21 sō Shōkai yuzurijō an, *KI*, 1: 409, doc. 528.

[56] 1197/6/15 Chōgen yuzurijō, in *Shunjōbō Chōgen shiryō shūsei*, p. 349.

[57] Document 11: 1200/12/19 Kashima sha ōnegi Nakatomi Chikahiro yuzurijō.

[58] Referred to in Document 59: 1239/11/5 Kantō gechijō an.

[59] *KB*, doc. 24: 1215/3/22 shōgun ke mandokoro kudashibumi an.

[60] *AK* 1210/9/14.

[61] *Sappan kyūki zatsuroku*, 1201/11/22 Kantō gechijō an, *KBSS*, 1: 5, doc. 4.

were developing among survivors. In a case that may have had wide-ranging influence, a mother brought suit against her son over possession of two *jitō shiki*. The dispute was precipitated by a decision of the Bakufu to assign the titles to the son of the former holder, a vassal who had fallen in battle in 1213. In her suit the mother claimed that the assignment was unjustified, but that if the error were corrected, she would keep them in trust for her son. When the Bakufu supported this claim in 1220, it was endorsing an important principle: from this point forward, tenures of both types—life and permanent—would be common, with feasibility governing the choice.[62]

A related circumstance that also promoted women as *shiki* holders was Kamakura's awarding of multiple *jitō* titles. Portfolios were large enough to guarantee largesse for all family members. Indeed, at the managerial level, the holding of widely dispersed assets was an entirely new phenomenon. For Kamakura's vassalage, it meant devising fresh strategies for administering often far-flung properties. Partible inheritance relieved some of this pressure; sons, daughters, and wives might receive their own *jitō shiki*. But such dispersal might also fragment families. For both the Bakufu and its followers, then, there were compelling reasons to enhance the authority of the house head.

It is important to note that the Bakufu neither curtailed the flow of new titles nor appreciably widened its distribution pool. In other words, honored easterners continued to receive new honors,[63] in contrast to less-esteemed westerners.[64] Indeed, these were developments that the core of the vassalage had little wish to disturb. The proliferation of collateral lines, newly endowed with *jitō* posts, might thus have seemed family-enhancing. But it also meant that coordination would be made more difficult. In the event, the principal heir would have to become the spokesman for and conduit to his siblings. This policy—replete with many unresolved issues—had its beginnings (as with so much else) in the period after 1205.

The creation of an administrative center for families, even as junior heirs were becoming *jitō*, took cognizance of the partible inheritance system and attempted to turn it to advantage. While in no way tam-

[62] Document 20: 1220/12/10 Kantō gechijō.

[63] The steady accumulation of *jitō* posts is graphically revealed in the cases of the Oyama and Nikaidō; Document 41: 1230/2/20 Oyama Tomomasa yuzurijō an; Document 60; 1240/10/14 Nikaidō Motoyuki yuzurijō.

[64] In fact, many westerners simply dropped off the vassal rolls. In Ōsumi Province, for instance, the numbers decreased from the original total of 33, mostly around 1204; Gomi Yoshio, "Ōsumi gokenin ni tsuite," p. 29. For the general subject of discrimination against non-easterners, see *DKR*, pp. 16–31.

pering with individual holdings, the Bakufu imposed vassal services and dues (*gokeninyaku* and *onkuji*) on sibling sets, with secondary heirs discharging obligations under the supervision of the head and in accordance with the sizes of their land shares. The head, meaning the principal heir, would receive the collection order from Kamakura, would inform his siblings of what they owed, and would coordinate both gathering and payment.

The earliest reference to this procedure appears in a vassal release of 1212. Significantly, it is also the first document to distinguish *chakushi* from *shoshi*, i.e., primary from secondary heirs.[65] We can only assume that the initiative here came from Kamakura, though no explicit statement is extant.[66] At any rate, the integrity of families was now bolstered, even while the potential for children's inheritances was enhanced. In effect, Kamakura was supporting the independence of junior heirs but depending for its services on senior heirs. From this point forward, *chakushi*, *shoshi*, *onkuji*, and *gokeninyaku* would become regular, intertwined features of the Kamakura vassal system.

There were no other inheritance-related innovations during the period before the Jōkyū War (1221). For example, the Bakufu's other officer network, the *shugo*, was not made subject to heredification or subdivision on the model of *jitō*. *Shugo* holders were frequently replaced by Kamakura, and the office retained its bureaucratic essence. Though a handful of releases in the 1220s and later did include *shugo shiki*, the posts were nevertheless considered reassignable.[67] In general, the period to 1221 experienced a natural maturation of all that had been introduced after 1205. The era was one in which the Bakufu's chancellery (*mandokoro*) exercised dominant power, implying a moderate level of collective rule.[68] The rivalries implicit behind this façade neither impeded the operations of Kamakura nor led to any additional shifts in its inheritance policies.

---

[65] *Mōri ke monjo*, 1212/8/19 Saeki Takatomo tō rensho yuzurijō utsushi, *KI*, 4: 35, doc. 1938. See also a follow-up release of two years later; *ibid.*, 1214/8/25 Saeki Takatomo yuzurijō utsushi, *KI*, 4: 140, doc. 2120.

[66] Many historians have noted this new responsibility of the house head. It is the only innovation in the list presented here to have been dealt with by previous scholars. See, e.g., Toyoda, *Bushidan to sonraku*, p. 187; Satō, "Bakufuron," pp. 16–17; and Kawai Masaharu, "Kamakura bushidan no kōzō," p. 3.

[67] The classic example concerned the Shimazu house head who prepared his will in 1227 and had it confirmed almost immediately; Document 36: 1227/10/10 shōgun sodehan kudashibumi. Though the confirmation included the *shugo* title for Echizen Province, the latter was reassigned within the year; *AK* 1228/5/16.

[68] For this story, see *DKR*, pp. 75–80.

Perhaps the most notable achievement overall was the advance during these years of Bakufu justice. In particular, Kamakura, which had earlier issued premature judgments and had then had to reverse itself, now gave greater attention to the review of evidence. As it turned out, the document type that proved most susceptible to forgery (or the charge of forgery) was the testament. Though countless suits would later come to hang on questions of document authenticity, even now there were accusations of bogus wills that needed to be checked. In an incident of 1213, for example, the outcome of a suit rested on a comparison of the seal on a conveyance written in the native syllabary with the seals appearing on other documents.[69] Two years later another charge of forgery was corroborated by means of a deposition submitted by a neighboring vassal.[70] The Bakufu was learning that the freedom of vassals to write wills meant the freedom to abuse them or to claim their abuse. At the same time, the heritability of *jitō* titles meant that contests over them, as valuable resources, could only increase. In the age of Yoritomo, the chieftain determined the contours of what was essentially his band of *jitō*. Now, in marked contrast, the Bakufu dealt with questions on the shape of a network increasingly set by the *jitō* themselves.

In the first month of 1219 the Shogun Sanetomo was murdered and the Minamoto line came to an end. Dramatic though this development was, the chieftainship had long since been superseded in practice by the senior vassalage, as we have noted. The real importance of 1219 lay in the opportunity it afforded to the Hōjō: in the absence of a titular head, the regent (Hōjō Yoshitoki) could rule in his place.[71] The question for us, therefore, is whether this seizure of power, at the expense of the vassalage, affected vassal inheritances. Did the Hōjō takeover promote the splits that broke into the open with the beginning of the Jōkyū War?

Unfortunately, there are few wills and even fewer adjudicated disputes for which information survives. Only a handful of cases is extant. In 1219, for example, a son was appointed to a *jitō* post vacated by his father. The father's departure had been involuntary, the result of an illegal banishment by the proprietor. By its action the Bakufu

---

[69] *Kawakami Tadafusa ichiryū kafu*, 1213/9/1 Tōtomi no kami Minamoto Chikahiro kudashibumi an, *KI*, 4: 85–86, doc. 2027. Chikahiro was a member of the Bakufu's chancellery (*mandokoro*).

[70] *DKR*, doc. 67: 1215/10/2 shōgun ke mandokoro kudashibumi an.

[71] The next shogun, a child of the Fujiwara family, would not be formally installed until 1226.

was affirming the heritability of the title even without a release by its holder.[72] A year later Kamakura made another decision that can only be considered favorable to the vassalage. This was the case, referred to above, in which a mother brought suit against her son. The Bakufu's verdict was to assign a life tenure to the mother, with possession promised eventually to the son.[73] The fact that such two-stage arrangements would soon become common is suggestive of their obvious appeal.

A third action taken during this period involved a confirmation in the wake of a theft of documents. The beneficiary here was the granddaughter of an original *jitō*—another case involving a woman.[74] A final sequence also involved women, though here the Bakufu's action followed, rather than preceded, the war. A month before the outbreak of hostilities a female released her *jitō* titles to an eldest daughter. At the same time, she promised the inheritance to her son. We see in this episode a classic example of an *ichigo* conveyance—arranged in this instance by a woman! The Hōjō-controlled Bakufu duly confirmed the release.[75]

The Jōkyū War of 1221 was sparked by an ill-fated attempt by the ex-emperor Go-Toba to defeat the Bakufu and oust the Hōjō. Dissatisfaction with the Hōjō is the usual explanation for the defections that marked the fighting. As just indicated, however, decisions bearing on inheritances (as few as they are) do not lend support to this view. Even the son who lost out to his mother is not known to have fought against the Bakufu.[76] Nevertheless, other easterners did defect and we need to understand why.

For the most part, loyalty or disloyalty was reducible to private ambition. Families split apart with as little hesitation as we saw in the Genpei War. Yet Yoritomo, building his regime at the time, had actually been more accommodating; he welcomed earlier recalcitrants and often rewarded them lavishly, and collateral heads might reasonably look forward to vassalage. The Jōkyū War was different. For one thing, enemies were not forgiven. For another, a common goal behind joining one side or the other was to replace family rivals, not to create space between them. The stakes were the extensive properties held by such kin and the prospect of a consolidated headship. Brief

[72] *DKR*, doc. 69: 1219/9/16 Kantō gechijō an.
[73] Document 20: 1220/12/10 Kantō gechijō.
[74] *KB*, doc. 25: 1220/10/14 Kantō gechijō.
[75] Document 24: 1221/11/21 Kantō gechijō an.
[76] Though he does disappear from view; Document 20, n. 5.

though the war was, it tore apart many families and led to major restructurings.

We need to look at several of the more dramatic examples. Clearly, antagonisms existed that were just waiting for an appropriate outlet. This is indicated by the absence of prior judicial cases (the normal route) for most of the families that divided. The Sasaki are a case in point. When the war broke out the clan head Hirotsuna, his uncle, and his cousin quickly joined the side of the Imperial Court. By contrast, Hirotsuna's younger brother Nobutsuna as well as other relatives remained loyal to the Bakufu. With Kamakura's victory, the family's headship was transferred to Nobutsuna, and there was a parallel shifting of land rights.[77]

The basic division in this instance was one between rival siblings. Just as likely were splits between generations. For example, the elder Gotō, a resident of Kyoto, opted for the Court, but his son fought for Kamakura. However, the elder Ōe sided with Kamakura, while his son fought for the Court.[78] Obviously, the divisions within families were idiosyncratic; older persons were neither more nor less likely to favor traditional authority, as exemplified by Kyoto. Stated differently, whereas individual participants may have borne old grievances, it was normally more than memory that moved them to choose sides. Though the war has always been depicted as a bloodletting between the two power centers, the dominant divisions were actually among fighting men. One of the principal axes on which participants separated was the splits that existed within their own families.

When the ex-emperor's declaration of war arrived in Kamakura, the Bakufu's leadership settled on a significant strategy. For the first time it decided to employ the command structure implicit in its bolstering of house heads. In other words, the Bakufu would eschew its regular provincial commanders, the *shugo*, and also avoid calling up collateral heads even though they might be vassals. It invoked instead the emergency dimension of the normal peacetime policy of having siblings discharge their vassal services under house-head brothers. Perhaps the Hōjō hoped that recruitment in this fashion would solidify families more effectively than individual call-ups, or call-ups by *shugo*, would.

Unfortunately, we are unable to judge the outcome of this policy. The Bakufu was able to field a great army and achieved its victory in less than a month. But the extent to which defections were fostered by

[77] *DKR*, p. 22.
[78] *DKR*, pp. 22–23.

the failure to utilize branches as separate fighting units is unknown. From the point of view of rival siblings, subordination under a brother might have seemed threatening. On the other hand, the prospect of fighting under a family banner, with no apparent risk to property, might have been appealing. The best that can be said is that Kamakura—and its official chronicle—made much of the defections. Yet the men who remained loyal emerged from the conflict much strengthened. In line now for rewards, they would be enriched beyond all expectations.

Though the Bakufu had tightened its own links with house heads, and had given them a prominent visibility, it could scarcely afford to limit its rewards to them. As we will see in the next chapter, the environment had been created for the term *sōryō*, in its meaning of house head, to assume its historic usage: in the aftermath of the war, the terminology would catch up to the reality. Yet despite this development Kamakura did not veer headlong into some exclusive dependence on house heads. Rather, it maintained its connections with all its men and women and by the end of the decade had even expanded them. Junior and senior heirs would have equal access to Kamakura's tribunals, and all who received inheritances would be in line for confirmations.

Stating it this way makes it seem as if progress was simple and direct. In fact, the first half of the 1220s (like the second half of the 1180s) was replete with half steps and missteps. Kamakura would need to put right all that had been put wrong by the war. For one thing, more than the meritorious had to be rewarded; so too did the survivors of the meritorious who had fallen.[79] In many cases this was straightforward. But in other cases there were family members on opposing sides, or claims that there had been. At the same time, there were claims of special honor or dishonor, and claims of not fighting at all.[80] In each of these situations, whom to credit, whom to condemn, and whom to ignore required a well-considered decision.

Second, families had to be realigned in ways that accorded with their own and Kamakura's best interests. Indeed, as complicated as the Bakufu's choices were, the vassalage in a sense faced something worse. Hitherto, few families had uprooted themselves from their eastern bases to take up residence in the west, the site, perhaps, of a second *jitō* post. But now the center of gravity for many families was

[79] E.g., *DKR*, docs. 13–16, 18; *KB*, doc. 28.
[80] E.g., doc. 21; *DKR*, docs. 31–32.

shifting. Such were the prospects beyond the Kantō that they represented a magnet—and therefore a source of tension. For the moment,
then, the basic problem was how to respond to the new opportuni-
ties—how to reconcile the new wealth with the existing family machinery for exploiting it. Various approaches were adopted: a greater
emphasis on partible inheritance, a reduced emphasis on it, an effort
to strengthen the bonds of family, an effort to weaken these bonds.
All of these approaches became part of the landscape of Japan in the
era after Jōkyū.

The vassals of Kamakura never enjoyed richer promises than they
did after 1221. How they handled what they now had is the subject of
our next chapter.

CHAPTER 3

THE SŌRYŌ SYSTEM

Compared with its companion institutions (shogun, *shugo*, *jitō*, and *gokenin*), the Kamakura *sōryō* has always seemed difficult to grasp. There are several reasons for this. The first is that the designation itself was not a title that the regime distributed. House heads may have been recognized as *sōryō*, but they received their status from a parent, not from Kamakura. The Bakufu neither selected *sōryō* nor terminated them. A second difficulty is the confusion over origins. Unlike the other institutions, which have been dated to specific years,[1] the *sōryō* system has defied such precision. A third problem is with parameters (i.e., what to include in the system); and a fourth is with periodization, itself a product of uncertainty over a definition.

Encapsulating all of these is the problem of how to introduce the subject. Previous studies have seen the system as stemming from the inheritance practices of provincial society in the late twelfth century. Many have seen it additionally, however, as a Bakufu policy invented to control the vassalage: without its "programmatic" element, it loses its nature as a system and becomes merely an aid to description. For historians in Japan, therefore, the *sōryō* system has social and political dimensions. In general, it is made to look back to the pre-Kamakura age for patterns of property transmission and family organization, but it is made to look to the Yoritomo period for the policies that gave it force.

As valuable as this dual approach may be, it is inadequate to the task. Indeed, it is based on mistaken assumptions. For example, it was

[1] See Mass, "The Early Bakufu and Feudalism," pp. 124–35; *WG*, pp. 93–102, 112–19.

the successors of Yoritomo, not the Bakufu founder himself, who actually promoted a "system."[2] Yoritomo's own encounter with kin groups, as we have noted, led him to judge them as unreliable: the period of his rulership witnessed a shaking out of family components with only limited efforts at integration. Indeed, he neither granted property that was heritable nor worked especially to bolster house heads. Even the term *sōryō*—the Kamakura equivalent for house head—did not acquire its historic meaning until after Yoritomo's lifetime.[3]

A related weakness of previous scholarship is the softness of its analysis on the system's supposed eastern roots. The problem here is that the *sōryō* pattern of organization is difficult to trace across Yoritomo's inactivity and backwards from the maze of changes attributable to his successors. Not only were warriors in the east not much different from warriors in other frontier areas; but they were as likely as not to incline toward greater or lesser integration. Everything considered, then, the *sōryōsei* is reducible to what was new. Its only meaningful origins are those we can actually see. In this sense, the innovations of 1205 deserve all of the emphasis we have given them.

Apart from such lapses over beginnings, Japanese scholarship has been superb in setting the agenda for debate, which we now must review. The division, as already indicated, has been between social and political (i.e., "legal") historians, with the former stressing house structure and inheritance practices, and the latter the effect of Bakufu policy on the authority of family heads. Most social historians point to Matsumoto Shinpachirō as their spiritual leader even as they reject his central argument. A Marxist, Matsumoto believed that the *sōryō* inherited full authority from his predecessor and held his family—siblings and children alike—in a condition of slavelike dependence. The *sōryō* possessed full responsibility for meeting the family's fiscal obligations (hence his usefulness to the Bakufu), and enjoyed full control over the means of production.[4]

Matsumoto's theory was rejected on the most fundamental of grounds: the pattern of succession was not from *sōryō* to *sōryō*, but rather from *sōryō* to *chakushi*, i.e., from the house head to a principal heir among other secondary heirs. In other words, it was the parent

---

[2] The argument that Yoritomo "adopted" the *sōryō* system (the position of Satō Shin'ichi; see chap. 2, n. 3) has never been seriously questioned.

[3] The earliest usage in this meaning dates from 1222; see n. 25.

[4] See, in particular, Matsumoto Shinpachirō, *Chūsei shakai no kenkyū*, chaps. 3, 5.

who partitioned his property, not the principal heir on behalf of his father. The main heir held little authority over his siblings. In retrospect, the theory of Matsumoto seems astonishingly naive. Compared with the thousands of releases to children, there are only a small number to siblings, and an even tinier handful at the start (rather than the end) of a main heir's tenure. Nevertheless, although Matsumoto had erred monumentally, his work proved enormously stimulating. The central question was now one of measuring the powers of the house head vis-à-vis his own siblings. It was still possible that, though he did not parcel land to them, he may yet have exercised other authority. With the degree of lateral integration the ultimate question here, this problem became the focus of most inquiry.

The debate over the nature and extent of this authority inevitably acquired a time dimension. As argued by Nagahara Keiji, though the *sōryō* did not exercise a significant right of command over his siblings in the early Kamakura age, he clearly did so later on. Thus the *sōryō* system, as defined by the strength of the *sōryō* himself, had its golden age at the end of the thirteenth century and the beginning of the fourteenth.[5]

That the yardstick had now become the balance between the *sōryō* and his siblings was given further impetus by Nitta Hideharu, who took the opposite line from Nagahara. Nitta, arguing for a progressive decline of the *sōryō*'s powers, claimed that the system's golden age was at the beginning of the Kamakura era. He admitted that this strength was undocumented, but attributed this fact to the secure dominance of the house head, a legacy of the patriarchal authority of late Heian times. By contrast, the powers of the house head declined in direct proportion to the advancing independence of collaterals. The greater documentation of the post-1250 era reflected fragmentation and weakness, not strength.[6]

Another prominent scholar who joined the debate was Toyoda Takeshi, who was less concerned with the forward or backward movement of the *sōryō*'s powers than he was with enumerating and emphasizing those powers. For Toyoda, in other words, the *sōryō*'s package of rights was substantial, not at the level posited by Matsumoto certainly, but sufficient to place the *sōryō* system at the center of Kamakura society. The value of Toyoda's work is that he attempted to spell out each dimension of the *sōryō*'s authority. Its weakness lay in its ad-

[5] Nagahara Keiji, "Tōgoku ni okeru sōryōsei no kaitai katei."
[6] Nitta Hideharu, "Aki no kuni Kobayakawa shi no sōryōsei ni tsuite."

vocacy: Toyoda claimed much more for the system *qua* system than seems warranted.[7]

Though there is no strict consensus on the issues of timing, extent, and direction, a majority view can perhaps be said to exist. As represented by historians such as Uwayokote Masataka and Haga Norihiko, the *sōryō*'s powers are viewed as weak at the beginning, stronger near the end, but never absolute.[8] Both scholars have emphasized what the house head was *not* able to do—in particular, confiscate the holdings of his siblings, a point we will return to later. At any rate, by positing a weak *sōryō* authority at first, these historians gave credence to a Heian legacy of impotence. As noted above, family heads did not bequeath to the Kamakura age a tradition of strong in-house leadership.

Satō Shin'ichi, a legal historian, has been the principal spokesman for the other major approach to the *sōryō* system. In his view, the Bakufu (Yoritomo, as he has argued it) took over the paternalistic command system of warrior society and bent it to its own needs. It made the *sōryō* responsible for military command of his family as well as for the collection of vassal dues. Thus, even though partible inheritance prevailed, the rights of junior heirs were incomplete. Later, these rights were advanced to a condition of true possession, and the *sōryō* system declined.[9] For Satō, then, as for other legal historians, the mainspring of the house head's power lay in his military command. It was a personalized authority, which, in its origins, had little to do with property and was therefore expressed by a different term. At the end of the Heian period, the house head was called *katoku*; only later would he be called *sōryō*. This condition developed when his rights came to embrace elements of land control.[10]

A major problem with the legalist view is its presumption of a *katoku* command over large groupings of relatives. As we have indicated, this may have been what Yoritomo hoped for, but it is not at all what he experienced. Nevertheless, the distinction between *katoku* and *sōryō*, grounded in the sources themselves, is a useful device for examining the origins and extent of the house head's powers. Both statuses had different beginnings, and both carried limited real authority.

During Heian times the term *katoku* was an occasional equivalent

---

[7] Toyoda, *Bushidan to sonraku*, chap. 3.

[8] Uwayokote Masataka, "Sōryōsei josetsu"; Haga, *Sōryōsei*.

[9] Satō, "Bakufuron."

[10] Nakada Kaoru, "Chūsei no katoku sōzoku hō"; Ishii Ryōsuke, "Chōshi sōzokusei." For a comprehensive review of the entire *katoku/sōryō* debate, see Suzuki Hideo, "Katoku to sōryō ni kan suru oboegaki," pp. 283–98.

for eldest son (usually denoted *chakushi*) in the meaning of a larger descent group's head-designate. The emphasis was on blood-line succession and titular leadership with little reference to property.[11] It was this usage that continued into the Kamakura age. For example, the term appears in at least ten entries of the *Azuma kagami* in its widest applicaton—as the equivalent for the head-designate of large families such as the Chichibu, Miura, Hōjō, and even Minamoto.[12] Ultimately, *katoku* would have its meaning superseded by that of *sōryō*, though the term experienced a resurgence later.[13] At any rate, it was the *sōryō* concept that was expanding—and is thus the one requiring scrutiny. Scholars in Japan use *katoku* in the explication of the *sōryō* system, but never the reverse.

The term *sōryō* has an ancient past and was first used in such eighth-century compilations as *Nihon shoki* and *Hitachi fudoki* in the meaning of a government-appointed provincial commander, e.g., the "Iyo [Province] sōryō."[14] By the eleventh century, when the term first appears in land and judicial records, its older meaning had lapsed and it was now used as a verb. To *sōryō* was to enjoy possession rights over land. The context in which these rights were exercised tended to be familial, that is, in one's capacity as an heir.[15] There was no restriction by class or by occupation.[16]

A second, less frequent context for the term was as a noun, a usage that no longer had any connection to a public authority or position.

[11] See, e.g., the reference in the *Honchō zoku monzui*, from 1040/8/13, cited in *Koji ruien, seiji bu*, 2: 84. Or the retrospective usages in slightly later sources, e.g., *Hōgen monogatari* (in reference to Minamoto Tameyoshi, grandson and heir to Yoshiie in 1108); and the Yūki family genealogy (in reference to Fujiwara Hidesato and the events of 940); *ibid.*, 2: 91, 85.

[12] In sequence, *AK* 1180/12/26, 1247/6/8, 1256/11/22, and 1203/1/22. The final reference states, in effect, that Ichiman, the half-brother of the future shogun, Sanetomo, should not succeed as *katoku*. *AK* 1195/3/16 refers to Yoritomo's heir, Yoriie, as the *katoku*.

[13] For the two terms—*katoku* and *sōryō*—used interchangeably, see Document 141: 1313/9/12 uhyōe no jō Norikane yuzurijō an. See also Document 142: 1314/5/12 Kantō gechijō. The term *katoku* continued to be used in post-Kamakura sources, e.g., in the *Taiheiki* and *Meitokuki*; *Koji ruien, seiji bu*, 3: 680ff.

[14] See these references in *Koji ruien, kan'i bu*, 2: 567. The term also appears in the *Shoku Nihongi* and *Harima fudoki*.

[15] For an example that is explicit, see *Nejime monjo*, 1147/7/15 saki no Ōsumi no jō Takebe Chikasuke mōshijō, *Nejime monjo*, 1: 5–6, doc. 7.

[16] See, e.g., the reference to a priestly exercise of *sōryō* rights over various *shōen*; *Iwashimizu monjo*, 1023/10/5 sō Kenshō ge, *HI*, 2: 668–70, doc. 487. This document is the one that contains the earliest usage of the term as a verb. But later documents similarly use it on behalf of courtiers.

Sōryō was used in the sense of "the whole land," a literal meaning implying an authority measurable by territorial expanse.[17] In total, there are at least eleven Heian-era records in which the term *sōryō* appears, and in every one it has one of the two meanings just cited.[18] This suggests that by the end of the Heian period the term already had a long association with land and land possession, but that the person exercising possession did so as a legatee. The exercise of *sōryō* authority, then, was not the same as the exercise of a *sōryō's* authority; the possession of such rights had not yet become the equivalent for house headship.

It is hardly surprising that the traditional usages continued into the early years of the Kamakura age, though now, significantly, with the "whole land" connotation clearly in the ascendant. This usage predominated in both the *Azuma kagami* and contemporary documents,[19] and it is the one that appears in the several Yoritomo orders that employed the word.[20] The emphasis on an authority that could be measured laterally had strong implications for the future and was actually reinforced by the few examples we find of "sōryō" used as a verb. While the possession of land was still the basic meaning, the land in question might have been not the legatee's own but rather that of a sibling or siblings. In a case of 1184, for example, a middle sister and her younger brother were accused by the eldest child of plotting to seize *sōryō* authority—rights of possession belonging to same-generation heirs.[21]

But it was an incident involving an officer of Usa Shrine in Kyushu that is the most revealing of all. In 1196, an eldest son, using that status as the basis for his action, conspired with his sister to violate the land shares of his brother.[22] Here we come very close to the later, his-

[17] E.g., *Higashi monjo*, 1164/7 Fujiwara bō shoryō mokuroku, *HI*, 7: 2616–17, doc. 3294. Here the usage is "*sōryō denchi*"—the full expanse of possessed paddy.

[18] There are actually twelve such documents, but one of these contains the term in a postscript that was added much later—in 1234; *Kawakami jinja komonjo*, 1091/8/11 Hizen no kuni sō Enjin ge, *HI*, 4: 1271, doc. 1299.

[19] See *AK* 1181/int.2/7 for a reference to Yoritomo's former wet nurse being made "*sōryō jitō*" for Hayakawa Estate, i.e., for her appointment as *jitō* over the whole estate (see also chap. 2, n. 28, n. 29). Also, *AK* 1186/11/24, which refers to despoilments over "*sōryō no jimoto*," i.e., over an entire area. For a document example, see *Tōji hyakugō monjo*, 1190/3/20 kurōdo Fujiwara bō haibunjo an, *KI*, 1: 347–48, doc. 432.

[20] See *Kujō ke monjo*, [1185]/1/20 Minamoto Yoritomo shojō, *HI*, 10: 190, supp. doc. 155; *Matsuura Kōshi kyūzō monjo*, [1186]/4/19 Minamoto Yoritomo shojō, *KI*, 1: 161, doc. 68.

[21] *Tōdaiji monjo*, 1184/10 Gamō Aneko ge, *HI*, 8: 3152–53, doc. 4214.

[22] *Usa Nagahiro monjo*, 1196/10 Usa Sadanari mōshijō an, *Ōita ken shiryō*, 3: 36, doc. 11.

toric meaning of the term *sōryō*, and indeed the language of the document is just vague enough for the term possibly to have been used as a noun.[23] Yet an eldest son's claiming of *sōryō* rights—rather than an eldest son's claiming to be *sōryō*—seems more likely and would constitute a transitional usage. By contrast, if the Usa head *were* to be interpreted as Japan's first *sōryō*,[24] we would need to explain why he had no counterparts until well into the next century. It thus seems more accurate to argue that the machinery for a *sōryō* system was being set into place after 1205, though without, as yet, an appropriate nomenclature. Because of its previous usages in a variety of related contexts, the term *sōryō* was ultimately fixed upon for this purpose.

The earliest clear use of *sōryō* as "house head" appears in a fascinating record of 1222 involving a dispute between two brothers over their late father's inheritance.[25] It is noteworthy that the case centered on a vassal family native to Kyushu, another indication that the Kantō did not make the sole contribution to the development of the Kamakura *sōryō* system. In its particulars, the dispute was based on an elder brother's unwillingness to recognize a younger brother as his father's choice as principal heir after the death of the eldest son. The father, in 1208, selected his third son, Kiramu, as house head-designate (*chakushi*), ignoring Ken, who was the second son. Yet Ken was not disinherited, merely passed over for the family's headship; on his deathbed the father bequeathed Ken a one-fourth portion. Ultimately, this share was deemed inadequate by Ken, who violated his brother's legacy, obliging Kiramu to lodge a lawsuit. The case was heard by the Dazaifu in 1222.

The principles enunciated in both the testimony and the verdict are of sufficient importance to be presented here in full. In Ken's rebuttal he stated, "In essence it was neither our father's intention, nor is it a principle of law, for a younger brother, Kiramu, to be house chieftain (*sōryō*), when Ken himself had been principal heir (*chakushi*)." Though this assertion by Ken of his own selection as successor was patently

---

[23] The key phrase can be read two ways: "because Motoshige was exercising *sōryō* rights, ..." (*Motoshige sōryō suru no kan*, . . .); or "because Motoshige was *sōryō*, ..." (*Motoshige sōryō taru no kan*, ...). "*Suru*" and "*taru*" are inserts regularly added in *kanbun* passages; no characters actually appear (though one for "*taru*" normally does appear, and would have made the meaning, as a noun, unmistakable).

[24] To my knowledge, no scholar in Japan has noticed this document in reference to the history of the *sōryō* system.

[25] Document 27: 1222/12/23 dazaifu shugosho kudashibumi an. Toyoda Takeshi cites an Ōtomo family document of 1223 (see n. 26) as the earliest to use the term "*sōryō*" in the meaning of a status; *Bushidan to sonraku*, p. 145.

false, he bolstered his argument by insisting that "the fact that Ken has been the principal heir is known by everyone in the Matsuura house. Thus, when the call was made last winter to stand palace guard duty (*ōbanyaku*) in Kyoto, [Ken] set out for the capital in his capacity as deputy (*daikan*) for his father." In other words, Ken was basing his claim on the rationale of common knowledge, of his being the eldest, and of his alleged deputyship on behalf of his father.

The weakness of Ken's position was made plain in the Dazaifu's verdict. It was Kiramu who received his father's conveyance in 1208, which stated that he was to be *chakushi*. Thus, "the disposition of property while parents are alive depends not on the distinction between older and younger (*chakusho*), but rather only on the discretion of the possessor (*zaishu*). Why, then, should Ken . . . pursue an argument calling himself an elder brother? Forthwith, Ken is to terminate his false suit."

In this episode it had been Ken, actually, who articulated the equivalency of *chakushi* and *sōryō*—a historic development. Part of his argument rested on his being the eldest. Yet when the Dazaifu rejected this premise it was really expanding the usage of *chakushi* and paving the way for *sōryō*. If *chakushi* (literally meaning eldest son) could now be applied freely to a younger son, a confusion existed that might require clarification. The present suit was an instance of such confusion. Thus to bolster his position Ken claimed to be *sōryō*, i.e., to exercise *sōryō* rights (the rights of a *sōryō*) over his family's holdings. A final indication that Ken had absorbed the lessons of the post-1205 world was his rush toward Kyoto to represent his family. The battleground for siblings was now taking on new spatial and symbolic forms.

It was not merely that the house head's share of the holdings exceeded that of the junior portions, a condition that had always been true. It was rather that the powers of the house head, now expanded, included rights over siblings' interests. These were "*sōryō* rights," yet to be defined, but sufficiently enticing to give new significance to battles over headships. In 1223, the full implications of the new authority were expressed in a will drawn up by one of the Bakufu's most influential vassals, Ōtomo Yoshinao.[26] In naming his *chakushi*, Yoshinao invested this successor with powers never before made explicit. He stated that the *chakushi*, "in his capacity as *sōryō*," was to allocate vassal

<hr />

[26] *Shiga monjo*, 1223/11/2 Ōtomo Yoshinao yuzurijō, *Hennen Ōtomo shiryō*, 1: 309–10, doc. 346. The property conveyed here (as in the Usa and Matsuura cases) was in Kyushu, though Yoshinao was himself an easterner. Traditional genealogies list him as a possible "illegitimate" son of Yoritomo; *Sonpi bunmyaku*, 3: 296–97.

dues corresponding to the size of sibling inheritances. Though the release in question (the only one surviving to a child) was in fact addressed to a junior heir, we can safely surmise that each child (including the *chakushi*) received a similar stipulation.[27] At any rate, by virtue
of this invested authority and the explanation included in each testament, the *chakushi* was transformed into a *sōryō*.

Yoshinao did not stop there, however. He made a further statement, which has frequently been cited by scholars. He asserted that
should junior heirs fail to heed his successor, control of their lands
would be taken over by that successor. Most historians believe that this
warning was no more than a hope, since in practice house heads did
not come to exercise confiscatory powers over the land shares of their
siblings.[28] Nevertheless, the expression of such a wish so early is revealing. In the wake of the Bakufu's victory in the Jōkyū War, there were
obviously senior vassals who sought to tighten controls within their
families as a way of safeguarding their recent gains.

For our purposes, Yoshinao's release demonstrates that the basic
elements of the *sōryō* system had at last come of age. The timing was
indeed appropriate since the 1220s witnessed conveyances far more
geographically diverse than any issued in the past. In 1222, for instance, a vassal transmitted holdings in five provinces to a son. The
areas in question had been acquired under Yoritomo, Sanetomo, and,
most recently, Hōjō Yoshitoki.[29] A year later the Bakufu, in another
case, confirmed testamentary passage of holdings in four provinces;[30]
and in 1230, a pair of vassal brothers wrote releases that conveyed,
respectively, property in nine and five provinces.[31]

The cases just cited meant an obvious need for coordination at the
top, which could be accomplished in several ways. One way was to
concentrate a holder's entire portfolio in the hands of a single suc-

[27] Indeed, the surviving release was to the youngest child, still a minor (n. 26). A
Bakufu confirmation of the second son's inheritance is extant; *Takuma monjo*, 1224/4/26
Kantō gechijō an, *Hennen Ōtomo shiryō*, 1: 311, doc. 348. A release to Yoshinao's wife is
discussed below.

[28] E.g., Haga, p. 72, or Uwayokote, p. 81.

[29] *Mogi monjo*, 1222/2/21 Fujiwara bō yuzurijō, *KI*, 5: 88, doc. 2927. In other words,
the vassal's homelands in Shimotsuke along with properties in Shinano and Echigo had
been confirmed or granted by Yoritomo; a holding in Noto (perhaps in 1213) had been
awarded by the third shogun, Sanetomo; and a post-Jōkyū award in Kii had been made
by the Bakufu regent.

[30] *Tashiro monjo*, 1223/6/20 Kantō gechijō, *KI*, 5: 208, doc. 3120.

[31] *Minagawa monjo*, 1230/8/13 Naganuma Munemasa yuzurijō, *KI*, 6: 212, doc. 4011;
Document 41: 1230/2/20 Oyama Tomomasa yuzurijō.

cessor, as Shimazu Tadahisa may have done in 1227.[32] In this instance, no property is known to have been transmitted to younger offspring, though one of Tadahisa's sons may have been honored independently by Kamakura.[33] In the two 1230 cases cited above, and in the case of Ōtomo Yoshinao, there were multiple potential heirs. Accordingly, all three donors made use of the *sōryō* system. Thus Naganuma Munemasa admonished his successor to apportion obligations among the junior heirs (*shoshi*) and also authorized him to possess (*ryōchi*) the properties Munemasa had disbursed to them if they were disobedient.[34] Oyama Tomomasa, the second testator of 1230, confronted a different situation. He had already designated his eldest son as *chakushi*, but the head-designate had died in 1229. The second son was passed over for the headship (though he did apparently receive a share) in favor of the deceased son's own son, i.e., the testator's grandson. It was this fourteen-year-old boy who received the "*sōryō*'s portion" (*sōryōbun*), consisting of property in five provinces.[35]

It was Ōtomo Yoshinao, however, who used the *sōryō* system in the most interesting way of all. On the same day that he designated his son as his successor, he named his wife as coheir. In a separate release he granted her two of his most important holdings—the family's homeland area in the east and a key *jitō* office in the west (Ōno Estate in Kyushu's Bungo Province). Noting their long years of marriage and the fact of his wife's being the mother of many children, he bequeathed these holdings to her in perpetuity.[36] Seventeen years later it was the widow who divided that inheritance among the couple's various children, with the homeland area going exclusively to the *chakushi*, and Ōno Estate parceled minutely among the others.[37] In this instance,

---

[32] Document 36: 1227/10/10 shōgun sodehan kudashibumi. This practice, if it existed at all, was very rare until later; see Chapter 4.

[33] Four sons are listed in the Shimazu genealogy, with Tadayoshi, his father's successor, appearing first but referred to as "Saburō"; perhaps two older brothers had died and were not listed. See *Zoku Gunsho ruijū*, 5: 457–58. The other son about whom we have information is Tadatsuna, who became influential in Echizen; *ibid.*, and *AK* 1248/8/15, 10/25. The fates of the final two sons are unknown.

[34] According to the Naganuma genealogy, there were only two sons (*Oyama shishi*, 806; *Sonpi bunmyaku*, 2: 402; *Zoku Gunsho ruijū*, 6: 606), though other children, including daughters, may have been omitted; the conveyance (n. 31) implies several offspring.

[35] Document 41: 1230/2/30 Oyama Tomomasa yuzurijō.

[36] *Shiga monjo*, 1223/11/2 Ōtomo Yoshinao yuzurijō an, *Hennen Ōtomo shiryō*, 1: 310, doc. 347.1. The Bakufu confirmed this transmission several months later; *ibid.*, 1224/4/24 Kantō gechijō an, *ibid.*, 1: 310–11, doc. 347.2.

[37] *Ibid.*, 1240/4/6 ama Shinmyō yuzurijō, *ibid.*, 1: 361–63, 365–66, docs. 416, 418.

then, the *sōryō* system had taken on a more complex character. Mother and son administered the family's interests together, and it would not be until late in her lifetime that Ōtomo Chikahide, his father's choice as *sōryō*, would assume that authority entirely in his own right. In the mother's releases of 1240, his brothers and sisters were enjoined to discharge their dues obligations to the Bakufu in accordance with the allocations of Chikahide.[38]

It will be useful to summarize the lessons of these several examples. By the end of the 1220s the separate pieces of the *sōryō* system were fully in place. Inducing this development were land rights legacies that were increasingly diffuse, vassals' desires to maintain family coherence into the next generation, and the need of the Bakufu to have its dues payments guaranteed. It was this triangle of sometimes contradictory practices that created the tension between unitary headship and multiple inheritances that was the essence of the *sōryō* system. Perhaps the ultimate expression of that tension was the appearance of the term *sōryōbun*, a clear indication that corporate and individual interests might coexist: there could be no "*sōryō* portion" without the corresponding presence of "*shoshi* shares." The releases issued by vassals neatly captured this duality. House heads would have to be obeyed but only within the limited parameters of their Bakufu-mandated authority. Sibling groups thus had one trunk and several limbs; but each limb was itself potentially a trunk with smaller limbs of its own. As the years passed, a hierarchy of *sōryō* systems (i.e., limbs) evolved, which made the articulation between earlier and later systems increasingly remote. How effective the historical "*sōryō* system" was in dealing with these conflicts of family organization and vassalage is ultimately the central issue of this study.

It was during the 1220s that the Bakufu's certification of vassals' releases began to impinge on the prerogatives of central proprietors in new ways. As it happened, the holdings of vassals constituted an assemblage of old and new titles which tended to be conveyed without distinguishing them on the basis of their originating source. When the Bakufu validated such transmissions it was exceeding a jurisdiction that was technically limited to *jitō shiki*. A case in point is that of Oyama Tomomasa, cited above (n. 35), whose release of 1230 included an array of pre- and post-1180 lands and offices. Thirteen

---

[38] It is noteworthy that the threat of a confiscation, so prominent in the father's testament of 1223, is absent in the mother's wills of 1240.

years later, in another case, the Bakufu confirmed a testament that conveyed only non-*jitō* estate titles.[39]

The Bakufu's policy was accommodating to vassals in other ways, too. As indicated earlier, a father's division of property and selection of heirs were seemingly never questioned. Knowing this in advance freed donors from considering anything other than the dynamics of their own families. In this regard, donors regularly exhorted offspring to be responsible in discharging their obligations,[40] but we search in vain for selections of heirs citing desirability from the point of view of Kamakura. The Bakufu never knew in advance which son or daughter would hold which property, and even after it was so apprised, it was expected to certify the maze of transfers routinely.[41] The matter was of even greater moment when the selection involved a principal heir, who would serve as the liaison with the Bakufu and its agents. But here too Kamakura was expected to acknowledge the current holder's choice, whether a younger son,[42] a younger brother,[43] a grandson,[44] a daughter,[45] or an adoptee.[46]

Not only did Kamakura not interfere with the prerogatives of parents in these areas, it actually bolstered them by enacting certain normative regulations that gave them virtual carte blanche authority in matters involving the division of assets. The background to Kamakura's new role as lawgiver was its victory in the Jōkyū War and the appearance on the scene of its greatest figure after Yoritomo, the

[39] Document 64: 1243/7/28 shōgun ke mandokoro kudashibumi.

[40] E.g., Document 42: 1230/int.1/14 Yamanouchi Shigetoshi yuzurijō.

[41] See, e.g., the references to multiple parcels being distributed to various sons and daughters in Document 42: 1230/int.1/14 Yamanouchi Shigetoshi yuzurijō; Document 55: 1237/8/25 Fujiwara Iekado yuzurijō; or—most explicitly of all—Document 65: 1243/10/6 Shigeno Mitsuuji yuzurijō an.

[42] E.g., a third son—Documents 29–31: 1223/5/26 jitō Sainin yuzurijō an, 1224/5/29 jitō Sainin yuzurijō an, 1224/11/30 Kantō gechijō an. Or again a third son—Documents 55–56: 1237/8/25 Fujiwara Iekado yuzurijō, 1237/10/11 dazaifu shugosho kudashibumi an.

[43] E.g., Document 35: 1227(?) Kanto gechijō.

[44] E.g., Documents 33–34: 1226/2/18 Nagano Kagetaka yuzurijō an, 1228/8/17 Hōjō Tomotoki gechijō an. Or—once again—the case of Oyama Tomomasa; Document 41: 1230/2/20 Oyama Tomomasa yuzurijō.

[45] E.g., Document 24: 1221/11/21 Kantō gechijō an (though in this case the daughter's younger brother[?] was earmarked for the inheritance later). Or in a case without any encumbrances, Documents 57–58: 1239/7/17 Kakuzen yuzurijō, 1239/8/3 Kantō gechijō.

[46] See, e.g., the reference in *DKR*, doc. 140: 1239/5/25 Kantō gechijō. Also, Document 49: 1235/8/28 Kantō gechijō, in which, however, an adopted son and his uncle fought over unbequeathed property.

shogunal regent Hōjō Yasutoki. It was Yasutoki who stabilized conditions after the war, and who gave the Bakufu and its vassalage the country's first warrior law code, the Goseibai Shikimoku. The code, of course, did not issue afresh from the fertile mind of one man, though Yasutoki's personal stamp was clearly on it. Its Confucian tone reflected his own training and predilections. But the great majority of its 51 clauses can best be thought of as paraphrases of current practices reconsidered and spun out now under the imprimatur of the Kamakura Bakufu. The emphasis in the Shikimoku was on making "old ground" the basis for conservative decision-making. On the subject of family and inheritance the objectives were to capture the essence of practices already in place and to protect the status quo by warning against special dangers. The restrictions on the freedom of the junior generation are as noteworthy as the glorification of license by their parents.

Among the nine clauses dealing expressly with the transfer of property, three may be said to deal with the powers of parents, two with the conditions of children, and four with the rights and obligations of women.[47] Summarized briefly, the first group confirmed parents in two basic privileges: the right to revoke releases to offspring of either sex, even releases already approved by the Bakufu; and the right to reclaim the grants to offspring who had predeceased their parents.[48] The practical effect was to invest in seniors absolute authority: no circumstances existed in which a child might make a claim on his parents. The second group, though continuing this basic orientation, did at least focus on the children: the disposition of intestate property was to be in accordance with performance and ability; and elder sons who were not disinherited were not to be neglected entirely.[49] The third group dealt with women in several of their most common life phases or experiences: marriage, childlessness, divorce, and widowhood. Vassal daughters who married courtiers were not to shirk the dues owed on lands received from their parents; landed women without children were free to adopt heirs; blameless women divorced by their husbands were to retain property assigned by their spouses; and unremarried widows holding lands from their husbands were not to be obliged to surrender them to their children.[50] Clearly, the emphasis

[47] The numbers here as well as their characterization represent my own conclusions. Obviously there are other clauses that also deal with property.

[48] *Goseibai shikimoku*, nos. 18, 20, 26, in *CHS*, 1: 44–46.

[49] *Ibid.*, nos. 22, 27.

[50] *Ibid.*, nos. 21, 23, 24, 25.

here was on permitting women the means to an independent existence free from the most flagrant handicaps deriving from their sex.[51]

Save for the attempt to legislate more equitable treatment for neglected elder sons, none of the injunctions broke new ground. In some instances the Shikimoku actually noted that a particular practice was the prevailing one, perhaps dating it from the era of Yoritomo. The history was not always accurate here,[52] but it did reflect an awareness of the need to justify such practices—as well as the Shikimoku's inclusion of them. On the other hand, the term *sōryō* does not appear in the law code, and there is much else that is left out and even much that is included that is extraneous.[53] In other words, in spite of the Shikimoku's pronouncements on family organization and the transmission of property, the *sōryō* system can only be examined from the releases, confirmations, and judicial edicts that were at its center. Though the more generalized, legislative sphere was important, the major initiatives came from the vassalage, not from the Bakufu.

In the post-Jōkyū era, the right of seniors to be entirely arbitrary in the disposition of property and the naming of house heads became the cornerstone of both the vassal and the inheritance systems. The Bakufu's laws and tribunals reinforced this notion time and again. Further ballast came in the form of a wave of disinheritances, rewritten wills, younger sons named as successors, and wives given precedence over children. The many forms that this downward flow of power took will serve as a useful foil for the limited authority of house heads vis-à-vis siblings. At any rate, it is these two sets of relationships, under the umbrella of the Bakufu, that constitute the main chapters of the *sōryō* story. The question of what parents could do—and brothers and sisters could not do—captures the essence of the tale. We begin with parents, concentrating on the middle third of the Kamakura age.[54]

[51] Of course this was true only for women who were "blameless," i.e., who were divorced for reasons not of their own making and who did not remarry. A darker interpretation can certainly be applied to the Shikimoku's handling of "women's issues."

[52] E.g., the attribution to the Yoritomo period of women's engaging in adoption, a practice with roots deep in the Heian age; see Chapter 1.

[53] As an example of the second, the Shikimoku (no. 22) specifies a one-fifth portion to be assigned to improvident elder sons from the main heir's share when a younger son had been selected as house head-designate. I have found no examples of an actual arrangement based on this formula.

[54] For the period after c. 1230 the data base expands enormously and it will not be practical to cite more than representative examples chosen mostly from the Documents section of this book.

In the first place, there appears to be little correlation between the amount of property available for distribution and the size of individual vassal houses. Warrior heads, whether of trunk or secondary lines, did not artificially limit the number or sex of their offspring. Genealogies and wills amply corroborate this and enumerate as many as 12 or 15 children, or even more.[55] By the same token, few families could boast of full strength: the harshness of life in medieval times imposed a natural limitation on size. As already noted, house heads, their plans for the next generation seemingly settled, often had to deal with unforeseen child deaths.[56] At the other end of the spectrum, infertile wives were not made the objects of public opprobrium, in part because divorce required no rationale and because secondary wives were a regular feature of medieval warrior families. It follows that no sharply defined legal distinction existed between legitimate and illegitimate offspring; bastardy was not the hopeless curse that it was in the premodern West. When it did become an issue, the matter had little to do with religion or morality—it was a question of greed. Disputes among half bloods were almost invariably over property.[57]

A further retardant to a sense of crisis over too few children was, as we saw for the Heian period, the ease of adoption. The Bakufu made no distinction between natural and adopted heirs (or, for that matter, between heirs born of principal wives and those born of concubines). Heirs, if required, could be created on demand, subject only to the availability of candidates. Perhaps the truest indicator of the universality of adoption was that it was freely engaged in even when heirs were not needed.[58] Nephews were often picked up in this fashion, but in other instances it was unrelated persons who were added. In this sense adoption served a purpose not dissimilar to that of marriage— the binding, at least by intent, of families and branches of families.

[55] Huge offspring lists are common in the standard genealogies of warrior houses; *Zoku Gunsho ruijū, keizu bu*, vols. 5–7. See, e.g., the 15 children of the Takeda scion during the second half of the twelfth century (*ibid.*, 5: 537–38); and the 15 children of the Kōsokabe head early in the fourteenth century (Document 135: 1306/4/16 Nakahara Shigemichi yuzurijō).

[56] E.g., Document 27: 1222/12/23 dazaifu shugosho kudashibumi an; Documents 30–31: 1224/5/29 jitō Sainin yuzurijō, 1224/11/30 Kantō gechijō an; and Document 41: 1230/2/20 Oyama Tomomasa yuzurijō.

[57] E.g., Document 142: 1314/5/12 Kantō gechijō, in which being born of the true mother was a point of contention. In 1269, a *jitō* holder thought it necessary to explain that his heir was a "younger sister born of the same father and mother," i.e., a true sister; Document 101: 1269/8/21 Fujiwara Tadaakira yuzurijō.

[58] A graphic example appears in Document 100: 1268/int.1/28 saemon no jō Kiyotoki yuzurijō an.

Only later in the Kamakura period would conditions begin to change. Though adoption continued to be practiced, there was now a rising tide of criticism against it.[59]

There is no way to determine what the normal life span was or to comment with any confidence on the usual timing of family successions. Men and women were often remarked to have lived to great ages, not uncommonly into their eighties. Moreover, there is an abundance of evidence to suggest that house heads were not expected to retire—if by retirement we mean the handing over of authority to a successor. Thus in a will of 1230 the donor asserted that he would retain "management and possession" (*shintai ryōshō*) until his own death, whereas in 1258 another donor ordered his successor to obey him under threat of a confiscation.[60] Nor is the timing of release documents—or the Bakufu's confirmations of them—much help here: men and women prepared *yuzurijō* over the course of their lifetimes,[61] and even after approvals by Kamakura they were revokable by a new release. Even the Bakufu's twenty-year statute of limitations, included in the Goseibai Shikimoku, did not compromise this fundamental privilege of parents.[62]

Grandfathers, especially, were the heads of families in the fullest sense. They not only acted peremptorily toward their own children but attempted to control the destinies of their grandchildren. In a case of 1238, for example, a father disinherited his daughter but acted as master of ceremonies for the coming of age ritual for her son. In the words of a Bakufu judgment of a suit brought by the daughter, "Is it not a regular practice for grandchildren to be supported, even when progeny have been disinherited?"[63] Moreover, with increasing frequency grandfathers made bequests to favored grandchildren (for

[59] Indeed, this criticism is heard as early as the 1260s; Document 92: 1264/10/3 Hioki Masaie yuzurijō an. For details on this subject, see Chapter 4.

[60] Document 41: 1230/2/20 Oyama Tomomasa yuzurijō; Document 84: 1258/7/19 Kobayakawa Shigehira yuzurijō an.

[61] The time span was from soon after receiving property until the deathbed. For the former, see *KB*, doc. 103: 1208/int.4/27 shōgun ke mandokoro kudashibumi; for the latter, Document 27: 1222/12/23 dazaifu shugosho kudashibumi an. Or see Document 59: 1239/11/5 Kantō gechijō, for releases prepared by the same donor in 1210 and again in 1239.

[62] This is graphically revealed in Document 59. Circumstances, however, could complicate things, e.g., in the case of a conflict between a dead parent's will and a long possession that was contrary to it; see the reference in the third-to-last item in Document 75: 1288/6/2 Kantō gechijō.

[63] *DKR*, doc. 138: 1238/10/27 Rokuhara gechijō. The suit itself was between the grandfather's widow and the latter's disinherited stepdaughter.

instance, to the son of a Jōkyū traitor),[64] and sought to influence the choice of house head for the grandchildren's generation.[65] The effective family unit can thus be viewed as a pyramid with one or two tiers. The father dominated his children but might in turn have been dominated by his father. Authority always ran vertically. Indeed, the only limitations on senior heads were the entails or other regulations laid down by their own predecessors.[66]

Fathers and grandfathers, then, could be petty tyrants. Failures of loyalty, constancy, filial devotion, and talent were balanced on a subjective basis by achievements in the same areas. The records of the period are filled with illustrations of children being threatened and punished. For example, unspecified "disturbances" by offspring were regularly made the basis of charges of unfiliality (*fukō*) by will-writing fathers.[67] The loss of an inheritance or even expulsion from the family might result.[68] The lack of ability, regularly cited as the justification for bypassing elder sons, was the most demeaning and embittering of a parent's accusations. It was also, unhappily, one of the most common.[69] At the same time, fathers took considerable pains to establish a system of checks and balances to militate against siblings falling upon one another. The granting of wills to individual heirs was one obvious device here,[70] as was the requiring of countersignatures on each re-

[64] Document 45: 1258/12/23 shōgun ke mandokoro kudashibumi. Also see the same-day bequests to three sons and a grandson in 1270 (Documents 102–5: 1270/8/25 Shami Gyōnin yuzurijō); and the bequest to a granddaughter in 1243 (Document 65: 1243/10/6 Shigeno Mitsuuji yuzurijō an).

[65] Sometimes he actually made the choice, e.g., Documents 93–94: 1264/2/18 Taira Shigesuke yuzurijō, 1270/8/28 Kantō gechijō; or, a bit later, Document 118: 1287/9/1 Kantō gechijō; and Document 121: 1295/3/29 Yamanouchi Tokimichi yuzurijō. In a bequest of 1259, the father-donor literally directed his *chakushi* to transmit the inheritance to his own *chakushi* at the end of his life; *Nejime monjo*, 1259/int.10/5 Takebe Kiyotsuna yuzurijō, *KI*, 11: 365, doc. 8424.

[66] For example, a fourth-generation male *jitō* holder bequeathed his inheritance to his sister "in accordance with the final wishes (*yuigon*) of our late father"; Document 101: 1269/8/21 Fujiwara Takaakira yuzurijō. Such final wishes, however, could readily be circumvented.

[67] E.g., Document 30: 1224/5/29 jitō Sainin yuzurijō.

[68] For the threatened loss of holdings, see Document 55: 1237/8/25 Fujiwara Iekado yuzurijō; and Document 86: 1260/3/15 Minamoto Yorinaga yuzurijō. For the threat of an expulsion, see Document 42: 1230/int.1/14 Yamanouchi Shigetoshi yuzurijō.

[69] E.g., Document 55: 1237/8/25 Fujiwara Iekado yuzurijō; Document 68: 1249/12/15 Nakano Yoshinari yuzurijō.

[70] E.g., three same-day *yuzurijō* to two sons and a nephew, and another *yuzurijō* to a daughter; the Bakufu confirmed all four in same-day edicts of its own; Documents 76–79: 1257/9/14 shōgun ke mandokoro kudashibumi. Or again, four same-day testa-

lease.[71] Similarly, junior heirs were regularly admonished to obey their *chakushi* brothers,[72] and the *chakushi* themselves were warned not to violate the holdings of their siblings.[73] To ensure compliance the Bakufu took care to make explicit in its confirmations the division of landholdings set down by the donor. No one, it enjoined, was to violate anyone else's share.[74]

Such efforts, however, had only mixed success, and families became arenas of competition for parental favor. Losers in these contests had no recourse; it was one of the foundations of the system that the disenfranchised could not bring suits against their fathers. The result was to set the stage for the monumental sibling battles that dominated the judicial scene for the remainder of the era. In one remarkable case, an eldest son deprived of an inheritance by his father spent the rest of his life, some 40 years, quarreling with his brothers and sisters.[75] Moreover, if the house headship was the prize that was at stake, an elder son might await his father's death and then find grounds to lodge a complaint against his brother who was *sōryō*. Naturally, when the wishes of the late father were clear in such matters, no countervailing argument could win.[76]

To this point we have had little to say about the powers exercised by mothers. Mothers were at least as peremptory as fathers and were necessarily more calculating. The major reason for this behavior was that mothers, if they became widows, were under a variety of limitations not applicable to their late husbands. For one thing, widows were obliged not to remarry under penalty of surrendering land rights conveyed to them by their spouses. The existence of such a rule

---

ments to three sons and a grandson; Documents 102–5: 1270/8/25 shami Gyōnin yuzurijō.

[71] E.g., Document 86: 1260/3/15 Minamoto Yorinaga yuzurijō. See also a Bakufu confirmation of a will to a junior heir that had been countersigned by the house headdesignate; Document 63: 1242/10/23 shōgun ke mandokoro kudashibumi.

[72] E.g., Document 84: 1258/7/19 Kobayakawa Shigehira yuzurijō an; Documents 103–4: 1270/8/25 shami Gyōnin yuzurijō.

[73] E.g., Document 42: 1230/int.1/14 Yamanouchi Shigetoshi yuzurijō; Document 55: 1237/8/25 Fujiwara Iekado yuzurijō; Document 65: 1243/10/6 Shigeno Mitsuuji yuzurijō an; 1295/3/29 Yamanouchi Tokimichi yuzurijō.

[74] E.g., Document 31: 1224/11/30 Kantō gechijō an; Documents 47–48: 1231/10/18 shōgun sodehan kudashibumi an, 1233/4/15 shōgun ke mandokoro kudashibumi; Documents 69–70: 1252/12/26, 1254/12/12 shōgun ke mandokoro kudashibumi; Document 94: 1270/8/28 Kantō gechijō an.

[75] Document 61: 1241/8/22 Kantō gechijō.

[76] E.g., Document 69: 1252/12/26 shōgun ke mandokoro kudashibumi.

worked to invite charges of remarriage, both real and fancied. For instance, in 1292 a widow who had remarried was stripped of her late husband's inheritance after her son proved that his new stepfather was attempting to succeed his real father.[77] The verdict might just as easily have gone the other way, as occurred in a case of 1239. On that occasion, the Bakufu, after obtaining depositions from various witnesses, ruled that no remarriage had taken place.[78] Experiences of this kind created an epidemic of estrangements between mothers and children, particularly when the mother was a stepparent.

Mothers were not always blameless in the controversies that enveloped them. If their desire to remarry evokes our sympathy, their arbitrariness in redirecting husbands' property does not. As we noted in Chapter Two, a mother, following a lawsuit against her son, was awarded a *jitō shiki* under condition that it devolve upon the son at her death. In effect, the verdict granted her a life tenure; she was not to break the entail established by the court. The mother, however, had other plans—and 18 years later successfully shifted the inheritance to a different son.[79] Machinations such as these did not always succeed, of course, as in another case in which a mother's efforts in this direction were stymied.[80] But the ambiguities attendant on life tenures often led to trouble. When the issue was a late husband's legacy for which an entail might or might not have been created, the Bakufu had no recourse but to hear the matter and render judgment. By contrast, the issue would not have come to trial if the property in question was the mother's by inheritance from her parents. Only fathers, who received no property from their wives,[81] were immune from legal actions by their children.

Naturally, it was not always true that mothers achieved positions of dominant influence within their families. If the bequests from their own fathers were small or were promised to a brother under a life-tenure formula, or if their husbands outlived them or bequeathed them only a small parcel, the effective power of a mother would be reduced. A typical case was that of Shigeno Mitsuuji, who in 1243 divided his holdings among children, grandchildren, and his wife, but placed his principal heir rather than his wife in the central position;

[77] *Itōzu monjo*, 1292/5 Usa Motohiro mōshijō, *Ōita ken shiryō*, 1: 117–18, doc. 86.

[78] *DKR*, doc. 144: 1244/4/23 Kantō gechijō.

[79] Document 20: 1220/12/19 Kantō gechijō; Documents 21–23: 1238/4/4 Taira no uji yuzurijō (2), 1241/5/1 shōgun ke mandokoro kudashibumi.

[80] Documents 38–40: Fukabori Nakamitsu yuzurijō, 1232/2/18 Fukabori Nakamitsu goke ama yuzurijō an, 1234/2/13 bikuni ama yuzurijō.

[81] This subject is dealt with below, pp. 78–79.

the latter received only a tiny entailed portion.[82] On the other hand, a surprisingly large number of women *were* given the dominant responsibility by fathers, mothers, and husbands. For example, a father who had received his inheritance from his mother now bequeathed it in perpetuity to his eldest daughter; she became house head and a Kamakura vassal in 1239.[83] Or again, a wife made heir by her late husband in place of his daughter worked cooperatively with an adopted son who was his parents' mutual choice as her successor.[84] There was one other situation that placed women in the middle—being widowed unexpectedly by a husband who left no will. On some occasions, it was the widow who decided the inheritances of the children.[85]

In between, however, there were all manner of possible arrangements. Most common here were permanent, though clearly secondary, bequests to a wife or daughter. In 1274 we encounter both of these situations—a mother conveying property to a daughter that she had received as a secondary share from her late husband. In this instance, the husband's principal heir was a son who had been obliged by his father to give formal assent to a share for his mother. The mother bequeathed this share to the young house head's sister rather than to him.[86] On other occasions, a mother who was an heiress but who had a living husband might yet exercise considerable leverage. A notable example was the wife of Yamanouchi Munetoshi, a prominent vassal. Both husband and wife prepared their wills at approximately the same time, but while he was concentrating on the principal heir, she was bequeathing to a younger son.[87] Finally, in intestate cases, there were instances in which a widow did not automatically step into the breach but had to be placed there by the Bakufu or else made a legatee alongside rather than in lieu of her children.[88]

[82] Document 65: 1243/10/6 Shigeno Mitsuuji yuzurijō an.

[83] Documents 57–58: 1239/7/17 Kakuzen yuzurijō, 1239/8/3 Kantō gechijō.

[84] *DKR*, doc. 140: 1239/5/25 Kantō gechijō.

[85] Document 80: 1257/7/6 Kantō gechijō. Or see Document 113: 1282/7/16 shōgun ke mandokoro kudashibumi an, for a widow's taking charge of allocations (*haibun*) in accordance with a statement on the subject (but not a will) of her late husband.

[86] Document 72: 1274/5/21 Kantō gechijō.

[87] For his wills, see Documents 43–44: 1248/12/21, 1249/8/21 Yamanouchi Munetoshi yuzurijō. For hers, Document 64: 1243/7/28 shōgun ke mandokoro kudashibumi.

[88] E.g., Document 83: 1272/10/29 Kantō gechijō. I do not agree with the view of Prof. Haga, therefore, who argues in favor of the widow in this context, or, if she were dead too, the main heir; Haga, *Sōryōsei*, p. 77. Things were never so categorical. For three alternative possibilities, see Documents 81–82: 1259/12/23 Kantō gechijō, 1265/12/27 Kantō gechijō an; and Document 134:1304/4/24 Kantō gechijō an. Or again, the survivors (mother and children) might decide to sell the husband/father's legacy in this situa-

As noted above, wives did not release property to their husbands. In fact, for the whole of the Kamakura period I have found no instances of a wife, anticipating death, devolving a permanent or entailed portion on a spouse. Instead, there is an extraordinary episode of 1264 that illuminates not a relationship that had deepened but one that had failed and ended in divorce.[89] The case involved a wife who had transferred her entire inheritance to a husband who then divorced her. She sought to retrieve her holdings on the grounds that their transmission was revocable in the same manner as releases to children. Her ex-husband countered, however, that "a former wife is [like] a stranger (*gainin*)," by which he meant that the transaction, as in a land sale, was between "unrelated people" (*tanin*). Only releases to relatives could be retrieved; those to outsiders were nonrescindable. The Bakufu concurred in this reasoning and in the process may have inflicted a mortal wound on the possibility of regular wifely bequests to husbands. Women might flee their husbands, and obtain their freedom in that fashion, but only husbands could initiate regular divorce. In addition, husbands might now retain property acquired from a marriage—if indeed there was such property.

The converse situation in divorce cases did not exist, however. Husbands might continue, without risk, to make provision for their wives because the latter were handicapped in two ways not applicable to their husbands. Women were unable to consummate divorce except by flight, which was a punishable offense leading to loss of property from a spouse; and women were unable as widows to remarry without surrendering their late husband's lands. The result was a freedom for husbands to deal with their wives much as they dealt with their children. They could grant or not grant them a bequest, make it permanent or temporary, or change their minds on these subjects. In a case of 1260, for example, a wife's portion was reduced in size but granted now in perpetuity.[90] But in another case, an entailed portion that a widow later attempted to bequeath was deemed as already "accounted for" by the Bakufu.[91] Both of these examples might just as easily have involved children instead of wives. The major difference with chil-

tion, or decide to divide it into equal and permanent shares; see *Tōdaiji monjo*, 1291/4/22 chakushi haha tō rensho baiken, *KI*, 23: 100–101, doc. 17601; and *Yamanaka monjo*, 1291/5/10 chakushi shoshi goke rensho haibunjō, *KI*, 23: 106–7, doc. 17613.

[89] Document 95: 1264/10/10 Kantō gechijō.

[90] Documents 86–87: 1260/3/15 Minamoto Yorinaga yuzurijō, 1261/8/29 Kantō gechijō an.

[91] Document 119: 1290/5/12 Kantō gechijō.

dren was that wives often had their own property—shares from their own parents that they could freely sell or pawn, commend to religious institutions, or assign or bequeath to natural or adopted children of either gender.[92] Moreover, when their husbands were dead, and if their husbands' property had been made subject to their jurisdiction, they could distort the intentions of those spouses. Upon the pretext of disloyalty they were able, in at least some instances, to disinherit children.[93] As we shall see shortly, women were also formidable opponents as sisters.

As we have noted repeatedly, the central question for historians of the *sōryō* system concerns men and women as brothers and sisters: what was the nature of the interaction between the sibling selected for headship and the rest? The authority of parents (except for widows and stepparents in some circumstances) required no justification in premodern Japan. But the authority of a brother—at times a younger brother—could always be questioned, despite the best efforts of parents to tie their transfer of power to that brother to filial piety toward themselves. The conflict was exacerbated by the desire of most parents to divide their holdings among all children, giving only the largest relative share to the main successor. The dilemma was never resolved. The senior generation wished to hand down sufficient power for the corporate interests and responsibilities of the familiy to be protected, but the step that was needed to ensure this condition—a transfer of the distribution privilege for house assets to the main heir—would have involved surrendering their own authority and placing at risk the principle of partible inheritance. Parents had no problem with the prospect of sharing their possessions with offspring. But for a brother to view his siblings as he did his own children was simply to run against human nature. And so the *sōryō* system—a compromise if it worked, a contradiction if it did not—evolved. That scholars see it as strong or weak, early or late, itself captures the ambiguity—and/or flexibility—of that system.

[92] For sales by females, see Documents 53–54: 1237/7/17 Minamoto no ujime baiken an, 1237/8/6 Fujiwara no ujime baiken an; for a reference to a pawning by a mother and her son, *Kanchūki ura monjo*, 1292/3 bō mōshijō, *KI*, 23: 228, doc. 17864; for a commendation, *Katsuodera monjo*, 1232/2/23 ama denchi kishinjō, *Minoo shishi, shiryō hen*, 1: 68, doc. 100; for bequests to, respectively, an adopted son and an adopted daughter; Document 109: 1274/3/21 Inukai Ken yuzurijō, *Tōdaiji monjo*, 1288/1/10 goke denchi shobunjō, *KI*, 21: 382, doc. 16476.

[93] For the disinheritance of a son, see *Kōyasan monjo*, 1290/8/10 ama Shin'a gizetsu kishōmon, *DNK, iewake 1*, 8: 119–20, doc. 1776. For the grandmother's disinheritance of the same son, *ibid.*, 1290/8/10 Saia gizetsu kishōmon, *ibid.*, 8: 119, doc. 1175.

In much the same fashion that we have examined the powers of parents vis-à-vis children, let us now attempt the same for the house head and his siblings. Our point of reference is what Japanese historians call the *sōryōken*—the powers of the *sōryō*. The term has meaning only in a horizontal sense, since the downward flow of power derived naturally from the status of a parent. Perhaps the central questions can be put this way: What did the *sōryō* receive from his parents (and from the Bakufu)? How were these different from what were received by his brothers and sisters? And how did these rights meld and conflict?

As we have seen, a father might choose his successor at any time, might grant or reclaim land rights at any time, and might invest as much or as little authority in his main heir as he wished. In other words, the heir did not become *sōryō*—house head in his own right—until his father's ashes were safely in the ground. Nevertheless, whether early or late, he did receive certain things from his father (or mother) before that parent's death. He received his designation as principal heir, at first probably informally, but later in a written release;[94] he received a document (or documents) of release from his father, with some movables and/or land rights transferred on a pre-obit basis but with the bulk to be treated as a bequest;[95] and he received from his father an irregular deputation to stand in for him in the performance of military or peacetime vassal duties,[96] to act as his representative in a court of law,[97] and to serve as his proxy in myriad other ways that would establish the son as the successor-designate of the father.

At some indeterminate point the family's treasured documents would also be transmitted to him, including original deeds and investitures plus the sequence of testaments, confirmations, and judgments,[98] but also including house genealogies or ancestral admoni-

[94] See Document 25: 1222/12/23 dazaifu shugosho kudashibumi an, for a dispute over an informal designation.

[95] The point of actual transfer is rarely specified; nor did it necessarily follow directly upon the receipt of a release, the submission of that release to Kamakura, or the Bakufu's approval. Indeed, there was no standard formula connecting these three actions: there were pre-obit releases that were approved immediately or were delayed, and probated wills coming soon or years after the death of the donor. See the Documents section for examples.

[96] See *KB*, doc. 21: 1221/7/26 Kantō gechijō (military); and Document 25: 1222/12/23 dazaifu shugosho kudashibumi an (peacetime).

[97] For a *chakushi* representing his father, see Document 61: 1241/8/22 Kantō gechijō; for a *chakushi* representing his mother, see Document 95: 1264/10/10 Kantō gechijō.

[98] See, e.g., the list of documents supposedly appended to a testament of 1243; Document 65: 1243/10/6 Shigeno Mitsuuji yuzurijō an.

tions, if such existed.[99] The family's hereditary banners, armor, and weapons would also be transferred as additional symbols of house headship,[100] as would the father's main residence, his core homeland area, and his key *shiki*.[101] It is noteworthy that the principal heir's right to all these was rarely questioned: what might become an issue, particularly in intestate cases, was the identity of that heir, not his special perquisites. For example, two brothers took their case before a tribunal in 1314 to contest the possession of armor, banners, and documents—in effect, a quarrel over who was to be the next house head.[102] But the clearest proof that the *sōryō*-designate had a right to such symbolic representations was the frequent inclusion of a disclaimer regarding missing ancestral documents in the releases granted to junior heirs. In cases where the land rights being conveyed constituted a portion of an original holding, the earlier documents could obviously not be appended. Instead, they would become the possessions of the principal heir.[103]

Apart from these unique resources attaching to house headship, main heirs received a variety of tangible perquisites that differed more in quantity than in kind from those received by their siblings. The complement of "typical" benefits for which all children might be eligible included *shiki* and parts of *shiki*, parcels of dry land and paddy, residential structures and compounds, and service households.[104] Less frequent were temples and shrines, boats, slaves and other dependents, designated income shares, and cash annuities.[105]

[99] For a genealogy (*keizu*), *Ōmi Mizuhara monjo*, 1229/8/11 Ōmi Sanekage yuzurijō, in *Hokuetsu chūsei monjo*, doc. 1, p. 36; for house rules, Documents 84–85: 1258/7/19 Kobayakawa Shigehira yuzurijō an, 1289/2/16 Kobayakawa Masakage yuzurijō.

[100] See n. 102 and (for swords) *Kuchiki monjo*, 1328/6/13 Taira Munenori yuzurijō, *Kuchiki monjo*, 1: 74, doc. 131.

[101] This is amply borne out in the Documents section, e.g., Document 41: 1230/2/20 Oyama Tomomasa yuzurijō an.

[102] Document 142: 1314/5/12 Kantō gechijō. Or see an inheritance dispute in which a family that was splitting irrevocably divided not only the real property but also the important movables: the main residence and banners to one side, the armor and long swords to the other; Document 148: 1323/12/12 Kantō gechijō.

[103] In cases of partible inheritance the *chakushi* also would have held only a portion of the original holding; but he was entrusted with the hereditary documents, e.g., Document 42: 1230/int.1/14 Yamanouchi Shigetoshi yuzurijō. The same problem was especially common in land sale transactions; see the disclaimer in Document 54: 1237/8/6 Fujiwara no ujime baiken.

[104] See, e.g., Documents 43–44 (to a *chakushi*): 1248/12/21, 1249/8/21 Yamanouchi Munetoshi yuzurijō; and Document 84 (to a second son): 1258/7/19 Kobayakawa Shigehira yuzurijō.

[105] For the first, Document 41: 1230/2/20 Oyama Tomomasa yuzurijō an; for the sec-

During the middle decades of the thirteenth century, conveyances often became highly complex documents as donors sought to cut and paste in an effort to be equitable but precise.[106] The inheritance disputes that were rife during this era reflected this complexity as well as an environment in which brothers and sisters jostled against one another in cramped and adjacent shares.[107] But quarrels of this kind, which had been common for centuries, were not necessarily a product of the *sōryō* system per se. Only where the principal heir was in conflict with his siblings (or, viewed more broadly, with his "cousins") was the *sōryō* system itself a factor. In other words, it was only when the issue derived from the exercise of authority over and within the family that the *sōryō* system proper was involved.

For historians, the only completely uncontroversial aspect of the *sōryō*'s authority is the fact that he allocated and collected the vassal dues (*onkuji*) owed to the Bakufu. Earlier we noted that this responsibility emerged as one of the key reforms affecting family and property in the period after 1205. In an era in which war occurred only infrequently, the exercise of this duty became the core element of the *sōryō*'s peacetime administrative authority. The issue for historians has been the degree of leverage accruing to him as a result, as well as his punitive rights in the event of noncompliance by siblings. On these two points, indeed, rests much of the debate surrounding the *sōryō* system itself. The lack of agreement about *onkuji* is largely rooted in the sources.

The sources in question are surprisingly limited in context and content. Most of what we know derives from wills and is prescriptive in nature; little survives on actual mechanics.[108] Because of this, the linkage between the *onkuji* and *sōryō* systems has become very largely a question of definition. For some historians, *onkuji*, a privilege enjoyed

---

ond, *Daitokuji monjo*, 1292/int.6/10 Hata Nagahisa yuzurijō, *KI*, 23: 257–58, doc. 17,948; for the third, *DKR*, doc. 141: 1239/5/25 Kantō migyōsho; for the fourth (a 50 *koku* stipend to a younger daughter), Document 84: 1258/7/19 Kobayakawa Shigehira yuzurijō; for the fifth (a 30 *kanmon* cash stipend, along with a *jitō shiki*, to a fourth daughter), Document 97: 1265/9/23 shami Iren yuzurijō. In 1260, a widow even fell heir to a grove of cherry trees; Document 86: 1260/3/15 Minamoto Yorinaga yuzurijō.

[106] See, e.g., the amounts cited in Documents 76–79: 1257/9/14 shōgun ke mandokoro kudashibumi.

[107] See also, e.g., Document 63: 1242/10/23 shōgun ke mandokoro kudashibumi; and Documents 102–5: 1270/8/25 shami Gyōnin yuzurijō.

[108] Twenty years ago Prof. Haga noted that *onkuji* had not yet been systematically studied (*Sōryōsei*, p. 100). An introductory look appeared only in 1981: Yasuda Motohisa, "Kantō onkuji kō," pp. 437–61.

by all house heads, represented the basis for the *sōryō*'s advancing superiority. For others (myself included), *onkuji* were simply vassal dues: a burden by definition, they were of limited value to the house heads who coordinated them. When *sōryō* were strong, it was for reasons other than their responsibility for collecting these tributes.[109]

The basis for this second view lies in the restraints on house heads imposed by their own parents. Though commissioned by parents to be the expediting agents for *onkuji*, *sōryō* were constantly reminded not to be neglectful of that duty. At the same time, a formula for parceling the tax load allowed them little discretion: payment shares were to be a function of the sizes of relative land shares. Finally, *sōryō* were not to exploit their siblings in the matter of *onkuji*, nor, it should be added, were the siblings to disobey the *sōryō*.[110]

From the point of view of the senior generation, then, the equitable distribution of the dues burden, rather than its collection by the *sōryō*, was the main issue. *Onkuji* were to reflect and bolster the parents' own property dispositions as well as the rank-ordering implied therein. It was for this reason that violators of the resulting equilibrium encountered opposition on all sides. The Bakufu, which had obligated itself to protect the aggregate of interests, permitted suits to be lodged against *sōryō* in which the latter's own siblings were the plaintiffs.[111]

Sōryō who were aggressive could even lose the limited prestige that did accrue from *onkuji* collection. This occurred when junior heirs were released from their obligations to pay through the house head. The dues themselves would still be incumbent upon them, but they could now discharge them as individuals.[112] Greater precision in speci-

[109] My views are akin to those of Uwayokote ("Sōryōsei josetsu," pp. 84–88, 92) and Haga (*Sōryōsei*, pp. 100–106). The chief spokesman for the other position is Toyoda (*Bushidan to sonraku*, pp. 186–91).

[110] For the linkage between payment shares and the sizes of land shares, see, e.g., *Shiga monjo*, 1240/4/6 ama Shinmyō shoryō haibunjō, *Hennen Ōtomo shiryō*, 1: 361–63, doc. 416; *Iriki-in monjo*, 1245/5/11 Shibuya Jōshin okibumi, in Asakawa Kanichi, *The Documents of Iriki*, doc. 13, pp. 121–27; and Document 121: 1295/3/29 Yamanouchi Jizen yuzurijō. For standard admonitions stressing obedience to the *sōryō*'s requisitioning orders, see, e.g., Documents 44, 84, and 103 (1249/8/21 Yamanouchi Shinnen yuzurijō, 1258/7/19 Kobayakawa Honbutsu yuzurijō an, 1270/8/25 shami Gyōnin yuzurijō). For a warning aimed at a *sōryō*, Document 65: 1243/10/6 Shigeno Mitsuuji yuzurijō an; and for a warning to junior heirs, *Minagawa monjo*, 1230/8/13 Fujiwara Munemasa yuzurijō, *KI*, 6: 212, doc. 4011.

[111] Uwayokote, "Sōryōsei josetsu," p. 82. Prof. Gomi refers to a bitter dispute within the Nikaidō *jitō* family of Satsuma over the apportionment of *onkuji* shares; Gomi Yoshio, "Chūsei shakai to gokenin—sōryōsei to gokeninsei," p. 50.

[112] E.g., *Sappan kyūki zatsuroku*, 1292/4/7 Izumi Yasumichi yuzurijō an, *KI*, 23: 230–31, doc. 17869.

fying the payment formula was yet another defense against *sōryō*, though here the protection could cut both ways. Depending on who was the aggressor, strict rules for calculating dues totals would serve as an obvious deterrent.[113]

The converse side to controls on the *sōryō* was his range of responses to the recalcitrance of junior heirs. Toyoda and other historians, reflecting the dire warnings contained in a small number of wills, have asserted a clear right of confiscation. Uwayokote and another group of scholars have argued the opposite, noting that there were but a handful of confiscations, none unqualified.[114] In fact, *sōryō* had only two basic options when challenged by coheirs. Unable to exact sanctions on their own, they had to win a court order through victory in a lawsuit or else obtain the backing of their own cohort of peers. The second situation might involve convening a "family council" (*yoriai*), an outlet for settlements increasingly encouraged by parents. Typically, however, the council might also be the forum for charges brought against the *sōryō*.[115] As brothers, then, *sōryō* could not act peremptorily against their own kin. Their responsibility for *onkuji* yielded only limited leverage.[116]

Before turning to the other parts of the *sōryō*'s rights package, it will be useful to distinguish between "primary" and "secondary" heads. Theoretically, a main line was the one that was descended from the "first" *sōryō*, i.e., from an original Kamakura vassal. As noted earlier, however, Yoritomo often recognized multiple sons of his first-generation vassals. In other words, a "*sōryō* system"—involving a single line above the others—emerged only after Yoritomo's death. In this sense, main lines dated from the period after 1205. But the Jōkyū War followed soon thereafter, and when headships were shifted new

---

[113] Uwayokote, "Sōryōsei josetsu," p. 92. For this greater specificity, see, e.g., the references in Document 86: 1260/3/15 Minamoto Yorinaga yuzurijō (though here the goal was to protect a wife from the donor's children); Document 88: 1260/8/27 Chikakazu yuzurijō (to protect a daughter); and Document 135: 1306/4/16 Nakahara Shigemichi yuzurijō (to protect 15 sons and daughters, a wife, and a grandson).

[114] Toyoda, *Bushidan to sonraku*, pp. 181–86; Uwayokote, "Sōryōsei josetsu," pp. 83–84; Haga, *Sōryōsei*, p. 72.

[115] As one will-writing father put it, "Accordingly, should there be any grievances that arise involving Yoshikado [the *sōryō*-designate], such matters shall be dealt with in family council, with all members of one mind." Document 55: 1237/8/25 Fujiwara Iekado yuzurijō.

[116] In 1270, for example, a *sōryō*, who was also an adopted son, was obliged to bring suit against his elder stepsister for failure to pay *onkuji*; Ōtomo monjo, 1270/3/25 Kantō gechijō, *KI*, 14: 138, doc. 10,617.

main lines were created. It was not until the 1230s that *sōryō* lines tended to become stabilized.[117]

At the same time, secondary *sōryō* were appearing. Each time the Bakufu confirmed a partible inheritance, it was establishing a son or daughter as a potential house head. With each new generation there would be further proliferation, and the distance between the main *sōryō* and these offshoots would increase.[118] How this fragmentation affected the *onkuji* obligation is largely moot. A pyramid of secondary heads, each collecting for his own siblings and then delivering to the next level up (or was it to the main *sōryō*?) may be more image than reality; it reminds us of the feudal pyramid. At all events, to the extent a pyramid existed here, it must have been a structure with little articulation among its parts. For this reason, the narrowest usage of *sōryō* (a principal heir, whether far or near to the main line) seems appropriate.

The remaining powers of the *sōryō*, following the list compiled by Toyoda, underscore the difficulty of making a case for strong house heads. In addition to his responsibility for *onkuji*, the *sōryō* exercised limited degrees of (1) religious authority, (2) military command, (3) homelands possession, (4) policing authority, (5) agricultural supervision, and (6) dominance over females.[119]

Although the first three may be called regular powers, each in its own way needs to be qualified. For example, religious authority varied widely. At the top end of the scale, a *sōryō* might function as the priest-administrator (*kannushi*) of his family's ancestral shrine, a point emphasized by Toyoda.[120] However, only a minority of *sōryō*, even representing trunk lines, probably did so.[121] In general, house heads

---

[117]Two sequences of releases and confirmations—those of the Yamanouchi and Kobayakawa—show this stabilization clearly. For the former, KB, doc. 21: 1221/7/26 Kantō gechijō; and Documents 42–46: 1230/int.1/14 Yamanouchi Shigetoshi yuzurijō, 1248/1/21 Yamanouchi Munetoshi yuzurijō, etc. For the latter, *DKR*, doc. 41: 1240/int.10/11 Kantō gechijō; and Documents 84–85: 1258/7/19 Kobayakawa Shigehira yuzurijō an, 1289/2/16 Kobayakawa Masakage yuzurijō.

[118]A valuable case study of this proliferation of secondary *sōryō* is Toyama Mikio, "Kamakura ki ni okeru Ōtomo shi no dōkō."

[119]Toyoda, *Bushidan to sonraku*, pp. 160–218. The classifications I have used borrow from Toyoda's own but also combine several of his.

[120]*Ibid.*, pp. 192–95.

[121]It has been argued, for example, that the *sōryō* line of the Ōtomo, which retained its base in the east while various junior lines moved westward, failed to exercise more than a modest religious authority over the larger kindred; Toyama, "Kamakura ki ni okeru Ōtomo shi," p. 65. For an extended treatment of this subject, which underscores

ministered to tutelary deities, administered burial grounds, and offici-
ated at important ceremonies. But whether these activities may be
equated with "control of a family's religious life" seems uncertain.
Moreover, any attempt to exercise dominion through religious sanction would doubtless have been contested.[122]

The *sōryō's* military command is controversial for a different reason.
It was the Bakufu's intention for house heads to serve as the instruments of its recruitment calls; *sōryō* would lead their families to battle
as well as to peacetime guard duty. In both activities, however, performance ran short of expectations. Guard call-ups were not only too infrequent to have contributed much to the *sōryō's* authority,[123] but the
guard duty itself was often avoided altogether. Parents' wills commonly divested the heir apparent of any right of personal command
by stipulating a commutation of service or even an exemption.[124]
Sometimes the length of service became an object of dispute between
a *sōryō* and his relatives.[125]

The *sōryō's* command authority proved even more vulnerable in
time of war. The difficulty here was that families broke apart easily
when confronted by genuine crisis. Naturally, not all families succumbed in this fashion, and a danger faced in common, e.g., a challenge from a proprietor, might even cause a closing of the ranks, albeit usually a temporary one.[126] At any rate, it was not merely that
trunk line heads could not be counted on to control their cousins; the
loyalty of even brothers might be just as uncertain.

Sōryō, as mentioned earlier, normally received their predecessors'
homelands, key *shiki*, and the other concrete manifestations of a fam-

---

the range of possibilities here, see Kawai Masaharu, "Chūsei bushidan no ujigami
ujidera."

[122] Though Toyoda cites the power to divest a sibling of the family name as an example of such a sanction (*Bushidan to sonraku*, p. 195), most scholars deny this.

[123] Prof. Gomi argues that many vassals were called on to serve only once in a generation, perhaps only once in a lifetime; Gomi Yoshio, "Kamakura gokenin no banyaku
kinshi ni tsuite," p. 33.

[124] For both of these (though benefiting a wife), see Document 86: 1260/3/15 Minamoto Yorinaga yuzurijō. Commutations into cash became increasingly common, e.g.,
for the benefit of a daughter, referred to in 1277/6/23 Owari Tadashige yuzurijō, *Tottori
kenshi*, 2: 738, doc. 131; not in *KI*. Most exemptions, of course, were granted by the
Bakufu; Gomi, "Kamakura gokenin no banyaku," pp. 32–33.

[125] In a case of 1302, for instance, a twenty-day service obligation was divided on a
9:11 basis; *Saisho monjo*, 1302/6/13 Saisho Munenari wayōjō, *KI*, 28: 14, doc. 21098.

[126] A classic example occurred in 1302 when lineages that had spent decades fighting
one another allied now to defend against the estate owner; Document 133: 1302/7/7
Kantō gechijō an.

ily's corporate identity. As time passed, however, these exchanges often lost their initial directness and simplicity. One common occurrence was for widows to be entrusted with homelands for the duration of their lifetimes; in the interim, the principal-heir-designate had to wait.[127] Moreover, if the portfolio was small and concentrated and the sibling group reasonably large, inheritances, including the *sōryō's* "homelands," would inevitably shrink in size.[128] Nevertheless, the identification between the *sōryō* and family homelands remained strong and even began to take on a fresh dimension: secondary heads, frequently bearing new surnames, established their own homelands wherever their inheritances took them.[129]

The remaining three items on Toyoda's list, as noted by various scholars, are problematic in more serious ways. For instance, intrafamily policing authority was an exceptional circumstance and therefore extrinsic to the status of *sōryō.* Much the same is true for agricultural authority. Though situations occurred in which, for example, water rights, commons, or labor privileges were bequeathed to a *sōryō,* there are at least an equal number of cases in which this was not so.[130] As we will note shortly, it was more likely anyway that such authority, when it did develop, did not derive from parents or the Bakufu. It was assigned instead by estate owners.

The relationship of house heads to their sisters is (once again) subject to opposing views. It is true that some sisters had their lands physically situated within the *sōryō's* holdings or even reduced to annuities paid or guaranteed by him.[131] Yet the most disproportionate of these arrangements occurred in the post-Mongol era, when the independence of junior heirs (brothers as well as sisters) did decline (see Chapter Four). Much more common in the decades under review here were properties entailed to a brother who was *sōryō.* The question thus becomes, What rights did he exercise before the entail took effect? In fact, apart from the current holder's inability to alienate such properties, there were no other encumbrances. Moreover, when

[127] See, e.g., Document 113: 1282/7/16 shōgun ke mandokoro kudashibumi an.

[128] See, e.g., Document 63: 1242/10/23 shōgun ke mandokoro kudashibumi.

[129] For case studies of the Masuda and Ōtomo, for example, see Kobayashi, "Iwami no kuni Masuda shi no ryōshusei," and Toyama, "Kamakura ki ni okeru Ōtomo shi."

[130] For the debate on this subject, see Toyoda, *Bushidan to sonraku,* p. 206, and Haga, *Sōryōsei,* pp. 91–92.

[131] For the holdings of a sister located within a *sōryō's* sphere, see Documents 69–70: 1252/12/26 and 1254/12/12 shōgun ke mandokoro kudashibumi. For a lifetime annuity of 50 *koku* of rice to be paid by a *second* son (not a *sōryō* in this case) to his younger sister, Document 84: 1258/7/19 Kobayakawa Shigehira yuzurijō an.

sisters' lands were violated by brothers, justice was close at hand. A life tenure was inviolate until death and implied no coparceners.

With the foregoing as background, we are now in a position to appreciate why most *sōryō* enjoyed limited real authority. They dominated their own heirs, but not their coheirs. On the other hand, some *sōryō* did come to transcend the institutional restraints on their positions, and we need to know why. The whimsy of parents, the ambitions of the children, the particulars of the family portfolio and its partitioning, and the patronage of higher authority were the main variables here.

As we already know, parents might contribute to the strength of a future house head in a number of ways. Selecting the eldest son was one of these ways, since the choice was not likely itself to become an issue. (Conversely, eldest sons who had been passed over frequently initiated very bitter lawsuits.)[132] Sometimes the rationale for favoring an eldest son was noted in a father's will, e.g., as a means of guaranteeing the collection of vassal dues.[133] Most often, however, such explanations were unnecessary; the pattern was simply the normal one. On the other hand, promotion of a younger son required extra effort. An early selection was obviously helpful here, but providing a rationale was still almost mandatory. References to the unfiliality and other defects of the children passed over became a regular feature of such wills.[134]

Parents were forever attempting to predict the vigor, abilities, and ambitions of their children. Despite such efforts, some families were continually wracked by disputes, whereas others were quiescent or were contumacious only occasionally. In other words, satisfaction with one's lot was only sometimes an objective condition; discontent stemmed from many factors. The willingness of siblings (*sōryō* included) to sacrifice family solidarity is the main point here. For many

---

[132] See, e.g., Document 27: 1222/12/23 dazaifu shugosho kudashibumi an; Document 61: 1241/8/22 Kantō gechijō; and Documents 68–69: 1249/12/15 Nakano Yoshinari yuzurijō, 1252/12/26 shōgun ke mandokoro kudashibumi. A daughter's being bypassed in favor of grandsons might also lead to a dispute, e.g., Document 118: 1287/9/1 Kantō gechijō an.

[133] *Kamada monjo*, 1310/2/7 Kantō gechijō, *KBSS*, 1: 330–31, doc. 256, which cites a testament of 1247/11/24 (not extant) in which this explanation appears.

[134] In 1237, for instance, a father cited a lack of ability on the part of his two eldest sons; Document 55: 1237/8/25 Fujiwara Iekado yuzurijō. In 1239, another father cited a daughter's unfiliality as his rationale for nominating her younger brother; Document 59: 1239/11/5 Kantō gechijō an. And in 1249, a third father cited both these deficiencies as the reason for bypassing his eldest son; Document 68: 1249/12/15 Nakano Yoshinari yuzurijō.

house heads, personal aggrandizement—the inflating of invested rights by unlawful means—seemed the only effective way to advance their interests. The most "successful" *sōryō* were in this sense those most amenable to ravaging their own families. Failing that, a richly endowed, fully intact, entirely accessible *jitō shiki* was the only kind of legacy for a *sōryō* to build upon. Yet this condition would not have prevailed if the siblings of the head either shared in his inheritance or received *jitō shiki* of their own.

In an era of partible inheritance, the numbers simply worked against most house heads. Bequests to them were reduced by the total of itemized exceptions allocated to their siblings.[135] By quantifying the commodities in which wealth and prestige were measured (paddy, upland, residences, service households, etc.), and then by factoring in standards of quality (location, productivity, degree of servility, etc.), donors could achieve the balance they desired. The problem for most *sōryō* was that only gross inequality really served their interests. In too many of the property dispensations of the era, there was a heavier emphasis on equity than on inequity.[136]

If house heads often felt handicapped by deficiencies in their inheritances, they sometimes received a boost from an unlikely source—estate owners. Their patronage took several forms. First, proprietors, as mentioned before, might assign water rights and other "agricultural" privileges to *sōryō*. Second, house heads might be called on to collect a series of Kyoto-imposed tributes comparable to Kamakura's *onkuji*.[137] Third, and most important, the authority to collect the annual land rent (*nengu*) from kin was occasionally awarded to *sōryō*.

This last requires some elaboration. In effect, *sōryō* could be empowered to collect the heaviest and most regular of all local levies, now from their closest relatives.[138] Opposition was not long in form-

[135] For a graphic example, Document 76: 1257/9/14 shōgun ke mandokoro kudashibumi.

[136] As we shall see in Chapter 4, this would change in the final third of the Kamakura age.

[137] Referred to by the same term, these *onkuji* are frequently cited in parents' wills, e.g., Document 42: 1230/int.1/14 Yamanouchi Shigetoshi yuzurijō ("public and private dues" [*kōshi no onkuji*]); *Takuma monjo*, 1288/4/25 Takuma Tokihide yuzurijō an, *KI*, 22: 36–37, doc. 16583 (*kuge Kantō no onkuji*); and *Irobe monjo*, 1292/10/22 shami Dōgan yuzurijō an, *Essa shiryō*, 2: 122–23 (*Kyōto Kamakura no onkuji*).

[138] We see this authority noted in various wills, e.g., Document 100: 1268/int.1/28 saemon no jō Kiyotoki yuzurijō an; Document 121: 1295/3/29 Yamanouchi Tokimichi yuzurijō; and Document 141: 1313/9/12 uhyōe no jō Norikane yuzurijō an. Haga reminds us (*Sōryōsei*, pp. 85–86) that arrangements of this kind with proprietors were far from being universal, however.

ing, as in the case of a ten-year refusal by a coheir to pay through his
sōryō.[139] At any rate, in much the same way that *jitō*, as tax agents, ex-
ploited peasants, *sōryō* might also seek to exploit their kin. Yet even
having said that, the question arises of whether such leverage—the
gift of estate owners—fits within the framework of the "*sōryō* system."
Bearing no relation to the Bakufu, it may be thought of as mostly an
accessory. Yet however extraneous to the *sōryōsei*, it might nonetheless
be important to *sōryō*.

Though much of this book is about the adversarial relations of kin,
we have not yet examined when these rivalries were most likely to sur-
face, who the principals tended to be, and what they were fighting
over. Where was the *sōryō* in this constellation of antipathy? The
Documents section that constitutes Part Two provides chapter and
verse on the disputes themselves. The cases are often fascinating because the clashes involve "domestic" issues. Whereas landlord-tenant
troubles may seem real enough, they are scarcely as engrossing as
family discord, which is experienced by everyone. At all events, so vo-
luminous is this record that we need to establish criteria for examining it. Let us first consider timing.

Anthropologists commonly note that the timing of family fission
(i.e., the point at which children leave the home) directly affects the
authority of parents. In the case of medieval Japan, this principle has
only limited application. Parents retained their dominance because of
the absence of dowry and because of their ability to rewrite wills. This
meant that sibling rivalry, at least in its unconcealed form, was postponed. Conditions were ripest for trouble as soon as the family head
died. Yet as we shall see, disputes might occur (or recur) at any time
thereafter.

The lineup of interests in these quarrels took different forms. Perhaps the most common pattern was for coheirs to seek protection
against their *sōryō* brother. Two cases, of 1252 and 1254, show this in
an interesting way. In the first case, an eldest son, who had not been
named successor by his father, complained to the Bakufu about the
smallness of his share. Kamakura rejected the claim and confirmed
the younger brother who was *sōryō*.[140] Two years later, however, a
younger sister of both brothers forced the *sōryō* to issue a quitclaim
renouncing his claims on her portion. The Bakufu, citing the will
from her father and the quitclaim from her brother, confirmed the

---

[139] Cited by Hirayama Kōzō, *Wayo no kenkyū*, pp. 178–79.
[140] Document 69: 1252/12/26 shōgun ke mandokoro kudashibumi.

sister in her share.[141] In effect, the *sōryō* had lost to his sister but defeated his brother.

A second pattern was when the *sōryō* was not the lone defendant. In a case of 1267, for instance, a *sōryō*, who once again was not the eldest, formed an alliance with a brother and sister in defense against the first-born. The courtroom battle hinged on accusations of forgery, with the main (though not all) issues settled in favor of the three siblings.[142] Yet a third pattern, by no means uncommon, was for the battle to bypass the *sōryō*, as for example in the case of two sisters who were fighting over property in four provinces.[143] In a final pattern, the *sōryō* was himself the plaintiff.[144] In other words, there were no constitutional restrictions based on relational status inhibiting sibling lawsuits.[145]

All of these disputes had a starting point but no terminal date; they began with the death of a donor but could continue for generations. Those harboring grievances had access to Bakufu courtrooms for their lifetimes, after which their children, who would be cousins, might continue the fight.[146] Such long-running disputes often convey the impression of great kindreds with interlocking interests, yet the original quarrels were normally among siblings—collaterals tended to be drawn in only later.

The major exception to this rule relates to the settlements of property upon siblings, nephews, and grandchildren. The first two practices were never very common,[147] but the last increasingly became

[141] Document 70: 1254/12/12 shōgun ke mandokoro kudashibumi.

[142] Document 99: 1267/10/27 Kantō gechijō. For a second example, see Document 134: 1304/4/24.

[143] E.g., *Okamoto ke monjo*, 1291/8/28 Kantō gechijō an, translated in Asakawa, *The Documents of Iriki*, p. 174.

[144] See. e.g., Document 73: 1254/3/8 Kantō gechijō. In another *sōryō*/younger brother dispute, the former accused his own widowed mother (allied with his brother) of incursions! Though the mother rejoined that her late husband had failed to leave her an inheritance, the Bakufu awarded victory to the *sōryō*; *Tashiro monjo*, 1291/6/8 Kantō gechijō, *KBSS*, 1: 250–51, doc. 186. The historical debate over whether the Bakufu regularly judged in favor of house heads is discussed in Chapter 4.

[145] Ishii Ryōsuke has summarized the Bakufu's regulations regarding intrafamily lawsuits: prohibitions were limited to suits against parents and grandparents, though the second of these proved difficult to enforce. All other suits were allowed. See Ishii Ryōsuke, *Chusei buke fudōsan soshō hō no kenkyū*, pp. 69–74.

[146] E.g., Document 75: 1288/6/2 Kantō gechijō; and Document 107: 1272/5/10 Kantō gechijō an.

[147] For examples of releases to siblings, see Document 35: 1227 Kantō gechijō (a brother); and Document 101: 1269/8/21 Fujiwara Takaakira yuzurijō (a sister). For releases to nephews, Document 78: 1257/9/14 shōgun ke mandokoro kudashibumi, and

so. At any rate, dispositions of these kinds confused the natural hierarchy between the generations and opened the way for trouble; uncles and aunts, for example, might find themselves obliged to pay *onkuji* through someone of the junior generation.[148] In fact, the backgrounds to these intergenerational disputes tended to be diverse. To cite just one example, in 1235 an entire family (parents and children) were murdered by outsiders except for a single son. The survivor and his uncle (who claimed to possess a testament) sought a judgment against the killers, but then sought judgments against one another. The documentation on both sides was weak, and the Bakufu, uncertain how to proceed, divided the assets.[149]

When grandchildren were the beneficiaries at the expense of a child, the same kind of trouble might develop. Once again the disputes were between uncles and nephews, albeit one generation forward. In 1287, for instance, an excluded daughter (hence an aunt, not an uncle) brought suit against three nephews, two of whom were the grandsons of her father. The nephews, who were judged to hold valid testaments, were correspondingly confirmed in their inheritances.[150]

As the volume of lawsuits increased, their processing was often slowed and justice could be delayed. One result was that siblings who were quarreling had reason to seek their own solutions. The Bakufu encouraged these efforts in two ways. First, it promised to endorse all private agreements, whatever their terms, by issuing a judicial edict that quoted from the accord.[151] And second, it frequently scheduled a trial in hopes of forcing "out of court" settlements.[152] At any rate, this was the context in which quitclaims and compromises (*wayo*) became adjuncts to Kamakura justice.[153]

A second result of the increase in sibling disputes was unintended. Although private accords helped ameliorate Kamakura's burden, the

Rusu monjo, 1294/10/13 Hōgen Ryōben yuzurijō, *Kaisetsu Rusu ke monjo*, doc. 7, pp. 14–15. This last case is worth summarizing: a nephew in line for an inheritance died leaving no heirs, so the nephew's own nephew was made the recipient. This second nephew also died, prompting the current bequest to that nephew's father!

[148]Citing a document of 1336, Toyoda points to an uncle who was referred to as a "junior heir" (*shoshi*) vis-à-vis his *sōryō* nephew; Toyoda, *Bushidan to sonraku*, p. 154.

[149]Document 49: 1235/8/28 Kantō gechijō.

[150]Document 118: 1287/9/1 Kantō gechijō an.

[151]See, e.g., Document 73: 1254/3/8 Kantō gechijō; and Document 120: 1294/12/2 Kantō gechijō.

[152]E.g., Document 73: 1254/3/8 Kantō gechijō; Document 111: 1277/1 Kantō gechijō; and Document 120: 1294/12/2 Kantō gechijō.

[153]For details, see Hirayama, *Wayo no kenkyū*, pp. 174–79.

intensity of the remaining cases had the opposite effect. Rokuhara, the Bakufu's branch in Kyoto and a tribunal in its own right, ceased to be a forum for intrafamily judicial cases. Only Kamakura, the court of final resort, could hope to exact compliance from the most disputatious of siblings.[154]

Because the objective was peace before all else, siblings who were frequent litigants were not normally discriminated against. Indeed, individuals might actually win a suit, then lose, then win again.[155] It follows that private vengeance was not tolerated; justice in the form of a judgment was the only acceptable outlet.[156] The point was amply made when two brothers concocted a false testament following the violent deaths of their parents. Rather than confront them directly, the final brother brought suit—and was rewarded with the entire inheritance.[157]

During the middle decades of the thirteenth century the Bakufu's primary role in government—to mediate between the classes—began to be superseded by the need to mediate among warriors. Moreover, the warriors who tended to oppose one another were more often than not close relatives: in a very real sense, the link of kinship, never very strong in Japan, was becoming the tie that could no longer bind.[158] Such a deterioration would naturally have grave consequences for the future. At the same time, how we interpret that change has a direct bearing on our view of the *sōryō* system. As we shall see in the next chapter, the *sōryō* system was moving toward either its acme or its nadir depending on the answer we give.

[154] Though the shrinking involvement of Rokuhara proved to be permanent, a third tribunal, established in Kyushu during the 1290s, did handle inheritance cases. But there were special reasons for this, relating to the anti-Mongol defense effort; see Chapter 4.

[155] See Document 106: 1271/11/19 Kantō gechijō an (especially notes 1–2).

[156] This point is forcefully argued by Ishii Ryōsuke, *Chūsei buke fudōsan*, pp. 102–3. Even if one had a legitimate claim, one had to work through regular channels.

[157] Document 134: 1304/4/24 Kantō gechijō an.

[158] Marc Bloch's conclusion that "feudal ties proper were developed when those of kinship proved inadequate" is certainly relevant to the case of Japan, as we shall see in Chapter 4. Bloch, *Feudal Society*, vol. 2, p. 443.

FAMILY AND INHERITANCE UNDER THE LATE BAKUFU

The late Kamakura age was a time of profound social and economic change in Japan, with much of the change centering on inheritance practices. Gradually, the partible principle, the norm for as far back as we can discern such things, came under attack, and a new restrictiveness began to characterize transmission strategy. When unigeniture was introduced, a tradition seemingly as old as Japanese history itself came under fire.

Behind these developments were the major upheavals of the era—the Mongol invasions and the Bakufu's efforts to deal with them, and an economic crisis that promoted dangerous fissures within society. Reinforcing these strains were unprecedented cracks in the estate system: one's place in society and level of permissible *shiki* holding no longer were perfectly congruent.[1] In short, the moorings of society were becoming loosened, and men felt threatened or challenged as never before.

Yet change was scarcely all-encompassing. For each testament that was written to exclude potential heirs, another was drafted to include them. For each vassal who suffered from indebtedness, another showed signs of prosperity. Such disparate conditions contributed to the era's volatility; a variety of situations was possible.

As in past decades, the policies of the Bakufu were a key influence on the general atmosphere. In this regard, scholars have traditionally

[1] There are many dimensions to this story, among them (1) the rise of bandit groups (*akutō*) who began to reject higher authority; (2) the division of estates (*shitaji chūbun*) between proprietors and *jitō*; (3) the rise of non-*jitō* managerial titles to a status competitive with *jitō*; and (4) the upsurge of *shiki* sales themselves. For the first, see Harrington, "Social Control and the Significance of *Akutō*"; for the second and third, Mass, "*Jitō* Land Possession in the Thirteenth Century"; the last is discussed below.

identified 1271 as marking the beginnings of significant change, citing two policy decisions. In the first, Kamakura introduced a new way to distinguish among heirs: principal heirs would be confirmed by *kudashibumi*, whereas junior heirs would be issued *gechijō*.[2] Hitherto, the *kudashibumi* had been standard for everyone,[3] though at different times the *gechijō* had come to replace it.[4] In a way that was new, therefore, Kamakura was seeking now to elevate family heads. On the other hand, the dual-format system was not used in all cases, and implementation throughout may have been selective.[5] Behind this absence of uniformity may have lain the policy's potential to sow discord.[6]

The second, more important decision of 1271 seems to have preceded the first by several months. As part of its anti-Mongol defense strategy, Kamakura decreed that vassals holding property in Kyushu would be obliged to proceed there in person.[7] Here was a plan that would inevitably strain the solidarity of families, with the greatest potential damage to *sōryō*. Though never enforced with any regularity, it did lead to large numbers of kin moving westward.[8] The two policy

[2] This distinction was first noted by Satō Shin'ichi; see "Bakufuron" and *Komonjogaku nyūmon*, pp. 127–28. Also see Toyoda, *Bushidan to sonraku*, p. 230, and Haga, *Sōryōsei*, pp. 105–6. The earliest actual examples are *Hirabayashi ke komonjo*, 1271/12/22 shōgun ke mandokoro kudashibumi, and 1271/12/22 Kantō gechijō, *KI*, 14; 337–38, docs. 10943, 10942.

[3] E.g., Documents 69–70: 1252/12/26 shōgun ke mandokoro kudashibumi (main heir), and 1254/12/12 shōgun ke mandokoro kudashibumi (secondary heir).

[4] In 1270, a *sōryō*, his two brothers, and his own son were confirmed by individual *gechijō* issued on the same day; *Irobe monjo*, 1270/12/14 Kantō gechijō (4), *Irobe shiryō*, 9, 4, 5, 14. (The testaments leading to these confirmations were also issued on the same day; Documents 102–5: 1270/8/25 shami Gyōnin yuzurijō.) Also see Document 58: 1239/8/3 Kantō gechijō, for a *gechijō* used to confirm a main heir.

[5] See, e.g., the Bakufu's issuance of individual *kudashibumi* to three grandsons—two brothers and a cousin; *Nakajō ke monjo*, 1278/5/18 shōgun ke mandokoro kudashibumi, *KI*, 17: 261–62, docs. 13047–49.

[6] This explanation is speculative; it discounts pure arbitrariness on the part of the Bakufu. At any rate, the dual-format system may be considered standard, with many exceptions. For a typical usage involving a brother and sister, see *Ōmi Nagahara monjo*, 1287/10/8 shōgun ke mandokoro kudashibumi, and 1287/10/8 Kantō gechijō, *Hokuetsu chūsei monjo*, 40–41, doc. 5–6.

[7] *Shōdai monjo*, 1271/9/13 Kantō migyōsho, *KI*, 14: 300, doc. 10873; *Nikaidō monjo*, 1271/9/13 Kantō migyōsho, *KI*, 14: 301, doc. 10874. The general application of what were individual orders here is an assumption made by all scholars.

[8] Exceptions were of two kinds—those who never moved, at least not fully, and those whose moves were delayed until after the first invasion (e.g., the Shimazu head to 1275). To put this in a different perspective, Prof. Toyama has calculated that of 59 outsiders who held *jitō shiki* in Bungo Province, not more than 29 had moved there as

decisions, the one undermining, the other strengthening the *sōryō*, seem thus to have been somehow connected. The threat to the *sōryō* of the defense plan may have been compensated for by the underpinning provided by the dual-confirmation system. At any rate, the two policy innovations were introduced in the second half of 1271.[9]

The effects of the defense strategy need to be amplified. Since the beginning of the Kamakura era, eastern vassals had received generous reward lands beyond the Kantō, although only a minority of house heads had emigrated.[10] As time passed and as the internal conditions of some families came to require it, an increasing number began to shift their bases westward even while normally retaining their eastern homelands. The removal of the Kobayakawa and Kumagai to Aki, and the Yamanouchi to Bingo, are well-known cases from mid-Kamakura times.[11] However, these decisions—whether to continue relying on deputies or to relocate—remained discretionary with vassals until 1271. The Bakufu's new defense strategy introduced an element of coercion into the process, with results that could be unpredictable. New arrivals might be thrust into close proximity to earlier immigrants who were relatives, thereby increasing tensions. Similarly, when a clan head, himself a landholder in Kyushu, moved westward and attempted to seize control, the consequences might be even more disruptive.

The best-known example of the latter problem centers on the Ōtomo, whose interests extended across several Kyushu provinces up to the level of *shugo* posts. The intrahouse rivalries within this family (which, along with the Shimazu and the Mutō, dominated affairs in Kyushu) have been much studied by scholars in Japan.[12] As these historians have made clear, conflicts among kin led to free-floating alliances as major and minor branches and individuals jockeyed for ad-

---

late as 1285; Megura Hiroshi, "Kamakura ki Kyūshū ni okeru gokenin oyobi zaichi ryōshu kenkyū," p. 9, citing Toyama Mikio, "Bungo no kuni Kamakura gokenin ni tsuite."

[9] No actual announcement seems to have been made of the dual-format policy; we only have the earliest surviving examples (from 1271/12), cited in n. 2. Perhaps the two policies were devised simultaneously, or the sequence of the two even reversed.

[10] Prof. Seno has argued that in the Yoritomo era possibly only the Mutō became naturalized to Kyushu; "Chinzei ni okeru Tōgoku gokenin," pp. 41–42. Gomi has cited the case of the Sameshima, and there are probably other examples; Gomi Yoshio, "Tōgoku bushi saisen no keiki—Satsuma no kuni no baai," p. 21.

[11] Kawai Masaharu, "Kamakura bakufu no seiritsu to saigoku no dōkō," p. 32.

[12] An excellent monograph on the Ōtomo, for example, is Fukuda Toyohiko, "Dainiji hōken kankei no keisei katei—Bungo no kuni Ōtomo shi no shujūsei o chūshin to shite."

vantage. In the most celebrated of all episodes, a member of the Shiga collateral line petitioned to serve with the Ōtomo chieftain (who was also *shugo*) as a way of distancing himself from his own branch head. To his credit, the chieftain, confronting the implications of overlapping *sōryō*, ordered service under the petitioner's immediate head.[13] As reflected in this incident, then, clan, branch, and individual interests might readily diverge, a circumstance built into a system that permitted multiple heirs and as many vassals as legatees.

As we have noted repeatedly, the Bakufu's *sōryō* system was most effective in the absence of a crisis. In Kyushu, where defense preparedness became an ongoing requirement, the separate parts of the system became antagonistic. It was one thing to expect junior heirs to pay vassal tribute through a brother; it was another to expect them to submit to that brother's military command. The result was military service disputes in which the issue became independent performance. By contrast, peacetime disputes tended to be over the size of relative tribute shares.[14] The Bakufu, once it realized that its vassal system was essentially a peacetime structure that was inadequate to meet the Mongol threat, simply went beyond it. Once having done so, however, new and even more serious problems developed.

As early as 1274 (the year of the first invasion) Kamakura authorized the recruitment of non-vassals,[15] who, in return for their duty, came later to claim status as *gokenin* in large numbers. Service affidavits, issued by *shugo*, formed the basis for such claims, which threatened to dilute the exclusiveness of vassal rank.[16] Ten years later the Bakufu adopted another policy that led to much the same result. It offered to confirm smallholders (*myōshu*) in Kyushu, persons hitherto outside (or on the fringe of) its orbit.[17]

---

[13] *Ibid.*, pp. 36–37; and Haga, *Sōryōsei*, p. 110.

[14] Gomi, "Kamakura bakufu no gokenin taisei—Kyōto ōbanyaku no tōsei o chūshin ni," p. 18.

[15] *Ōtomo monjo*, 1274/11/1 Kantō migyōsho, *KI*, 15: 332, doc. 11742; and Nitta Hideharu, "Kamakura bakufu no gokenin seido," p. 254.

[16] These documents, called *fukkanjō*, were issued by *shugo* between 1272 and 1310 and recognized peacetime guard duty as well as anti-Mongol service; Kawazoe Shōji, *Mōko shūrai kenkyū shiron*, pp. 33–35.

[17] *Shinpen tsuika*, [1284]/9/10 Hōjō Naotoki shojō, *KI*, 20: 213–14, doc. 15302. For an appeal for such a confirmation, see Document 112: 1282/3/11 Hashiguchi Ietada mōshijō. According to most scholars, the objective here was to increase Kamakura's service pool by explicitly recognizing more vassals. By so doing, however, it undermined local *sōryō* and also undermined prestigious easterners (*sōjitō*) who, frequently, had confirmed *myōshu* on their own; see, e.g., the references in *KB*, doc. 45: 1248/9/13 Kantō gechijō.

Though the status question was scarcely a new one, policies such as these brought it into sharper relief. As early as 1222, an heir had argued that the receipt of a will from a vassal was tantamount to becoming one himself.[18] Indeed, by confirming such wills, the Bakufu had implicitly agreed with that idea, leading to a condition in which the vassalage, rather than its leadership, was essentially determining the membership. However, beginning in the 1270s, the question took on greater complexity. No longer a matter of status conferred by inheritance, vassalage could now be obtained through service.[19] Beyond that it soon became an object of purchase. Though the Bakufu vigorously opposed such sales, the practice, once begun, rapidly expanded.[20]

On top of these developments were the consequences of the twin victories over the Mongols.[21] Though the rejoicing was heartfelt and countrywide, there were no reward lands to distribute, as in a civil war, and there was also the specter of a third invasion. Unable to reward the deserving, and unable to quiet the undeserving, the Bakufu was also unwilling to dismantle its defense apparatus. A military deployment of eastern vassals gradually became a resettlement, and ultimately a permanent colonization. Easterners were forbidden to return home and even forbidden to argue their suits in Kamakura.[22] This latter was a condition that paved the way for the opening of a quasi-judicial agency in Kyushu (the Chinzei *dangijo*), followed in the 1290s by a full Bakufu branch (the Chinzei *tandai*).[23] Yet nothing could disguise the fact that tiny fragments of property were all that

[18] *Isshi monjo*, 1222/12/23 dazaifu shugosho kudashibumi an, *KI*, 5: 138, doc. 3032, item 2.

[19] So intent was the Bakufu on securing vassal services that it moved to affirm the status of currently landless persons if their grandfathers (later changed to great-grandfathers) had been *gokenin*; *Shinpen tsuika*, 1287/5/25 Kantō hyōjō kotogaki, *KI*, 21: 268, doc. 16264; and *ibid.*, 1293/5/25 Kantō hyōjō kotogaki, *KI*, 23: 372, doc. 18205.

[20] Kamakura's efforts in this regard began in 1232 and continued, with increasing restrictiveness, into the future. For details, see Nitta, "Kamakura bakufu no gokenin seido," pp. 251–52.

[21] The fullest account in English remains Kyotsu Hori, "The Mongol Invasions and the Kamakura Bakufu" (Ph.D. dissertation, Columbia University, 1967).

[22] From the 1220s forward, Kyushu was technically under the jurisdiction of Rokuhara, the Bakufu's branch in Kyoto. However, virtually all Kyushu suits had been heard in Kamakura; Seno Seiichirō, "Chinzei ni okeru Rokuhara tandai no kengen."

[23] A special review board of 1284 was superseded by an expanded agency in 1286 (the *dangijo*), which in turn was replaced by the *tandai* in 1293; Seno Seiichirō, "Kamakura bakufu metsubō no rekishiteki zentei—Chinzei tandai saikyojō no bunseki"; Satō Shin'ichi, *Kamakura bakufu soshō seido no kenkyū*, p. 295; and Aida Nirō, *Mōko shūrai no kenkyū*, pp. 330–34. Unlike the case of Rokuhara, many inheritance disputes were heard by the *tandai*'s tribunals; see *KBSS*, vol. 2.

Kamakura could muster for rewards.[24] The regime's desire to maintain its military capability precluded the disbursement of *jitō* titles outside Kyushu.[25]

This, then, was the altered state of the vassalage in the post-Mongol era. A major but unknown percentage of easterners had moved westward, with probably fewer economic resources to draw upon and with unpredictable consequences for their kin. By contrast, houses without Kyushu interests were only indirectly affected by the invasions. The earlier status advantage favoring families from the Kantō was being narrowed, in a sense, to those whose *sōryō* had remained stationary. There were other continuities as well. Kamakura's courts remained active and retained all of their earlier prestige; and most probate matters continued to be discharged routinely. There were even some favored older houses that might expect to receive new *jitō* titles.[26] Yet it is equally true that more and more of the Bakufu's judicial and administrative time seemed to be taken up with internal rather than external vassal problems; the hearing of family quarrels—particularly in its Kamakura-based tribunals—began to crowd out disputes involving estate owners. Changes in the *sōryō* system would inevitably reflect this altered condition.

In general, current and prospective landholders reacted differently to the mounting social and economic pressures. If the former came to rely more on entails and other centralizing techniques, the latter, potentially threatened by these devices, began to think more of autonomy. Nevertheless, those who wrote wills tended to set the terms against which recipients had to respond; the senior generation continued to retain the initiative. But heirs who were successful then themselves became the new elders, and often accepted alternatives earlier rejected.

Adding to the disorder was the fact that inheritance strategies did not narrow suddenly to some dominant single mode. Rather, new for-

[24] See Kyotsu Hori, "The Economic and Political Effects of the Mongol Wars," pp. 184–91.

[25] No rewards outside Kyushu were ever granted to vassals; Seno Seiichirō, "Kamakura bakufu no seiritsu to Kyūshū chihō no dōkō," p. 44. Moreover, no rewards were ever granted to vassals who had not taken up residence there; Seno, "Chinzei ni okeru Tōgoku gokenin," p. 41. Finally, even the palace guard duty in Kyoto seems to have been suspended for vassals now on permanent watch in Kyushu; Gomi Yoshio, "Kamakura gokenin no banyaku kinshi ni tsuite," pp. 29–31.

[26] E.g., the receipt of a new *jitō shiki* by Kobayakawa Masakage in 1288; *Kobayakawa ke monjo*, 1288/11/21 shōgun ke mandokoro kudashibumi, *DNK, iewake 11*, 1: 18, doc. 29. The title (over Mokake Estate in Bizen Province) was bequeathed by Masakage three months later; Document 85: 1289/2/16 Kobayakawa Masakage yuzurijō.

mulae were introduced, to exist side by side, in different kin groups, with more traditional techniques. Thus, partible inheritance continued to be practiced, as the following example graphically illustrates. In 1292, the holder of a one-fifth interest in a *benzaishi shiki* bequeathed a one-twentieth portion (i.e., a one-hundredth of the whole!) to an heir.[27] In other words, the partible principle was being clung to, in many cases beyond the point of economic rationality.

Part and parcel of the survival of multiple shares for offspring was the continuation of inheritances by women. Both major types of female bequests continued—settlements in perpetuity and life tenures. In fact, even at the end of the period, wives, true daughters, and female adoptees were still receiving property, and the Bakufu was issuing approvals.[28] Even much later (though the instances were fewer) the same was essentially true.[29] But practices were changing, as we need to examine in closer detail.

Perhaps the earliest indication of a new restrictive thinking was the onset of warnings against alienation to outsiders. Strictly speaking, such admonitions were not new,[30] and the very earliest examples date back to the Yoritomo era.[31] Moreover, sales rather than inheritances had been the principal target here, since outsiders by definition were not members of the kin group. Later on, the familial distinction was sometimes blurred when outsiders-turned-adoptees became the focus. Yet the rise in admonitions remained at all times situational. Thus a father rich in progeny (like the Kōsokabe head with fifteen) might eagerly exhort an heir to select a brother over an adoptee.[32] But a fe-

---

[27] *Sappan kyūki zatsuroku,* 1292/3/14 Tomo Morokazu yuzurijō, *KI,* 23: 223, doc. 17848 (a *benzaishi shiki* was a financial officership common to Kyushu).

[28] See, e.g., *Eikōji monjo,* 1329/3/15 Yoshimi Enchū yuzurijō an, *Zōtei Kano komonjo,* doc. 209, p. 123 (to a wife); and *Kutsuna ke monjo,* 1325/7/3 ama Shinmyō yuzurijō, *Ehime ken hennen shi,* 2: 524 (to an adopted daughter). The Bakufu's confirmation of the last was dated 1327/6/20; *ibid.*

[29] In 1385, a main heir was bequeathed one-half of a donor's assets with the remainder divided among other sons and daughters; *Hiraga ke monjo,* 1385/11/15 Hiraga Sadamune yuzurijō, *DNK, iewake 14,* doc. 134, pp. 598–99. Even in 1451 daughters were receiving shares; *ibid.,* 1451/6/17 Hiraga Yorimune yuzurijō, doc. 146, pp. 605–6. See also Wakita, "Marriage and Property," pp. 90–91. Suzanne Gay makes the interesting point that wealthy peasants continued to engage in partible inheritance during Muromachi times; "The Kawashima: Warrior-Peasants of Medieval Japan," p. 112.

[30] See, e.g., the reference to such an admonition in a will of 1229; cited in *Nitta jinja monjo,* 1289/4/7 Kantō gechijō, *KBSS,* 1: 240, doc. 175.

[31] E.g., Document 7: 1191/3/1 Kumagaya Renjō yuzurijō; and Document 8: 1193/1 kannushi Kaya ason bō yuzurijō.

[32] Document 135: 1306/4/16 Nakahara Shigemichi yuzurijō.

male who was childless saw the world differently; for her, adoption was the solution, hardly the problem.[33]

Since necessity in these matters affected people in different ways, the experiences of the Kuchiki and their kin may not be unusual. One branch of the family was apparently able to ignore the new environment: in 1292, its head, a female, proceeded to disinherit her son in favor of a nephew, whom she adopted. Twelve years later the nephew bequeathed his inheritance to his own daughter, in perpetuity.[34] Here, then, were several of the older and more familiar patterns. But another branch of the family chose a different path. In 1322, the male head here eschewed his younger children in favor of a single son. As he expressed it, his assets would otherwise be dispersed, and, accordingly, his daughters in particular were to receive nothing.[35] However, the story was to have an ironic ending. Since the inheriting son was himself childless, he was obliged to bequeath to an adoptee.[36]

It is clear from these and other examples that the new forms of restrictiveness could be adopted at any time that conditions might warrant them. But whether sooner or later,[37] the new possibilities were now taking root. And from prohibitions aimed at outsiders, restrictions against kin, especially female kin, soon followed. When gender-blind legacies became the new target, women started to lose what had hitherto been a birthright.

As early as 1286, the Bakufu had decreed against female inheritances out of a desire to maintain a continuous anti-Mongol guard effort.[38] This enactment, intended only for Kyushu, seems to have been effective: we find no wills addressed to women for the remainder of the thirteenth century (though neither do we find specific invocations of that prohibition). But whatever the situation in Kyushu, women were now beginning to be excluded in other parts of the country as well.

The strategies of exclusion were diverse. Most frequent were wills to daughters containing a strict reversion clause: should the receiving

[33] Note the simple rationale put forward by such a woman—the absence of a child; Document 109: 1274/3/21 Inukai Ken yuzurijō.

[34] *Kuchiki monjo*, 1292/10/24 ama Myōgo yuzurijō, *Kuchiki monjo*, 1: 57–58, doc. 107; *ibid.*, 1304/8/5 Yokoyama Yorinobu yuzurijō, *ibid.*, 1: 59, doc. 109.

[35] *Ibid.*, 1322/11/28 Taira Munenori okibumi, *ibid.*, 1: 68–69, doc. 122.

[36] *Ibid.*, 1330/9/22 Taira Akimori yuzurijō, *ibid.*, 1: 75–76, doc. 133.

[37] The points at which donors were ready to bequeath obviously differed. Thus age and similar variables often distorted the meaning of "sooner or later."

[38] *Shinpen tsuika*, 1286/7/25 Kantō hyōjō kotogaki, *KI*, 21: 122, doc. 15946.

daughter bear no sons, her legacy was to revert to her *sōryō* brother.[39] Stipulations of this kind were different from those in the past; they marked a compromise between a life tenure and a bequest made in perpetuity, both of which (in opposite ways) were categorical. Under the new arrangement, the settlement was to be permanent only if the inheriting daughter bore sons. In other words, the exclusion of females was to be delayed by a generation.

A second pattern, increasingly common, was more direct. In releasing property to a son (not a daughter), the donor stipulated what should happen in future: in the absence of sons, settlement should be to a nephew or brother.[40] Daughters were to be excluded, or, in a variation, given only modest parcels.[41] A third pattern followed logically— the start of a process in which secondary sons, in addition to daughters, began to feel pressure. Life tenures to males, highly unusual earlier, were the natural result here.[42]

In this light, the final pattern seems almost inevitable: unitary inheritances in which junior males joined all females in being excluded. This development was mostly delayed until the 1330s, though earlier instances, such as a case of 1301, can be cited.[43] At any rate, the Yamanouchi adopted this pattern in 1330, the Ōtomo in 1333.[44] In 1335, a donor placed the issue in definitive perspective: because of the

---

[39] E.g., *Irobe monjo*, 1298/5/11 shami Anin yuzurijō, *Essa shiryō*, 2: 155; *Yasuda monjo*, 1310/6/18 Kantō gechijō, *KBSS*, 1: 331–32, doc. 258; and *Ōishidera monjo*, 1312/11/11 Fujiwara Yorimichi tō rensho yuzurijō, *Miyagi kenshi, 30, shiryōshū*, 1: 188–89, doc. 119. This last release enumerated four conditions: (1) upon the widow's death her entire share was to go to the *sōryō*; (2) if either of the two daughters had no sons, their shares would go to the *sōryō*; (3) if there was anything left over (i.e., left intestate?), it would go to the *sōryō*; and (4) if any of the junior heirs reneged on *onkuji* payments, their shares would revert to the *sōryō*.

[40] E.g., *Kondō monjo*, 1297/10/22 Ōe Sōshin tō rensho yuzurijō, *Kyūshū shōen shiryō sōsho*, 14: 35–43, doc. 14 (nephew); *Ichikawa monjo*, 1321/10/24 Ichikawa Morifusa yuzurijō, *Shinano shiryō*, 5: 20–22 (nephew or brother).

[41] E.g., *Rusu monjo*, 1300/5/21 Rusu Iemasa yuzurijō, *Kaisetsu chūsei Rusu ke monjo*, doc. 11, pp. 25–26. In this instance the release to a grandson stipulated as follows: should you have no sons, only daughters, settle upon them a total of 2 service households and 5 *chō* of paddy; the remainder should go to your nephews. (This bequest, in northern Japan, would have been considered modest.)

[42] See, e.g., the life tenure bequests for three sons, an adopted son, and a widow in Document 144: 1318/4/3 shami Ennin yuzurijō. Also see *Shinpen Hitachi kokushi*, entry for 1330/2/2: "Secondary shares (*shoshi haibun no chi*) shall all be returned to the *sōryō* after a generation" (cited by Toyoda, *Bushidan to sonraku*, p. 240).

[43] Document 132: 1301/4/22 saki no ōnegi Nakatomi Tomochika yuzurijō. The wording of this testament is very explicit.

[44] Document 150: 1330/3/18 Yamanouchi Chōkai yuzurijō; *Ōtomo monjo*, 1333/3/13 Ōtomo Sadamune yuzurijō, *Hennen Ōtomo shiryō*, 2: 134, doc. 188. In the words of the

fragmentation of his family's holdings, there were to be no transmissions except to a single son.[45]

Yet counterexamples continued, e.g., a father's *jitō* transfer to a daughter "since I have no sons,"[46] and a husband's bequest to his wife, under the following stipulation: the wife would be free to release her widow's share to daughters, but only if the respective sons-in-law should show themselves to be loyal.[47] It is worth noting that in both of these cases the donors had grasped the new situation. Requiring no justification earlier, bequests to women now needed to be explained.[48]

Contributing to the new conditional releases to women was a heightened concern over their spouses, as just noted. The problem was underscored when, in a celebrated case, a daughter's release to her husband was deemed non-rescindable since the spouse in question issued from a different kindred.[49] In other words, just as sale transactions could not be invalidated by a seller who had changed his mind, so a wife stood to lose her inheritance by releasing it to an "unrelated" husband. The permanency of such transfers stood in sharp contrast to a donor's continuing ability to overturn any releases made to children.[50] Just at the point, then, that fathers were becoming more restrictive anyway, a decision was rendered that threatened seepage through their daughters' husbands. An emphasis on in-marriage was one result.[51] A second result was to cut back directly on female inheritances.

---

latter, "All landholdings and offices are to be transmitted to my son Chiyomatsumaru, who is made my successor. All his siblings are to be given stipends under [his] authority."

[45] *Amano monjo*, 1335/3/17 Amano Taneari yuzurijō, *Zōtei Kano komonjo*, doc. 247, p. 138.

[46] *Hagi han batsuetsu roku*, 1281/7/10 Naitō Tamehisa yuzurijō an, *KI*, 19: 211–12, doc. 14361.

[47] *Saitō monjo*, 1292/3/6 nakatsukasa no jō Korehide yuzurijō, *Miyagi kenshi, 30, shiryōshū*, 1: 167–68, doc. 65.

[48] Nevertheless, as noted earlier, there were many transmissions to women that were not being explained, e.g., those cited in n. 28.

[49] Document 95: 1264/10/10 Kantō gechijō.

[50] According to the *Satamirensho*, a legal primer prepared under Bakufu auspices in 1319: "Regarding gifts to descendants, the more recent of two conflicting documents stands; but as regards gifts to relatives or other 'strangers,' the earlier of the two documents should be relied on." Translated by Carl Steenstrup, "Sata Mirensho: A Fourteenth Century Law Primer," p. 432. The distinction between relatives and descendants is noteworthy, but its applicability earlier was probably inconsistent. To the extent that fraternal bequests were considered non-rescindable, donors, normally wary anyway, would have been even more reluctant to grant them.

[51] Toyoda, *Bushidan to sonraku*, p. 237. Fathers, in short, may have viewed family assets administered by blood-related sons-in-law as being more easily retrievable.

The question arises of whether mothers contributed to the tide of restrictiveness now beginning to engulf women. In fact, mothers who had property to dispose of continued to bequeath to sons and/or daughters on the basis of mostly discretionary criteria. Gender was much less a factor for them than it was for their brothers. Thus, mothers transmitted to daughters, natural or adopted, in ratios that seem mostly unchanged. Equally interesting, the Bakufu supported them in these decisions, and even allowed sisters to assume pride of place over brothers, if that is the way donors had willed it. To illustrate the point, in 1295 the Bakufu probated a will in which a granddaughter had been designated the principal heir, with only tiny portions allotted to her brothers.[52] This arrangement represented an obvious reversal of the normal division of authority between the genders. But it also shows that, whereas women may have had much to fear from their brothers (and, increasingly, from their fathers), they had little to fear from Kamakura, save perhaps in Kyushu.[53] Within the family, if much less so within the Bakufu, gender was becoming a potentially explosive issue.

With more men than women receiving free inheritances, gender confrontations now began heating up. Disputes took several forms, chief among them female attempts to override restrictive entails.[54] When the Bakufu rejected such claims, it was not revealing a bias against women as much as it was affirming a long-held principle: to possess a life tenure was to be considered ineligible to sell or bequeath.[55] Though persons of both sexes might have been affected by

[52] In other words, the main heir was the granddaughter, with the grandsons strictly secondary; *Rusu monjo*, 1295/7/23 Kantō gechijō, *Kaisetsu chūsei Rusu ke monjo*, p. 18, doc. 9.

[53] Prof. Hirayama has argued that the Bakufu moved to an outright policy of denying females. But even he admits that it defended lawful female inheritances—and this is precisely the point. See Hirayama, *Wayo no kenkyū*, p. 201.

[54] In 1290, a widow holding a life tenure from her husband was denied the right to issue a will even though the father's intended heir, a son, had already died; Document 119: 1290/5/12 Kantō gechijō. In 1318, a life tenure holder (in this case a male) was made the object of a suit for selling his land; *Hōzawa monjo*, 1318/4/28 Kantō gechijō, *KBSS*, 1: 347–48, doc. 274.

[55] Kamakura stated the point succinctly in a case of 1293: "The current holder is a lifetime lord (*ichigo ryōshu*); there can thus be no testament." *Kashima ōnegi ke monjo*, c. 1293 monchū no ki, *KI*, 24: 60–64, doc. 18370. Toyoda has argued that secondary heirs required the permission of *sōryō* when they wished to sell; *Bushidan to sonraku*, pp. 180–81. But he fails to make the crucial point that this would likely have been the case only if the affected lands had been promised to the *sōryō*, i.e., if they were currently being held as life tenures.

such decisions, women of course were the more frequent losers. Yet the blame for these defeats lay clearly with their fathers, who had set the original conditions of their inheritances.

A second category of dispute also involved wills—those prepared at different times and those alleged to be forgeries. Though charges of this kind might be brought by sisters or brothers, sisters here tended to have more at stake. Thus in one instance, a daughter, bypassed by her father, leveled an accusation of forgery; in another, a daughter, older than her adopted brother, claimed blood descent and the possession of a lawful will. Both daughters lost their cases, however—the first because the charge was proved false, the second because the adopted son had a later-sealed will.[56] But once again the responsibility lay with the two fathers. Indeed, in the second episode, the adopted son was simultaneously battling his stepmother—a side issue that ended in a compromise.[57]

A third category of dispute took in the most ground of all—charges by women of property violations by men. These were dealt with in the standard fashion, with women the victors or losers depending on the strength of their claims.[58] A subgroup here involved thefts of the wills themselves, with sisters the fairly frequent victims. When this happened, brothers were attempting, in a sense, to shed their sisters by destroying all proof of female inheritances.[59] And in one remarkable case, involving property left intestate, a brother insisted that in fact he had no sister, a claim that led to a decision to conduct an investigation.[60] At any rate, the problems encountered by females stemmed initially from the fathers who would deny them, and/or later from the brothers who sought to complete the process. Yet, as always, there were exceptions—fathers who took pains to protect their daughters,

---

[56] Document 118: 1287/9/1 Kantō gechijō an (the daughter in this case was battling against nephews—the sons of her brothers); and *Nogami monjo*, 1270/4/26 Kantō gechijō, *Hennen Ōtomo shiryō*, 1: 439–40, doc. 527. To help neutralize the increase of suits concerning wills, donors frequently added a disclaimer that the current will was the only one being recorded; all others were in fact forgeries. See, e.g., *Sagara ke monjo*, 1287/5/2 Sagara Geiren yuzurijō, *KI*, 21: 261–62, doc. 16252.

[57] *Nogami monjo*, 1270/5/6 Kantō migyōsho, *Hennen Ōtomo shiryō*, 1: 440, doc. 528. It is not clear whether the two women involved here were mother and daughter, though even if they were, the fact of their different surnames (Kiyohara no uji and Taira no uji) was entirely natural. Women's names harked back to their families of descent.

[58] A private agreement (*wayo*) was another possibility, e.g., Document 120: 1294/12/2 Kantō gechijō.

[59] In 1310, a *sōryō* brother was convicted on such a charge; *Yasuda monjo*, 1310/6/18 Kantō gechijō, *KBSS*, 1: 331–32, doc. 258.

[60] *Nejime monjo*, 1279/3/26 Kantō migyōsho, *Nejime monjo*, 1: 68, doc. 84.

and brothers who were concerned and fraternal.[61] For that matter, disputes could erupt between sisters, just as they continued to occur between brothers.

The role of the Bakufu in nurturing these new restrictions has always generated controversy among scholars.[62] As I have argued, the issues for Kamakura were not inherently gender-based; they concerned the ability of vassals to discharge services. Except for the anti-Mongol defense effort, these services mostly involved peacetime tribute. Moreover, by the 1280s, the Bakufu had placed economic goals above all others. Thus, among other things, it legislated a tightening of tribute collection, adopted measures aimed at ending vassal indebtedness, and moved to protect weaker vassals being threatened by proprietary dismissals.[63] Yet at the same time, the Bakufu's leading family, the Hōjō, was moving vigorously to neutralize certain older families. As part of this effort, new rank-and-file dues payers might have been viewed as a financial wedge against traditional rivals. The question that arises, then, is how these various activities affected the *sōryō* system. In the post-Mongol era, what was the condition of the house head in his relationships with kin and Kamakura?

Not surprisingly, given the contradictory nature of much of the evidence, scholars have interpreted the data in different ways. Satō Shin'ichi, for example, has argued that the Hōjō, in their drive toward autocracy, were responsive to junior heirs and others who were seeking greater independence by becoming vassals. Thus, Kamakura weakened its support of *sōryō* by moving to end the practice in which house heads and their siblings were confirmed by separate document types. In Satō's most important observation, he noted that all wills after 1303 were validated by a terse approval (*gedai ando*) appearing in the empty space at the end of testaments. Thus, they were not even on separate papers; Kamakura's support of the *sōryō* was reduced to the most bureaucratic of procedures.[64] Satō went on to argue that a

---

[61] For example, a father in 1294 warned his son, under threat of partial confiscation, not to intrude upon the share of his sister; *Nakajō ke monjo*, 1294/6/12 Wada Shigetsure yuzurijō, *Okuyama-no-shō shiryōshū*, pp. 103–4, doc. 25.

[62] See, e.g., n. 53 above.

[63] For the *onkuji* legislation, Toyoda, *Bushidan to sonraku*, pp. 232–33; for the laws up to and including the famous debt cancellation order of 1297, Nitta, "Kamakura bakufu no gokenin seido," pp. 251–52; and for the Bakufu's effort to defend vassals against estate owners' arbitrariness, n. 86 below.

[64] Satō, *Komonjogaku nyūmon*, pp. 127–28, and other studies by him. All scholars writing on the subject credit Satō's discovery (though not necessarily his interpretation) of the change that began in 1303. The sources bear him out. In early 1303 the dual-

judgment of 1312 (by the Chinzei *tandai*) reinforced the Bakufu's policy of liberating junior heirs.[65] In essence, the *sōryō* system, in decline anyway, was no longer Kamakura's favored vehicle for coordinating the vassalage.

Seno Seiichirō has reached a different conclusion by looking at the Bakufu's verdicts in lawsuits pitting *sōryō* against *shoshi*. He argues that in seventeen such cases handled by the Chinzei *tandai*, fifteen judgments favored the *sōryō*, with the remaining two settled by compromise (*wayo*). In his view, then, the Bakufu's support of junior heirs was limited to performance of the anti-Mongol defense service; once the crisis had ended, there was a return to reliance on the *sōryō*.[66]

The views of Satō and Seno are symptomatic of much of the debate, which turns, as suggested above, on different criteria. Whereas Seno's argument rests exclusively on data from Kyushu, Satō's conclusion derives largely from a single observation—the status-free confirmations after 1303.[67] Because this latter is a legalist position that ignores the major trends of the era, it might be useful to summarize and compare those trends here.

Lending weight to the progress of *sōryō* was, above all, the rise of exclusionist inheritance practices, up to and including unigeniture. By the end of the period, there were thus *sōryō* in possession of the resources needed to control their kin. Sustenance shares to siblings might replace the partible bequests from parents, which were now becoming scarcer. In short, the potential for constructing lordships based on kin would finally have become a reality.[68]

Yet the negative evidence seems much the more persuasive here. For a majority of *sōryō*, their inventory of problems was simply too for-

---

format policy was still in effect, but by late in the year we find the first *gedai ando*; see *Kuchiki monjo*, 1303/8/5 Yokoyama Yorinobu yuzurijō, *KI*, 29: 5, doc. 21935, bearing a *gedai ando* dated 1303/11/17.

[65] Many other scholars have also cited the 1312 decision, e.g., Gomi, "Chūsei shakai to gokenin—sōryōsei to gokeninsei," p. 50; and Haga, *Sōryōsei*, p. 111.

[66] Seno, "Kamakura bakufu metsubō no rekishiteki zentei," pp. 101–2.

[67] There are, of course, countless examples of these confirmations. For a sampling, see Document 135: 1306/4/16 Nakahara Shigemichi yuzurijō (*gedai ando* dated 1314/12/20); Document 140: 1312/4/14 Naganuma Munehide yuzurijō an (*gedai ando* dated 1312/4/22); and Document 141: 1313/9/12 uhyōe no jō Norikane yuzurijō an (*gedai ando* dated 1325/5/4). The practice was used even for wills prepared much earlier but not submitted for probate until after 1303, e.g., Document 108: 1273/10/5 sō Kakujitsu yuzurijō an (*gedai ando* dated 1318/4/29).

[68] In 1313 a father vested in his son the power to allocate such small shares (though with some qualifications); Document 141: 1313/9/12 uhyōe no jō Norikane yuzurijō an.

midable. Not only was there an unprecedented dispersal of house members geographically, but there was an increase of persons with legitimate grounds for calling themselves house heads. The notion of chieftains of large kin groups was thus the ultimate casualty: the system declined when there were too few kin willing to submit themselves to extended unions based on blood. With a minority of heads advancing but the majority probably declining, the *sōryō* system, predicated on a balance between the trunk and its limbs, increasingly became an anachronism.[69]

The emergence of a new concept, that of *sōryō shiki*, captures this duality neatly. In the early fourteenth century fathers began releasing *sōryō shiki* in two contexts.[70] In the first, donors were seeking to strengthen their successors' authority, especially in the face of some threat. The *sōryō* was the chieftain and now had the title to prove it. But in the second, a weakened connotation was clear. Here a *sōryō shiki* meant little more than a package of land rights, in other words, the "share of the *sōryō*." Partible inheritance was thereby sustained, expressed by the vocabulary of *shiki*.[71] Once again, therefore, *sōryō* might be on an upward or downward trajectory.[72]

The condition of house heads was thus a function of the particular mix of same-generation relatives acted upon by the degree of restrictiveness of senior-generation inheritance strategies. But even as vassal families were experiencing drastic changes in their power compositions, the inheritance system as a whole was developing a wider currency. Indeed, from the level of *myōshu* upward, persons obtained, administered, and transmitted property in ways that were now drawing closer. One aspect of this was that *shiki* were ceasing to mark the boundaries of status and were becoming mere tokens of wealth; they were commodities to be exchanged in the marketplace.[73] A second as-

[69] As described by Prof. Haga, the kindred-based *sōryōsei* became obsolete as more and more branch lines broke off; *Sōryōsei*, pp. 103–4.

[70] The earliest usage of this term may be in a document of 1291 (dated "Bun-ō 4" [1263], corrected by Takeuchi to "Shō-ō 4" [1291]); *Nabeshima ke monjo*, 1291?/5/28 Taira bō kakikudashi an, *KI*, 23: 110, doc. 17623.

[71] See, e.g., Document 143: 1316/7/7 Kiyohara Moroyuki yuzurijō.

[72] Seno, Haga, and other scholars have provided illustrations of strong and weak unions under *sōryō*. Thus, for example, the Matsuura exhibited strong *shoshi* independence early in the period, but united in search of rewards later; then they divided again. Seno, "Chinzei ni okeru tō—Matsuura tō no baai," pp. 70–71. Haga (*Sōryōsei*, pp. 114–16) provides a similar look at the Sagara house.

[73] Thus they were now being sold; *Tōdaiji monjo*, 1276/11 gesu shiki baiken, *KI*, 16: 363, doc. 12587; and *ibid.*, 1284/int.4/13 gesu shiki baiken, *KI*, 20: 170, doc. 15176 (the 1276 buyer of the *gesu* title resold it eight years later).

pect centered specifically on inheritance patterns. When priests and aristocrats bequeathed, the language of their wills expressed concepts increasingly shared at all levels.

Transmissions by priests provide an illustration of this national experience. Clerical wills show only one minor difference from warrior testaments: for priests who did not father children, disciples were the natural substitute. Thus, priests demanded loyalty and obedience instead of requiring filiality. Moreover, since partible inheritance was the norm for clerics, priests manipulated their protégés, just as warrior parents did with children. Accordingly, clerics wrote and rewrote wills, practiced disinheritance, and imposed entails, exactly as we have seen with fighting men. An abbot of Chūsonji engaged in all three practices in 1280.[74] At the same time, priests admonished their disciples not to make bequests to outsiders; legacies were to stay within the "same line of scholar priests."[75]

In circumstances such as these, conflict became a common phenomenon, both clashes among priests and clashes between priests and lay relatives. For example, in one early episode, a cleric conveyed his title to his sister who later transmitted it to her son; a lawsuit by an original disciple soon followed.[76] In other cases, priests released property to persons who were true offspring and to a variety of other relatives as well.[77] It was the breadth of this priestly inheritance pool that helped fuel the potential for trouble.

How then were such disputes resolved? Just as Kamakura judged the suits of its vassals, so Kyoto heard the cases of its clients. Moreover, the techniques and guidelines of the one became essentially the techniques and guidelines of the other. The only major differences were that the suits heard in Kyoto were more diverse than those handled by Kamakura; and that aristocratic justice remained two-tiered, with proprietary and imperial levels.[78] The cases themselves ranged across the entire hierarchy, from proprietors' and patrons'

[74] *Chūsonji monjo*, 1280/5/25 Chūsonji kyōzō bettō yuzurijō, *Ōshū Hiraizumi monjo*, p. 20, doc. 48.

[75] E.g., *Daigoji monjo*, 1289/3/15 Kenyū yuzurijō an, *KI*, 22: 212, doc. 16928.

[76] Document 25: 1222/6 Hōrenga-in mandokoro kudashibumi.

[77] For land conveyed to an eldest daughter, *Kasuga jinja monjo*, 1288/2/11 sō Ryūjitsu shobunjō, *KI*, 22: 6, doc. 16511. For an administrative position within Chūsonji transmitted to the holder's uncle, *Chūsonji monjo*, 1302/4/5 sō Chōken yuzurijō, *Ōshū Hiraizumi monjo*, pp. 23–24, doc. 45.

[78] For a description of the mid- and late-period imperial judicial agencies (the *in-no-hyōjōshū*, *kirokujo*, and *fudono*), see Kiley, "The Imperial Court as a Legal Authority in the Kamakura Age."

titles at the top, to management-level posts, to strictly local offices.[79] But the process of reaching verdicts displayed familiar patterns. The list includes pretrial exchanges of charges and refutations,[80] face-to-face encounters by litigants in courtrooms,[81] tribunal reports that paraphrased testimony,[82] and later wills credited over earlier ones.[83] Even the Court's most prestigious decrees, the edicts of emperors and retired emperors (*rinji* and *inzen*), now came into regular usage as vehicles of probate, emulating the confirmations of shoguns.[84]

A discordant note might still be struck by estate proprietors. It was one thing for Kamakura to assume that *jitō* appointed to lands not owned by itself would be hereditary, but quite another for the estate holders themselves to do so. The latter continued to oppose the presence of *jitō* and continued to seek leverage over other managers. Confirmations were thus frequently conditional, a situation not found when the Bakufu was the probating authority. In the hands of priests and aristocrats, then, the future of a local tenure might be linked directly to performance of service.[85] At any rate, it was this absence of security, as it affected *gokenin*, that caused the Bakufu periodically to intervene. In the early 1290s, it admonished proprietors not to disrupt the tenures of law-abiding vassals.[86]

[79] E.g., *Tōji monjo*, 1290/3/30 Go-Fukakusa inzen an, *KI*, 22: 371, doc. 17298 (*ryōke shiki*); *Kanchūki ura monjo*, undated Shinkei mōshijō, *KI*, 23: 357–58, doc. 18157 (*honke* and *azukari dokoro shiki*); *Takamure monjo*, 1293/12/23 kanpaku ke migyōsho, *KI*, 24: 90, doc. 18432 (*doki-chō* [chief potter's] *shiki*).

[80] E.g., the reference to two such stages (*nimon-nitō*) in *Kuzukawa Myōōin monjo*, [1295]/int.2/2 Fushimi tennō rinji an, *KI*, 24: 232, doc. 18752.

[81] E.g., the call for such a *taiketsu* before the *kirokujo* agency; *ibid.*, 1294/12/2 Fushimi tennō rinji an, *KI*, 24: 208–9, doc. 18703. To expedite such *taiketsu*, the *kirokujo* issued summonses, on the model of Kamakura; e.g., *Kanchūki ura monjo*, 1293/8/4 kirokujo meshibumi, *KI*, 24: 46, doc. 18338.

[82] *Mibu ke monjo*, 1292/7/3 kirokujo chūshinjō an, *KI*, 23: 263–64, doc. 17962.

[83] *Ibid.*, 1295/4/22 kirokujo chūshinjō, *KI*, 24: 267–68, doc. 18813. For a local court's application of the same principle, see Document 123: 1298/2 Ajisaka no shō kagura mandokoro shiki buninjō.

[84] E.g., *Daigoji monjo*, 1293/1/22 Fushimi tennō rinji, *KI*, 23: 321, doc. 18096; and *Kanchūki ura monjo*, 1290/6/27 Go-Fukakusa inzen an, *KI*, 23: 7, doc. 17373.

[85] E.g., *Hayamura monjo*, 1289/2/29 Haya no shō ryōke gechijō an, *KI*, 22: 197, doc. 16904. In this instance, disloyalty to the proprietor or his agent (the *azukari dokoro*) would lead to revocation of the *shiki*. In another example, disloyalty by the appointee's children would be suitable grounds for dismissal; *Tōji monjo*, 1291/5 Hiranodono no shō gesu shiki buninjō, *KI*, 23: 108–9, doc. 17618.

[86] *Shimazu ke monjo*, 1292/8/7 Kantō migyōsho an, *KI*, 23: 268, doc. 17976. On the other hand, *gokenin* were not to disregard proprietors' administrative orders by invoking vassal status; see the reference to such activity in *Kitano jinja monjo*, 1280/4/7 Rokuhara gechijō an, *KBSS*, 2: 34–36, doc. 19.

When it came to their own inheritances, priests and aristocrats, not surprisingly, sought problem-free transfers. Yet even at the highest levels, this hope might be disappointed, with inheritance disputes reaching inside the imperial family itself. The alternating succession scheme between the Daikakuji and Jimyōin branches of the imperial house not only divided it into rival factions, but caused a ripple effect through much of the aristocracy.[87] Clearly, competition among kin was scarcely an affliction known only to warriors.

During the post-Mongol era, commendation of land, an older form of property disposition, once again came into vogue. Only now it was not for the purpose of creating *shōen* as a means of blocking the intrusions of governors.[88] In a world beset with economic difficulties, land sales and loans based on land had soared.[89] When higher authority sought to limit such transactions, commendation became a new outlet. There were several potential benefits here. By packaging a transfer as a commendation, a vassal (or anyone) might disguise an exchange that was in fact a land sale.[90] Conversely, one might strengthen (rather than alienate) a tenure by promising it as a later endowment.[91] This second practice had the effect of expanding, in a sense, the inheritance pool. Unlike the situation in Europe, where the Church regularly received property that had been willed, in Japan property could only be commended. Thus post-obit transfers broke free of the kin group, and, for vassal holdings, broke free in part of the Bakufu also.

[87] For a detailed treatment of this subject, see Goble, "Go-Daigo and the Kemmu Restoration," chap. 1.

[88] This was the rationale for the explosion of commendations in the twelfth century; *WG*, pp. 46–48, and Chapter 1 above.

[89] For a major sequence of sale deeds and related records, see Documents 124–31. Loan tickets survive in large numbers, e.g., *Kanazawa bunko shozō monjo*, 1294/8/6 Matajirō zeni shakuken, *KI*, 24: 176, doc. 18618. Under the terms of this loan of 1 *kanmon* cash, 10 percent of the principal plus 6 percent interest were to be repaid monthly. Larger loans were also possible, e.g., one for 70 *kanmon* cash in which collateral—landed property plus the borrower's residence in Kyoto and other possessions—was required; referred to in *Kanchūki ura monjo*, 1292/5/3 bō mōshijō, *KI*, 23: 228, doc. 17864.

[90] I.e., two documents would have been prepared—a sale deed and a commendation deed. The latter would be deposited with a religious institution and brought out in the event of a sale invalidation order (*tokusei*); Satō, *Komonjogaku nyūmon*, pp. 226–27.

[91] I.e., the commendation would take full effect only upon the death of the donor. For the retention of rights earmarked later for a temple, see, e.g., *Katsuodera monjo*, 1280/11/8 ama Myōshin kishinjō, *Katsuodera monjo*, pp. 295–96, doc. 326. In a variation, a commender stipulated that a person being named was to hold the area's administrative post for the duration of the person's lifetime. In effect, the commendation was deferred (at least potentially) beyond the donor's *own* lifetime; *Chōmyōji monjo*, 1290/7/29 Enkei ate-okonaijō, *KI*, 23: 16, doc. 17397.

Since commendations could be framed as filial good works,[92] they were immunized from the prohibitions that followed sales.

Taking refuge in the law and its loopholes, however, marked a strategy that could potentially cut two ways. In a reversal from earlier times, when the terms more than the terminology were what counted, vocabulary might now thwart intent: to fail to use the accepted language of a transaction was to risk having that transaction invalidated.[93] And thus the interpretations of higher authority still mattered. In the case of the vassalage, since the majority was willing to abide by this condition, no innovative minority could do otherwise. Vassal wills and vassal disputes continued to be submitted to Kamakura, which remained the principal source of legitimacy between the generations.

In such an environment, the destruction of Kamakura led not to some rush to break free from dependence but rather to a search for new patrons. As in previous crises (the 1180s and 1221), political alignments in 1333 were quite volatile. On this point, the Bakufu's defeat has been explained by some scholars in terms of the division between *sōryō* and *shoshi*. In this reading, *sōryō*, who had traditionally been favored by the Bakufu, now repaid their debt by remaining mostly loyal. Kamakura was destroyed because the essence of *sōryō* power had dissipated, a product of the autonomy of rival *shoshi*.[94]

More recent scholarship has tended to discount this view, on the grounds that *sōryō* and *shoshi* did not line up, *en bloc*, to fight one another. Indeed, according to Andrew Goble "there appear to be no instances when different members of a family fought on opposite sides because a family rival fought on the other."[95] Goble, it should be noted, was referring to strictly Kantō-based houses, where timing and proximity favored joint action. Farther afield, and in cases where branches of families had established separate identities, individual responses must have been the norm. In short, the crisis of a rapidly changing situation came to be acted upon by a warrior class more disparate in every way than ever before. In the spring of 1333, Japan's Imperial Restoration was proclaimed, and the country was engulfed in civil war.

[92] See, e.g., a commendation in memory of the donor's parents; *Kan'onji monjo*, 1280/12 Enchi kishinjō, *KI*, 19: 140, doc. 14227.

[93] In particular, testamentary look-alikes, e.g., *haibunjō*—blueprints for asset distribution—were not considered an acceptable substitute; Haga, *Sōryōsei*, p. 77. Thus, for instance, a mother was obliged to issue a *yuzurijō* to make effective her late husband's *haibunjō*; Document 113: 1282/7/16 shōgun ke mandokoro kudashibumi an.

[94] Toyoda, *Bushidan to sonraku*, pp. 146–47, and elsewhere in his writings.

[95] Goble, "Go-Daigo and the Kemmu Restoration," p. 195.

The sudden appearance of a new, unified polity under the Emperor Go-Daigo posed a serious threat to all warriors. Suppressing or exaggerating their earlier leanings, they began flooding the Court now with petitions. As we have come to understand it, the regime of Go-Daigo responded to these claims with vigor and insight.[96] Nevertheless, conditions remained highly fluid and inheritances proved especially vulnerable. Political loyalty, only rarely an issue in the relatively crisis-free Kamakura age, now became very much a factor.

In 1336, a reconstituted Bakufu was established under the Ashikaga, who had spearheaded the attack against the Hōjō and made possible the Restoration of Go-Daigo. Takauji, its head, fell heir to the confusion of the times, which required him to make exacting demands on his followers' loyalty. As part of this effort, probate matters were now made objects of a much closer scrutiny. The marginal confirmations, symbolic of the earlier Bakufu's bureaucratized procedures, were dropped in favor of individual edicts bearing a personal seal. Tadayoshi, the brother of the Shogun Takauji, affixed his name to the new government's confirmations.

A single example, with pre-regime origins, will illustrate how this might work. In the final month of 1332, a *jitō* of Mino Province issued a will on behalf of a son still a minor.[97] The collapse of Kamakura followed quickly, and it was not until 1345 that an edict of confirmation was granted, "in accordance with the testament of the late father."[98] Continuity was thus preserved, though in countless other cases it was not.

In fact, new considerations, chief among them military, were now influencing the choice of heirs. If administrative talent (*kiryō*) was highly prized earlier, the new conditions of warfare demanded other skills. In 1345, for instance, a father cited military loyalty and filial piety as the twin bases for his selection.[99] Nor was this thinking misplaced. To fail to be prepared for war was to risk losing favor with the Ashikaga.[100] At the same time, since the requirements of the age favored consolidation, partible holdouts, it appears, became fewer. Prominent houses like the Shiga, a major collateral of the Ōtomo, now adopted unigeniture.[101]

---

[96] *Ibid.*, chaps. 4–6.

[97] Document 145: 1332/12/14 Fujiwara Shigechika yuzurijō.

[98] Document 146: 1345/5/27 Ashikaga Tadayoshi sodehan kudashibumi.

[99] *Kōsokabe kaden shōmon*, 1345/9/26 shami Shōkai yuzurijō, *Kōsokabe shiryō*, p. 157.

[100] Many scholars have noted that the Ashikaga regime grasped the power to grant or confiscate *sōryō* titles; see, e.g., Kawai, "Kamakura bushidan no kōzō," p. 8.

[101] Toyoda, *Bushidan to sonraku*, p. 242.

Yet the process, as we know, was still not uniform. Where partible inheritance was continued, the affected house heads might find themselves severely handicapped. In the face of autonomy on the part of collaterals, they might be able to arrange no more than temporary alliances. The Nitta house, under the illustrious Yoshisada, provides an example. By the 1330s, Yoshisada effectively controlled only one of four Nitta branches that had split off earlier. Among these branches, the Satomi were now considered entirely separate, and the Yamana went into service with the Ashikaga. Even the Ōshima, technically subservient to Yoshisada, aligned with the Ashikaga and later became *shugo* by their favor. The authority of Yoshisada as *sōryō*, then, was limited to his own branch, and further limited by defections from within.[102]

In fact, to emphasize a *sōryō*'s military authority is to suggest that the term's meaning had now changed. Having nothing to do with the land rights of kin, it had been divorced in effect from inheritance practices. Indeed, it was now separable from the head's own holdings: *sōryō shiki* were now transmittable as command rights that were listed apart from the bequeathing person's assets.[103] This change had profound implications for the future. With increasing frequency, the bonding of kin through the instrument of family holdings was giving way to ties cemented by military service. In the past, same-generation kin were almost equal: as recipients of *jitō* rights from their parents, they would be recognized as vassals by the Bakufu. Personal fealty to the *sōryō* had only rarely been a necessity or a requirement. By the 1340s, however, conditions were becoming vastly different. Either a command structure under a *sōryō* would be fostered, or kin groups would continue to fragment. Either the *sōryō* would become a true lord, or his family would lapse into inconsequence. The *sōryō* system, a product of partible inheritance in an era of relative stability, now itself lapsed into irrelevance.

[102] Haga, *Sōryōsei*, pp. 119–20.
[103] Kawai, "Kamakura bushidan no kōzō," p. 8.

CHAPTER 5

PERSPECTIVES

During the Kamakura era warrior lordship operated on two major levels, that of the Bakufu and that of the *sōryō*. In both instances the powers inherent in the lordship were weak. A vassal who received a *jitō* title could expect that post to be hereditary, and also expect to be called to service only infrequently. Moreover, the Bakufu confirmed the transfers between the generations, without the exaction of any "relief,"[1] and indeed without any substantive interference. Vassals were free to revoke and rewrite wills, to add and subtract heirs by adoption and disinheritance, and to choose the next head (male or female, youngest or eldest) who would become, by the parent's decision, the next *sōryō*—the person through whom the Bakufu would collect its dues. Only during the trauma of the Mongol invasion crisis did Kamakura demand more from its men than they in turn had long received. And that crisis helped to create the conditions for the *sōryō* system's decline.

If the vassalage had the better of the exchange with Kamakura, its own internal exchanges partly negated that advantage. Partible inheritance, the practice in Japan from its historical beginnings, was the instrument of most of that weakness. As long as donors gave generously to multiple heirs, a principal heir would have trouble in controlling his brothers and sisters. When he tried they opposed him; and in their opposition they could rely on the recorded wishes of a late parent, which the Bakufu almost invariably upheld. Moreover, since holdings were frequently scattered, geography was the junior heir's ally.

[1] In medieval Europe, a "relief" was a payment to the lord on the occasion of a vassal's inheritance.

Though a *sōryō* had responsibility for collecting *onkuji*, he enjoyed no other authority affecting his siblings' holdings. In particular, he had no involvement in approving, much less validating, their wills, or, conversely, in prohibiting their sales. He was the chieftain writ small of his sibling group. His brothers and sisters, the majority among the vassalage, favored this arrangement; and so in some measure did the Bakufu. Above all else, Kamakura predicated its rulership on its ability to block rival lordships.

The weaknesses inherent in this inheritance-cum-vassalage system distinguish it from what came next. By the mid-fourteenth century, the powers of lordship had vastly increased at both the Bakufu and the *sōryō* levels. For example, the shogun now claimed an authority that was wholly without precedent—the right to choose a *sōryō* and also, if necessary, to dismiss him. Under the Ashikaga, the position of house head had become, to a degree, appointive.[2] The conditions inducing this change are noteworthy—the shogun's need for great men, yet the risks inherent in allowing them excessive autonomy. Concern over the latter provided much of the spark for the intrusions of higher authority into family matters. The control techniques of the later daimyo, and ultimately the escheats and attainders of the Tokugawa, may be thought to have had their genesis here.[3] As we know, during the Kamakura age, current heads, almost never the regime, were responsible for selecting their own successors.

Though the approval of the Bakufu became an active requirement under the Ashikaga, *sōryō* were enhanced, not diminished, as a result. Privileged brothers in the Kamakura age, they now became house chieftains to a much greater degree. Unigeniture was the key innovation here, since the sustenance needs of siblings would as a result now fall to a brother. In other words, when bequests were replaced by same-generation grants or even annuities, a condition of true dependence would follow. The bonds of feudalism (or patrimonialism) would be in process of supplanting the ties of kinship. In practice, of course, a trunk line's appropriation of its newest limbs was inordinately easier than its reapprehension of older ones.

[2] According to Andrew Goble, the restorationist Emperor Go-Daigo had asserted this right vis-à-vis the Saionji and Yūki families, the first an aristocratic house, the second a warrior house.

[3] There is now a considerable literature on the control devices of the daimyo, e.g., Hall, *Government and Local Power*, chaps. 8 and 9; Totman, *Politics in the Tokugawa Bakufu*, chap. 1; and especially Arnesen, *The Medieval Japanese Daimyo*. For the attainders of the Tokugawa, see Bolitho, *Treasures Among Men*.

In fact, these developments seem logical and familiar in the context of Japan's fourteenth century. The heightened tensions of the era produced a natural tightening of command systems and the emergence of war bands that were now operational. By contrast, the thirteenth century continues to yield seeming paradoxes. For example, what are we to make of parents who terrorized their children yet resisted leaving assets to only one; of men and women who adopted heirs even when they did not need them; and of brothers and sisters who preferred to weaken the links of kinship rather than strengthen them against neighbors who were rivals? The role of the Bakufu was obviously central here, even if decoding it resists easy explication. On the one hand, Kamakura served its vassals well by providing them with *jitō* titles, justice, and job prestige. It also confirmed their asset transfers and allowed them to subdivide land and people almost freely. But on the other hand, it created an environment in which families would be too weak to make war on each other. Stated differently, it allowed the natural contentiousness of kin to hold sway. Yet by permitting such freedom the Bakufu also gave up much that other regimes might have held dear. Exercised mostly through its tribunals, the hand of Kamakura's governance would be felt in practice only very lightly.

Ultimately, it is the autonomy of parental decision-making that is most striking, a condition nourished by values embedded in the national psyche. The society's idealization of filial piety was one such value, which was expressed in the form of parents' absolute authority. Immune from criticism in the abstract, it could only be sustained by the Bakufu through its decisions. In the lawsuits that Kamakura judged and also refused to judge, and in the regime's morally laden legislative pronouncements, the Bakufu widened the gulf between the generations, even as it narrowed the distance that separated siblings. Moreover, there were no countervailing values or influences to help break this dominant grip of parents. For example, unlike the case in medieval Europe, where the Church penetrated to the very core of the family, religious sanctions in Japan all but bypassed the intersection of parents, children, and property. Save for Buddhism's prohibition against widows publicly remarrying (which might lead to the assignment to children of inheritances received from late husbands), it had little to say that was negative about improper family behavior. On this point, Christianity's interference with the family was so much more pronounced than that of Buddhism that it affords us a useful comparison.

If the Buddhist establishment in Japan seems never to have conceived of manipulating the relationships among kin as a means of augmenting its own wealth, the Church in Europe owed much of its great treasure to precisely this kind of activity. For example, if adoption could be made an outlawed practice, childless elders might be obliged to will property to the Church. Similarly, if monogamy were strictly enforced, there would be no half-blood offspring to compete with the Church for inheritances. Related to this, if divorce were strictly prohibited, childless couples might also have to bequeath to the Church. Finally, if persons who were widowed were restricted in whom they could remarry, the Church once again stood potentially to profit.[4]

Indeed, we can go further by arguing that it was the Church's specific goal to loosen the bonds of kinship for its own purposes. This motivation was revealed in many ways. For example, kin were denied the right to marry a wide range of other kin, a net whose scope was unimaginable in Japan. Secondly, it was the Church that made bastardy the status of outcasts in an attempt to remove illegitimates from their own families. Even the writing of wills, actively promoted by the Church, can be portrayed as a means of monitoring, and hence restricting, parishioners' bequests. By overseeing what was proper and correct, and by linking this to the will-writer's own salvation, the Church virtually guaranteed for itself at least a portion of every legacy.[5] In Japan, by contrast, warrior wills almost never transmitted anything to religious institutions. Descendants might be reminded to discharge services on behalf of a sectarian proprietor; but the property rights involved would fall exclusively to themselves. Indeed, multiple marriages and unlimited adoption meant that persons with property would never lack for descendants.[6]

The foregoing describes the experience for most of the Kamakura period. Near the end of that era, restrictive strategies, as we have seen, became commonplace. In those instances in which unigeniture was introduced, the stakes being played for were now vastly increased. Yet since fathers were still autonomous in the decisions they made,

[4]Though the motivations of the Church are sometimes viewed less darkly, recent opinion tends to emphasize its acquisitiveness. See, e.g., Goody, *The Development of the Family and Marriage in Europe*; Herlihy, *Medieval Households*; and Sheehan, *The Will in Medieval England*.

[5]One need only peruse the wills of Anglo-Saxon England, for example, to see that testaments virtually never neglected the Church; see Whitelock, ed., *Anglo-Saxon Wills*.

[6]This does not preclude the increase in religious commendations noted in Chapter 4.

they had only to draw up proper testaments to settle the matter. The Bakufu simply confirmed these choices. However, with the onset of the succeeding era, the power balance among the major families now became a factor. Takauji could not afford to ignore what the Hōjō had scarcely worried about—the identities of rival *sōryō* atop the leading families. In a world in which siblings were less equal, and in which the top prizes were less frequently divisible, alliances began to form across family lines and among individuals at several levels. Succession politics, reaching up to and inside the Bakufu, became structured around factions that supported candidates for the principal house headships.[7] And yet, though the winners might still be called *sōryō*, they were no longer expressive of a "*sōryō* system." This last had been a means of dividing assets among heirs, along with a means of designating a coordinator of vassal dues.

The Kamakura period may thus have been Japan's final premodern era in which the separate parts were more important than their sum total. There was a highly developed concept not only of two parents, but of individual inheriting children as well. Centrifugal tendencies clearly outweighed centripetal ones. The Bakufu tended to validate this situation by confirming the inheritances of all will-receiving offspring, and then by judging the suits they brought against one another. In this environment, the collective had no one to defend it except the donor-elder, who was thinking not of his peers but only of his descendants. It was only by the fourth or fifth generation, coincident with the onset of other problems, that the extravagance favored by the earlier situation now started to become an impediment. As shares became smaller, rivalries intensified, and many families began not only to divide but to break apart. The strategies contrived in the late Kamakura age were designed to stem this tide of disintegration. For some families at least, a rewelding occurred, but with the constituent parts now cemented by ties that were only in part blood-based. Warriors became the leaders and followers of other warriors, who only sometimes belonged to the same kin groups. This experience, blocked for a hundred years by the Kamakura *sōryō* system, could now in the fourteenth century no longer be held back.

[7] For a discussion of such succession disputes among the leading families in the fifteenth century, see Varley, *The Ōnin War*, chap. 5.

PART TWO

DOCUMENTS IN TRANSLATION

The documents that follow represent a selection of the source materials I have used in the preparation of this book. I have been guided in my choices by the need to illustrate the evolution of warrior inheritance practices, the range of these practices, and the role of higher authority in sustaining them. In a few cases the documents illustrate other means of property transmission, as well as other classes and their inheritance techniques. I have drawn my sources from all parts of Japan.

I have added an introduction to each document (or related sequence of documents) as a way of facilitating access to what, after all, are difficult materials. For the same reason, I have not scrimped on annotation, since these records clearly call out for constant explication. For the less industrious, the introductions can be read, without the translations, as an addendum to Part One.

DOCUMENTS 1–4

A Local Chieftain Transmits a Provincial Title to His Son and Has It Confirmed by the Governor in the Pre-Kamakura Era, 1149, 1175, 1187

Before the establishment of the Kamakura Bakufu the validation of warrior land conveyances (pre- and post-obit) and the resolution of warrior inheritance disputes were the responsibility of estate proprietors in the *shōen* sector and of civil governors in public lands. In the sequence depicted here, a prominent chieftain of southern Kyushu deeded his headship of the provincial headquarters to a second son and thereby precipitated a long-running family feud. Ultimately the governor dismissed the claim of the older brother, who was the challenger, and in the final document the victor conveyed the provincial authority to a nephew (not the son of his rival) whom he had adopted. By this juncture the Bakufu had appeared and would shortly accept this nephew into vassalage. Thereafter, the Bakufu would serve as final arbiter, replacing the governor.

1

san-i Kusakabe Naomori
conveys: the resident provincial governor's post (*zaikokushi shiki*) and the paddy and upland of Umatsu Village.[1]

Although Morihira is my second son, he is designated my principal heir (*chakushi*).[2] Accordingly, the resident provincial governor's post and the paddy and upland of Umatsu village, along with the sequence of entitlements (*daidai no kugen*),[3] are herewith conveyed to him. The boundaries of Umatsu are Akasaka to the east, the river to the south and west, and the Nakaya-Kayo Bridge to the north. The paddy acreage is 30 *chō*. Thus, in accordance with the rights of ancestral succession,[4] possession (*ryōchi*) shall be exercised [by him], free of disturbance. By this document our conveyance is thus.
5th year of Kyūan [1149], 3d month, 10th day
san-i, Kusakabe Naomori seal

2

The governor's office decrees: to the absentee provincial headquarters (*rusudokoro*).
That appointment shall be made to the resident provincial governor's post:[5] to *gon no suke san-i* Kusakabe *no sukune* Morihira

The aforesaid person is appointed to the resident provincial governor's post. Our decree is thus. The absentee headquarters shall know this and abide by it accordingly. Wherefore, this edict.
5th year of Kyūan [1149], 7th month,   day
ōsuke, Fujiwara ason seal

3

The governor's office decrees: to the absentee provincial headquarters.
Concerning appointment to the resident provincial governor's post: to *gon no suke san-i* Kusakabe *no sukune* Morihira

Moritoshi's [claim] is dismissed,[6] and Morihira shall possess the resident provincial governor's post. Our decree is thus. The absentee headquarters shall know this and abide by it accordingly. Wherefore, this edict.

5th year of Shōan [1175], 4th month,   day

ōsuke, Fujiwara ason seal

4

san-i Kusakabe Morihira respectfully announces: his conveyance of the resident provincial governor's post and the paddy and upland of Umatsu village

[to:] Tabe Eimyō [7]

appended: entitlements (*kugen*) and the succession of documents.[8]

Morihira has reached old age and feebleness (*rōmō*), but because he has no true sons or daughters, he deeds the said *shiki* to Eimyō, along with the sequence of documents. The boundaries and area of Umatsu are indicated in the previous conveyance. Thus, in accordance with the rights of ancestral succession, possession (*ryōshō*) shall be exercised [by him], free of disturbance.

3d year of Bunji [1187], 2d month, 10th day

san-i, Kusakabe Morihira . . . [9] seal

SOURCES: Document 1: *Kusakabe keizu shoshū monjo*, 1149/3/10 Kusakabe Naomori yuzurijō, *HI*, 6: 2238–39, doc. 2661. Document 2: *ibid.*, 1149/7 Hyūga kokushi chōsen, *HI*, 6: 2255, doc. 2673. Document 3: *ibid.*, 1175/4 Hyūga kokushi chōsen, *HI*, 7: 2852, doc. 3684. Document 4: *ibid.*, 1187/2/10 Kusakabe Morihira yuzurijō, *KI*, 1: 126–27, doc. 205.

1. The *zaikokushi* post was the effective local headship of the governor's headquarters here in Hyūga Province. Throughout these translations, the words "convey," "deed," "release," and "transmit" will be used more or less interchangeably as equivalents for "*yuzuru*." "Bequeath" and "devise," which are specific to postmortem conveyances, will be used only when the document functioned explicitly as a will. Even here there is some confusion since the original intent (as opposed to actual usage) may not have been testamentary. There is no fully satisfactory way for the translator to deal with this problem.

2. The donor's first son, Moritoshi, was later to challenge this; see Document 3.

3. Deeds to property issued by the governor's office; they would specify boundaries and other relevant information.

4. Naomori himself received the resident governorship in 1132 when his father, Naosada, who had been appointed in 1123, reached "old age" and could no longer effectively discharge the office's duties. Both appointments came via governor's edicts, with no hint of a written conveyance by the holder (see *Kusakabe keizu shoshū monjo*, 1123/1/25 Hyūga kokushi chōsen, *HI*, 5: 1722, doc. 1981; *ibid.*, 1132/10 Hyūga kokushi chōsen, *HI*, 9: 3692, doc. 4697). Indeed, it would appear that Naosada (also known as

Hisasada) was the initial appointee to the post, which would make the present "ancestral" inheritance quite brief; the present deed of release is possibly the first.

5. Formalization thus came via a governor's appointment.

6. The present reappointment of Morihira was in effect a confirmation necessitated by the challenge of his elder brother, Moritoshi. Again, it is the governor who serves as legitimator and arbiter.

7. Tabe Eimyō was a nephew of the donor Morihira who became the latter's adopted son (*yōshi*). See *Hyūga Kusakabe keizu*, reprinted in Nishioka Toranosuke, *Shōen shi no kenkyū*, 2: 437–40. Eimyō (also known as Sanemori) became a Kamakura *jitō* and substituted the Bakufu for the governor's office as the legitimator of his authority; *ibid.*

8. This entire line is omitted from the *KI* transcription; but see *ibid.*, p. 439.

9. Two half-size characters appear here out of context.

DOCUMENT   5

An Estate Custodian Has His Petition Approved for Confirmation of a Conveyance, 1187

Only a small minority of landholders became part of the Bakufu's system of protection. In the case described here, the hereditary custodian of a pair of estates appealed to their patron, the highest-ranking officer, for confirmation of the petitioner's release to his son. The request was made during the troubled middle years of the 1180s. Even so, the estate system remained operational with those at its summit continuing to serve as probate-granting authorities. As an indication of this, the custodianships in question were over estates in different provinces. Yet at the highest administrative levels they were clearly linked.

The chancellery of the minister of the right (*udaijin*) directs:[1]

> That in accordance with the deed of release by Kamo *gon negi* Sukeyasu, his son Kamo Yoshihisa shall administer (*chigyō*) Kisaichi Estate in Tanba Province and Kawachi Estate in Mimasaka Province.

The aforesaid two estates, under the jurisdiction (*sata*) of this house,[2] were commended to the bloc of holdings (*goryō*) belonging to the Kamo detached shrine (*betsu-gū*)[3]—at Shijōbōmon and Abura-no-kōji.[4] Accordingly, since this authority (*sata*) has been entrusted to Sukeyasu over many years, he has petitioned that his son Yoshihisa might succeed to it.[5] In accordance with the father's conveyance, let Yoshihisa enjoy this possession.[6] Our command is as above. Both estates shall observe this and not be negligent. Wherefore, this order.

3d year of Bunji [1187], 10th month, 5th day

anzu, Ōe

daijū mondo no ryōshi, Kiyohara

ryō, taikō daigōgū no daisakan, Sugano ason

bettō jokyō ken Ōi no kami, Nakahara ason (monogram)

san-i, Fujiwara ason

Mutsu no kami, Fujiwara ason

kōtai gōgū shōshin, Fujiwara ason (monogram)

san-i, Fujiwara ason (monogram)

SOURCE: *Kamowake Ikazuchi jinja monjo*, 1187/10/5 udaijin ke mandokoro kudashibumi, *KI*, 1: 165, doc. 271.

1. Tokudaiji (Fujiwara) Sanesada, who had succeeded Kujō (Fujiwara) Kanezane as *udaijin* in 1186, and who was patron (*honke*) of the estates in question.

2. I.e., the house of the patron, Tokudaiji Sanesada.

3. This transaction was recognized by decree of the Tanba governor in 1160; see Hosomi Sueo, *Tanba no shōen*, p. 135.

4. Two streets in Kyoto, designating the location of the shrine; in half-size characters.

5. Several years earlier, a petition from Sukeyasu had appealed against local outlawry in these estates by someone in the Kamo hierarchy. The retired emperor Go-Shirakawa issued an injunction, which was then strengthened by a decree from Kamakura confirming Sukeyasu's rightful authority. Sukeyasu was thus "physically" secured by the emerging Bakufu, but would be guaranteed in his family's hereditary possession by the patron. See *Kamowake Ikazuchi jinja monjo*, 1185/6/6 Minamoto Yoritomo kudashibumi, *HI*, 8: 3178, doc. 4257.

6. Yoshihisa joined the Court side in the Jōkyū War and was replaced as custodian (*azukàri dokoro*) over the two estates by another Kamo Shrine official, possibly a relative. See *ibid.*, 1222/3 Tokudaiji udaijin ke mandokoro kudashibumi, *KI*, 5: 91–92, doc. 2936, and *Tanba no shōen*, p. 135. We thus see three levels of authority: patron, proprietor, and custodian. There was also a managerial officer (*kumon*) in Kisaichi Estate who attempted to claim for himself *jitō*-level privileges: *ibid.*, 1232/4/17 Kantō gechijō, *DKR*, doc. 38.

DOCUMENT 6

A Local Priest Chooses a Younger Brother as His Successor, 1188

Pre- or post-obit transmissions were not limited to rights in the public and private land sectors (*shōen* and *kokugaryō*). As we see here, priestly titles could also be conveyed, in this instance, to a younger brother. It is noteworthy that a resident governorship (Documents 1–4), an estate custodianship (Document 5), and a temple's headship could all be denominated *shiki* and be made the objects of written conveyances. Indeed, any prestigious authority was potentially a *shiki* (a heritable authority) and citable as such in deeds of release. In the present instance, the theft of hereditary documents posed a threat to the transfer of the priesthood.

Conveyed: the head priesthood (*inju shiki*) of Naisanji Temple, Mie gō.[1]

[To:] zenshūbō Kakushū

The head priesthood of this temple is the inheritance of Kikaku from generations past. This being the case, it is conveyed in perpetuity to my true younger brother (*chakutei*), Kakushū. However, though the generations of releases by priests prior to Kikaku should [rightfully] be appended here, these were entrusted to Tamata Tarō on the occasion of a trip by Kikaku to the capital, owing to [Kikaku's] fear of the dangers posed by wind, waves, and robbers. [Tamata, however,] appropriated the entrusted documents (*shōmon*), claiming that they had burned up when his lodging place (*shukusho*) was destroyed by fire. After Kikaku's death, in the event anyone causes trouble to the temple by claiming that he possesses the documents, that person should be declared a thief and his assertions disregarded. For the future, this conveyance is thus.[2]

4th year of Bunji [1188], 3d month, 10th day

dai hosshi Kikaku seal

SOURCE: *Ōtomo monjo*, 1188/3/10 dai hosshi Kikaku yuzurijō an, *Hennen Ōtomo shiryō*, 1: 177–78, doc. 175 (*KI*, 1: 183, doc. 316).

1. In Bungo Province.

2. A century and a half later the original of this release (along with later *yuzurijō*) was itself lost in a fire. A petition reproducing all of these records was then submitted for validation. See *Ōtomo monjo*, 1335/3 Shoei funshitsujō an, *Hennen Ōtomo shiryō*, 2: 198–210, doc. 315.

DOCUMENT 7

A Father Urges Family Solidarity and Protection of the House Patrimony, 1191

During Kamakura times donors regularly wrote individual releases to sons, daughters, and other close relatives who might be receiving portions. A donor's own documents, however, could be transmitted to only one person—

his primary heir, as we see in the present instance. Though partible inheritance was the norm, the symbols of a lineage's integrity—its original investiture decrees, its ancestral bequests, etc.—could not be divided. As a further protection against fragmentation, heirs were admonished not to dissipate inheritances. Occasionally this took the form of vague warnings of confiscation.

Conveyed:[1] one ancestral landholding.
   Located: within Kumagaya[2] *gō*, Ōsato District, Musashi Province
Boundaries: . . .[3]

The aforesaid landholding is hereby passed in perpetuity to Saneie[4] *ason*, our son. Because the proof records from generations past (*daidai shōmon*) are in a connected series (*renkan*), passage of the document sequence is made to our eldest son (*chakunan*), Naoie *ason*.[5] Nevertheless, among my descendants, if any unvirtuous person should appear and make [this land] another's by commending it to a central proprietor (*kenmon seika*), the bond of brotherhood will be broken and possession [reassigned] by ability (*kiryō*). As proof for the future, it is recorded thus.
   2d year of Kenkyū [1191], 3d month, 1st day

jitō, the priest Renjō[6] (monogram)

> eldest son (*chakushi*),[7] Taira Naoie
> (monogram)
> 2d son (*jinan*), Taira Sanekage
> (monogram)

SOURCE: *Kumagai ke monjo*, 1191/3/1 Kumagaya Renjō (Naozane) yuzurijō, *DNK*, *iewake 14*, p. 1, doc. 1 (*KI*, 1: 388, doc. 514).
   1. A note to the present document in *DNK* suggests that this release may have been written later in the Kamakura period and then predated. If true, this would make it a forgery in the strict sense, though its interest is little diminished.
   2. A *kana* identification on the reverse side of the document clarifies the pronunciation of this name; later, the name came to be read Kumagai.
   3. Specified here. According to *AK* 1182/6/5, Kumagaya *gō* was confirmed by Yoritomo to Kumagaya Naozane, the present donor.
   4. The characters are inverted here (Iezane), but a correction is included in the margin of the original. On the reverse side of the document Saneie is referred to as Shirō, sometimes "the 4th son."
   5. This makes the present conveyance one to a secondary heir; none of the others is extant.
   6. Kumagaya Naozane, the present donor.
   7. This term is interchangeable with *chakunan* above.

DOCUMENT 8

A House Chieftain Warns Against Fragmentation of the Family Estate, 1193

Sometimes the warnings of confiscation were more specific. In the present document, a priestly donor was obviously concerned with erosion of his family's holdings. The sale of inherited portions was not only to remain within the family; it was to be limited to persons of ability. Also, donees were not to adopt heirs from outside the family collective. This was a stricture that violated current practice; free alienation was the norm and would remain so for some time. Here and in Document 7 we see early examples of the partible–impartible tension that developed during the thirteenth century.

. . . should . . .[1]

chief priest (*kannushi*), Kaya *ason* (monogram)

A register of allocated shares of paddy and upland within Hisanari *myō*, Niwase *gō*.[2]

. . .[3]

Regarding the foregoing, our dispositions (*shobun*) are thus. However, there should be no sale to outsiders (*tanin*) of any of the said paddy and upland. If there is to be a sale, let it be [to someone] within our family, in accordance with his ability. In the absence of children, should there be a release to an outsider who is called an adoptive son (*yōshi*), even though this is a kind of son, [the parcels concerned] should be retaken and subsumed under the main holding (*hon myō*).[4] Wherefore, our allocation (*shihai*) is thus.

4th year of Kenkyū [1193], 1st month,   day

kannushi, Kaya ason (monogram)

SOURCE: *Kibitsu jinja monjo*, 1193/1 kannushi Kaya ason bō yuzurijō, *Okayama ken komonjo shū*, 2: 129–33, doc. 1 (*KI*, 2: 61–65, doc. 653).

1. All but two characters of a prescript added by the author of the present document have been lost.

2. In Bitchū Province.

3. The actual disposition specifications follow here, though with many characters lost. The apportionments are very detailed.

4. Half a century later we encounter a conveyance by the same family containing the same strictures: *Kibitsu jinja monjo*, 1245/10 kannushi Kaya bō yuzurijō, *Okayama ken komonjo shū*, 2: 133–36, doc. 2.

DOCUMENTS 9–10

A Fourth Son Receives a Family's Main Inheritance and Parcels a Portion of It to His Third Son, 1186, 1200

The complications emanating from a donor's absolute discretion in the division of property are highlighted in the present sequence. In 1186, a parceling among four sons was apparently achieved without incident. One reason for this was the donor's securing of the other sons' signatures (i.e., assent) to the individual allocations. One of these conveyances (the only one surviving) is presented here. In the second generation, however, the 1186 recipient elected to exclude his own eldest son from the inheritance and thereby triggered a dispute that would fester for decades. Of particular note are the signatures of persons representing three generations—the father of the donor, the donor himself, and the donor's sons.

9

Conveyed:
    Hereditary local titles for Usa Shrine holdings.[1]

The aforesaid titles are the ancestral [possessions][2] of Fujiwara *ason* Yukifusa. Accordingly, transmission is herewith made, along with the succession of proof records, to our fourth son, Fujiwara *ason* Yukiakira. Let there be no disturbances whatever. It is thus. Ifuku, Ōkawa, Iko, and Mihakano are so conveyed.[3]
    2d year of Bunji [1186], 4th month, 29th day

    san-i, Fujiwara ason[4] (monogram)
    Fujiwara Yukitada[5] (monogram)
    Fujiwara Yuki . . .[6]
    Fujiwara Yukihide . . .[7]
    . . .[8]

10

Fujiwara Yukiakira releases: to Fujiwara Matsukuma[9]
    The [coastal][10] paddy, upland, and open areas of Ifuku . . . ,[11] among our four holdings,[12] all [Usa][13] Shrine lands in Takaki District, Hizen Province.
        Boundaries: to the east, the Yokota-bito Trail
                to the west, the Yomi River

to the south, Tatabakara
to the north, the sea.

The aforesaid coastal paddy, upland, and open areas were received by Yukiakira from his father Ayabe *nyūdō*.[14] After that, the *benzaishi* title[15] allotted to Kayo-dono[16] was similarly passed on [to Yukiakira] by agreement of both men.[17] Even though [Yukiakira] has an eldest son (*chakushi*),[18] disposition shall [not][19] be to him. Accordingly, let there be no disturbances in future. It is thus.

2d year of Shōji [1200], intercalated 2d month, day

> shami, Jōshin[20] seal
> Fujiwara Michimune[21] seal
> Fujiwara Yukiakira[22] seal
> chakushi, dō Jirō[23] seal
> dō Tsuchikumi-Ō[24] seal

Yukitomo[25] will go on to the Kantō from Kyoto taking this copy (*anmon*) with him. Since the original has been lost, he will present this [copy].

> Yukitomo
> The seals of three magistrates (*bugyōnin*)
> seal   seal   seal

SOURCES: Document 9: *Ōkawa monjo*, 1186/4/29 Fujiwara (Ayabe) Yukifusa yuzurijō, *Ogashima monjo—Ōkawa monjo—Madarashima monjo*, p. 67, doc. 1 (*KI*, 1: 63, doc. 91). Document 10: *ibid.*, 1200/int. 2 Fujiwara Yukiakira yuzurijō an, *Ogashima monjo—Ōkawa monjo—Madarashima monjo*, p. 68, doc. 2 (*KI*, 2: 387, doc. 1123).

1. Usa Shrine was thus the proprietor (*ryōke*) of the lands in question. There are no Heian-period documents that clarify the background here.

2. Speculative; two or three characters are missing here.

3. These are the names of the four villages being conveyed. No confirmation from Usa Shrine is extant, and indeed there is no indication of interaction with the Bakufu until much later; see Document 61. Just when the family became *gokenin* is not clear.

4. I.e., the donor, Fujiwara Yukifusa.

5. The eldest son. There is no information regarding his inheritance and no indication of any special status accruing from his being the eldest. He disappears from view with the present document.

6. The second son; one character and the monogram have been lost.

7. The third son; the monogram has been lost. A fleeting reference to Yukihide appears in Document 61 below; see n. 14.

8. An addendum by Yukiakira, the investee here, appears in this place, obviously added later. Various characters are missing.

9. Known later as Ifuku Michiyuki, he was the donor's third son and victor in a 1241 inheritance dispute with his elder brother Yukimoto and the latter's son; see Document 61.

10. Characters missing but appearing later in the document.

11. Two or three characters lost.

12. Thus, only Ifuku of the donor's four possessions (see Document 9) was being transmitted here to the donor's third son.

13. Characters lost but interpolated.

14. Document 9.

15. A financial officership, common in Kyushu.

16. Kayo-dono would appear to be the brother of Ayabe *nyūdō*, designated below (see the second signature) as Fujiwara Michimune. The phrase "allotted to" is derived from the transcription in *Ogashima monjo—Ōkawa monjo—Madarashima monjo*; the *KI* transcription has an incorrect character.

17. The two men referred to here are the senior-generation brothers Ayabe *nyūdō* (Yukifusa) and Kayo-dono (Michimune).

18. "Eldest son" rather than "principal heir" is clearly the correct rendering here, since Yukimoto (the person referred to) would spend the rest of his life attempting to secure an inheritance; see Document 61.

19. The negative character is omitted in the document itself, but the transcription in *KI* assumes this to be an error; the editor adds it in the margin. So do the editors in another transcription, that in *DNS*, series 4, 6: 858. However, the version in *Ogashima monjo—Ōkawa monjo—Madarashima monjo* makes no such correction. The translation might then read, "Even though [Yukiakira] has an eldest son, disposition is to [Matsukuma]."

20. Ayabe *nyūdō* (i.e., Fujiwara Yukifusa), the technical donor's father. The placement of his name first is noteworthy.

21. Kayo-dono, Ayabe *nyūdō*'s brother.

22. The technical donor here.

23. Fujiwara Yukimoto, Yukiakira's eldest son. Note that he is a signatory to his own exclusion here.

24. Fujiwara Yukimura, Yukiakira's second son.

25. Appended here is a much later statement by Ōkawa Yukitomo (the son of Yukimoto), on the occasion of an inheritance dispute in 1241 (Document 61). The original (*shōmon*) of the 1200 document had been lost and the present copy (*anmon*) was being submitted in evidence.

DOCUMENT 11

A Portion of a Principal Heir's Inheritance Is Allotted as a Life Bequest to His Mother, 1200

One of the most important developments of the mid-thirteenth century was the growing currency of non-alienable life bequests for women. Hitherto, wives and daughters (and less frequently sisters) received inheritances totally without encumbrances. The present example is one of the earliest instances of an "entail" involving a woman. The release is to a son; but a portion of that inheritance was to be diverted to his mother for the duration of her lifetime. In effect, the mother was given user privileges but not ownership. Much more common at this time (as we shall see) were mothers in their widowhood literally dominating their families and largely controlling the flow of property.

Conveyed:

> The *ōnegi shiki*[1] plus paddy and upland in Mochishige *myō*; the *gō* units of Kanō, Asanama, Ōeda, and Tachibana, all within Namekata District.

Following longstanding practice, my principal heir (*chakushi*) Masachika is herewith conveyed these posts. However, Tachibana *gō* shall be held by Masachika's mother. Later, Masachika will assume authority.[2] It is thus.

> 2d year of Shōji [1200], 12th month, 19th day

> > Kashima ōnegi, san-i Nakatomi
> > (monogram)

SOURCE: *Hanawa Fujimaru shi shozō monjo*, 1200/12/19 Kashima sha ōnegi Nakatomi Chikahiro yuzurijō, *Ibaragi ken shiryō, chūsei hen* 1: 294, doc. 5 (*KI*, 2: 424, doc. 1173).
    1. A ranking priest-administrator's post within Kashima Shrine, Hitachi Province.
    2. It is unclear whether Masachika's mother (wife of the present donor) ever came to hold Tachibana. In 1205, the Bakufu canceled a *jitō shiki* wrongly assigned there in 1202 and used the occasion to confirm Masachika's possession of Tachibana. He was confirmed also in 1221. For these and further details, see *Kashima jingū monjo*, 1205/8/23 Minamoto Sanetomo kudashibumi, *KI*, 3: 250, doc. 1574 (*KB*, doc. 35), and *ibid.*, 1228/5/19 Kantō gechijō, *KI*, 6: 8285, doc. 3745. Masachika's own release of Tachibana was dated 1227/12/7; cited in *ibid.*, 1240/12/7 shōgun ke mandokoro kudashibumi, *KI*, 8: 191-92, doc. 5687.

DOCUMENTS 12–15

The Bakufu Confirms the Transmission of Jitō Shiki by Their Holders, 1205, 1208, 1212, 1215

From about 1205 it became standard practice for the Bakufu to confirm the land releases of its vassals. This was advantageous for both Kamakura and the warriors composing its band. For the former it permitted a periodic check on the disposition of land rights originally granted by itself but now alienable by the families that had received them. For the latter it meant a regular recertification of the legality of their possession, as well as reconfirmation of their status as vassals. As we note in the examples that follow, the right to dispose of *jitō* offices did indeed reside with their holders. Confirmations were linked to the death or retirement of the vassal, not of the lord, and in response to actions initiated by the vassal, not by higher authority. After only one generation, then, the conditional nature of the original grant had been reduced to a right of probate.

12

Directed: to the residents of Southern Fukazawa *gō*, Sagami Province.
      That Takai Tarō Shigemochi shall forthwith hold the *jitō shiki*, in accordance with the release of the late Wada Saburō Munezane.[1]

The aforesaid person has received this inheritance from Munezane, accompanied by [investiture] edicts of the late *[u]taishō* lord[2] as well as 15 *chō* of stipend paddy (*kyūden*).[3] In accordance with that document,[4] he shall possess the *jitō shiki*. By command of the Kamakura lord, it is so decreed. Wherefore, this order.
      2d year of Genkyū [1205], 2d month, 22d day

> Tōtomi no kami, Taira
> (monogram)

13

Directed: to the residents of Agana, Haruhara, Hirose *gō*, and Ogose *gō*, Musashi province.
      That Arimichi and Aritaka shall forthwith hold the *jitō shiki*, in accordance with the release of *uma no jō* Arihiro.[5]

The aforesaid person[6] shall possess these *shiki* in accordance with the conveyance by Arihiro. By command of the Kamakura lord, it is so decreed. Wherefore, this order.
      2d year of Jōgen [1208], 3d month, 13th day

> Koremune seal
> saki no zusho no jō, Kiyohara seal
> san-i, Nakahara ason seal
> san-i, Fujiwara ason seal
> sho hakase, Nakahara ason seal

14

The chancellery of the shogun's house directs: to the residents of the Hizen Province official temple (*kokubunji*).
      The appointment of a *jitō shiki*: Fujiwara Suetoshi.

The aforesaid person's father, Suenaga *hosshi*, was granted a chancellery edict[7] by the late *[u]taishō* lord, dated the 5th year of Kenkyū [1194], 2d month, 25th day,[8] and [thereafter] exercised possession.

Now, in accordance with the present deed of release,[9] Suetoshi shall hold the *jitō shiki*. Let authority be carried out pursuant to precedent. The command is thus. Wherefore, this order.

2d year of Kenryaku [1212], 10th month, 27th day

anzu, Sugano
chikeji, Koremune

ryō, zusho no shōjō, Kiyohara (monogram)
bettō, Sagami no kami, Taira ason (monogram)
ukonoe shōgen ken Tōtomi no kami, Minamoto ason (monogram)
Musashi no kami, Taira ason (monogram)
sho hakase, Nakahara ason (monogram)
san-i, Nakahara (monogram)

15

The chancellery of the shogun's house directs: to the residents of 12 *gō* within Nitta Estate, Kōzuke Province.

That Minamoto Tokikane shall forthwith be *jitō*: Tajima *gō*, Murata *gō*, Takashima *gō*, Narihaka *gō*, Futagohaka *gō*, Kami-Horiguchi *gō*, Chitose *gō*, Yabuhaka *gō*, Tabegai *gō*, Koshima *gō*, Yonezawa *gō*, Kami-Imai *gō*.

Appointment to the *shiki* for the aforesaid *gō* is in accordance with the register (*chūmon*) submitted by the widow of the *kurōdo*, Yoshikane.[10] As for the fixed annual tax and other services, these shall be paid in accordance with precedent. The command is thus. Wherefore, this order.

3d year of Kenpō [1215], 3d month, 23d day

anzu, Sugano seal
chike[ji], Koremune seal

ryō, zusho no jō, Kiyohara seal
bettō, Sagami no kami, Taira ason seal
minbu gon no shōsuke ken Tōtomi no kami, Minamoto ason
Musashi no kami, Taira ason seal
sho hakase, Nakahara ason seal
san-i, Fujiwara ason seal

SOURCES: Document 12: *Nakajō ke monjo*, 1205/2/22 Kantō gechijō, *Okuyama-no-shō shiryōshū*, p. 98 (*KI*, 3: 230, doc. 1519). Document 13: *Hōonji nenpu*, 1208/3/13 Kantō kudashibumi an, *KI*, 3: 343, doc. 1722. Document 14: *Taku monjo* 1212/10/27 shōgun ke mandokoro kudashibumi, *Saga ken shiryō shūsei*, 14: 41 (*KI*, 4: 47, doc. 1948). Document 15: *Iwamatsu Nitta monjo*, 1215/3/23 shōgun ke mandokoro kudashibumi an, *Masaki komonjo*, pp. 16–17 (*KI*, 4: 156, doc. 2151).

1. Munezane received the *jitō shiki* in 1192, ostensibly as a new investiture; see *Nakajō ke monjo*, 1192/10/21 shōgun ke mandokoro kudashibumi, *Okuyama-no-sho shiryōshū*,

p. 97. However, a much later document suggests that the original award was made to Wada Yoshimochi, elder brother of Munezane and a nephew of the Miura clan chieftain Yoshizumi; see *ibid.*, 1336/2 Wada Mochizane mōshijō, *Okuyama-no-shō shiryōshū*, p. 17. If this is true it would mean that the present transaction (confirmation of passage from Munezane to Shigemochi) was returning the Fukazawa *jitō* authority to the elder brother's line, since Shigemochi was Yoshimochi's son. The conveyance, at any rate, was clearly to a nephew. Munezane's daughter, however, was simultaneously married to Shigemochi, her cousin (*Echigo monjo hōkanshū*, p. 16), and it was she who eventually succeeded him after his death in the Wada Rebellion on the side of the Bakufu. Her tenure was rife with contention, as we see in Documents 20–23 below.

2. I.e., the 1192 document cited in n. 1 plus (possibly) the earlier award edict to Yoshimochi (n. 1).

3. See glossary in *KB*, p. 202.

4. I.e., the release by Munezane, which is not extant.

5. The document reads "sama no jō Arihiro," but *KI* has a correction in the margin; Arihiro was *uma no jō*. See *Musashi shichidō keizu, DNS*, Series 4, 10: 7; and *AK* 1189/7/19, 1190/11/7.

6. Though the meaning here is unclear, it seems possible that two sons (Arimichi and Aritaka) were to divide the several *jitō shiki*. The genealogy of Ogose Arihiro (*DNS*, Series 4, 10: 7) lists Aritaka as his successor.

7. I.e., investiture.

8. Extant but apparently not published.

9. Probably *Taku monjo*, 1212/8/20 Suenaga yuzurijō, *KI*, 4: 35, doc. 1939.

10. The widow herself had just received the *jitō shiki* for three other *gō* within Nitta Estate from her husband's will; *Nitta Iwamatsu monjo*, 1215/3/22 shōgun ke mandokoro kudashibumi an, *Nitta shi konpon shiryō*, pp. 110–11 (*KB*, doc. 24). (Yoshikane's own inheritance, from his father, dated from 1172, his *jitō shiki* from 1205; *Nitta shi konpon shiryō*, pp. 79, 109–10.) Clearly, she was representing her family at this time, since the awardee here (Tokikane) was her grandson. In 1224, she transmitted one of her three *gō*-level *jitō shiki* to him, a transaction that the Bakufu confirmed. *Ibid.*, 1224/1/29 Nitta no ama yuzurijō; 1226/9/15 shōgun ke kudashibumi, *Nitta shi konpon shiryō*, pp. 116–17. (*KI*, 5: 264, doc. 3208; *KI*, 5: 428, doc. 3524.)

DOCUMENT 16

A Mother and Her Eldest Son and Daughter Cosign a Conveyance, 1206

As mentioned before, women came to assume an increasingly prominent role in the disposition of property. Here we see the transfer of a parcel to a younger son with cosignatures added by the latter's eldest brother and eldest sister. Documents of this kind are very common.

Conveyance (*shobun*):[1] of privately owned paddy (*shiryōden*).
   In total: 2.5 *tan*, of which 1 *tan* has been sold.[2]

The aforesaid paddy is released to our second son, Shinjumaru. Therefore, as proof for the future, his grieving mother (*hibo*)³ Fujiwara *no uji* and his elder siblings clearly add their seals. Let there be no departure from this; accordingly, our conveyance for the future is so made.

1st year of Ken'ei [1206], 11th month, 3d day

> hibo, Fujiwara no uji (monogram)
> chakunan, sō (monogram)
> chakujo, Fujiwara no uji (monogram)

SOURCE: *Tōji hyakugō monjo*, 1206/11/3 Fujiwara no ujime denchi shobunjō, *KI*, 3: 292, doc. 1646.
   1. The *shobunjō* format is used since no *shiki* requiring confirmation is involved.
   2. The meaning here is not clear. No actual locale is specified.
   3. Is she grieving over the death of a child or the death of her husband? Since she does not call herself "widow" (*goke*), the land in question seems to come from her line.

DOCUMENT 17

A Jitō Changes the Course of a Portion of His Inheritance, 1208

Nowhere are the powers of a donor made clearer than in cases where wills were rewritten and donees divested of their promised inheritances. The Bakufu almost never questioned such reversals since its interests were only rarely affected by intralineal shifts of this kind. In the present instance Kamakura had been involved in an ongoing dispute between separate and competing lines over the property in question. But once it rendered its verdict it freed the victorious litigant to dispose of his interests as he saw fit. By the same token, a reversal of an earlier judgment would invalidate any release that had occurred in the intervening period. Disputes between siblings and other same-generation relatives were justiciable by the Kamakura Bakufu. By contrast, differences between property holders and their progeny were resolved unilaterally by the holders.

Conveyed: the *jitō shiki* over our original local lordship (*hon ryōshu*) of Ojika Island, an ancestral holding hereditary for 15 generations.
   Specifications: Ojika Island, within Uno Tribute Estate (*mikuriya*), Hizen Province.

The proof records (*shōmon*) are clear that the said island has been hereditary with the ancestors of Jinkaku for 15 generations. At present, since Jinkaku has already passed 80 years of age, he hereby conveys it and its sequence of proof records to his eldest son, Fujiwara Michitaka.[1] Although Urabe within Ojika Island[2] was released to Fujiwara Ietaka,[3] owing to disturbances by his heir Tarō,[4] a retrocession was in order, leading to a conveyance, as before (*moto no gotoku*), to Michitaka.[5] Henceforth, authority shall lie with Michitaka, free of any other disturbance. It is thus.

2d year of Jōgen [1208], 7th month,   day

Jinkaku dai hosshi[6] seal

Owing to the loss of the original of this document in Kamakura, acknowledgment is hereby given that the above is accurate. As proof for the future, the administrators (*jikinin*) and estate officials (*shōkan*) have added their signatures.

Fujii Tsunesada seal
Fujii Tokikatsu seal
Fujii Sadakane seal
Fujiwara Michiyasu seal
Fujiwara Hidekane seal
Fujiwara Yoshitaka[7]

SOURCE: *Aokata monjo*, 1208/7 Jinkaku yuzurijō an, *Aokata monjo*, 1: 6–7, doc. 7 (*KI*, 3: 361, doc. 1754).

1. A second reason for Jinkaku's action at this moment was a recent confirmation by the Bakufu of his authority there. Jinkaku had been struggling with relatives for control of the island for some years; see *KB*, docs. 19 and 20, and *DKR*, pp. 95–101. Michitaka later changed his name to Michizumi and is so named in subsequent documents and in the family's genealogy; *Aokata shi kafu*, in *Aokata monjo*, 2: 204.

2. Urabe was evidently an island within the Ojika Island orbit; *ibid.*

3. Jinkaku's second son.

4. The *Aokata monjo* transcription divides the clauses by a comma so that the meaning is as follows: "Although Urabe within Ojika Island was released by Fujiwara Ietaka to his heir Tarō, owing to disturbances, a retrocession was in order. . . ." However, no subsequent document refers to a transfer at this time *from* Ietaka; see, e.g., Document 107 below. The comma placement in the *KI* version (which I have followed) seems clearly correct.

5. It would seem, then, that Urabe had earlier been conveyed to Michitaka, was transferred to Ietaka, and was now being transferred back to Michitaka. This may be true, though later documents refer simply to a release to Ietaka, followed by the redisposition described here; see Document 107 below, and *Aokata monjo*, 1259/7/16 Kantō gechijō an, *Aokata monjo*, 1: 17–18, doc. 16.

6. Jinkaku died in 1213.

7. This addendum could either have been added to an existing copy or made part of a new copy.

DOCUMENT 18

The Bakufu Acknowledges a Divided Jitō Shiki, 1209

The Kamakura edict presented here is the very earliest to acknowledge the partibility of a *jitō shiki*. Hitherto land itself, along with movables, could be divided according to any scheme desired by a donor, but *shiki*, involving "offices" that had been granted by a higher authority, were impartible. The case presented here refers to a disposition that had split the property component of a *shiki* between two persons but, apparently, had said nothing about the splitting of *shiki*. The Bakufu, however, rendered a verdict in which it alluded to a one-half *shiki*. It was a portentous decision since, by mid-century, offices were being broken apart and shares freely dispersed. The Bakufu certified such dispositions—and in the process promoted a fragmentation of its own military stewardships. The parceling of other kinds of *shiki* followed, and a major buttress of the hierarchically arranged land system now came under attack.

The chancellery of the shogun's house directs: to the residents of Uchidono village, a Munakata Shrine land, Chikuzen Province.

That the depredations of Konomi *kannushi* Ujinushi shall forthwith cease, and that the priest Gyōsai shall hold a one-half (*hanbun*) *jitō shiki*.[1]

[Gyōsai stated:] "When my parents were alive, a one-half share of the paddy, upland, mountains, and fields of this village was split off and conveyed to Gyōsai. Nevertheless, Ujinushi disregarded this release,[2] and, neglecting an oath in his own hand (*jihitsu no kishō*),[3] wantonly committed encroachments."[4] If this is true, it is most disquieting. Forthwith, Ujinushi's depredations are to cease, and Gyōsai shall hold the *jitō shiki*.[5] Moreover, in accordance with the release, two *chō* out of the two *chō* five *tan* of *jitō* stipend paddy (*kyūden*) shall constitute Gyōsai's income share (*tokubun*).[6] The command is thus. Wherefore, this order.

      3d year of Jōgen [1209], 7th month, 28th day[7]

                            anzu, Kiyohara seal
                            chikeji, Koremune seal

ryō, zusho no jō, Kiyohara seal
bettō, sho hakase, Nakahara ason[8]
ukonoe shōgen, Minamoto ason seal

Suruga no kami, Taira ason seal
san-i, Nakahara ason seal

SOURCE: *Munakata jinja monjo*, 1209/7/28 shōgun ke mandokoro kudashibumi an, *Munakata gunshi*, 2: 146 (*KI*, 3: 381–82, doc. 1797).
    1. This is the earliest extant reference to a fractional *jitō shiki*. Though no other documents refer to Ujinushi and Gyōsai, it seems possible (see below) that they were brothers. The other one-half *jitō shiki* might then have gone to Ujinushi. None of this is discussed in *Munakata jinja shi*, 2: 656, which treats the present document.
    2. Unfortunately, not extant.
    3. This pledge (i.e., quitclaim) may have taken the form of a cosignature on the release to Gyōsai; or it could have been a separate document. Both practices were common for siblings.
    4. This is the end of Gyōsai's complaint to the Bakufu.
    5. That is, a one-half *jitō shiki*.
    6. Does this mean that Ujinushi received a 20 percent share from the stipend portion accompanying Gyōsai's one-half *jitō shiki*? Or had Ujinushi received but 20 percent of the stipend paddy of the whole *jitō shiki*?
    7. Three years earlier the Bakufu had prohibited violations against Uchidono and one other village, but other persons were involved and there is no reference to a *jitō shiki*; *Munakata jinja monjo*, 1206/7/14 Kantō kudashibumi, *Munakata gunshi*, 2: 144 (*DKR*, doc. 62).
    8. Nakahara Moritoshi, for a brief period the director of the shogun's chancellery. For a discussion of the significance of this, see *DKR*, 77–78.

DOCUMENT 19

An Estate Officer Dies Intestate, 1218

When *shiki* holders died intestate, their interests in property were increasingly succeeded to by their widows. In effect, the latter became the interpreters of their late husbands' "wills." Sometimes this proceeded smoothly, as seems to be the case here. But in many other instances sons and daughters chafed under an arrangement that might have been threatening to them. When the widow happened to be a stepmother, as was so commonly the case, the conditions for major trouble were now present.

Conveyed: the local managership (*gesu shiki*) of Kanshinji Estate.[1]

The aforesaid *shiki* is the hereditary office from generations past of the late priest Enson. However, he suddenly contracted an unexpected illness and died intestate. Consequently, in accordance with his expressed desire while he was still alive, Ōe Aneko, as his widow (*goke*), assumed jurisdiction. Conveyance of this *shiki* is now made to Ryūtamaru.[2] It is thus.

6th year of Kenpō [1218], 4th month, 28th day

widow, Ōe (monogram)

SOURCE: *Kanshinji monjo*, 1218/4/28 goke Ōe yuzurijō, *KI*, 4: 208–81, doc. 2369.
   1. In Kawachi Province.
   2. Ryūtamaru is evidently the couple's son, still a minor. Unfortunately, we do not know how much time has passed since Enson's death or whether the widow is making a free choice of heirs.

DOCUMENTS 20–23

The Bakufu Sides with a Widow Against a First Son; the Inheritance Becomes Confused, 1220, 1238, 1241

Since there was no fully standardized practice regarding the disposition of unbequeathed property, the Bakufu sometimes stepped in only to reverse itself later when it realized it had erred. In 1213, a major vassal lost his life in battle and Kamakura passed his property to his eldest son, thereby sparking a lawsuit by the widow. The latter argued for an interim authority by herself with the inheritance promised eventually to the son. The Bakufu agreed with this reasoning, but in the ensuing years the son in question dropped from sight. The widow now settled the property on another son, leading to a dispute among rival siblings, a compromise, and a follow-up Bakufu confirmation. Here was one instance in which a widow's own arbitrariness appears to have been the major cause of discord.

20

That the *jitō shiki* of Okuyama Estate, Echigo Province, and southern Fukazawa *gō*, Sagami Province, shall forthwith be administered (*sata*) by the widow-nun (*goke ama*) of Takai *hyōe no jō* Shigemochi.[1]

The aforesaid person has stated:[2] "Both of these places are lands which should be held (*chigyō*) by the mother nun. Their entrustment instead to our son, Tarō Shigetsuna,[3] is vigorously challenged. After the nun's possession (*chigyō*),[4] release shall be made [to him]."[5] In accordance with this petition, administration (*sata*) for the present shall lie with the nun. By this command, it is so decreed.

2d year of Jōkyū [1220], 12th month, 10th day

Mutsu no kami, Taira (monogram)

21

Conveyed: the Mandokoro sector (*mandokoro-jō*) of Okuyama Estate,[6] Echigo Province.

The aforesaid place is conveyed to my son Saburō.[7] Hereafter and for all time, there are to be no disturbances. Regarding boundaries, since this is not a new matter,[8] there is no need for particulars. Accordingly, our conveyance is thus.

4th year of Katei [1238], 4th month, 4th day

Taira no uji ama (monogram)

22

Conveyed: the Kurokawa sector of Okuyama Estate, Echigo Province.

The aforesaid place is conveyed to my son Saburō. However, during the lifetime (*ichigo*) of his elder sister, the nun, there are to be no disturbances whatsoever.[9] After that, as Saburō's possession, there is to be no trouble. Regarding boundaries, since this is not a new matter, there is no need for particulars. Our conveyance is thus.

4th year of Katei [1238], 4th month, 4th day

Taira no uji ama (monogram)

23

The chancellery of the shogun's house directs: to Taira Tokimochi.[10] That the *jitō shiki* shall forthwith be held for the residences (*ya-shiki*) and directly-owned fields (*tezukuri*) of southern Fukazawa [*gō*], Sagami Province—boundaries appear in the con-veyance[11]—and for the Mandokoro and Kurokawa sectors of Okuyama Estate, Echigo Province.

The aforesaid person shall exercise possession under these *shiki*, in ac-cordance with the mother's three releases—two from the 4th year of Katei [1238], 4th month, 4th day, one from the 2d year of Ninji [1241], 4th month, 17th day—as well as with a compromise record (*wayojō*) of the siblings (*kyōdai*) from the 2d year of Tenpuku [1234], 11th month, 8th day.[12] The command is thus. Wherefore, this order.[13]

anzu, sakon no shōsō, Sugano
chikeji, danjōchū, Kiyohara (monogram)

ryō, saemon no shōjō, Fujiwara (monogram)
bettō, saki no Musashi no kami, Taira ason (monogram)
kazue no kami, Nakahara ason (monogram)
saki no Mino no kami, Fujiwara ason
saki no Mutsu no kami, Minamoto ason
saki no Kai no kami, Ōe ason
Musashi no kami, Taira ason
san-i, Fujiwara ason (monogram)

SOURCES: Document 20: *Nakajō ke monjo*, 1220/12/10 Kantō gechijō, *Okuyama-no-shō shiryōshū*, p. 98 (*KI*, 4: 408, doc. 2688). Document 21: *ibid.*, 1238/4/4 Taira no uji ama yuzurijō, *Okuyama-no-shō shiryōshū*, p. 98 (*KI*, 7: 376, doc. 5229). Document 22: *Miura Wada monjo*, 1238/4/4 Taira no uji ama yuzurijō, *Okuyama-no-shō shiryōshū*, p. 1 (*KI*, 7: 376, doc. 5228). Document 23: *Nakajō ke monjo*, 1241/5/1 shōgun ke mandokoro kudashibumi, *Okuyama-no-shō shiryōshū*, p. 99 (*KI*, 8: 257, doc. 5827).

1. The widow-nun here was a cousin of her late husband, who had died on the Bakufu side in the Wada Rebellion of 1213. Her father, Wada Munezane, had received the *jitō shiki* from his elder brother, Yoshimochi, who was the father of Shigemochi. See Document 12, n. 1, *Miura-Wada shi ichizoku sō keizu*, in *Okuyama-no-shō shiryōshū*, p. 31 and *AK* 1213/5/2.

2. What follows is the gist of the widow-nun's suit against one of her sons.

3. I.e., by the Bakufu.

4. I.e., after her death.

5. In fact, as we will see, the nun never did make good on this promise; Tarō Shigetsuna (and his line) disappear from view, and the nun-mother's heir was another son, Saburō Tokimochi; see below. Shigetsuna does not even appear in the clan genealogy.

6. This probably refers to the region of the estate's administrative headquarters (*mandokoro*).

7. I.e., Tokimochi, the future household head.

8. The boundaries are well known.

9. In other words, the widow was making a one-generation disposition to an elder daughter.

10. This is the Saburō of Documents 21 and 22.

11. *Nakajō ke monjo*, 1241/4/17 Taira no uji ama yuzurijō, *Okuyama-no-shō shiryōshū*, p. 99. This release to Saburō Tokimochi contains the complex border dimensions of residence areas, etc., within southern Fukazawa *gō*.

12. This last document, unfortunately, is not extant. Presumably it would have helped unravel the mystery of what happened to Tarō Shigetsuna. Did the compromise occur upon his death? What was the mother's role in determining the nature of the agreement? What were the terms of the accord? At any rate, with the present edict, the Bakufu was confirming an arrangement very different from that which it had approved in 1220.

13. In the next generation, Saburō Tokimochi divided Okuyama Estate into three sectors and granted *jitō* authority to separate grandsons. He also granted small portions to two nephews. See Tokimochi's releases in *Okuyama-no-shō shiryōshū*, pp. 2–3, 100–101, 188–89, and also Document 118 below.

DOCUMENT 24

The Bakufu Confirms the Transmission of a Jitō Shiki from a Mother to a Daughter, 1221

As surprising as it may seem, the Bakufu early on began confirming mother-to-daughter conveyances of *jitō shiki*, the country's elite military titles. In the present instance, a woman's release to her daughter was certified—quite routinely—by Kamakura. At the same time, the bequest itself was of a type that later became standard (though in 1221 it was still innovative): following the daughter's death, the inheritance was to go to her brother (see n. 3). In other words, the daughter could not alienate the property; its inheritance was entailed to a male. Of special note is that the *jitō* offices involved were clearly in the mother's line—though how they got there is not explained.

That the *jitō shiki* of Yata and Ikewata, Kazusa Province, be possessed in heredity by the eldest daughter (*chakujo*), the nun Tomizuka, in accordance with the release of the Yata nun.

According to the letter of conveyance:[1] "As the ancestral private holdings of the nun,[2] these places are hereby released to our eldest daughter, the nun Tomizuka. After [the lifetime of] the nun Tomizuka, they shall be possessed by Jōkan."[3] In accordance with the conveyance of the Yata nun,[4] Jōkan shall succeed to these *shiki* after the hereditary tenure of the nun Tomizuka. By this command, it is so decreed.

3d year of Jōkyū [1221], 11th month, 21st day

Mutsu no kami, Taira seal

SOURCE: *Fūken monjo san*, 1221/11/21 Kantō gechijō an, *KI*, 5: 70, doc. 2888.
1. *Ibid.*, 1221/4/5 Yata ama yuzurijō an, *KI*, 5: 11, doc. 2736.
2. That is, the mother. The *jitō shiki* in question, then, were in the female line; they had not been transferred by the present donor's husband.
3. Identity unknown, but very likely Tomizuka's younger brother.
4. It is noteworthy that the Bakufu does not identify her in relation to her husband, i.e., as a wife or widow. This is because the husband had no involvement with these *jitō shiki*.

DOCUMENT 25

A Priest's Disciple Challenges an In-Family Inheritance, 1222

It was not only military titles that were being deeded to women; priestly and other administrative offices were similarly being transferred. In the present instance, a priest selected his younger sister as his heir, and she for her part chose her own son on the basis of this son's filiality. At this point, however, a priest-disciple of the original donor came forward and advanced his claim for the *shiki* in question. In denying this challenge the adjudicating authority enunciated an important principle: that a claimant's physical holding of documents of inheritance was no substitute for an explicit conveyance to the claimant. The original donor had transferred his legacy to his sister; the inheritance therefore properly lay in her line. The Bakufu could scarcely have said it any more effectively.

The chancellery of the Hōrenga-in directs: to the priests of Kagami-no-miya Shrine-temple (*jingūji*).[1]
> Appointment to the chief priest's position (*zasu shiki*) of Tono-bara Temple.[2]

"The aforesaid *shiki* is a title conveyed in heredity to the priest Gikaku. When he became seriously ill, however, he released it to his younger sister, Fujitsu *no uji*, and she possessed it for many years without incident. Then, owing to the sincerity of her son Fujii Sadashige's filial piety (*kōyō*), the conveyance was made to him, along with the sequence of proof records. But now, the priest Genjitsu, claiming to be a disciple (*montei*) of Gikaku and without holding any specific written promise (*keijō*), has interfered."[3] *Shiki* such as this one are subject to hereditary succession (*tetsugi no sōden*). Thus, even if original documents (*hon monjo*) had been held, in the absence of a written promise they would not constitute valid proof (*shōmon*). In pursuance of the principle of hereditary succession, Sadashige shall hold [this *shiki*], and the fixed religious dues and other obligations will be discharged without negligence. It is commanded thus. Shrine officers and temple priests shall know this and not be remiss. Wherefore, this order.
> 1st year of Jōō [1222], 6th month,   day
>> kumon hosshi, Gōshun
> jōza hokkyō shōnin-i (monogram)
> jishu daihosshi (monogram)
> tsuina daihosshi

SOURCE: *Kyōto daigaku shozō monjo*, 1222/6 Hōrenga-in mandokoro kudashibumi, *KI*, 5: 114–15, doc. 2972.

1. In Hizen Province.

2. The exact relationship of these religious institutions is not clear, though Tono-bara was either a local branch or subchapel of Kagami-no-miya, which itself was a subsidiary of Hōrenga-in.

3. This marks the end of the plaintiff's (Sadashige's) petition against Genjitsu.

DOCUMENT 26

The Bakufu Settles an Inheritance Dispute, 1222

The inheritance disputes regularly coming before the Bakufu often obliged it to probe the distant past for answers. The case described here involved a challenge by a latecomer who apparently argued that no explicit release had transferred property to the woman whose line then came to possess it. The proprietor, however, had confirmed the transfer anyway, and many years had passed without incident. The Bakufu reaffirmed this arrangement on the grounds that the challenger had acknowledged this long possession and was lodging his suit only now. This case was heard in 1222. Ten years later, when the Bakufu issued its historic law code, the Goseibai Shikimoku, a statute of limitations was included, which intended to block suits of the kind adjudicated here.

That the false claim (*hiron*) of Masahide shall forthwith cease, and that Usa Tsugusuke shall possess Koinumaru *myō*, in Ejima-no-befu, Buzen Province, an Usa Shrine land.

According to a report (*kanjō*) of the 3d month, 28th day last by the [*dazaifu's*] board of inquiry (*monchūjo*): "The statements of the two sides contained many details in the matter of Koinumaru *myō* of Ejima-no-befu.[1] In brief, however, although Hiroko did not receive the conveyance (*tetsugi*) from her father Masataka,[2] after his death in the 3d year of Chōkan [1165][3] she did come to hold the [*myō's*] original proof records (*hon shōmon*)[4] and was granted a 'marginal confirmation' (*gedai*) by the [Usa Shrine] priest-administrator (*daigūji*).[5] For a period of more than 50 years after the 3d year of Chōkan, Hiroko and her daughter Mitsuko—mother of Tsugusuke—enjoyed possession of this *myō*,[6] a condition already acknowledged by Masahide. Even beyond that, from the very beginning Masahide had no easy basis for launching a suit (*sōron*)."[7] In accordance with this report, Tsugusuke shall exercise possession over Koinumaru *myō* of Ejima-no-befu.[8] By this command, it is so decreed.

　　1st year of Jōō [1222], 7th month, 7th day

　　　　　　　　　　　　　　　　　　Mutsu no kami, Taira seal

SOURCE: *Masunaga ke monjo*, 1222/7/7 Kantō gechijō an, *KBSS*, 1: 24, doc. 27 (*KI*, 5: 115–16, doc. 2974).

　　1. The original petition of Usa Tsugusuke, the winner in the suit, is extant; *ibid.*, 1221/8 Usa Tsugusuke mōshijō, *KI*, 5: 43–44, doc. 2824. In it, we learn that Koinumaru *myō* was originally a holding of Tsugusuke's great-grandfather, who was followed in that tenure by his eldest daughter, Hiroko, in the 1160s. Hiroko's brother, Michimasa, apparently acquiesced in this. In 1188, however, her claim to the *myō* was challenged by Michimasa's son, Masanao (the present disputant, Masahide's, father), who, upon losing, acknowledged the possession of his aunt. Six years later, Hiroko deeded the *myō* to her own daughter, Mitsuko, the mother of Tsugusuke, victor in the current suit. In fact, Tsugusuke's petition for redress dealt with several land units and led eventually to a pair of edicts—the present document (treating Koinumaru *myō*) and a later one (*ibid.*, 1222/11 Kantō gechijō an, *KI*, 5: 132–33, doc. 3018).

　　2. According to Tsugusuke's brief (n. 1), Masataka, who was the acting priest-administrator (*gon no daigūji*) of Usa Shrine in the 1160s, had actually designated his eldest son Michimasa as his successor; see n. 4.

　　3. The 1221/8 petition records the death as having occurred in the 2d year of Chōkan, i.e., 1164.

　　4. Referred to in the 1221/8 petition as "*shidai kugen.*" This suggests that Hiroko came into possession of the entitlements (*kugen*) for Koinumaru *myō* even as her brother became house head.

　　5. The *gedai*—a validation recorded in the blank margin space at the end of a petition—was added to *Masunaga ke monjo*, 1166/9/25 Usa Hiroko ge an, *HI*, 7: 2677, doc. 3400. She also received a confirmation from the *dazaifu*; *ibid.*, 1166/9/25 dazaifu mandokoro chō an, *HI*, 7: 2677, doc. 3401.

　　6. See n. 1. Yet Mitsuko's possession was not without incident. According to Tsugusuke's brief, his mother actually lost the *myō* for five years, a condition put right by the Bakufu in 1220: *Masunaga ke monjo*, 1220/9/3 Kantō gechijō an, *KI*, 4: 394, doc. 2645.

　　7. That is, since Tsugusuke was the direct heir of Hiroko and Mitsuko, legitimate holders of the *myō*.

　　8. And so he did, though not without challenges along the way. See *Masunaga ke monjo*, 1244/4/27 Rokuhara migyōsho an, *KI* 9: 78, doc. 6311. Tsugusuke's own release—to his wife—was dated 1251/7/19 (not extant) and was confirmed by the Bakufu the following year: *Kongō monjo*, 1252/8/15 shōgun ke mandokoro kudashibumi, *KI*, 10: 328, doc. 7468.

DOCUMENT 27

The Dazaifu Resolves a Vassal-Related Inheritance Dispute but Defers to Kamakura, 1222

As mentioned before, a father's decision to name a younger son as principal heir involved considerable sacrifice by elder brothers. In the case presented here, an elder brother received an inheritance from his dying father—but it was not the main inheritance. Nevertheless, he claimed to have served as representative for his father and to have been recognized locally as his father's heir apparent. The document presented here, a judgment edict of the Kyushu government-general, provides an unusually graphic account of a deathbed bequest in the company of children who were worrying less about their father than about their inheritance shares. But the document's real importance lies in its rejection of the older son / younger son distinction as a factor affecting a father's free choice concerning the disposition of property. In addition, the term *sōryō*—house head—appears for the first time as an equivalent for *chakushi*—principal heir. Though the equivalency was articulated by the loser in the suit, the connection between the two terms—a principal heir acknowledged as the next house head—would quickly become the accepted usage.

Seal

The *shugo* headquarters[1] directs: to Isshi Jirō Kiramu.
    Instructions in two matters.[2]

Item: In the matter of Kiramu's complaint that his elder brother, Yamamoto Shirō Ken, in violation of the conveyance of their late father Kasan,[3] had seized uplands in the Kikushi-no-hara area of Isshi Village, Matsuura Estate; had plundered harvested wheat; and had undertaken to convert inherited paddy into a privately-owned administrative unit (*betsumyō*).

    In response to Kiramu's letter of accusation in this matter the two sides were summoned to trial. According to Kiramu's petition: "When our late father Kasan was alive, a written promise (*keijō*) was granted noting that the holdings called Osogi and Tomo within Isshi were to have been conveyed to Kiramu—child's name Kumaichi.[4] Likewise, in the 2d year of Jōgen [1208], intercalated 4th month, 10th day, Kiramu was named heir-designate (*chakushi*) and was deeded various paddy and upland,[5] accompanied by a [prior] edict (*onkudashibumi*) of the Kamakura lord and the sequence of hereditary proof records.[6] Subsequently, in the 1st month of the present year, Kasan became gravely ill, and various parcels among his holdings were allocated to his sons and daughters. At that juncture, Yamamoto Shirō Ken had settled upon him 10 *chō* of paddy, 3 homestead areas (*sono*) and 1 *chō* of exempt paddy (*menden*)—the *kumon* [officer's] stipend share (*kumon kyū*).[7] At present, though in possession of this conveyance, he has seized the wheat harvest from the Kikushi-no-hara area within Kiramu's sector, and concocted a scheme to disengage a small parcel of *myō* land from the original Fukunaga *myō*, converting it into a separate *myō* called Tokumoto. All of this is under the pretext of his being the elder brother, acts that are without justification"—so paraphrased.

According to Ken's defense statement: "The offspring of our late father Kasan *nyūdō* consisted of 3 sons and 3 daughters. However, many years have passed since the death of Genta Nanoru, the principal heir (*chakushi*).[8] Since then, the fact that Ken has been the principal heir is known by everyone in the Matsuura house.[9] Thus, when the call was made last winter to stand palace guard duty in Kyoto,[10] [Ken] set out for the capital in his capacity as deputy (*daikan*) for his father. However, on the 6th day of the 1st month while staying over in Imazu,[11] he was informed of the gravity of his father's condition, and he returned to Matsuura on the 14th. On the 18th day the father Kasan took priestly vows, and that evening Kiramu claimed that a document done in his own hand was in fact a release written by the priest.[12] Although [Kiramu] hoped to have Ken countersign it, he did not apply his seal. Then, on the 19th day, Kasan *nyūdō* died, and out of the more than 40 *chō* making up the Isshi [homelands], Ken's share was only 10 *chō* of paddy land and 2 or 3 local households (*zaike*), while Kiramu, a younger brother, seized the rest—more than 30 *chō* of paddy plus many tens of local households and movables within the Tomo Bay area. Now a suit exists, even though Kiramu, besides everything else, has cunningly broken precedent and committed violations by placing upland and local households belonging to Ken within his own sector of Kikushi-no-hara. [But] the present dispute over borders is [really] the least important matter. In essence it was neither our father's intention, nor is it a principle of law, for a younger brother, Kiramu, to be house chieftain (*sōryō*),[13] when Ken himself had been principal heir (*chakushi*). How can seizures take place on the basis of writings that are falsified? The paddy field total as well as the movable wealth should be equitably partitioned"—so paraphrased.

In response thereof the merits (*rihi*) of the two sides were duly examined. Deeds of conveyance were drawn up and distributed by Kasan *nyūdō* on two occasions, once much earlier and then again during

Jōgen [1208]. Likewise, on the occasion of parceling the paddy and uplands among the offspring when Kasan was on his deathbed, the share released to Ken was clearly 10 *chō* of paddy, 3 homestead areas (*sono*), and 1 *chō* of exempt paddy—the *kumon*'s stipend share. Indeed, the disposition of property while parents are alive depends not on the distinction between older and younger (*chakusho*), but rather only on the discretion of the possessor (*zaishu*). Why, then, should Ken, who has received a bequest from Kasan, pursue an argument calling himself an elder brother? Forthwith, Ken is to terminate his false claim (*hiron*) and is to possess his 10 *chō* of paddy, 3 local households (*zaike*),[14] and 1 *chō* of exempt paddy—the *kumon*'s stipend share. However, as regards the effort to disengage allocated paddy from the original *myō* and establish a separate *myō*, neither side has furnished any actual proof records (*shōmon*). Thus the issues remain cloudy and are difficult [to judge]. In essence, however, the customs of Matsuura Estate as a whole should be followed. . . .[15]

Though the foregoing matters should have been reported to the Kantō, a decree is now given, in accordance with [Kantō] decisions (*goseibai*), in order to terminate the current dispute and end despoilments. However, in the event any grievances should remain, the chancellery of the Kamakura lord should be petitioned and a judgment will be rendered there.[16] It is thus.

1st year of Jōō [1222], 12th month, 23d day

> taigen, Ōnakatomi ason seal
> kandai, Nakahara ason seal
> kandai, Fujiwara ason seal
> kandai, Koremune ason seal
> kandai ken kumon, Minamoto seal
> kandai, atae seal
> kandai ken kumon, Sugano seal
> kandai, Minamoto seal
> kandai, Ono seal

SOURCE: *Isshi monjo*, 1222/12/23 dazaifu shugosho kudashibumi an, *Hirado Matsuura ke shiryō*, pp. 146–48, doc. 6 (*KI*, 5: 136–38, doc. 3032).

1. It is possible that the reference here is to the Hizen Province *shugo* headquarters; cf. the citation in *Hirado Matsuura ke shiryō* and in *DNS*, Series 5, 1: 661–65. Volumes compiled by Prof. Takeuchi, however (*KI* and *Dazaifu-Dazaifu Tenmangū shiryō*, 7: 373–77), suggest the *dazaifu*, and I believe this is correct. It was during this period that the *dazaifu* was actively assisting Kamakura in the expediting of Kyushu judicial cases (see Document 26).

2. Only the first of the two matters is translated here.

3. *Isshi monjo*, 1208/int. 4/10 Minamoto Kasan yuzurijō an, *Hirado Matsuura ke shiryō*, pp. 144–46, doc. 5 (*KI*, 3: 354–56, doc. 1738).

4. Conveyed to Kiramu, in other words, while he was still a child. The background here is not clear.

5. This claim is borne out by Kasan's release of that date, cited in n. 3.

6. The Kamakura edict is not extant, but conveyances from 1102(2) and 1169 do survive; *Hirado Matsuura ke shiryō,* pp. 142–44, docs. 1–2, 4.

7. This last phrase is in half-size characters. Land designated as "*kyū*" would have been tax-exempt (i.e., "*men*").

8. Kasan's conveyance deed of 1208 (n. 3) refers to the early death of the heir-designate.

9. This is directly contradicted by Kasan's release of 1208, which named Kiramu as *chakushi.*

10. The so-called *ōbanyaku* service fell periodically on all Kamakura vassals.

11. In Kyushu's Chikuzen Province.

12. This is a difficult sentence. An alternative reading might be ". . . claimed that a document done by a priestly scribe was in fact [the father's] release."

13. This is the earliest reference I have found to the use of "sōryō" as "house head."

14. *Zaike* (local households) and *sono* (homestead areas) are thus used interchangeably here. Much scholarly dispute surrounds both terms.

15. The second "item" follows here and is a dispute over a residential compound (*yashiki*) between Kiramu and his father's brother. Since this uncle had cosigned the father's 1208 conveyance to Kiramu, victory was awarded to Kiramu.

16. There is no indication that this was ever necessary. In the next generation, Kiramu, who in the meantime was appointed administrator (*bettō*) of Matsuura Estate, transmitted his holdings to his own chosen heir, Saburō. See *Isshi monjo,* 1238/12 Matsuura-no-shō bettō shiki buninjō, 1252/3/27 Minamoto Kiramu yuzurijō, in *Hirado matsuura ke shiryō,* pp. 149–50, docs. 9, 11.

DOCUMENT 28

A Western Province Vassal Receives, Then Conveys, Confirmatory-Type Jitō Shiki, 1223

Warriors who were natives to western provinces were granted *jitō shiki* much less frequently than were their eastern counterparts. Yet when such awards were made, they became as instantly heritable as those made to easterners. The decision to convey the *jitō shiki* to a son soon after a vassal received it was often sound strategy—as may have been the case here. Nevertheless, the Bakufu did not confirm this transfer until after the death of the donor.

Conveyed: the *jitō shiki* for Mebogaki and Takadanohara-no-befu[1] and that for Nagata *gō,* Aki Province

As reclaimed lands, the aforesaid *befu* and Nagata *gō* have, for many generations, been hereditary possessions. By virtue thereof, a *jitō shiki* investiture (*onkudashibumi*) was entrusted to us in the 4th year of Kenpō [1216], 7th month, 16th day,[2] and there has been no change in that possession [since then]. Nevertheless, permanent release is now made to our son Takatōji Tamesada.[3] Let there be no disturbances against it. The shrine services and other obligations shall be performed without negligence, pursuant to precedent. As proof for the future, our release is thus.[4]

2d year of Jōō [1223], 3d month, 20th day

shami, Hōa seal

SOURCE: *Seijun shiryō gaihen*, 1223/3/20 shami Hōa yuzurijō an, *Hagi han batsuetsu roku*, 2: 248, doc. 64 (*KI*, 5: 178, doc. 3076).

1. Normally, lands added to a *shōen* after initial incorporation.

2. See *Hagi han batsuetsu roku*, 1216/7/16 shōgun ke mandokoro kudashibumi an, *Hagi han batsuetsu roku*, 2: 427–28, doc. 63 (*KI*, 4: 225, doc. 2252).

3. I.e., Saeki Tamesada. The donor here is Saeki Tamehiro, bearing the same surname as the prominent Aki family that earlier had served the Taira. Whether they were in fact related is open to question.

4. The Bakufu's confirmation of this release did not come until 16 years later: *Seijun shiryō gaihen*, 1239/7/1 shōgun ke mandokoro kudashibumi an, *Hagi han batsuetsu roku*, 2: 428, doc. 65 (*KI*, 8: 53, doc. 5447). A document of a century later reproduces the entire sequence of earlier records and shows that, following the initial appointment in 1216, releases and shogunal confirmations followed one another thereafter; *ibid.*, 1341/4/23 Ashikaga Tadayoshi funshitsujō an, *Hagi han batsuetsu roku*, 2: 430–32, doc. 72.

DOCUMENTS 29–31

A Jitō Names His Third Son Principal Heir, 1223, 1224

When sons predeceased their parents it tended to confuse the pattern of inheritance. In the present instance, the eldest son died young, the second son entered the priesthood, and the third son became the principal heir. A fourth son was given an allotment, as was a grandson—the son of the dead first son. As we shall see, grandsons came to be included in wills with increasing frequency during the course of the thirteenth century.

29

Conveyed: one of our landed holdings:

The *jitō shiki* of Niho Estate, Suō Province.

The aforesaid *shiki* is hereby deeded to Taira Shigesuke. It is released in order to ensure future administration. A dispensation (*goseibai*)[1] of the shogun's house shall be sought. It is thus.

2d year of Jōō [1223], 5th month, 26th day

jitō, shami Sainin[2] seal

30

The *jitō shiki* of Niho Estate, Suō Province, is conveyed to Taira-no-ko Saburō *saemon no jō* Shigesuke, who is designated my principal heir (*chakushi*). Because Jirō Tsunemura[3] has entered the priesthood and must attend to the service of our lord, the transfer of Tsunetomi *ho* is made to Shirō Shigetsugu.[4] In the event any of these sons should seek to create disturbances, he shall be considered unfilial (*fukō*). For the future we record this conveyance with our own hand.

3d year of Jōō [1224], 5th month, 29th day

jitō, shami Sainin seal

31

That Taira Shigesuke shall forthwith hold the *jitō shiki* for Niho Estate, Suō Province.

The aforesaid person shall hold this *shiki*, in accordance with the release of his father, Shigetsune *hosshi*. Also, there is to be no challenge to Fukano Village, which is Shigetsuna's share.[5] By this command, it is so decreed.

3d year of Jōō [1224], 11th month, 30th day[6]

Musashi no kami, Taira seal

SOURCES: Document 29: *Miura ke monjo*, 1223/5/26 jitō Sainin yuzurijō an, *DNK*, *iewake 14*, p. 285, doc. 1.4 (*KI*, 5: 204, doc. 3109). Document 30: *ibid.*, 1224/5/29 jitō Sainin yuzurijō an, *DNK*, *iewake 14*, p. 286, doc. 1.5 (*KI*, 5: 280, doc. 3242). Document 31: *ibid.*, 1224/11/30 Kantō gechijō an, *DNK*, *iewake 14*, p. 285, doc. 1.3 (*KI*, 5: 317, doc. 3316).

1. I.e., a confirmation.

2. Sainin (Shigetsune) received the *jitō shiki* for Niho Estate in 1197; in 1210 the Bakufu reappointed him; *Miura ke monjo*, 1197/2/24 saki no utaishō ke mandokoro kudashibumi an (*KB*, doc. 13); 1210/2/9 shōgun ke mandokoro kudashibumi an, *DNK*, *iewake 14*, pp. 283–84, docs. 1.1, 1.2.

3. The second son; *Miura shi keizu*, in *DNK*, *iewake 14*, p. 471.

4. Shigetsugu was the fourth son of Sainin; *ibid.*, p. 473. Tsunetomi *ho* was granted to Sainin at the same time as Niho Estate; see n. 2.

5. This conveyance to Shigetsuna, the son of Sainin's eldest son, Shigenao, is what

suggests that Shigenao was dead; it explains the deeding of the *jitō shiki* to the third son, Shigesuke. *Miura shi keizu,* in *DNK, iewake 14,* p. 471.

6. Five years later, the newly installed shogun issued a personal confirmation (*sode-han kudashibumi*) of the present Hōjō-signed writ (*gechijō*); *Miura ke monjo,* 1229/3/22 shōgun Fujiwara Yoritsune kudashibumi an, *DNK, iewake 14,* pp. 294–95, doc. 1.6. For the next generation's succession, see Documents 93–94.

DOCUMENT 32

A Priest Conveys Land Whose Sale and Other Documents Have Been Stolen, 1224

The heritability of any property was a product of lawful, not necessarily long, possession. Thus, property acquired by purchase was no different from property received by bequest. What made such transactions secure was the possession of appropriate documents. Here we encounter a case in which documents have been confiscated under cover of war. More commonly, records were destroyed in fires or were stolen by rival claimants. At any rate, the holder here, his property at risk, was attempting to transmit his holding and in the process establish a new legality for it.

Conveyed: paddy fields, one *tan* in total; name omitted.
    Within Kuragaki Village, Nose District, Settsu Province.

The aforesaid paddy was purchased during the 2d year of Kenpō [1214] from the former Bungo governor at a cash price of four *kan,* 500 *mon.* However, during the Jōkyū period, in the midst of the countrywide upheaval (*kokudo tairan*), the relevant proof records were requisitioned and seized. Notwithstanding, by virtue of internal and external cause (*innen*),[1] conveyance is made to Noma *uemon* Shirō.[2] As proof for the future, our deed of release is thus.[3]
    1st year of Gennin [1224], 2d month, 3d day

                                    sō, Rishin (monogram)

SOURCE: *Katsuodera monjo,* 1224/2/3 sō Rishin yuzurijō, *Katsuodera monjo,* p. 195, doc. 238 (*KI,* 5: 326, doc. 3328).
    1. An important Buddhist concept.
    2. The relationship between donor and recipient is unknown. The recipient's name, however, is not that of a priest and would therefore not seem to be that of a disciple.
    3. Takeuchi speculates in *KI* that the correct date may be the 12th month, since the period name Gennin had not yet been designated in the 2d month.

DOCUMENTS 33–34

A Release to a Grandson Is Challenged by a Local Rival, 1226, 1228

Here we see an explicit conveyance to a grandson, a situation induced by the death in battle of the grandson's father. Less than two years later a challenger appeared, leading to a suit by the grandson, a failure on the part of the challenger to appear for trial, and ultimate vindication for the holder.

33

Conveyed: hereditary proof records for Nagano *ho* [and][1] Shigetomo [Village][2]

[To:] Fujiwara Morikage

On the occasion of the Kyoto disturbance (*sōdō*),[3] Kagetaka's eldest son Nagano Saburō Iekage was executed by Hayashi Jirō Ietsuna.[4] Iekage's eldest son Nagano Jirō Morikage is therefore deeded the several proof records. In preservation of Kagetaka's legacy (*chigyō no ato*), his descendants shall, without fail, exercise this authority. It is thus.

    2d year of Karoku [1226], 2d month, 18th day

                       Fujiwara Kagetaka seal

34

In the matter of Shigetomo Village (*mura*) within Nomi Estate, Kaga Province.

On the occasion of a hearing in the 10th month of last year into Enuma Jirō Kageyoshi's claim that he held a deed of release,[5] the suit by Nagano Jirō Morikage argued that Kageyoshi was lying and that his own hereditary possession should be unchanged. [Kageyoshi] was repeatedly advised to appear for trial, but even now he has failed to do so. Therefore, Morikage shall retain possession as of old. If Kageyoshi should still bear some grievance, let him appear for judgment forthwith.[6] It is so decreed.

    2d year of Antei [1228], 8th month, 17th day

                    Echigo no kami, Taira[7] seal

SOURCES: Document 33: *Kikuōji ke monjo,* 1226/2/18 Nagano Kagetaka yuzurijō an, *Zōtei Kano komonjo,* p. 50, doc. 74 (*KI,* 5: 392, doc. 3465). Document 34: *ibid.,* 1228/8/17 Hōjō Tomotoki gechijō an, *Zōtei Kano komonjo,* p. 51, doc. 76 (*KI,* 6: 100, doc. 3775).

1. An incorrect character appears here; see n. 2.

2. In Kaga Province. The present recipient's own conveyance of half a century later establishes that these are separate places: *Kikuōji ke monjo*, 1279/9/24 Nagano Morikage yuzurijō an, *Zōtei Kano komonjo*, p. 71, doc. 115.

3. I.e., the Jōkyū War.

4. Hayashi Jirō Ietsuna was a powerful Court partisan from Kaga who submitted to Bakufu forces midway through the war; *AK* 1221/6/8. Subsequently, he and his sons were taken to Kamakura and executed; *Ishikawa ken no rekishi*, pp. 73–74. Since Nagano Iekage was killed by Ietsuna, he was probably a Bakufu loyalist.

5. The challenger Enuma Jirō Kageyoshi's relationship to Morikage is unclear, though earlier Shigetomo *ho* had been conveyed from one Enuma *suke* Jirō to the latter's second son, Enuma Saburō (*Kikuōji ke monjo*, 1201/7/20 Enuma suke Jirō yuzu-rijō an, *Zōtei Kano komonjo*, p. 39, doc. 60). This might suggest that the current Jirō Ka-geyoshi was the heir of Enuma Saburō. At all events, Kagetaka's release of 1226 consti-tuted a threat of some kind to the Enuma, seemingly the area's dominant family.

6. It seems clear that Kamakura itself was uncertain about which of its two vassals was in the right; hence the option granted to Kageyoshi. It was his rival, however, who retained the inheritance; in 1279, Morikage deeded it to his son (n. 2).

7. Hōjō Tomotoki, son of Yoshitoki, and the *shugo* of Kaga Province. Tomotoki was generally active in the Hokuriku region during the 1220s (*AK* 1223/10/1, 1224/2/29, etc.) and was the Kamakura general responsible for capturing Hayashi Jirō Ietsuna (*AK* 1221/6/8), the murderer of Nagano Morikage's father (Document 33).

DOCUMENT 35

The Bakufu Approves a Release to a Younger Brother, 1227

Though by no means a common practice, siblings occasionally passed on property to one another. Here an elder brother, barely a year before his death, settled his *jitō shiki* upon his younger sibling. Shortly after the donor's death the recipient petitioned the Bakufu for confirmation, which was imme-diately granted.

This order dates from the regency (*shikken*) of Tokifusa and Yasutoki.[1]

Directed: to the residents of the Hizen Province official temple (*kokubunji*).

That Enjirō shall forthwith hold the *jitō shiki*, in accordance with the conveyance of his elder brother, Suemasu.

According to [Enjirō's] petition: "This *jitō shiki* was transmitted to my elder brother, Entarō Suemasu, by deed from our father Suetoshi.[2] Possession was exercised, but upon the death last year of Suemasu, conveyance was made to Enjirōmaru, along with the hereditary proof records from generations past." [In accordance with] the release of Suemasu from the 2d year of Gennin [1225], 5th month,[3] Enjirōmaru shall hold this *shiki*. In the event of challengers, details will be investigated and a judgment rendered in accordance with justice (*rihi*). By command of the Kamakura lord, it is so decreed.

[date portion lost][4]

SOURCE: *Taku monjo* (Asohina ke monjo), 1227(?) Kantō gechijō, *KI*, 5: 353–54, doc. 3371.

1. Added later to this damaged document (date portion lost). See n. 4.

2. The father Suetoshi received his own inheritance and Bakufu confirmation in 1212; see Document 14. His subsequent release to Entarō was confirmed in 1220; *Taku monjo*, 1220/5/19 Kantō gechijō, *KI*, 4: 377–78, doc. 2608.

3. Not extant.

4. Several clues permit us to date this document from 1227 or 1228: (1) the reference to a conveyance of 1225; (2) the reference to a functioning Kamakura lord (Yoritsune was not so designated in documents until his formal investiture as shogun in 1226); (3) a format that combines features of the *kudashibumi* and *gechijō* (the document opens with "kudasu" and closes with "gechi kudan no gotoshi"), a particular style appearing in several documents from 1227–28 (e.g., Document 37).

DOCUMENT 36

The Heir to the Powerful Shimazu Family Is Confirmed in His Inheritance, 1227

The greatest warriors had enormous legacies to pass on, and few were wealthier than the first chieftain of the great Shimazu family, Tadahisa. Here we see the Bakufu's confirmation of his deeds of release, which included interests in three provinces, among them a pair of *shugo* posts, normally of weak heritability. Noteworthy about this conveyance is its seemingly early emphasis on unitary inheritance: save for the life tenure to his widow of a single portion of his estate, Tadahisa's legacy is not known to have been otherwise parceled. His heir became the second chieftain of the Shimazu house.

(Fujiwara Yoritsune's monogram)[1]

Directed: to *saemon no jō* Koremune Tadayoshi.[2]

That [the following] shall be possessed:[3] the *shugo* post of Echizen Province;[4] the *jitō* and *shugo* titles of Shimazu Estate's Satsuma sector[5] plus the *jitō shiki* for the "12 islands"—but minus Kawanobe and Yubusuki districts and Isaku Estate.[6] In addition, a [confirmatory] edict has been granted to the widow[7] for Izumi Estate,[8] [though] Tadayoshi will succeed to this inheritance after her lifetime (*ichigo*).[9] [The following shall also be possessed:] the *jitō shiki* for the 4 *gō* within Ōta Estate, Shinano Province: Kojima, Kashiro, Ishimura-minami, and Tsuno.[10]

The aforesaid person shall be confirmed in these *shiki*, in accordance with the deeds of release by the late father, the Bungo governor, Tadahisa *ason*. The command is thus. Wherefore, this order.

3d year of Karoku [1227], 10th month, 10th day[11]

SOURCE: *Shimazu ke monjo*, 1227/10/10 shōgun sodehan kudashibumi, *DNK, iewake 16*, 1: 18–19, doc. 27 (*KI*, 6: 50–51, doc. 3670).

1. I.e., the shogun's monogram.

2. Tadayoshi (later changed to Tadatoki) was the son of Koremune Tadahisa, southern Kyushu's dominant vassal from the late 1180s. The present confirmation is in response to several conveyances, only two of which survive: *Shimazu ke monjo*, 1227/6/18 Shimazu Tadahisa yuzurijō, *DNK, iewake 16*, 1: 18, doc. 26; *ibid.*, 1227/6/18 Shimazu Tadahisa yuzurijō an, *DNK, iewake 16*, 1: 296–97, doc. 305.1.

3. The list of titles in the original is expressed as a single sentence, which would be awkward in English.

4. This post had been held by Tadahisa since 1221 (*Shimazu ke monjo*, 1221/7/12 Kantō gechijō, *DNK, iewake 16*, 1: 13, doc. 17). Yet soon after the present confirmation it was transferred by Kamakura to someone else; see the reference in *AK* 1228/5/16.

`5. Shimazu Estate was larger than Satsuma Province. The authority referred to here dated back to the Yoritomo era; *Shimazu ke monjo*, 1186/4/3 Minamoto Yoritomo kudashibumi, *DNK, iewake 16*, 1: 4–5, doc. 5; *ibid.*, 1197/2/3 saki no utaishō ke mandokoro kudashibumi, *DNK, iewake 16*, 1: 8–9, doc. 11 (*KB*, doc. 137).

6. See the first of Tadahisa's releases, cited in n. 2. Regarding these exceptions, it is clear that Isaku Estate (for example) had a *gesu shiki* (often an identical authority to *jitō*) that was strictly accountable to the proprietor (*ryōke*); *Shimazu ke ta no ie monjo*, 1255/12/25 Kantō gechijō an, *Satsuma-no-kuni Isaku-no-shō shiryō*, pp. 16–19, doc. 20. Obviously, all three interior areas within Shimazu Estate had whole or partial exemptions from Shimazu family interference.

7. I.e., Tadahisa's widow.

8. Edict not extant. In fact, we have no information at all concerning this estate.

9. Everything from the words "12 islands" is in half-size characters.

10. Ōta Estate's *jitō shiki* was granted to Shimazu Tadahisa only days before the outbreak of the Jōkyū War; *Shimazu ke monjo*, 1221/5/8 Kantō gechijō an, *DNK, iewake 16*, 1: 12, doc. 16. A later genealogy refers to a paddy total of 340 *chō* but also classifies Ōta as a Jōkyū reward land. See *ibid.*, Shinano Ōta-no-shō sōden keizu, *DNK, iewake 16*, 1: 297, doc. 306.

11. A separate confirmation for the Kashiro and Tsuno *jitō shiki* of Ōta Estate was granted to Tadayoshi on the same day; *ibid.*, 1227/10/10 Kantō kudashibumi an, *KI*, 6: 51, doc. 3671.

DOCUMENT 37

The Bakufu Adjudicates an Intrafamily Dispute Involving a Woman Jitō, 1228

The classic rivalries of early medieval society in Japan were not so much between families as within families. And nowhere were the antagonisms more acute than among siblings, among siblings and their nephews and nieces, and among stepchildren and their stepmothers. In the present instance, a highly unusual division of authority between an elder sister, appointed *jitō* by the Bakufu, and her younger brother, who became her deputy, led ultimately to a falling out between the woman and a male relative, probably her nephew. Typically, the Bakufu was called on to untangle the confusion, which it did by stipulating a sharing of local authority.

Directed: to the residents of Tamagawa *gō*, Izu Province, a Mishima Shrine land.
    That the administration of *sanden*[1] shall lie with the *jitō*, the Lady Izu.

The said *gō* was commended (*kishin*) to this shrine in the 2d year of Genkyū [1205], intercalated 7th month, and after that the *gō* administrator's title (*gōshi shiki*) was possessed by Morishige, the shrine chieftain (*kannushi*).[2] Then, in the 2d year of Jōkyū [1220], 2d month, when the Lady Izu was appointed *jitō*,[3] Morishige, her younger brother, appealed privately to be assigned the deputyship (*daikan shiki*).[4] Thereafter, Morishige, Mitsumori, and Moritada all exercised an exclusive administrative authority (*ikkō sata*) as [successive?] deputies.[5] Now, however, on the occasion of a falling out between the *jitō* and Hisamori,[6] the *jitō* has brought suit against Hisamori's willful assertion that, apart from the two *chō*, seven *tan* constituting the *jitō*'s residential plot (*yashiki*), [the *jitō*] should have no involvement.[7] All during the period of exclusive administration, separate (*kakubetsu*) possessions existed. Why then should there be any difference now? Forthwith, in accordance with custom, the *sanden* shall be under the jurisdiction (*sata*) of the *jitō*, and tax collection (*shotō shūnō*) will be under the *gōshi*. Both sides will abide by this. By command of the Kamakura lord, it is so decreed.
    2d year of Antei [1228], 3d month, 30th day

                                             Musashi no kami, Taira (monogram)
                                             Sagami no kami, Taira (monogram)

SOURCE: *Mishima jinja monjo*, 1228/3/30 Kantō gechijō, *Shizuoka ken shiryō*, 1: 145–46, doc. 5 (*KI*, 6: 77–78, doc. 3735).

1. The term *sanden* has several meanings—scattered fields (cf. the note in *Shizuoka ken shiryō*), local privately held fields, fields directly owned by a proprietor and assigned to peasants, fields abandoned by peasants, etc. Perhaps the meaning here is the authority to reassign abandoned lands.

2. No record of this transaction survives.

3. No record survives here either. Nor can we identify "Izu-no-tsubone."

4. The circumstances here are unclear, though it is obvious that Morishige wished to maintain his actual local authority. Was his deputyship conceived of as a standard *jitōdai*'s authority, and why, moreover, had Kamakura appointed the lady as *jitō* instead of her brother who was *gōshi*?

5. Were Mitsumori and Moritada brothers (or perhaps sons) of Morishige? What were the circumstances of their assignments?

6. Hisamori was probably the son of Morishige and the successor of his *gōshi* post.

7. It would seem that Hisamori's control of day-to-day administration (in his capacity as *gōshi*) induced him to attempt to limit the *jitō*'s authority strictly to her residence area.

DOCUMENTS 38–40

A Jitō and His Widow Shift the Family Inheritance and Create Confusion, 1230, 1232, 1234

As mentioned earlier, meddlesome widows, left in charge by their late husbands, could wreak havoc by their attempts to alter their husbands' wills. A classic example is the sequence here in which a husband, out of gratitude to his wife, transferred his legacy to her but designated a second son as the ultimate heir. The lady, however, had other ideas and attempted to bypass her late husband's choice in favor of the latter's son—in other words, her and her husband's grandson. The plan failed and two years later she wrote a release in which her husband's choice was now her choice. One irony of this episode is that the favored son had actually been granted the legacy by his father several years earlier and the Bakufu had approved the transfer. But then the father had changed his mind by deciding to make his widow the interim legatee; the son would have to wait his turn. As we shall see, he very nearly lost his inheritance outright.

38

Released: one parcel of private land (*shiryō*): within the [former] holding (*ryō*) of Suesato *nyūdō*, Yoshii-shin Estate, Settsu Province.[1]

Paddy totals of 5 *chō*, 4 *tan*, 150 *bu*—of which 1 *chō* is stipend paddy (*kyūden*).

The aforesaid holding was awarded owing to my merit,[2] and the [investiture] edict is in my possession.[3] By virtue of our marriage over many years (*nenrai no fusai*), Taira *no uji*[4] is made this conveyance. After Nakamitsu's lifetime (*ichigo*), she shall possess it free of disruption. Likewise, after Taira *no uji*'s lifetime, it shall be conveyed to Gorō Yoshinaka.[5] Let there be no disturbance even though our principal heir (*chakushi*) is a second son (*jinan*).[6] Hence, for posterity, our release is thus.

  2d year of Kangi [1230], 8th month, 4th day

Taira Nakamitsu (monogram)

39

Transcribed copy (*an*) of the release by the widow-nun (*goke ama*)[7] of Fukabori Tarō *nyūdō*, [prepared by] Myōshin.[8]

Deeded: the *jitō* [*shiki*] of Yoshii-shin Estate, [Set]tsu Province.[9] Conveyance was made to me by Fukabori *nyūdō dono*, to take effect only after the *nyūdō*'s lifetime. After my own lifetime, I wish the inheritance to go to Kōichi, who is my adopted grandson (*yōshi no mago*).[10]

  4th year of Kangi [1232], 2d month, 18th day

seal

40

Released: the *jitō shiki* over the former holding (*ato*) of Suesato *nyūdō*, within Yoshii Estate, [Set]tsu Province.

The aforesaid *jitō shiki* was conveyed by Fukabori *nyūdō* to the nun. After her lifetime, Fukabori Gorō Yoshinaka is indeed to inherit it, free of disturbance, despite the existence of other sons and daughters.[11] Hence, for the future, this record (*chūmon*) is thus.[12]

  2d year of Tenpuku [1234], 2d month, 13th day

shami bikuni ama (monogram)

SOURCES: Document 38: *Fukabori ke monjo*, 1230/8/4 Fukabori Nakamitsu yuzurijō, *Saga ken shiryō shūsei*, 4: 26, doc. 49 (*KI*, 6: 212, doc. 4010). Document 39: *ibid.*, 1232/2/18 Fukabori Nakamitsu goke ama yuzurijō an, *Saga ken shiryō shūsei*, 4: 27–28, doc. 52 (*KI*, 6: 344, doc. 4278). Document 40: *ibid.*, 1234/2/13 bikuni ama yuzurijō, *Saga ken shiryō shūsei*, 4: 29, doc. 56 (*KI*, 7: 101, doc. 4614).

 1. We can surmise that this Suesato *nyūdō* had fought for the Court during the Jōkyū War and been replaced by the present donor, Taira (Fukabori) Nakamitsu. See the reference to Suesato *nyūdō*'s former holding (*ato*) in Document 40 and also the documents cited in n. 12.

2. I.e., it was granted by the Bakufu owing to valorous conduct in the Jōkyū War.

3. Not extant.

4. The donor Nakamitsu's wife.

5. Nakamitsu's son and principal heir.

6. Several readings are possible here, e.g., "Despite the existence of first (*chakushi*) and second (*jinan*) sons, let there be no disturbance." At all events, Yoshinaka is clearly not the eldest.

7. I.e., Nakamitsu's widow, referred to in Document 38 as Taira *no uji*.

8. Myōshin was a great-grandson of Nakamitsu who conveyed the holding in question to his own son in 1289; *Fukabori ke monjo*, 1289/8/11 Fukabori Myōshin yuzurijō an, *Saga ken shiryō shūsei*, 4: 56, doc. 94. The present document was probably copied—or authored?—by him around this time.

9. This is clearly different from the release of the single land parcel two years earlier (Document 38). In fact, there is a discrepancy here, since Nakamitsu's heir, Yoshinaka, had been confirmed by the Bakufu in this *jitō shiki* in 1229 following his father's release of 1226 (not extant); *Fukabori ke monjo*, 1229/9/8 shōgun sodehan kudashibumi, *Saga ken shiryō shūsei*, 4: 25, doc. 47. The explanation seems to lie in a reversion of the *jitō* post to Nakamitsu in 1230; see *ibid.*, 1230/12/26 Rokuhara shigyōjō, *Saga ken shiryō shūsei*, 4: 27, doc. 51. This would then have been followed by Nakamitsu's designation of his wife as interim legatee (conveyance not extant). By 1232, he was dead and she was clearly taking charge.

10. I.e., a true grandson adopted as heir. This was clearly a departure from Nakamitsu's original plan, and the new arrangement, if not in fact a fable invented by Myōshin (n. 8), was never put into effect. Kōichi was the future Yukimitsu, son of the 1230 heir Yoshinaka and father of Myōshin.

11. Evidently, the 1232 plan to bypass Yoshinaka, assuming it is authentic, had now been dropped.

12. At the same time, the Fukabori were struggling with a locally entrenched family in their award area (see *DKR*, docs. 74–75) and appealing for a transfer away from Settsu Province (*DKR*, docs. 34–46).

DOCUMENT 41

A Great Vassal Retains Active Possession After Bequeathing to His Principal Heir, 1230

Great houses had great riches to distribute, as this example, a bequest by the Oyama chieftain to his principal heir, makes clear. Explicitly called the "chieftain's share," the package included extensive holdings spread across five provinces. It is noteworthy that the release was made to the donor's grandson as a substitute for the donor's son, who had died young. In this way, lineality was preserved and the integrity of a great family's most important holdings maintained. It is also of interest that the rights involved covered a combination of ancestral and Bakufu-granted holdings and that the document transferring them was indeed a will to take effect only upon the donor's death.

Testament of Shimotsuke *nyūdō*—chieftain's share (*sōryōbun*)[1]

Bequeathed: lands and offices (*shoryō shoshiki*) belonging to Jōsai:[2]
   The share of our grandson and heir-designate (*chakuson*) Gorō
   Nagamura.[3]
In total:
Shimotsuke Province:[4]
   The provisional governorship (*gon no ōsuke shiki*); Samukawa
   Tribute Estate (*mikuriya*)—known as Oyama Estate,[5] our home-
   land from generations past (*jūdai yashiki*).[6]
   Within the provincial capital district:
   Hinatano *gō*;[7] Sugata *gō*; Fukijima *gō*; the old provincial capital
   (*furu-kokufu*); Daikōji Temple; the provincial temple grounds;
   the provincial shrine grounds—plus the plain area and unused
   dwellings of that shrine;[8] Miyanome Shrine; Ōtsuka Plain.
   Higashitakei *gō*.
   The added fields (*kanō*) of Nakaizumi Estate.
Musashi Province:
   Kamisuga *gō*.
Mutsu Province:
   Kikuta Estate—including Yugama *gō*.
Owari Province:
   The three estates in Kaitō [District]—with the exception of Tai-
   zanji Temple.
Harima Province:
   The office of *shugo* (*shugo bugyō shiki*).[9]
   Takaoka Estate.
   Takaoka-Hōjō *gō*.

The aforesaid lands and offices, which are either Jōsai's inheritance
from past generations or benefices granted him (*go-onshi*) by the shogunal house, have been possessed by him without interruption.[10] Accordingly, when our heir (*chakunan*)[11] *saemon no jō* Tomonaga was
alive, conveyance was made to him, but he passed away prematurely.[12]
While still in good health, [Tomonaga] determined that, among his
sons, Gorō Nagamura should be heir (*chakunan*)[13] and should carry on
the family's affairs (*kagyō*). Therefore, in accordance with that intent,
and in order for Nagamura's succession to be recognized, the hereditary proof records and sequence of shogunal house orders for these
lands and offices are put in order now and are devised. However, for
the remainder of Jōsai's lifetime (*ichigo*), he shall exercise management and possession (*shintai chigyō*). After his death (*botsugo*), Naga-

mura shall enjoy such possession (*ryōshō chigyō*) without interference, in accordance with the present deed of bequest. Our devise is thus.

2d year of Kangi [1230], 2d month, 20th day

> saki no Shimotsuke no kami Fuji-
> wara Tomomasa nyūdō Jōsai[14]
> (monogram)

SOURCE: *Oyama monjo*, 1230/2/20 Oyama Tomomasa yuzurijō, *Oyama shishi, shiryō hen, chūsei*, pp. 80–81, doc. 102 (*KI*, 6: 179–80, doc. 3960).

1. Identification added by the recipient or his heirs to the reverse side of the document.

2. Oyama Tomomasa (1155–1238), a leading stalwart of the Bakufu whose mother had been Yoritomo's wet nurse. For more on the Oyama, see also n. 14.

3. The reasons for designating a grandson as principal heir are explained below. Nagamura, a second son, died in 1269.

4. The home province of the Oyama, a family with roots there going far back into the Heian period. Its titles and landed interests derived from close ties with the Shimotsuke provincial government. See *WG*, pp. 43–44.

5. At first a holding of the ex-emperor, it was commended to Ise Shrine in 1166; hence its designation as "mikuriya" (*Oyama shishi*, p. 41). The *jitō* authority for the larger Samukawa District (*gun*) was awarded early on to the testator's mother (Yoritomo's wet nurse); *AK*, 1187/12/1.

6. Not the normal usage for *yashiki*, which means residential plot or compound. The phrase is in half-size characters.

7. The testator was appointed *jitō* of Hinatano *gō* in 1192; *Oyama shishi*, p. 43.

8. In half-size characters.

9. The testator was granted this post in 1199; *KB*, doc. 138. Following a hiatus the post was reassigned to him in 1221 and was held by his family until the 1270s; *WG*, p. 216, *DKR*, p. 177.

10. Presumably, all of the holdings outside Shimotsuke were awards of the Bakufu. Full investiture records have not survived, however.

11. The term *chakunan* can mean eldest son or principal heir. Here it means heir, as we see from a reference later in the document.

12. The conveyance referred to here does not survive, though it is known that To-monaga died in 1229; *Oyama shishi*, p. 79.

13. Nagamura, we recall, was Tomonaga's second son.

14. Tomomasa's two brothers, Munemasa and Tomomitsu, were, respectively, progenitors of the Naganuma and the Yūki, branch houses of the Oyama. All three families were richly endowed by the Bakufu, with holdings all across Japan. Munemasa, for example, conveyed property in nine provinces in the same year that Tomomasa bequeathed the present inheritance; see *Minagawa monjo*, 1230/8/13 Naganuma Mune-masa yuzurijō, *Tochigi kenshi, shiryō hen, chūsei*, 1: 152–53, doc. 2.

DOCUMENTS 42–46

A Prominent Eastern House Divides Its Patrimony but Continues to Add New Holdings, 1230, 1248, 1249, 1258, 1270

There were basically three ways for warrior houses to be able to continue the practice of making all children heirs and heiresses. One was to allow individual parcels to grow ever smaller. A second was to maintain equilibrium between beneficiaries and holdings by receiving new properties from the Bakufu and by exploiting more ruthlessly the lands that were already held. A final technique was to begin offering life bequests to an ever-greater number of heirs. A by-product here was a new concentration of authority in the hands of the house chieftain. The Yamanouchi, like most other warrior houses, sought to emphasize the second approach—and were more or less successful at it. Nevertheless, the first and third approaches, which we gain only hints of here, became more prominent as time went on (see Documents 121–22). Eventually, the family's age-old practice of distributing to multiple heirs was dropped in 1330 in favor of a single heir (Document 150).

42

Conveyed: to our principal heir (*chakunan*), sa *hyōe no jō* Fujiwara Munetoshi: paddy fields and service households (*zaike*) within Ittoku *myō*, in Hayakawa Estate, Ashinoshimo District, Sagami Province.[1]

Totals: . . .[2]

Among the shares distributed to our sons and daughters from within Ittoku *myō*, paddy and service households are herewith deeded to Munetoshi. If from among [my children] any troublemakers should appear, let them be expelled from the family; there is to be no enmity. On the occasion of public or private tribute levies (*kōshi no onkuji*) on paddy and service households within peasant areas, these should be discharged by all, cooperatively and without negligence. The basic sequence of documents (*honken monjo*) for this *myō* is entrusted to Munetoshi as our principal heir (*chakushi*). However, he is not to interfere with the paddy and service households earmarked for inheritance by his siblings (*shoshi*)[3] on the pretext that he holds this basic sequence. Thus, for the sake of posterity, these details are recorded. Our conveyance is thus.

2d year of Kangi [1230], intercalated 1st month, 14th day

> nakatsukasa no jō, Fujiwara Shige-
> toshi (monogram)

43

Conveyed:[4] the *jitō shiki* of Tomishima *hon-shō*, Settsu Province.
[To:] Fujiwara Tokitoshi

The aforesaid estate is a place [awarded] for merit in the Jōkyū [War].[5] As our principal heir (*chakushi*), Tokitoshi is made this conveyance, accompanied by a [Kantō] edict (*gechijō*) and an order of the two governors (*ryō shuden no onfumi*).[6] Let there be no disturbances in future. Our disposition[7] is thus.

> 2d year of Hōji [1248], 12th month, 21st day

> shami, Shinnen[8] (monogram)

44

Conveyed:
> [to:] our son, Fujiwara Tokitoshi: paddy fields, a residence compound, and service households within Ittoku *myō*, Tanoko *gō*, Hayakawa Estate, Ashinoshimo District, Sagami Province.

Item: paddy fields: . . .[9]
Item: the ancestral residence compound: . . .[10]
Item: service households within peasant areas: . . .[11]
The aforesaid paddy land, residence compound, and service households are the hereditary ancestral holdings of Shinnen.[12] Accordingly, our third son, Tokitoshi, who is recognized as our principal heir, is herewith made this conveyance, accompanied by the sequence of hereditary instruments as well as proof records. However, on the occasion of public or private tribute levies on paddy and service households within peasant areas, these should be discharged without negligence by all the siblings, under the apportionments (*shihai*) of Tokitoshi.[13] Thus, for the sake of posterity, these details are recorded. Our disposition is thus.[14]

> 1st year of Kenchō [1249], 8th month, 21st day

> shami, Shinnen (monogram)

45

The chancellery of the shogun's house directs: to *saemon no jō* Fujiwara Tokinari *hosshi*—Buddhist name, Myōdō:[15]

That he shall possess forthwith the *jitō shiki* of Shimobara Village, in Jibi Estate, Bingo Province;[16] the Hanya *isshiki*;[17] and 4 *tan* of *myō* paddy plus one service household in Hayakawa Estate, Sagami Province.

Authority shall be exercised under these *shiki*, pursuant to precedent, in accordance with two conveyances of the late grandfather *nakatsukasa no jō* Shigetoshi *hosshi*—Buddhist name, Saimyō—dated the 3d year of Antei [1229], 3d month, 3d day, and the 1st year of Jōei [1232], 12th month,   day.[18] It is commanded thus. Wherefore, this order.

2d year of Shōka [1258], 12th month, 23d day[19]

> anzu, Kiyohara
> chikeji, Kiyohara

ryō, saemon no jō, Fujiwara
bettō, Sagami no kami, Taira ason (monogram)
Musashi no kami, Taira ason (monogram)

46

That Fujiwara *no uji*—named Kametsuru[20]—shall forthwith possess the *jitō shiki* for 2 residence compounds and 1.4 *chō* of *myō* paddy within Ittoku *myō*, Hayakawa Estate, Sagami Province; for Shimobara[21] Village and the Hanya *isshiki* within Iyonishi Village, Jibi Estate, Bingo Province, plus the precincts of the new main temple (*shin-midō*) of the Hon-*gō* [region] of that same estate; for Upper Udagawa Estate, Hōki Province; and for Yoshino Village, in Momonobu District, Mutsu Province.[22]

Authority shall be exercised under these *shiki*, pursuant to precedent, in accordance with the release by the late father *saemon no jō* Tokinari *hosshi*—Buddhist name, Myōdō—dated the 1st year of Bun'ō [1260], 7th month, 8th day, and in accordance with 4 releases of this past year [1269], 9th month, 16th day, and also 2d day.[23] By this command, it is so decreed.

7th year of Bun'ei [1270], 6th month, 13th day

> Sagami no kami, Taira ason (monogram)
> sakyō gon no daibu, Taira ason (monogram)

SOURCES: Document 42: *Yamanouchi Sudō ke monjo*, 1230/int.1/14 Yamanouchi Shigetoshi yuzurijō, *DNK, iewake 15*, pp. 2–3, doc. 3 (*KI*, 6: 168, doc. 3927). Document 43: *ibid.*, 1248/1/21 Yamanouchi Shinnen (Munetoshi) yuzurijō, *DNK, iewake 15*, pp. 3–4, doc. 4 (*KI*, 10: 48, doc. 7019). Document 44: *ibid.*, 1249/8/21 Yamanouchi Shinnen (Munetoshi) yuzurijō, *DNK, iewake 15*, pp. 4–5, doc. 5 (*KI* 10: 113–14, doc. 7110). Document 45: *ibid.*, 1258/12/23 shōgun ke mandokoro kudashibumi, *DNK, iewake 15*, p. 37, doc. 31 (*KI*, 11: 325, doc. 8328). Document 46: *ibid.*, 1270/6/13 Kantō gechijō, *DNK, iewake 15*, pp. 37–38, doc. 32 (*KI*, 14: 149, doc. 10636).

1. Ittoku *myō* in Sagami was the home area of one branch of the Yamanouchi house; cf. *Yamanouchi shi keizu*, in *DNK, iewake 15*, p. 556. The present conveyance is from Yamanouchi Shigetoshi (1157–1242) to his chosen heir, Munetoshi.

2. These are divided into three groups: field specifications (4.9 *chō* spread over 13 itemized units within Ittoku *myō*), one ancestral residence compound (with north-south-east-west boundaries), and service households (a total of 5 *zaike*).

3. The donor, then, clearly issued other conveyances to his children, though none survives. He also issued releases to (at least) one grandson; cf. the reference in Document 45.

4. The donor here is Munetoshi, who was the donee in Document 42.

5. The merit must have been Munetoshi's personally, since his elder brother Toshinari had died fighting on the side of the Court, and their father (then aged 64) had apparently remained home. See *Yamanouchi Sudō ke monjo*, 1221/7/26 Kantō gechijō, *DNK, iewake 15*, p. 1, doc. 1 (*KB*, doc. 21).

6. The edict was probably the post-Jōkyū investiture order, which is not extant. The other reference is to the Hōjō regent and vice-regent (Yasutoki and Tokifusa), respectively governors of Musashi and Sagami.

7. An incorrect character is here, but this is the probable meaning.

8. Yamanouchi Munetoshi.

9. The total here is only 1.7 *chō*, much smaller than the 4.9 *chō* received in inheritance by the present donor in 1230 (see n. 2).

10. Only two of the four boundaries are the same as in 1230 (n. 2). This suggests a parceling here, too.

11. Two *zaike* are listed here; in 1230 (see n. 2) the number was five.

12. This release is for the mainline inheritance that Munetoshi (Shinnen) had received from his own father (Document 42). The transfer a year earlier of the Tomishima Estate *jitō shiki* (Document 43) was for a holding received by Munetoshi directly from the Bakufu.

13. The authority of the chieftain-designate is thus much more explicit here than in the conveyance of 1230 (Document 42).

14. Kamakura's edicts of confirmation for Documents 42–44 do not survive.

15. Tokinari was the son of Toshinari, who had fought for the Court in 1221; cf. n. 5. Thus, the son of a traitor was being confirmed by the Bakufu in a bequest made to him by his grandfather, Shigetoshi.

16. It was the *jitō shiki* of the full estate that was confirmed to Shigetoshi in 1221; cf. the document cited in n. 5. Obviously, Shigetoshi had decided to parcel it. For further details on Jibi, see Document 99.

17. A certain designated land area in Iyo-nishi Village, Jibi Estate (see Document 46).

18. Neither of these conveyances is extant; but it is noteworthy that Shigetoshi elected to care for his traitor son's own son.

19. Why was the Bakufu's confirmation coming only now? The donor Shigetoshi had died at the age of 85 in 1242.

20. Fujiwara Kametsuru was a daughter of Tokinari *hosshi*, the present donor and recipient of his own inheritance (from his grandfather) twelve years earlier; cf. Docu-

ments 45 and 99. The *Yamanouchi shi keizu* lists only one child (a daughter) for Tokinari, but does not record her name: *DNK, iewake 15*, p. 538. More than 50 years later we see her conveyance to an adopted son: *Yamanouchi Sudō ke monjo*, 1323/3/29 ama yuzurijō, *DNK, iewake 15*, pp. 38–41.

21. The text has it "Harashimo" Village, but this is an inversion of "Shimobara"; see Document 45.

22. Where did these holdings from Hōki and Mutsu provinces come from? Certainly they are not referred to in the Bakufu's 1258 confirmation of the present donor, Tokinari. May we conclude that they were new awards to this minor branch of the Yamanouchi?

23. None of these is extant.

DOCUMENTS 47–48

The Bakufu Orders Separate Jitō Confirmees to Honor the Land Shares of Their Sisters and Brothers, 1231, 1233

In the two unrelated documents here we see the Bakufu confirming inheritances in the standard fashion but adding admonitions that the recipients, both principal heirs, not violate the smaller bequests of their siblings. As we have noted in previous examples, house heads were seeking to exercise new powers vis-à-vis coheirs. Thus it was often left to the Bakufu to guarantee the security of those heirs as part of its effort to base the vassal system on the senior generation's right to define authority within families. The converse to this was a hedging of the arbitrary lateral powers of house heads, which might easily violate the plans for children left by parents.

47

Directed: to the residents of Tajiri Estate, Nose District, Settsu Province.

That Minamoto Yorinaka shall forthwith hold the *jitō shiki*.

The aforesaid person shall exercise this possession without disturbance, in accordance with the conveyance of the 12th day of this month by his father Yorisada *ason*.[1] Similarly, regarding the shares for three daughters, let there be no violations, in pursuance of the same document. It is [commanded] thus.

3d year of Kangi [1231], 10th month, 18th day[2]

48

The chancellery of the shogun's house directs:[3] to Taira [Tsune]hisa.[4] That the *jitō shiki* of Ishikawa Village, within Hirago *gō*, Kuraki District, Musashi Province, as well as that of Yamada *gō*, Echigo Province, shall forthwith be possessed.

The aforesaid person shall enjoy this possession, in accordance with the conveyance of the 3d year of Kangi [1231], 3d month, 10th day, by his father Tsunesue.[5] Nevertheless, he is not to commit incursions against the shares of his two younger brothers. The command is thus. Wherefore, this order.

    2d year of Jōei [1233], 4th month, 15th day

                     anzu, sakan no shōsō, Sugano
                     chikeji, utoneri, Kiyohara (mono-
                     gram)
ryō, saemon no shōjō, Fujiwara (monogram)
bettō, Sagami no kami, Taira ason (monogram)
Musashi no kami, Taira ason (monogram)

SOURCES: Document 47: *Kakiage monjo*, 1231/10/18 shōgun sodehan kudashibumi an, *KI*, 6: 313, doc. 4233. Document 48: *Shoshū komonjo*, 1233/4/15 shōgun ke mandokoro kudashibumi, *KI*, 7: 21, doc. 4473.

    1. Document not extant.

    2. Years later the Bakufu confirmed Yorinaka's release of 1268 to his own son; *Nose monjo*, 1284/7/8 shōgun ke mandokoro kudashibumi, *Shōen shiryō*, 1: 381. By this juncture, a *jitō shiki* from Shikoku's Awa Province had been added to the family's holdings.

    3. Note the difference in format between this document and the last. In 1232, the shogun Yoritsune achieved Court rank sufficient to warrant the opening of a chancellery.

    4. The first character here has been lost; but a traditional genealogy informs us that the heir of the donor was named Tsunehisa. See *Musashi shichidō keizu*, in *DNS*, Series 5, 8: 819.

    5. Document not extant.

DOCUMENT 49

An Adopted Son and His Uncle Dispute a Vacated Inheritance, 1235

As we have seen several times earlier, the unexpected death of a property holder often meant property left intestate and an almost open invitation to rival claimants. In the fascinating episode presented here, an uncle and a nephew joined forces against their kinsman's murderer, the area's *jitō*, and once having succeeded in gaining his ouster, turned on each other in their drive to become the dead relative's successor. Specifically, the victim's brother and adopted son vied for the vacated inheritance, but the Bakufu, unclear as to which side had the stronger case, divided the estate between them.

> That Taira Shigehide shall forthwith possess a one-half share of the former holdings (*ato*) of Tadahide, his foster father (*yōfu*), consisting of the Satsuma Province Ibusuki District headship (*gunji*), nine locales within a plain area under development [characters indecipherable],[1] the head priesthood (*gūji*) of Daimyō Shrine, and the headship (*myōshu*) of Akitomi *myō*, along with its paddy and upland.

When Tadahide, his relatives, and his personal servants were killed by the deputy (*daikan*) of Bungo Shirō *saemon no jō* Tadatsuna, *jitō* for this district, a suit was lodged by Tadahide's younger brother, Kojirō Tadanari, and by [Tadahide's] adopted son (*yōshi*), Taira Jirō Shigehide—originally named Jirō *hosshi*, Tadahide's nephew.[2] It stated: "How could such outrages have been committed by the deputy if not upon an order (*gechi*) from his lord (*shujin*), Tadatsuna?" Tadatsuna rejoined that as he had no knowledge whatever of the details, he would summon and forward the offender to Rokuhara, or else would behead him. According to a deposition (*mōshijō*) by Ayazaburō Nobumoto, the head oarsman (*kajitori*) of Tadatsuna and a prominent personage (*jūnin*) of Yamakawa, [Ibusuki] District: "It is my understanding that Tadatsuna took over the *myō* paddy and upland left by Tadahide and his relatives and transferred it to his deputy Takashi Shirō Yukishige." Inasmuch as Tadatsuna's defense statement is thus a palpable lie, his *shiki* has been confiscated and reassigned.[3] At present, Tadanari has undertaken to appear here, stating as follows: "If there is no challenge to my explanation, what need is there for further jurisdiction?[4] Inasmuch as I served Tadahide loyally, the *shiki* and fields comprising his estate (*ato*) should be awarded to me." For his part, Shigehide, claiming to possess a release from his adoptive father Tadahide, has argued that he should succeed to the family headship (*sōryō*). Yet the details of his statement are unclear, and, anyway, Tadanari's statement is not easily dismissed. Shigehide and Tadanari are therefore each to possess one-half of the *shiki* and *myō* paddy and upland in question; and in accordance with the precedent of Tadahide, the *jitō*'s authority (*shomu*) shall be heeded. By command of the Kamakura lord, it is so decreed.

2d year of Bunryaku [1235], 8th month, 28th day[5]

Musashi no kami, Taira (monogram)
Sagami no kami, Taira (monogram)

SOURCE: *Ibusuki monjo*, 1235/8/28 Kantō gechijō, *Sappan kyūki zatsuroku, zenpen*, 2: 106–7, doc. 232 (*KI*, 7: 203, doc. 4815).

1. Translation here is problematic; also, the phrase "characters indecipherable" actually appears in the *Sappan kyūki zatsuroku* transcription.

2. Apparently, Shigehide was originally the nephew of both Tadahide and the latter's younger brother, Tadanari. Tadahide adopted Shigehide, but Tadahide and his immediate family (save for Shigehide) were murdered. This led to Tadanari's and Shigehide's suit against the murderers, who were seeking to seize the inheritance. As we shall see, however, uncle and nephew hoped as well to exclude the other from the inheritance.

3. For his role in the murder, in other words, the Ibusuki District *jitō* had been replaced. The identity of the new appointee is not disclosed.

4. Other interpretations of this sentence are possible.

5. No related documents survive.

DOCUMENT 50

A Recently Appointed Official Conveys Land Rights Within the Traditional Estate System, 1236

Though most of our examples have dealt with families that were within Kamakura's orbit, inheritance practices in general were more or less uniform. Here we see a managerial *shiki*, granted by an estate proprietor three years earlier, being conveyed to a principal heir. Speedy conveyances of this kind (though hardly implying an immediate transfer) were a common device of recent acquirers of *shiki*.

Conveyed:

The Iyatomi *gesu* [*shiki*]—for half the estate[1]—and the *kumon shiki*—for the full estate[2]—[both within] Nagataki Estate, Izumi Province, a Tōhoku-in land.

The aforesaid *shiki* were bestowed to me by decree (*onkudashibumi*) of the Fujiwara (*denka*) chancellery in the 1st year of Tenpuku [1233], 5th month,   day,[3] and I exercised possession. Details can be seen in that decree. Now, however, I make this conveyance, along with accompanying proof records, to *shami* Jōgan, who is my principal heir. There are to be no disturbances in future. It is thus.[4]

2d year of Katei [1236], 11th month, 15th day

saemon no jō, Nakahara Morizane
(monogram)

SOURCE: *Hine monjo*, 1236/11/15 Nakahara Morizane yuzurijō, *KI*, 7: 315, doc. 5085.
1. Iyatomi presumably refers to that sector of the estate for which the one-half *gesu shiki* is released.
2. Phrase in half-size characters.
3. Not extant.
4. No related documents seem to survive.

DOCUMENTS 51–52

The Hōjō Confirm the Passage of Jitō Deputyships, 1237, 1249

Within Kamakura warrior society only two families, the Hōjō and the Ashikaga, issued confirmatory edicts for the testamentary passage of deputy *jitō shiki*. In other words, these two families exercised explicit rights of lordship at a level once removed from the shogun's own confirmatory privilege vis-à-vis *jitō* offices proper. At the same time, we know that the majority of *jitō* holders appointed deputies who were posted to their appointment areas as stand-ins for their lords. These deputy *jitō* obviously came to exercise hereditary rights —but they wrote no wills and thus had none confirmed. Only vassals of the Hōjō and Ashikaga enjoyed this extra measure of security.

51

(Hōjō Yasutoki's monogram)

Directed: to the Lady Izu Tadokoro.
That the deputy *jitō* title for Iwatate Village, Hiraga District,[1] shall forthwith be possessed.
The aforesaid person shall enjoy possession in accordance with a deed of release of the 2d year of Katei [1236], 3d month, 6th day,[2] by her husband, *shami* Saishin;[3] it is recorded [further] that after her lifetime, Iyajirō shall exercise this possession.[4] It is thus. Wherefore, this order.

3d year of Katei [1237], 3d month, 13th day

52

(Hōjō Tokiyori's monogram)

Directed: to Kojirō *hyōe no jō* Suketoki.

That the deputy *jitō* titles for Asō Estate, Nozura Estate, and Kōzuyaku *gō*, [all] within Yamaga Estate, Chikuzen Province, shall forthwith be possessed.

The aforesaid person shall exercise authority under these titles, in accordance with the deed of release of this month[5] by his father, Jirō *nyūdō* Sainen.[6] It is thus.

1st year of Kenchō [1249], 6th month, 26th day

SOURCES: Document 51: *Nitobe monjo*, 1237/3/13 Hōjō Yasutoki kudashibumi, *Iwate ken chūsei monjo*, 1: 2–3, doc. 8 (*KI*, 7: 328, doc. 5116). Document 52: *Asō monjo*, 1249/6/26 Hōjo Tokiyori kudashibumi, *Asō monjo*, p. 1, doc. 2 (*KI*, 10: 97, doc. 7088).

    1. In Mutsu Province.

    2. Not extant.

    3. *Shami* Saishin, originally Taira Hirotada, was appointed deputy *jitō* by Hōjō Yoshitoki in 1219; *Nitobe monjo*, 1219/4/27 Hōjō Yoshitoki kudashibumi, *Iwate ken chūsei monjo*, 1: 1, doc. 1.

    4. In half-size characters from "it is recorded. . . ." Iyajirō, subsequently Soga Daijirō, later conveyed the same *jitō* deputyship to his own wife, who in turn was confirmed by the Hōjō chieftain-designate, Masamura; *Saitō monjo*, 1264/5 Hōjō Masamura andojō, *Iwate ken chūsei monjo*, 1: 7, doc. 24 (*KB*, doc. 110).

    5. Not extant.

    6. An additional confirmation was issued to Suketoki after his father Sainen's death; *Asō monjo*, 1264/3/29 bō jitōdai shiki andojō, *Asō monjo*, pp. 1–2, doc. 3 (perhaps the author here was Hōjō Masamura; see n. 4). Eight years later Suketoki himself was dead and was succeeded by his son Sukeuji; *ibid.*, 1272/4/27 bō kudashibumi, *Asō monjo*, p. 2, doc. 4.

DOCUMENTS 53–54

Women Devise, Inherit, Sell, and Buy Land, 1237

As we now know, land that had been purchased could be passed on, and land that had been passed on could be purchased; the possession of ownership papers meant that the possessor could transfer them—by sale, bequest, or commendation—as he saw fit. Nor were there any gender barriers here: in the two cases described below all of the principals were women. From these and other examples we gain the impression of wealthy men and women engaging in land speculation. Transactions in real estate merely required the transfer of paper—title deeds from one owner to another.

53

Sold: one landed holding (ryōchi).
. . .¹

The aforementioned land was purchased in perpetuity from the Lady Fujiwara for a cash price of 20 kanmon in the 2d year of Kangi [1230], 2d month. The substance of this is clearly noted in the deed of sale.² However, by reason of current need, the said land, along with a dwelling, is sold in perpetuity to our grandmother for a cash price of 17 kanmon, along with the [original?] deed of sale. In the event any challengers should arise in future, the stated cash price shall be returned. Moreover, even after our lifetime if such claimants arise, assumption of authority by them will be grounds for return of the cash price. Thus, as proof for the future, this new deed is hereby constituted.

3d year of Katei [1237], 7th month, 13th day

Minamoto no ujime seal

54

Original deed for the southern sector.³
Sold: the Ōtani plot.
. . .⁴

The aforesaid land parcel was deeded to me by my late mother. However, by reason of current need, it is hereby sold to the Lady Minamoto for 17 kanmon cash.⁵ Nevertheless, although the original deed ought to accompany [this transaction], it includes other items and so cannot be transmitted.⁶ The present document shall constitute the new deed and is designed to serve as proof for the future. Let there be no violations. It is thus.

3d year of Katei [1237], 8th month, 6th day

Fujiwara seal

SOURCES: Document 53: Honganji monjo, 1237/7/13 Minamoto no ujime baiken an, KI, 7: 346, doc. 5156. Document 54: ibid., 1237/8/6 Fujiwara no ujime baiken an, KI, 7: 350, doc. 5164.
    1. Size, boundaries, and location follow here.
    2. See Honganji monjo, 1230/2/23 Fujiwara no ujime baiken an, KI, 6: 181, doc. 3962. Noted therein is the fact that the seller received the land from her mother during the Kenpō era (1213–19).

3. This second transaction is distinct from that recorded in Document 53. The seller here is the same seller as in 1230; see n. 2.

4. Only the size is specified. This is presumably because the unit is named and therefore cannot be confused with other units.

5. Evidently, then, the seller in Document 53 (to her grandmother) is the buyer here in Document 54. The prices were the same—17 *kanmon*—thus suggesting a deliberate substitution of properties.

6. It would seem, in other words, that the Lady Fujiwara was slowly selling off the inheritance from her mother; see n. 2.

DOCUMENTS 55–56

A Father Chooses His Heir on the Basis of Ability, 1237

As we have repeatedly noted, the freedom of a father to divide his estate was without limit. The two most common reasons for bypassing elder sons were a lack of filiality and a lack of ability. Here the pretext offered for making the third son principal heir was the ineptness of his two seniors. Yet these two, as well as the other children and even the grandchildren, were granted small land shares. Moreover, the donor was anxious to protect all offspring from the ambitions of any sibling, in particular, the ambitions of the principal heir. Any untoward behavior by the latter was to be subject to the censure of a family council, while, conversely, the violations of a junior heir had to be reported to the Bakufu, not dealt with independently by the new chieftain. Here once again, then, we see the weak lateral integration that a dominant house headship might have compensated for.

55
Conveyed: the post of shrine head (*daigūji shiki*) for Takeo Shrine, Hizen Province.

The aforesaid post is Iekado's inheritance from past generations, with investiture edicts (*onkudashibumi*) granted by successive shoguns.[1] Now I have possessed it for many years, and although I have both eldest and second sons, they are lacking in ability (*kiryō*). In consequence, I have made my third son, Yoshikado, my principal heir (*chakushi*).[2] Conveyance of this *shiki* is made to him in perpetuity, along with the generations of proof records. Each of my sons shall pay due respect to Yoshikado's authority. However, small parcels of paddy and upland have been allotted to my male and female children, as well as to my grandchildren.[3] Accordingly, should there be any grievances that arise involving Yoshikado, such matters shall be dealt with in family council (*yoriai*), with all members of one mind.[4] Moreover, concerning shrine affairs, prayers for the shogunal house are to be performed respectfully, with no individual negligence, and in accordance with precedent. Should there be any who contravene this covenant (*keijō*), Yoshikado will report particulars,[5] and the landed holdings (*shoryō*) [of such persons] shall be terminated, even though they may possess releases from Iekado.[6] For the future record, our deed of conveyance to Yoshikado is thus.

    3d year of Katei [1237], 8th month, 25th day

                        Fujiwara (monogram)

56

                         seal

The *shugo* headquarters[7] directs: to Fujiwara Yoshikado.

    That, in accordance with the intent of a shogunal house chancellery edict,[8] he shall possess forthwith the headship of Takeo Shrine, Hizen Province.

Regarding the above, a [shogunal] edict of the 9th month, 5th day of this year arrived here today. It states: "That [Yoshikado] shall forthwith possess the *daigūji* post for Takeo Shrine, Hizen [Province]. The aforesaid person shall possess this *shiki*, in accordance with the deed of conveyance by his father Iekado, dated the 8th month, 25th day of this year. The command is thus. Wherefore, this order."[9] This *shiki* shall be possessed in compliance with the intent of the [shogunal] edict. It is thus.

    3d year of Katei [1237], 10th month, 11th day[10]

                      taigen, Ōnakatomi ason
                      taigen, Koremune ason seal
                      kandai, Fujiwara ason seal
                      kandai, atae sukune
                      kandai, Fujiwara ason seal
                      kandai, Ono ason seal
                      kandai, Minamoto ason
                      kandai, Nakahara seal

SOURCES: Document 55: *Takeo jinja monjo*, 1237/8/25 Fujiwara Iekado yuzurijō, *Saga ken shiryō shūsei*, 2: 41–42 (*KI*, 7: 352–53, doc. 5170). Document 56: *ibid.*, 1237/10/11 dazaifu shugosho kudashibumi an, *Saga ken shiryō shūsei*, 2: 85–86 (*KI*, 7: 358, doc. 5183).

1. For details on these earlier confirmations, see *DKR*, docs. 57, 67, 98, and the list of documents in Iekado's possession referred to in *Takeo jinja monjo*, 1239/6/27 Kantō gechijō, *Saga ken shiryō shūsei*, 2: 42.

2. Earlier in the year, Iekado, the donor, had issued a similar release decrying the lack of ability of his first two sons; *ibid.*, 1237/5/10 Fujiwara Iekado yuzurijō, *Saga ken shiryō shūsei*, 2: 41. The present document, at any rate, is the one that was confirmed by the Bakufu.

3. On the same day, the first and second sons and a daughter were granted such parcels; *ibid.*, 1237/8/25 Fujiwara Iekado okibumi an, *Saga ken shiryō shūsei*, 2: 113. This document is misplaced in *KI* under the year 1238; *KI*, 7: 402, doc. 5298.

4. This stricture is not present in the 5/10 devise; see n. 2.

5. I.e., to the Kantō.

6. Evidently, Yoshikado himself could not take action against his siblings; the Bakufu had the sole right of confiscation.

7. I.e., the *dazaifu*.

8. This is the Bakufu's confirmatory edict; *Takeo jinja monjo*, 1237/9/5 shōgun ke mandokoro kudashibumi, *Saga ken shiryō shūsei*, 2: 85. Note that the *dazaifu's* response is to a formal Kamakura decree, not to the original deed of conveyance.

9. This is identical to the original of this edict, cited in n. 8.

10. Two years later a legal challenge to Iekado, who was still in authority, was branded a "false suit" (*ranso*) by the Bakufu; *Takeo jinja monjo*, 1239/6/27 Kantō gechijō, *Saga ken shiryō shūsei*, 2: 42.

DOCUMENTS 57–58

A Gokenin Appeals for a Bakufu Confirmation, 1239

In the absence of gender restrictions, property often shifted from males to females—or females to males—and back again quite normally. The Bakufu took little note of these shifts and simply issued its confirmations. The present case is peculiar only because one of the two *shiki* involved—and that a *jitō shiki*—was not included in the edict of confirmation. It is also worth noting that the Bakufu's edict—which was in fact a reconfirmation—was issued only two weeks after the conveyance itself was prepared.

57

Conveyed: Senbu Estate plus residence compounds and *myō* paddy and upland in Sugai Village, within the northern sector of Toshima [District], Settsu Province.

    Proof records appended.

The aforesaid holdings have been hereditary for generations with [the forebears of] the monk (*shamon*) Kakuzen's mother, the Lady

Minamoto. Accordingly, during the time of the late *udaijin*,[1] an [investiture] edict (*onkudashibumi*) was bestowed for *jitō* and *gesu shiki*.[2] After that a *soebumi*[3] was authorized by the *sakyō no daibu*.[4] Nevertheless, owing to Kakuzen's severe illness of recent days, he once again deeds [these holdings] to his eldest daughter (*chakujo*), the Lady Fuji[wara].[5] In order that there might be security (*ando*) for the future, we therefore desire a second edict (*kasanete no onkudashibumi*)[6] to serve as proof [of possession]. Our deed of release is thus.

1st year of En'ō [1239], 7th month, 17th day

> shamon, Kakuzen (monogram)

58

That the daughter of Kagenari *hosshi*[7] shall forthwith hold the *gesu shiki* for Senbu Estate, within the northern sector of Toshima [District], Settsu Province.[8]

The aforesaid person shall hold this title in accordance with the release of her father, dated the 7th month, 17th day of the present year.[9] By command of the Kamakura lord, it is so decreed.[10]

1st year of En'ō [1239], 8th month, 3d day[11]

> saki no Musashi no kami, Taira (monogram)
>
> shuri gon no daibu, Taira (monogram)

SOURCES: Document 57: *Tosa monjo*, 1239/7/17 Kakuzen yuzurijō, *Tosa monjo kaisetsu*, pp. 2–3 (*KI*, 8: 56, doc. 5453). Document 58: *ibid.*, 1239/8/3 Kantō gechijō, *Tosa monjo kaisetsu*, pp. 3–4 (*KI*, 8: 60, doc. 5463).

1. Minamoto Sanetomo, the third lord of Kamakura (r. 1203–19).

2. *Tosa monjo*, 1204/7/26 Kantō kudashibumi, *Tosa monjo kaisetsu*, p. 1. The grant was to Kakuzen (Kagenari), the present donor. Evidently, his mother had already transferred her interests to him.

3. A *soebumi* functioned as a kind of "cover letter," though here it seems to mean a confirmation; see below. For examples of *soejō* (= *soebumi*), see *Nihon no komonjo*, 2: 246–47, docs. 446–49.

4. The reference is to Hōjō Yasutoki, regent for the shogun during 1224–42 and a signatory to the present document.

5. Why an additional release was needed is unknown. It would seem that there is a connection here with the *soebumi* of Hōjō Yasutoki just mentioned. At all events, the initial conveyance is not extant.

6. I.e., a further confirmation.

7. The version in *Tosa monjo kaisetsu* has it "Kagenari *hosshi*," whereas *KI* renders it "Yoshinari *hosshi*." But Kagenari (i.e., Kakuzen) is the name appearing in the original investiture of 1204; see n. 2.

8. Why was the Bakufu not confirming *jitō* and *gesu shiki*, pursuant to its original authorization of 1204? We note also that Sugai Village, which was not included in the 1204 grant (but is included in Document 57), is similarly not referred to here.

9. I.e., Document 57.

10. Why was this confirmation granted as a *gechijō* rather than as a shogunal *kuda-shibumi*, which was normal?

11. There are no additional Kamakura-period testamentary materials bearing on Senbu Estate.

DOCUMENT 59

The Bakufu Credits the Later of Two Deeds of Conveyance, 1239

In this extraordinarily vivid account we see once again that there was no legal recourse against a father's changing the direction of an inheritance. The bequest had originally gone to his daughter, but she proved unfilial (which had only to be asserted by a parent). This alone would have been reason for the reacquisition of an inheritance. But then she died prematurely, another reason for redirection. The present judgment is unusual in that one of the litigants (the victor) was the donor. This is because his opponent was his son-in-law—his late daughter's husband and thus not a junior-generation blood relative. Though in our eyes the donor's grandchildren through his daughter ought to have had a claim on the inheritance, neither the Bakufu nor the society it served felt that way. The donor was awarded the right to reallocate the disputed property, which was promptly settled upon a son rather than a daughter. It seems possible that cases of this kind might have influenced donors who were contemplating leaving parts of their estates to daughters.

> That, in accordance with the later-sealed (*gohan*) conveyance of the former Satsuma governor, Kinnari *hosshi*—Buddhist name Kōren—the *jitō shiki* for the harbor at Yugawasawa, Akita District, Dewa Province, shall forthwith be held by his son Kinkazu.

According to Kōren's conveyance to Kinkazu dated this year, 6th month,   day:[1] "The aforesaid place was granted for my military merit (*gunkō*) by the late [*u*]*taishō* lord on the occasion of the Northern Campaign.[2] Although I deeded it to the wife of the Izu governor— Kōren's second daughter, Kusunoue[3]—she was unfilial (*fukō*) to Kōren and then died. Though her children could not have known of this, [her inheritance] is rescinded and Kinkazu is made our heir (*chaku-shi*), with the bequest conveyed to him.[4] [Authorization for such] is recorded in the [Jōei] Formulary (*shikimoku*).[5] Let there be no departure whatever from Kōren's decision." Abridged into Chinese characters (*kanji*) from [the original in] the Japanese syllabary (*wa no ji*).[6]

According to the brief forwarded by Yorisada *ason*:[7] "On the 29th day, 9th month, 1st year of Genkyū [1204], Kōren transferred his investiture edict (*kudashibumi*) to his late wife, Fujiwara *no uji*, who in turn deeded it to their daughter Kusunoue—Yorisada's wife, Suke-no-tsubone[8]—on the 29th day, 7th month, 4th year of Jōgen [1210]; Kōren added his seal to this document.[9] In pursuance thereof, a petition was made on the 23d day, 12th month, 1st year of Jōō [1222], to the Lady of the Second Rank (Nii *dono*)[10] to which a reply was given that no deviations were possible.[11] In the 3d year of Kangi [1231], 4th month, a [Kantō confirmation] edict was awarded.[12] Now Suke-no-tsubone has suddenly passed away this 4th month, 8th day. Though she left no testament, she did leave three sons. Heredity should certainly prevail here, and it is difficult to assuage our grief over Kōren's sudden allocation to another child.[13] There is a regulation against overturning any settlements from the time of the Lady of the Second Rank.[14] How can there be an exception here?"

The rule regarding judgments rendered by successive shoguns and by the Lady of the Second Rank is limited to disputes between an original holder (*hon ryōshu*) and a current recipient (*tō-kyūnin*). It is not a clause that affects a father and daughter.[15] As regards property disposal to children, the same regulation avers that the later [of two] documents shall prevail.[16] Thus, in accordance with both the rules as well as established custom, Kinkazu shall possess the *jitō shiki* for the harbor, pursuant to Kōren's later-sealed conveyance.[17] By this command, it is so decreed.

1st year of En'ō [1239], 11th month, 5th day

> saki no Musashi no kami, Taira
> ason seal
> shuri gon no daibu, Taira ason seal

SOURCE: *Ogashima monjo*, 1239/11/5 Kantō gechijō an, *Ogashima monjo—Ōkawa monjo—Madarashima monjo*, pp. 3–5, doc. 5 (*KI*, 8: 72–73, doc. 5496).

1. *Ogashima monjo*, 1239/6 Tachibana Kinnari yuzurijō an, *Ogashima monjo—Ōkawa monjo—Madarashima monjo*, pp. 2–3, doc. 4 (*KI*, 8: 53, doc. 5446).

2. The Ōshū War (in which Bakufu forces defeated the armies of the Northern Fujiwara) occurred in 1189. The original investiture edict is not extant.

3. As we will note shortly, the present suit was brought by Kusunoue's husband, the Izu governor, Yorisada *ason*. The conveyance to Kusunoue (dated 1210/7/29; see below) is not extant.

4. The conveyance of 1239/6 (n. 1) makes clear that Kusunoue had broken all ties with her father; thus her children would not have been aware of their grandfather's reconveyance.

5. Article 20 of the Formulary permits parents to revoke a release to an heir at any time, but especially if the child has predeceased the parent. Similarly, Article 18 permits disinheritance of daughters who are unfilial.

6. The original release was indeed in *kana*; see n. 1.

7. At last we learn that Kōren's revised conveyance of 1239 is being challenged. The suit was brought by Kōren's son-in-law, Yorisada *ason*, the governor of Izu.

8. Thus Kusunoue = Suke-no-tsubone = Kōren's daughter = Yorisada's wife.

9. Not extant; this alleged involvement of Kōren's wife seems very doubtful.

10. I.e., Hōjō Masako, widow of Yoritomo.

11. This seems a bit curious, since Bakufu confirmations were all issued by Hōjō Yoshitoki, Masako's brother. In fact, no petitions to Masako survive—and no replies by her either. Yet various later documents (as in the present case) refer to her influence during the early 1220s.

12. The only extant confirmation from this period was in response to a deed by Kōren to a son, Otsuōmaru (= Kinkazu?), not a daughter; *Ogashima monjo*, 1231/3/27 shōgun ke kudashibumi an, *Ogashima monjo—Ōkawa monjo—Madarashima monjo*, p. 1, doc. 1 (*KI*, 6: 251, doc. 4119). The release in question occurred in the 7th month of 1230 and was for *jitō* rights in Iyo and Dewa provinces. However, the Dewa bequest was not the same as that being contested here.

13. I.e., to Kinkazu, his own son. Yorisada, the plaintiff, is claiming that the bequest should have gone to one of his own sons, who would have been a grandson of Kōren.

14. See Article 7 of the Jōei Formulary; also n. 15.

15. Article 7, which provides security against challenge from former holders, excludes parents as testators from its scope.

16. In this case, the more recent of two testaments; see Article 26 of the Formulary.

17. Kōren's conveyance of 1239/6 (n. 1) clearly took precedence over his assignment to his daughter of 1210.

DOCUMENT 60

The Head of a Branch Line Within a Senior Kamakura Family Deeds His Inheritance, 1240

As we have seen, certain families continued to receive new *jitō* posts from a Bakufu that valued their services. A classic example was the Nikaidō family, one of whose branches became a bureaucratic line within the Bakufu, and the other (represented here) a warrior line, much honored, which also served at times within the central Bakufu. Especially noteworthy is the timing of this family's acquisition of some of its holdings—after each of the major political or military incidents of the period. These episodes saw persons on the winning side being granted land rights confiscated from the losers.

Conveyed:[1]

> Futokorojima-Tonobara *gō*, Sagami Province;[2]
> Shigenohara Estate, Mikawa Province;[3]
> Nishikadoma Estate, Owari Province;[4]
> Masuda Estate, Ise Province;
> Kagami Shrine, Hizen Province;
> (Toriwada Village, in Shinobu Estate, Mutsu [Province] . . .[5]
>   [monogram])[6]
> [To:] *saemon no jō* Yukiuji[7]

The aforesaid places and accompanying investiture edicts are conveyed. Let there be no disturbances. It is thus.

1st year of Ninji [1240], 10th month, 14th day[8]

                                             shami[9] (monogram)

SOURCE: *Nikaidō monjo*, 1240/10/14 Nikaidō Motoyuki *yuzurijō*, *Kanagawa kenshi, shiryō hen*, 1: 587, doc. 349 (*KI*, 8: 158–59, doc. 5627).

1. Though not so specified, *jitō* titles were being deeded (see the confirmatory edict cited in n. 8). The author of the present document, Nikaidō Motoyuki (1198–1240), was appointed to the Bakufu's Board of Councillors (*hyōjōshū*) in 1239. The Nikaidō family occupied numerous senior positions within the Kamakura bureaucracy.

2. Acquired in 1213 in the wake of the Wada Rebellion; see *Nikaidō monjo*, 1213/5/9 Minamoto Sanetomo *sodehan kudashibumi*, *Kanagawa kenshi, shiryō hen*, 1: 549, doc. 278 (*KB*, doc. 26).

3. Acquired in 1221 after the Jōkyū War; *ibid.*, 1221/7/12 Kantō *gechijō*, *Aichi kenshi, bekkan*, p. 378.

4. The investiture documents for this and the remaining places do not survive. In 1247, in the wake of the Miura War, the present recipient (Yukiuji) was granted still another *jitō shiki* (in the Kantō's Awa Province); *Nikaidō monjo*, 1247/6/23 shōgun *sodehan kudashibumi an*, *KI*, 9: 385, doc. 6846.

5. A corrupt term of two characters appears here.

6. The section in parentheses was evidently inserted after the document had been prepared. It may represent a kind of afterthought on the part of Motoyuki, and hence the additional monogram (his own) to give it authenticity. For a photograph of this document, see *Kanagawa kenshi, shiryō hen*, 1: 587.

7. Nikaidō Yukiuji, the son and principal heir of Motoyuki, the donor. Motoyuki died just two months after recording this will; see *AK*, 1240/12/15.

8. The Bakufu's confirmation was issued a month later; *Nikaidō monjo*, 1240/int. 10/20 shōgun *ke mandokoro kudashibumi*, *Kanagawa kenshi, shiryō hen*, 1: 588, doc. 350. A generation later Yukiuji, the recipient here, bequeathed only a portion of this inheritance to his own primary heir (the *jitō* titles in Sagami and Mikawa provinces, plus the Awa holding cited in n. 4); *ibid.*, 1272/5/26 shōgun *ke mandokoro kudashibumi an*, *Kanagawa kenshi, shiryō hen*, 1: 771, doc. 641. Evidently, Yukiuji was dividing his estate among more than one heir, though we have no explicit information on this.

9. Nikaidō Motoyuki.

DOCUMENT 61

An Eldest Son Left Out of an Inheritance Brings Suit and Loses, 1241

It is hardly surprising that the competing claims for property on the part of relatives often included charges of forgery. Indeed, no document type of the Kamakura era was more frequently labeled a counterfeit than the deed of conveyance. This is because property holders prepared conveyances for multiple children—and then rewrote them (or had scribes rewrite them) entirely according to whim. It often happened, moreover, that a charge of forgery elicited a countercharge of the same crime—as we see in the present case in reference to a disinheritance. It was left for the Bakufu to unravel the contradictory claims, which it succeeded in doing on the basis of an earlier accord that made unlikely a "release" not cited at that time. We also see in this episode the tightness of available land for the number of candidates hoping to succeed to it.

> Concerning a dispute over Ōkawa and Ifuku villages between Ōkawa Jirō Yukimoto of [Hizen][1] Province, represented by his son Shintarō Yukitomo, and Ifuku Saburō Michiyuki, represented by Daizanji Gorō Toshiyuki.[2]

On the occasion of a trial (*taiketsu*), Yukitomo stated:[3] "The aforesaid two villages were the hereditary private holdings of our great-grandfather, Yukifusa *hosshi*—Buddhist name, Jōshin. Subsequently, his son Yukiakira *hosshi*—Buddhist name, Sainen—had them deeded to him.[4] On the occasion of the allocation of these villages by Sainen to his sons in the 3d year of Kenpō [1215], 2d month, 15th day, conveyances were prepared and given to the younger children (*shoshi*), after which a release for the remaining land was received by Yukimoto, the eldest (*chakushi*), authorizing him to enjoy possession.[5] Thus, pursuant to that document, [Sainen] sought to grant [to Yukimoto] that which was not parceled among [Yukimoto's] younger brothers."

According to Toshiyuki's statement: "The two villages were of course the hereditary private holdings of Jōshin. Accordingly, both villages were deeded by Jōshin to Sainen in the 2d year of Bunji [1186].[6] Moreover, in the 2d year of Shōji [1200], Ifuku Village was disengaged, with a deed going to Michiyuki under countersignatures of Michimune, Sainen, Yukimoto, and Motomura,[7] [a dispensation] arranged by Jōshin.[8] After that, Sainen released the bounded region of the Ōkawa open areas to his fourth son Yukinori in the 3d year of Kenpō [1215], obtaining countersignatures from Yukimoto and Michiyuki.[9] Additionally, Otohime and Esaburō Yukiyoshi were deeded units (*myō*) lying outside that bounded region.[10] In this way [Sainen] made allocations to his sons and daughters so that nothing remained. How, then, could Sainen have written a conveyance in the 3d year of Kenpō stating that the remainder should be held by Yukimoto?[11] Clearly, [this document] is a forgery. When a complaint was lodged with the former Buzen governor Sukeyoshi at the *shugo* headquarters,[12] a bill of accusation (*sojō*) was accordingly sent out.[13] In consequence of this, Ayabe Gorō Yukihide *hosshi*[14]—Buddhist name, Chōshu—as well as Gyōsai,[15] acting as representatives for Michiyuki and Otohime, undertook to go to the Daizanji villa (*bessho*)[16] for the purpose of drafting a rebuttal statement (*chinjō*); but Yukimoto followed and caught up with them proclaiming that even though he had initiated the suit, a compromise (*wayo*) was now in order. Whereupon Chōshu, lecturing both sides, argued that indeed an agreement should be reached. Accordingly, a compact (*keijō*) was drawn up in the 1st year of Kangi [1229],   month, to which Gyōsai added his seal on behalf of Otohime, and to which Yukimoto and Michiyuki also added their signatures: 3 *chō* of paddy and 5 homestead areas (*sono*) were now relinquished to Yukimoto. Sukeyoshi added his seal to this quitclaim (*saribumi*), and it was conveyed to Yukimoto.[17] But most particularly, the deed of release from the 3d year of Kenpō [1215] is patently a forgery by virtue of its presentation now but nonsubmission at the time of Sukeyoshi's earlier review.[18] Besides that, Yukimoto was disinherited (*gizetsu*) by Sainen in the 2d year of Antei [1228]. This fact is attested to by signatures of the family's membership."[19]

According to Yukitomo's statement: "There is no dispute regarding Jōshin's release to Sainen in the 2d year of Bunji [1186] of Ōkawa and Ifuku. Next, there is no need to pursue the release of Ifuku to Michiyuki in the 2d year of Shōji [1200] for which Jōshin obtained the signatures of Michimune, Yukimoto, and Yukimura.[20] However, following Sainen's parceling of shares in the two villages among his younger children (*shoshi*) in the 3d year of Kenpō, 2d month, he recorded that the remainder was to be Yukimoto's share, though [Sainen] held it for the duration of his lifetime.[21] The conveyance from the 2d year of Shōji [1200] bears an earlier seal; the conveyance from the 3d year of Kenpō [1215] bears a later seal. That the conveyance from the 2d year of Shōji was invalidated is made clear by the release in the 3d year of

Jōō [1224]²² of a portion of Ifuku to the daughter Otohime.²³ Yet even
after this later-sealed deed, the leftover portion remained with Michiyuki: why was this not transferred to Yukimoto? Next, regarding the
allegation of a disinheritance, this is entirely false. Next, the 3 *chō* of
paddy and 5 homestead areas were of course relinquished [to us]. But
actually it was 3 *chō* 2 *tan* and 6 homestead areas."

According to Toshiyuki's statement: "We have already acknowledged the compact (*keijō*) of the 1st year of Kangi [1229]. As for the
discrepancy in paddy and homestead totals, let the [original] quitclaim be called in."²⁴

Yukitomo²⁵ does not dispute the conveyance from the 2d year of
Shōji [1200] possessed by Michiyuki; it does not list any leftover area.²⁶
Moreover, it hardly seems credible to claim possession of a release
from the 3d year of Kenpō [1215] when that deed was not submitted
in the suit before Sukeyoshi in the 1st year of Kangi, and when the 3
chō of paddy and 5 homesteads, obtained by a compromise, were anyway later sold off.²⁷ Next, concerning the document of disinheritance
(*gizetsujō*), Yukitomo has labeled it a forgery.²⁸ Although the cosigners
ought, correspondingly, to be interrogated, this will not be done since
no other disputed matters remain.²⁹ In consequence, Yukimoto's false
charges (*ranso*) are dismissed, and individual possessions shall continue as before, in accordance with the [lawful] deeds of conveyance.³⁰
By command of the Kamakura lord, it is so decreed.

2d year of Ninji [1241], 8th month, 22d day³¹

saki no Musashi no kami, Taira
ason (monogram)

SOURCE: *Ōkawa monjo*, 1241/8/22 Kantō gechijō, *Ogashima monjo—Ōkawa monjo—
Madarashima monjo*, pp. 75–77, doc. 9 (*KI*, 8: 300–301, doc. 5918).

  1. Characters lost but determinable from related documents. In various other
places I have borrowed from a *dazaifu* edict of several months later (see n. 31), which
reproduces the present document with no characters lost.

  2. Toshiyuki was married to Michiyuki's sister, Otohime, and was thus a brother-in-
law; see *Ōkawa monjo*, 1241/5/2 Kantō gechijō, *Ogashima monjo—Ōkawa monjo—Madarashima monjo*, pp. 74–75, doc. 8 (*KI*, 8: 258, doc. 5831).

  3. Yukitomo was the plaintiff and ultimate loser in this dispute with his uncle
Michiyuki. Several months earlier Yukitomo (on behalf of his father Yukimoto) had lost
a separate suit with another uncle, Yukinori; see the document cited in n. 2.

  4. The release for four villages (including Ōkawa and Ifuku) occurred in 1186 and
was signed by the donor (Jōshin) and the recipient's three elder brothers; see Document 9.

  5. As we shall see, this was the hub of the dispute: Yukimoto's conveyance of 1215
(not extant) was branded a forgery.

6. Document 9. Both sides agree on this point.

7. The text is in error here and should read "Yukimura"; see Document 10.

8. Document 10. Noteworthy here is that Yukitomo, the plaintiff, had pointedly failed to mention this release to Michiyuki, which had in fact been cosigned by his father (Yukimoto).

9. This conveyance is not extant. Jōshin had now died and Sainen was creating shares for his sons on his own. Yukimoto, we recall, was the eldest, and Michiyuki, his brother, was the recipient in 1200 (see Document 10).

10. The references are to a daughter and a fifth son of Sainen.

11. The condition of Yukimoto is in fact puzzling. He was the eldest son but obviously had to struggle to acquire any property at all. It would seem that the *chakushi* in this instance was barely the equal of his brothers.

12. Mutō Sukeyoshi, ranking officer of the *dazaifu* and also the *shugo* of Hizen Province. The reference here is to the *dazaifu* (= *shugosho*). This is the earliest indication (1229) that Sainen's family had achieved *gokenin* status.

13. In other words, Yukimoto's suit was accepted for litigation and his formal accusation statement was sent to the defendants (Michiyuki and Otohime, as noted below). What prompted Yukimoto's suit against his brother and sister was his disinheritance a year earlier; see below.

14. Yukihide was a brother of Sainen and uncle of Michiyuki and Yukimoto; he was probably the family's senior surviving member. For his name, see Document 9.

15. Identity unknown.

16. We recall that Otohime was married to Daizanji Toshiyuki, who in 1241 (the present suit) would act as representative for his brother-in-law Michiyuki.

17. Not extant.

18. Yukimoto, in other words, would not have needed the compromise of 1229 if he had held a valid conveyance from his father, Sainen.

19. Here is the real reason why Yukimoto, hoping to salvage something, agreed to the compromise of 1229. What is unclear is the background to his disinheritance—or its meaning for someone who was landless. Why did Sainen, who was now an old man, take this action against his first-born?

20. The plaintiff's acknowledgment of this release (not included in his opening statement) is not, however, what it appears to be; he would shortly attempt to claim its invalidity.

21. Unfortunately, we do not know when Sainen died. Perhaps his disinheritance of Yukimoto in 1228 was his last important decision; the compromise of the following year does not mention him.

22. The original has it this way, though the 3d year of Kenpō [1215] would seem to make better sense.

23. In other words, Otohime's receiving a portion of Ifuku made clear that the earlier grant of *all* of Ifuku to Michiyuki was now rendered invalid.

24. The document itself, we recall, was cosigned by Mutō Sukeyoshi and conveyed to Yukimoto.

25. The Bakufu's verdict begins here.

26. The release of 1200 (Document 10) granted the entire village of Ifuku to Michiyuki, a transaction to which Yukimoto added his own signature. As we have seen, however, Yukitomo was attempting to argue its invalidity, on the basis of a later-sealed conveyance.

27. We are not prepared for this reference to Yukimoto's disposal by sale of the holdings he received in 1229. Yukitomo, as Yukimoto's son, evidently had no inheritance coming to him.

28. Thus both sides had claimed the use of forged documents: Yukimoto had labeled the *gizetsujō* a counterfeit, whereas Toshiyuki had argued the same for the 1215 release to Yukimoto.

29. Yukimoto's case had already been discredited; there was no need to pursue the investigation further.

30. I.e., those of 1200, 1215, and (possibly) 1224, but excluding the alleged conveyance of 1215 to Yukimoto.

31. A *dazaifu* validation was issued several months later; *Ōkawa monjo*, 1241/11/12 dazaifu shugosho kudashibumi, *Ogashima monjo—Ōkawa monjo—Madarashima monjo*, pp. 78–81, doc. 11 (*KI*, 8: 319–20, doc. 5960).

DOCUMENT 62

The Bakufu Transfers Jitō Rights to an Elder Brother, 1242

The Bakufu dispossessed *jitō* holders for certain capital crimes, for blatant instances of forgery before Kamakura's judges, and for the act of treachery. In all three cases a likely candidate for the vacated position was a relative—often a brother—of the person who had been dispossessed. During Kamakura times there was scarcely a presumption of guilt by association, since the fraternal relationship, far from being the bedrock of solidarity, was the most common basis for discord. As in the present instance, the bad fortune of one brother turned out to be the good fortune of another.

The chancellery of the shogun's house directs: to Minamoto Yorinaka.
    That he shall forthwith possess the *jitō shiki* vacated by his younger brother, the Nose [district] *kurōdo*.

Despite long residence in Kyoto the aforesaid *kurōdo*[1] has been dismissed (*kaieki*) for disloyalty (*fuchū*).[2] In his place, Yorinaka is granted [this appointment] by virtue of his service (*hōkō*) in the capital. He is to exercise possession under this title.[3] The command is thus. Wherefore, this order.[4]
    3d year of Ninji [1242], 3d month, 21st day

                                    anzu, sakon no shōsō, Sugano seal[5]
                                    chikeji, danjōchū, Kiyohara seal
ryō, saemon no shōjō, Kiyohara seal
bettō, saki no Musashi no kami, Taira ason seal

saki no Settsu no kami, Nakahara ason seal
saki no Mutsu no kami, Minamoto ason seal[6]
saki no Mino no kami, Fujiwara ason seal
saki no Kai no kami, Ōe ason seal
Musashi no kami, Taira ason seal
san-i, Fujiwara seal

SOURCE: *Komonjo shū*, 1242/3/21 shōgun ke mandokoro kudashibumi an, *KI*, 8: 341, doc. 6003.

1. An archivist or secretary.

2. The Emperor Shijō had just died (1242/1/9), and Kyoto and Kamakura disagreed vigorously over his successor. The Bakufu's views ultimately prevailed, leading to Go-Saga's enthronement just three days before the present document. The charge of disloyalty may be related to this situation.

3. The location (or nature) of the *jitō shiki* is not specified.

4. Rokuhara issued an enforcement edict eleven days later; *Kakiage komonjo*, 1242/4/2 Rokuhara shigyōjō an, *KI*, 8: 345, doc. 6012.

5. A different copy of this document lacks the character for "seal"; *Kakiage komonjo, DNS*, Series 5, 14: 294–95.

6. See n. 5.

DOCUMENT 63

The Bakufu Confirms a Release to a Second Son Countersigned by the Principal Heir, 1242

During the middle decades of the thirteenth century releases tended to become more complicated as donors felt obliged to spell out the conditions of the complementary bequests in somewhat greater detail. The Bakufu's confirmatory edicts reflected this new complexity by noting the special conditions. The pie could be cut up into any number of equal or unequal pieces; but the sum total of the pieces still equaled the pie.

The chancellery of the shogun's house directs: to Fujiwara Sanetoki.
    That he shall forthwith possess the *jitō shiki* for a portion of Minochi Village, in Nagano Estate, Iwami Province[1]—boundaries recorded in the release; minus the third son Sanetaka's share.[2]

Possession shall be in accordance with the release of the father, Sanemori, dated the 2d year of En'ō [1240], 3d month, 9th day[3]—countersigned by the principal heir (*chakushi*).[4] The command is thus. Wherefore, this order.

3d year of Ninji [1242], 10th month, 23d day[5]

anzu, sakon no shōsō, Sugano

chikeji, danjōchū, Kiyohara

ryō, saemon no shōjō, Kiyohara (monogram)

bettō, saki no Settsu no kami, Nakahara ason (monogram)

saki no Mino no kami, Fujiwara ason

saki no Kai no kami, Ōe ason

Musashi no kami, Taira ason

sa konoe shōgen, Taira ason (monogram)

san-i, Fujiwara ason

SOURCE: *Mōri ke monjo*, 1242/10/23 shōgun ke mandokoro kudashibumi, *KI*, 8: 399–400, doc. 6127.

1. Nagano Estate was a stronghold of the Masuda family, the dominant *gokenin* house of Iwami Province. The Masuda held three *gō*-level *jitō* titles there; see *Masuda ke monjo*, 1203/12 Masuda Kanesue mōshibumi an, *Shinshū Shimane kenshi, shiryō hen*, 1: 542–43 (*KI*, 3: 120, doc. 1418), and *ibid.*, 1223/5/25 Kantō gechijō an, *KI*, 5: 204, doc. 3108 (*DKR*, doc. 70). It seems likely that the recipient here (Fujiwara Sanetoki) was related or was otherwise subject to Nagano Estate's leading family.

2. In half-size characters from "boundaries recorded. . . ."

3. Not extant.

4. The present recipient then was probably the second son (Sanetaka, referred to above, was the third son). The principal heir's name is not given. Phrase in half-size characters.

5. No related documents appear to survive.

DOCUMENT 64

The Bakufu Confirms a Broad Range of Non-Jitō Titles Released by a Mother, 1243

Here we see a "same-day" confirmation by the Bakufu of a variety of *shiki* released by the wife of a Kamakura vassal. The recipient here, a son, would also have been eligible to receive a share of assets from his father, though whether he did in this instance is not clear. Double inheritances were not very common, suggesting the reluctance of partners (especially women) to merge properties with those belonging to their spouses. More normal was for a husband and wife to deed rights to different children. Even so, the wealth of two people must be taken into account when measuring the assets of families.

The chancellery of the shogun's house directs: to *san-i* Fujiwara Kiyotoshi.[1]

That forthwith he shall possess the local lordships (*ryōshu shiki*) of Ayukawa Estate, Sagami Province, and of Northern and Southern Ahiru Estate, Kazusa Province; also the custodial (*azukari dokoro*) and managerial (*gesu*) titles of Hota Estate, Bitchū Province, all holdings of Kumano [Shrine].

In accordance with the conveyance of this day by the mother,[2] Kakuyū—details recorded therein—authority shall be exercised, pursuant to precedent, under these *shiki*. The command is thus. Wherefore, this order.

    1st year of Kangen [1243], 7th month, 28th day

                  anzu, sakon no shōsō, Sugano
                  chikeji, danjōchū, Kiyohara
                  (monogram)

ryō, saemon no jō, Kiyohara (monogram)
bettō, saki no Settsu no kami, Nakahara ason (monogram)
saki no Mino no kami, Fujiwara ason (monogram)
saki no Kai no kami, Ōe ason (monogram)
Tōtomi no kami, Taira ason (monogram)
Musashi no kami, Taira ason (monogram)
san-i, Fujiwara ason (monogram)

SOURCE: *Mōri ke monjo*, 1243/7/28 shōgun ke mandokoro kudashibumi, *Kanagawa kenshi, shiryō hen*, 1: 596–97, doc. 366 (*KI*, 9: 23, doc. 6207).
    1. Yamanouchi Kiyotoshi, a younger son of the Yamanouchi house head, Munetoshi (see Documents 42–44).
    2. The release of these non-*jitō* titles, then, issued from Kiyotoshi's mother, not from his Kamakura-vassal father. Although the mother's identity is unknown, there seems a likely connection with Kumano Shrine. The deed of release itself is not extant, though we should note the Bakufu's remarkably rapid movement here—a "same-day" confirmation. The conveyance was obviously drawn up in Kamakura.

DOCUMENTS 65–67

A Warrior Provides Land Shares for the Members of His Family, 1243, 1244, 1254

Maintaining a partible-inheritance strategy was difficult enough when a donor was rich. But when a single unit of land was held, and when the donor wished to make bequests to secondary heirs such as a younger son, a daughter, a granddaughter, and his own wife, the parcels necessarily became tiny. In the best of circumstances relatives felt crowded by one another; in cramped circumstances the pressures for abjuring parcelization and for placing increased authority in the hands of one person became stronger. In the present case, two of the four secondary recipients (the daughter and the wife) were given only lifetime tenures. The example represents, then, an inheritance package with permanent and impermanent components. It is typical of the mid-thirteenth century.

65

Conveyed: Tanaka *gō*, an added land (*kanō*) of Umino Estate, Shinano Province.

> Appended: two [shogunal] edicts; the release of my father, Mitsunao; the release of [Tsuneuji's] grandmother, Saimyō[1]— along with the [full] sequence of releases (*tetsugi yuzurijō*).[2]
> [To:] Shigeno Tsuneuji

The aforesaid Tanaka *gō*, the [shogunal] edicts, and the conveyance of my father, Mitsunao, are hereby deeded to Shigeno Tsuneuji.[3] However, the residence area (*yashiki*) of Kotarō[4] plus one *chō* of paddy within this *gō* were released to my son Kagemitsu. Moreover, the residence area of Miyami *nyūdō*[5] plus six *tan* of paddy appurtenant to a service household (*zaike*) were released to my daughter, the Lady Urano. Similarly, the service household of Fuji *nyūdō*[6] plus six *tan* of paddy were released to my granddaughter, Masu-gozen.[7] Also, the residence area and adjoining compound (*hori no uchi*) of my father, Mitsunao, along with two *chō* three *tan* of cultivated paddy located therein (*naisaku*) were released to my wife, Ono *no uji*. Tsuneuji is not to cause disturbance either to my offspring[8] or to Ono *no uji*. Nevertheless, at the end of their lifetimes, the share of Ono *no uji* and that of my daughter will become the possessions of Tsuneuji. As concerns the residence area of my father plus the interior paddy (*naisaku*), these, along with Mitsunao's deed of conveyance, were deeded by Saimyō—Tsuneuji's grandmother—to Mitsu. . . .[9] The boundaries of the said residence area as well as paddy fields appear in the original documents (*hon monjo*). Wherefore, our conveyance is thus.

> 1st year of Kangen [1243], 10th month, 6th day

> > Shigeno Mitsuuji seal

66

seal

Directed: to the residents of Tanaka *gō*, an added land of Umino Estate, Shinano Province—minus those land shares of relatives (*shinrui*).[10]

That Shigeno Tsuneuji shall forthwith hold the *jitō shiki*.

Pursuant to precedent, authority shall be exercised under this *shiki*, in accordance with the conveyance of last year, 10th month, 6th day, by the father Mitsuuji—particulars contained therein. It is [commanded] thus.

2d year of Kangen [1244], 12th month, 30th day[11]

67

The chancellery of the shogun's house directs: to the residents of Tanaka *gō*, an added land of Umino Estate, Shinano Province—minus the land shares of a younger brother, of females,[12] and of the mother.

That *saemon no jō* Shigeno Tsuneuji shall forthwith hold the *jitō shiki*.[13]

Pursuant to precedent, authority shall be exercised under this *shiki*, in accordance with the conveyance of the 1st year of Kangen [1243], 10th month, 6th day, by the father Tanaka Shirō Mitsuuji—particulars on excludable shares recorded therein. The command is thus. Wherefore, this order.

6th year of Kenchō [1254], 11th month, 5th day[14]

anzu, Kiyohara
chikeji, Kiyohara

ryō, saemon no shōjō, Fujiwara
bettō, Mutsu no kami, Taira ason seal
Sagami no kami, Taira ason seal

SOURCES: Document 65: *Usuda monjo*, 1243/10/6 Shigeno Mitsuuji yuzurijō an, *Shinano shiryō*, 4: 112 (*KI*, 9: 38, doc. 6241). Document 66: *ibid.*, 1244/12/30 shōgun sodehan kudashibumi an, *Shinano shiryō*, 4: 117 (*KI*, 9: 159–60, doc. 6430). Document 67: *ibid.*, 1254/11/5 shōgun ke mandokoro kudashibumi an, *Shinano shiryō*, 4: 203–4 (*KI*, 11: 55, doc. 7818).

1. As we see later, Saimyō is the grandmother of the recipient (Tsuneuji), not of the donor (Mitsuuji). This would seem to make Saimyō the mother of Mitsuuji, though why she is not so described is unclear. Also, we will see that Mitsunao apparently made Saimyō executrix of his estate during her lifetime and that she then passed the inheritance to Mitsuuji.

2. None of these earlier documents is extant.

3. The *KI* version omits the character *tsune*, an obvious error.

4. Not identified.

5. Not identified.

6. Not identified.

7. Whose daughter is this? Tsuneuji's?

8. I.e., to Tsuneuji's siblings.

9. A character was deliberately omitted here. Could this be Mitsu*uji*, the author of the present release? At the front of this document we see that both Saimyō's and Mitsunao's conveyances were held by Mitsuuji. As implied here, then, Saimyō received the family estate as a life bequest and then deeded it (as per her husband Mitsunao's instruction) to Mitsuuji.

10. The version in *KI* (also *Ibaragi ken shiryō, chūsei hen,* 1: 421) is clearly correct: *shinrui* = relatives, rather than *Shinano shiryō*'s "Chikayori," a personal name.

11. The format of this edict is different from that of shogunal decrees a year earlier (Documents 62–64). This is because a child shogun, Yoritsugu, had been appointed in the meantime (1244/4/28). A formal chancellery would not issue edicts until 1251 (see, e.g., Document 71), when Yoritsugu was promoted to high Court rank; see *AK*, 1251/7/4.

12. The term here is *joshi* (also pronounced *nyoshi* or *onago*), meaning girl, woman, daughter, etc. It is probably not daughter, since the Lady Urano (Document 65) was Tsuneuji's sister (unless the Bakufu scribe was simply confused here). In fact, there were two female shares cited in Document 65—that of Tsuneuji's sister and that of his daughter (or niece—we cannot tell which). The present translation reflects this condition. (Of course, Tsuneuji's mother—Ono *no uji*—was also included in Document 65.)

13. Why, after ten years, did the Bakufu issue this new investiture? Could it be that the donor, Mitsuuji, had finally died?

14. The next surviving document in the sequence is dated 1310; Tsuneuji had died and his principal heir, Tsunenaga, is confirmed in a portion of Tanaka *gō: Usuda monjo,* 1310/3/7 Kantō gechijō an, *Shinano shiryō,* 4: 544.

DOCUMENTS 68–70

An Elder Brother Is Barred from the Family Headship, Brings Suit, and Loses, 1249, 1252, 1254

As mentioned earlier, eldest sons passed over for the house headship often became understandably resentful. Such was the case here even though the neglected first son was granted his own land share. The father seems to have been aware of the potential for trouble created by his decision, and he appealed to the Bakufu to heed his own (and his heir's) words in the event of a dispute. At the same time, a daughter was given a minor share, which made her vulnerable to her brother. And thus—typical of the age—two brothers and a sister were at loggerheads, with the Bakufu, as in so many similar instances, thrust into the role of arbiter.

68

In the matter of conveyance of family lands (*shoryō*).

With the exception of paddy and service households in Nakano and Shikumi *gō*, which I have divided among other descendants,[1] I deed in perpetuity the main *jitō* title (*sōjitō shiki*) to Jirō Tadayoshi, who has been made my principal heir, accompanied by [Kantō] edicts and other original records.[2] Tarō Mitsunari has not been named principal heir because he has disregarded his father's wishes and because he lacks ability (*kiryō*).[3] In order that [the authorities] heed the claims of Tadayoshi and render judgment, in the event of a suit, following Myōren's will, our deed of release is thus.

　　　1st year of Kenchō [1249], 12th month, 15th day

　　　　　　　　　　　　　　　　　shami, Myōren (monogram)

69

The chancellery of the shogun's house directs: to Fujiwara Tadayoshi.
　　　That he shall forthwith possess the *jitō shiki* for Nakano-Nishi-jō and for Shikumi *gō* within the private lands (*ryō*) of Haruchika,[4] Shinano Province—minus designated shares for the elder brother Tarō *nyūdō* Saigan[5] and for [Myōren's] daughter.[6]

Regarding the above, Saigan has presented various details, but they are without foundation.[7] Therefore, in accordance with the release of the late father *sama no jō* Yoshinari *hosshi*—Buddhist name, Myōren—from the 1st year of Kenchō [1249], 12th month, 15th day[8]—in which Saigan's faults are detailed—[Tadayoshi] shall exercise authority under this *shiki*, pursuant to precedent. The command is thus. Wherefore, this order.[9]

　　　4th year of Kenchō [1252], 12th month, 26th day

　　　　　　　　　　　　　　　　　anzu, Kiyohara
　　　　　　　　　　　　　　　　　chikeji, Kiyohara
ryō saemon no jō, Fujiwara
bettō, Mutsu no kami, Taira ason (monogram)
Sagami no kami, Taira ason (monogram)

70

The chancellery of the shogun's house directs: to Fujiwara *no uji*.[10]
　　　That she shall forthwith possess five *tan* of paddy and one service household within Nakano-Nishi-jō, Shinano Province.

Possession shall be exercised in accordance with the release of her late father [*sa*]*ma no jō* Yoshinari *hosshi*—Buddhist name, Myōren—from the 2d year of Tenpuku [1234], 10th month, 25th day,[11] and in accordance with the quitclaim (*saribumi*) of this past month, 17th day, by her elder brother Tadayoshi.[12] The command is thus. Wherefore, this order.

6th year of Kenchō [1254], 12th month, 12th day[13]

anzu, Kiyohara

chikeji, Kiyohara

ryō, saemon no shōjō, Fujiwara

bettō, Mutsu no kami, Taira ason (monogram)

Sagami no kami, Taira ason (monogram)

SOURCES: Document 68: *Ichikawa monjo*, 1249/12/15 Nakano Yoshinari yuzurijō, *Shinano shiryō*, 4: 147–48 (*KI*, 10: 128–29, doc. 7149). Document 69: *ibid.*, 1252/12/26 shōgun ke mandokoro kudashibumi, *Shinano shiryō*, 4: 183–84 (*KI*, 10: 342, doc. 7506). Document 70: *ibid.*, 1254/12/12 shōgun ke mandokoro kudashibumi, *Shinano shiryō*, 4: 205 (*KI*, 11: 63, doc. 7829).

1. At least three "descendants" (*shison*) appear in our documents, two sons and a daughter; see Documents 69–70.

2. Surviving records go back to the late Heian period, with Kamakura investiture edicts dating from the age of Yoritomo. See especially *Ichikawa monjo*, 1192/12/10 shōgun ke mandokoro kudashibumi, *Shinano shiryō*, 3: 440. The entire Ichikawa collection appears in *Shinpen Shinano shiryō sōsho*, 3: 1–60.

3. In other words, the first son has been passed over by his father in favor of a second son.

4. These designations evidently correspond to the *sōjitō* authority conveyed in Document 68.

5. Thus a first son passed over for the family headship was still allotted a land share.

6. The bequest to this daughter is dealt with in Document 70.

7. Thus the expected suit (see Document 68) was indeed lodged; with the father now dead, Saigan was seeking to oust his younger brother from the family headship.

8. I.e., Document 68.

9. The *kudashibumi* format for a suit settlement of this kind is unusual; *mandokoro* edicts were normally reserved for simple appointments and confirmations. Thus, two days after the present document Kamakura issued a standard confirmation for a grandson of the same donor, Myōren, based on a conveyance (not extant) of 1240/1/25; *Ichikawa monjo*, 1252/12/28 shōgun ke mandokoro kudashibumi, *Shinano shiryō*, 4: 185.

10. This is the daughter of Myōren referred to in Document 69.

11. Not extant, though it is noteworthy that Myōren made provision for his daughter as early as 1234. This was much earlier than the 1249 conveyance to Tadayoshi, suggesting a late decision to substitute Tadayoshi for Mitsunari as principal heir. We can imagine that Mitsunari possessed an earlier deed from his father, which was then superseded in 1249.

12. It seems possible that Fujiwara *no uji* had undertaken legal action to induce both the quitclaim and the Bakufu's present confirmation. This would mean that the new house head had been subjected to two suits: his elder brother's losing suit to wrest the family headship from his younger brother, and his younger sister's winning suit to seek protection of her holdings.

13. Eleven years later there occurred a major legal battle over Tadayoshi's own legacy; *Ichikawa monjo*, 1265/int. 4/18 Kantō gechijō, *Shinano shiryō*, 4: 255–57.

DOCUMENTS 71–72

The Bakufu Confirms Mother-to-Daughter Conveyances, 1251, 1274

The second half of the thirteenth century witnessed a marked decrease in the number of transfers of unencumbered property rights for women. This decrease, however, did not affect all women; nor did it occur in some uniform way or at a "standard" rate of speed. In the first of two unrelated cases here, a two-thirds share of a *jitō shiki* was transmitted, in perpetuity, by a mother to a daughter. A generation earlier the mother had received the entire *jitō shiki*, suggesting that partible inheritance, not the life-tenure mode of compromising women's rights, would affect this particular line of women. In the second example, a father had earlier deeded secondary shares to his wife, a younger son, and a younger daughter; an eldest son had been made the principal heir. Now, however, the widow deeded her share to the daughter, which meant a merging of assets for her benefit rather than for the male-dominated main line. There is no visible evidence of "decline," then, for this woman at this particular stage.

71

The chancellery of the shogun's house directs: to the residents of Mikata, the two-thirds sector of Osa *gō*, Tajima Province.[1]

That the Date nun[2] shall forthwith possess the *jitō shiki*.

Pursuant to precedent, authority shall be exercised under this *shiki*, in accordance with the release of the nun-mother, Hitachi-no-tsubone, dated the 30th day of this past month—boundaries recorded therein.[3] The command is thus. Wherefore, this order.

3d year of Kenchō [1251], 12th month, 12th day

anzu, Sugano
chikeji, Nakahara

ryō, saemon no shōjō, Fujiwara
bettō, Mutsu no kami, Taira ason (monogram)
Sagami no kami, Taira ason (monogram)

72

That Fujiwara *no uji*, the daughter of Hakazaki Jirō Naoaki *hosshi*—Buddhist name, Jōshin—shall forthwith possess paddy, upland, residence plot(s), and the former . . . ,[4] all within Hakazaki Village, Hizen Province—names (*myōji*) and totals (*inzu*) recorded in the deed of release.[5]

Possession shall be exercised in accordance with the release of the 2d year of Kōgen [1257], 3d month, 2d day[6]—details recorded therein— by the widow of Jōshin, the daughter's mother.[7] By command of the Kamakura lord, it is so decreed.

11th year of Bun'ei [1274], 5th month, 21st day

> Musashi no kami, Taira ason
> (monogram)
> Sagami no kami, Taira ason
> (monogram)

SOURCES: Document 71: *Date monjo*, 1251/12/12 shōgun ke mandokoro kudashibumi, *KI*, 10: 279, doc. 7389. Document 72: *Gotō ke monjo*, 1274/5/21 Kantō gechijō, *Saga ken shiryō shūsei*, 6: 65, doc. 5 (*KI*, 15: 289, doc. 11660).

1. In a Tajima Province field register of 1285, Osa *gō* is recorded as split among four *jitō* (*Tajima no kuni ōtabumi*, *KI*, 21: 38, doc. 15774); and in Document 115 below, a dispute of 1286 concerns a fractional portion of the *jitō* rights there (*ichibu jitō shiki*). By 1285, in other words, a two-thirds sector was no longer intact. Earlier in the century, a single *jitō shiki* existed for the whole of Osa *gō*; see n. 3.

2. In Document 115 below, the Date nun is referred to as the nun-widow of Date *shuri no suke* Tokitsuna.

3. This release is not extant. Hitachi-no-tsubone was confirmed by the Bakufu in her own inheritance of the *jitō shiki* for the entire Osa *gō* in 1221; *Kōta Naritomo shi shozō monjo*, 1221/8/25 Kantō gechijō, *KI*, 5: 40, doc. 2812.

4. Several characters (with one lost) referring to a commutation rate of some kind follow here.

5. Fujiwara *no uji* was a younger sister of Jōshin's principal heir, Ujiaki. In the father's conveyance to Ujiaki, reference is made to shares granted to Ujiaki's mother, younger brother, and younger sister; see *Gotō ke monjo*, 1247/2/14 shōgun sodehan kudashibumi, *Saga ken shiryō shūsei*, 6: 63, doc. 3 (the conveyance itself, dated 1242/7/2, is not extant).

6. Not extant.

7. In a Bakufu confirmation of 1248 addressed to Jōshin's widow, we see that her share was originally announced in her husband's deed to Ujiaki in 1242, and that Ujiaki had countersigned that release, in effect agreeing to its terms; *Gotō ke monjo*, 1248/2/29 Kantō migyōsho, *Saga ken shiryō shūsei*, 6: 63–64, doc. 4. At present, then, the widow was transmitting her share of the inheritance to her daughter, who, in her own right, had received a portion much earlier from her father. This daughter (Fujiwara *no uji*) thus received land in perpetuity from both her mother and father, though both sectors

had originally belonged to the father. By contrast, in Document 71 the inheritance issued clearly from the mother.

Two Brothers Reach a Compromise over a Disputed Inheritance, 1254

Here we encounter a dispute between two brothers that began with a charge of possession of a forged deed of conveyance but that ended with a compromise agreement worked out between them. The Bakufu, as was standard, approved the dispensation as outlined by the brothers themselves. Other smaller shares were also involved, and the brothers promised not to violate these parcels, which belonged to their siblings and mother.

> Concerning a dispute between *saemon no jō* Shigetoshi and his younger brother over the *jitō shiki* of Kutsuna Island—plus Matsuyoshi *myō*—Iyo Province, the legacy of the late father *sama no jō* Kunishige *hosshi*—Buddhist name, Saishin.[1]

A summons for trial was issued in response to Shigetoshi's suit that the conveyances of Saishin in Shigeyasu's possession were forgeries (*gisho*).[2] However, according to a written compromise (*wayojō*) of the 14th day of last month:[3] "The western bay area shall be Shigeyasu's share, and the eastern bay area Shigetoshi's[4]—in addition, the spheres of the widow and other siblings[5] shall not be disrupted by the mainline possessions (*hon chigyō*)."[6] There is no need for additional information. Forthwith, authority shall be exercised free of interference by either side, in accordance with generations of [Kantō] edicts and pursuant to the mutual compromise. By this command, it is so decreed.

6th year of Kenchō [1254], 3d month, 8th day

> Sagami no kami, Taira ason
> (monogram)
> Mutsu no kami, Taira ason (monogram)

SOURCE: *Kutsuna ke monjo,* 1254/3/8 Kantō gechijō, *Kutsuna ke monjo,* pp. 135–36, doc. 5 (*KI,* 11: 14, doc. 7719).

1. For Kunishige's investiture (in 1208) and struggles with the proprietor (1232–33), see *KB,* docs. 103–6.

2. No conveyances of Saishin (Kunishige) are extant.

3. Not extant.

4. Shigetoshi was the new house chieftain. A similar east-west division between brothers within this family occurred in 1205; *Kutsuna ke monjo*, 1205/5/6 Kantō gechijō an, *Kutsuna ke monjo*, pp. 131–32, doc. 1 (*KB*, doc. 100).

5. In addition to Shigetoshi and Shigeyasu, there were four other brothers as well as two sisters; see *Kutsuna shi keizu*, in *Kutsuna ke monjo*, pp. 37–38. For one of the brothers, Michishige, see Documents 74–75.

6. Everything from "in addition" to this point appears in half-size characters—a continuation of the content of the compromise record.

DOCUMENTS 74–75

The Bakufu Confirms the Inheritance of a Secondary Line Within a Vassal House, and Later Defends It Against a Tertiary Line, 1256, 1288

The suit presented here was the culmination of a long-festering dispute between an uncle and a nephew, which, in its trial stage, saw the son of the late uncle pitted against his cousin. The case involved a blatantly illegal attempt on the part of the uncle's line to violate a proper release, which led to the Bakufu's confirmation of it. Kamakura's anger is apparent here and it did something quite rare for it—it imposed a punishment in the form of a partial confiscation of the offender's holdings. On a secondary point, the Bakufu expressed its uncertainty about whether a long possession in violation of a release should—on the basis of its own statute of limitations—be allowed to stand. On this and one other item the Bakufu postponed its verdict pending further investigation.

74

The chancellery of the shogun's house directs: to Fujiwara Iyakame-maru.[1]

That he shall possess forthwith the constable's (*sōtsuibushi*) [title] and *myō* paddy and upland—names recorded in the conveyance —of Kutsuna Island's western bay area, Iyo Province.

Possession shall be exercised in accordance with the compact (*keijō*) of the 5th year of Kenchō [1253], 2d month, 29th day,[2] issued by the father *saemon no jō* Michishige.[3] The command is thus. Wherefore, this order.

8th year of Kenchō [1256], 7th month, 9th day

anzu, Kiyohara
chikeji, Kiyohara

ryō, saemon no shōjō, Fujiwara
bettō, Mutsu no kami, Taira ason (monogram)
Sagami no kami, Taira ason (monogram)

75

The terms of a dispute between *sa hyōe no jō* Saneshige *hosshi* of
Kutsuna Island, Iyo Province—Buddhist name, Shōun; child's
name, Iyakame—and Tōshige, the son of Jūrō *saemon no jō* Shigeyasu, now deceased.[4]

Item: the *sōtsuibushi shiki* of the western bay.

Item: Matsushige *myō*.

According to the bill of accusation (*sojō*): "Confirmation was granted
for the said *shiki*, in accordance with the conveyance of my late father
Shirō *saemon no jō* Michishige.[5] Even so, Shigeyasu intruded upon it."[6]
According to the defense statement (*chinjō*): "There has been no interference by Shigeyasu with the holdings of Saneshige. Therefore,
the charge of a takeover (*ōryō*) is absurd." According to the renewed
bill of accusation: "In addition to an acknowledgment [of our charges],
we desire formal judgment (*ongechi*)." According to the renewed defense statement: "The holdings in question were a [new] award (*onkyū*)
made to Michishige. However, after his death they were succeeded to
[by Shigeyasu], and the aggrieved Saneshige complained. Moreover,
the settlement upon [Shigeyasu] was [approved]."[7]

According to the document (*jō*) submitted by Shōun dated the 3d
year of Kenchō [1251], 4th month, 28th day, which was conveyed by
the original holder (*honshu*) Saishin—Saneshige's and Tōshige's grandfather—to his principal heir (*chakushi*) Michishige, Shōun's late father:[8] "Concerning the release of portions (*shobun*) within Kutsuna Island. Item: the *sōtsuibushi shiki* of the western bay. Item: Matsushige
myō. Disposition is made to Michishige in accordance with our hereditary documents. Let there be no disturbances"—remaining matters
omitted.[9] According to the document from Michishige to Shōun dated
the 5th year of Kenchō [1253], 2d month, 29th day: "Item: the *sōtsuibushi shiki*. Item: Matsushige *myō*. These are to be held by our principal heir Iyakame without interference by other persons"—remaining matters omitted; a rendering in Chinese characters (*kanji*) of the
Japanese syllabary (*wa no ji*) [release].[10]

According to the [confirmation] edict of the 8th year of Kenchō
[1256], 7th month, 9th day, granted to Shōun:[11] "The chancellery
of the shogun's house directs: to Fujiwara Iyakamemaru. That the
sōtsuibushi shiki and *myō* paddy and upland—names recorded in the

release—of Kutsuna Island's western bay area, Iyo Province, shall forthwith be possessed. Possession shall be exercised in accordance with the compact of the 5th year of Kenchō [1253], 2d month, 29th day, issued by the father *saemon no jō* Michishige."

The aforesaid holdings were received in inheritance by the principal hair, Michishige, from the original holder Saishin. Michishige deeded them to Shōun, and Shōun, in accordance with that document, was awarded the Kenchō [era] confirmation edict.[12] Notwithstanding, Tōshige, representing the line of the third son,[13] brazenly claims that a [new] grant (*onkyū*) was made [to his father, Shigeyasu]: is this not the most evil of schemes? Worst of all, after initially claiming no involvement, Tōshige then goes on to assert an *onkyū*. The discrepancy between his earlier and later statements reveals this to be nothing but a deception. Accordingly, Tōshige's incursions against these *shiki* are to cease, and Shōun shall exercise possession in accordance with Saishin's and Michishige's deeds of release and with the confirmatory edict.

Next, concerning the punishment for this takeover, Tōshige's assumption of the said *shiki* has already been acknowledged by him. His violation of both his grandfather's release[14] and a [Kantō] confirmation[15] constitutes more than an encroachment: by intruding upon someone else's holding and then brazenly calling it a benefice (*onko no chi*) he most certainly invites punishment. In consequence, his holdings shall be catalogued and a portion of them confiscated.

Next, concerning income [obtained] in the wake of his takeover, it is to be returned.

Next, concerning the accusation bill's charge of a fictitious land grant, [clearly] this warrants punishment. However, beyond the recall of a portion of [Tōshige's] holdings owing to his criminal seizures, there seems no need for a double punishment. For that reason, the matter will not be acted upon.

Item: Kunimune *myō*.

Just at the point that this matter was to be taken up in response to plaintiff and defense statements, Saneshige issued a document canceling his suit. Beyond that there is no discrepancy of views.

Item: the Daimarushi[16] paddy area.

Shigeyasu petitioned[17] that it should be awarded [to himself] in accordance with Saishin's conveyance. Shōun defended that possession [in his line] already exceeded 20 years.[18] It is unclear whether a deed of release should prevail as against a statutory possession (*chigyō nengi*). Accordingly, Rokuhara has been ordered to send a report after conducting a full investigation.

Item: the charge of Shigeyasu's plot to murder Saneshige. Beyond the fact that there is a heated dispute, there is no actual proof here. Hence the matter cannot be acted upon.

Item: private servants (*shojū*).

Rokuhara has been ordered to investigate and judge the matter.

By command of the Kamakura lord, the foregoing points are so decreed.

1st year of Shōō [1288], 6th month, 2d day[19]

> saki no Musashi no kami, Taira ason (monogram)
>
> Sagami no kami, Taira ason (monogram)

SOURCES: Document 74: *Kutsuna ke monjo*, 1256/7/9 shōgun ke mandokoro kudashi-bumi, *Kutsuna ke monjo*, pp. 138–39, doc. 7 (*KI*, 11: 171, doc. 8010). Document 75: *ibid.*, 1288/6/2 Kantō gechijō, *Kutsuna ke monjo*, pp. 139–43, doc. 8 (*KBSS*, 1: 232–34, doc. 170).

1. The child's name of Kutsuna Saneshige, the nephew of Shigetoshi and Shigeyasu; see Documents 73 and 75. The *Kutsuna ke monjo* version has an incorrect character in the name; but see *KI* and also *Ehime ken hennenshi*, 2: 309.

2. Not extant, though see Document 75 for part of it. One wonders why it is not referred to here as a deed of release (*yuzurijō*), since that is what it was.

3. Michishige was a brother of Shigetoshi and Shigeyasu (Document 73) and had received his own inheritance in 1251; see Document 75. He quickly transmitted it to his son two years later.

4. Saneshige (Shōun) and Tōshige were cousins. As we note from the content of the lawsuit, Tōshige's father (Shigeyasu) was the original defendant in the case, but he died leaving his son to take over for him. There are no surviving documents between 1256 (Document 74) and 1288 (Document 75).

5. The original of the release referred to (that of 1253/2/29) does not survive, but a portion of it is reproduced later in the present document. For its confirmation, see Document 74.

6. In other words, Saneshige was bringing suit against his father's brother, Shigeyasu.

7. Meaning speculative here. The argument of the defendant, Tōshige, seems to be that Shigeyasu's line (his own) properly took over from Michishige's and that Kamakura gave its blessing. As we shall see, this was patently untrue.

8. The Bakufu has apparently erred here by referring to Michishige as Kunishige's chosen heir. As we know, Michishige's elder brother, Shigetoshi, became *sōryō*; see the house genealogy in *Kutsuna ke monjo*, p. 37, and an imperial guard service (*ōbanyaku*) order to Shigetoshi presumably in his capacity as house head; *Kutsuna ke monjo*, 6/2 Nikaidō Yukiaki shojō, *KI*, 11: 14, doc. 7720. Unfortunately, the original of the document from Saishin (Kunishige) that is partially reproduced here is not extant.

9. In the section of Saishin's document appearing here we see no reference to Michishige as primary heir. The phrase "remaining matters omitted" is in half-size characters.

10. The original of this *kana* document is not extant. Michishige, at any rate, was passing his inheritance to his son less than two years after his own receipt.

11. I.e., Document 74.

12. *Ibid.*

13. The Bakufu is incorrect here; Tōshige's father, Shigeyasu, was the fourth son. See *Kutsuna ke monjo*, pp. 29–30, 37.

14. I.e., the testament of 1251/4/28 from Saishin to Michishige.

15. Document 74.

16. The *KBSS* transcription has it "Daikushi," but both *Ehime ken hennenshi* (2: 382) and *Kutsuna ke monjo* (p. 142) have Daimarushi.

17. Evidently, the suit was originally brought by Shigeyasu, who then died; see n. 4. His son Tōshige continued it.

18. According to the Jōei Formulary, a 20-year possession would render a holding invulnerable from legal challenge.

19. A Rokuhara validation of the full Kantō settlement was issued in the ninth month; *Kutsuna ke monjo*, 1288/9/17 Rokuhara shigyōjō, *Kutsuna ke monjo*, pp. 144–45, doc. 9. For further trouble on Kutsuna Island, see Document 133 below. Note 1 of that document contains an abbreviated genealogy.

DOCUMENTS 76–79

The Bakufu Issues Confirmatory Edicts to Four Members of a Family on the Same Day, 1257

Nowhere is the complexity of partible inheritance more vivid than in the present sequence involving a father's division of his holdings among two sons, a daughter, and a nephew. Since all four legatees required protection, the Bakufu confirmed each by way of a separate document. Moreover, it is apparent that there were yet additional bequests as well as cosigned agreements among various family members to insure compliance. At this stage each of the shares, including the daughter's, was intended to be alienable; there are no references to reversions in future to the main line. At any rate, the cutting and pasting required of the father is the dominant image here. The recipients could either cooperate and forbear or else engage one another and squabble.

76

The chancellery of the shogun's house directs: to Fujiwara Yoritoshi *hosshi*—Buddhist name, Kōren.

That the *jitō shiki* shall be held for [the following units] in the southern sector of Hitoyoshi Estate, Kuma District, Higo Province:[1] Keitoku *myō*, minus 9.3 *tan* of temple paddy (*jiden*), 7 *chō* belonging to Tōji,[2] 1.5 *chō* of paddy belonging to the daughter of

Munakata,[3] and 2.5 *chō* of irrigated paddy which had been converted within the Samuda residence area (*hori no uchi*);[4] Jōraku *myō*; Ryūman *myō*; 4 *tan* in Yaguro; 2.3 *chō* of shrine paddy; 3.93 *chō* of new paddy scattered within the village; 15 service households within the Samuda residence area—specifications on all of the above in the deed of release and succession permit (*sōdenjō*).[5] Also, the *jitō shiki* of Naritsune *myō* in Kamutsumike District, Buzen Province.[6]

Pursuant to precedent, let authority be exercised under these *shiki*, in accordance with a release of the late father Nagayori *hosshi*—Buddhist name, Renbutsu—dated the 4th year of Kangen [1246], 3d month, 5th day,[7] and in accordance with a succession permit of Renshin, dated the 6th year of Kenchō [1254], 11th month,   day.[8] The command is thus. Wherefore, this order.

    1st year of Shōka [1257], 9th month, 14th day

                         anzu, Kiyohara
                         chikeji, Kiyohara

ryō, saemon no shōjō, Fujiwara
bettō, Sagami no kami, Taira ason (monogram)
Musashi no kami, Taira ason (monogram)

77

The chancellery of the shogun's house directs: to Fujiwara Yorikazu.[9]
    That [the following] shall be held[10] within the southern sector of Hitoyoshi Estate, Kuma District, Higo Province: 26 *chō* within Matsunobe *myō*, minus 7 *tan* belonging to the daughter of Munakata; plus 1.7 *chō* of new paddy; and 16 service households, minus 1 household, which belongs to the daughter of Munakata.

Possession shall be exercised in accordance with a release of the late father Nagayori *hosshi*—Buddhist name, Renbutsu—dated the 4th year of Kangen [1246], 3d month, 5th day.[11] The command is thus. Wherefore, this order.

    1st year of Shōka [1257], 9th month, 14th day

                         anzu, Kiyohara
                         chikeji, Kiyohara

ryō, saemon no shōjō, Fujiwara
bettō, Sagami no kami, Taira ason (monogram)
Musashi no kami, Taira ason (monogram)

78

The chancellery of the shogun's house directs: to Taira Nagatsuna
hosshi—Buddhist name, Saishin.[12]

That [the following] shall be held within the southern sector of
Hitoyoshi Estate, Kuma District, Higo Province: 7 *chō* within
Keitoku *myō*,[13] of which 2.5 *chō* are *shutsuden*;[14] 2.03 *chō* within
Matsunobe *myō*, minus 3 *tan* of paddy, which belongs to the
daughter of Munakata; 4 *tan* within Toyonaga-Fujiyoshi; 5.3 *tan*
of new paddy; and 4 service households.

Possession shall be exercised in accordance with a release of the uncle,
Nagayori *hosshi*—Buddhist name, Renbutsu—dated the 4th year of
Kangen [1246], 3d month, 5th day.[15] The command is thus. Where-
fore, this order.

1st year of Shōka [1257], 9th month, 14th day

anzu, Kiyohara
chikeji, Kiyohara

ryō, saemon no shōjō, Fujiwara
bettō, Sagami no kami, Taira ason (monogram)
Musashi no kami, Taira ason (monogram)

79

The chancellery of the shogun's house directs: to Fujiwara *no uji*—
given name, Ushi.[16]

That [the following] shall be held within the southern sector of
Hitoyoshi Estate, Kuma District, Higo Province: 7.22 *chō* and 5
service households within Toraoka *myō*—field specifications and
names recorded in the cosigned quitclaim (*rensho sari*[*jō*]).

Possession shall be exercised in accordance with a quitclaim—details
recorded therein—cosigned by Yoriuji, Yoritoshi, and Yorisada, dated
the 4th year of Kenchō [1252], 3d month, 25th day.[17] By this command, it is thus.

1st year of Shōka [1257], 9th month, 14th day[18]

anzu, Kiyohara
chike[ji], Kiyohara

ryō, saemon no shōjō, Fujiwara
bettō, Sagami no kami, Taira ason seal
Musashi no kami, Taira ason seal

SOURCES: Documents 76–78: *Sagara ke monjo*, 1257/9/14 shōgun ke mandokoro kudashibumi, *DNK, iewake* 5, 1: 42–44, docs. 14–16 (*KI*, 11: 241–42, docs. 8145, 8147–48).

Document 79: *ibid.*, 1257/9/14 shōgun ke mandokoro kudashibumi an, *DNK, iewake* 5, 1: 102–3, doc. 48.3 (*KI*, 11: 241–42, doc. 8146).

1. The recipient, Yoritoshi, was chieftain of the southern branch of the Sagara house, succeeding his father, Nagayori, who had issued the release (see n. 7) now being confirmed. The *jitō shiki* for Hitoyoshi Estate dated back to 1205, but had been divided, after a family dispute in 1243, into northern and southern sectors; see *Sagara ke monjo,* 1205/7/25 Kantō kudashibumi an, *DNK, iewake* 5, 1; 6, doc. 3, and *ibid.*, 1243/12/23 Kantō gechijō, *DNK, iewake* 5, 1: 8–13, doc. 5.

2. This refers to a release by Nagayori of these 7 *chō* to Tōji Nagatsuna, his nephew; see Document 78.

3. Identity unknown, but possibly the widow of the donor. It will be noticed that the Lady Munakata received an exempt share within the holdings of Yoritoshi, Yorikazu, and Nagatsuna, the confirmees in our first three documents here.

4. In half-size characters from the word "minus." These exceptions, then, all concerned Keitoku *myō*.

5. See below and n. 8.

6. This *jitō shiki* in Buzen Province was received from the Bakufu in 1249 (*Sagara ke monjo,* 1249/3/27 shōgun ke sodehan kudashibumi, *DNK, iewake* 5, 1: 35–36, doc. 10), and deeded to the present recipient in 1251 (*ibid.*, 1251/3/22 Sagara Nagayori yuzurijō, *DNK, iewake* 5, 1: 40, doc. 12). By contrast, the bequests from Hitoyoshi Estate were deeded in 1246; see n. 7.

7. *Ibid.*, 1246/3/5 Sagara Nagayori yuzurijō, *DNK, iewake* 5, 1: 26–30, doc. 7. The present Bakufu confirmation abbreviates and summarizes this very detailed conveyance, and does not even refer to the 1251 release (n. 6) that transmitted the Buzen Province holding.

8. Renshin was probably Yorichika, an elder brother of the present recipient who had once been his father's choice for branch head but who had elected to become a priest. The father's death evidently prompted this permit statement, which is not extant.

9. A younger son of the donor, Nagayori.

10. There is no mention here of a *jitō shiki*. The new branch chieftain, Yoritoshi, held that title.

11. *Sagara ke monjo,* 1246/3/5 Sagara Nagayori yuzurijō, *DNK, iewake* 5, 1: 30–33, doc. 8.

12. A nephew of the donor, Nagayori.

13. See n. 2.

14. Meaning unclear, though perhaps these 2.5 *chō* lay adjacent to Keitoku *myō* proper.

15. *Sagara ke monjo,* 1246/3/5 Sagara Nagayori yuzurijō, *DNK, iewake* 5, 1: 33–35, doc. 9. This is the third of the four surviving *yuzurijō* of Nagayori; the fourth was from 1251 (see n. 6). But obviously there were others as well.

16. A daughter of the donor, Nagayori.

17. *Sagara ke monjo,* 1252/3/25 Sagara Yoritoshi tō rensho sarijō an, *DNK, iewake* 5, 1: 100–102, doc. 48.2. The three signatories were all Ushi's brothers, with Yoritoshi (as we have seen) head of the Sagara southern branch, and Yoriuji head of the northern branch as well as overall house chieftain (*sōryō*). In the quitclaim itself we see that the father Nagayori had ordered Yorisada to give up part of his own legacy in order to create a share for his sister. The two branch heads (along with Yorisada himself) were

then obliged to sign the quit document. It is noteworthy, then, that the present confirmation by the Bakufu was not actually of a father's conveyance deed.

18. The full complement of extant records relating to Hitoyoshi Estate (including those from collections other than the Sagara) appear in *Higo-no-kuni Kanokogi—
Hitoyoshi-no-shō shiryō*, pp. 73ff.

DOCUMENTS 80–83

Four Gokenin Die Intestate, 1257, 1259, 1265, 1272

In a society so utterly dependent on valid (and validated) release documents,
the death of a vassal whose legacy had not been devised or disposed of led to
several possible results. Each of the unrelated cases here had a different outcome. In the first, the widow divided the holdings by her free choice. In the
second, the two sons divided the estate by their free choice. In the third, an
only son was confirmed by the Bakufu. And in the fourth, the widow and as
many as nine sons were granted shares, seemingly with the help of the Bakufu.

80

That the priest Ryōen shall forthwith possess 3 *chō* . . .[1] [within]
New Nuta [Estate],[2] Aki Province—names (*myōji*),[3] taxes (*shotō*),
and service obligations (*kuji*) appear in the allotment register
(*haibunjō*).[4]

Because the late father *saemon no jō* Kunihira [died] intestate,[5] [his leg-
acy] was parceled (*haibun*) by his widow on the . . .[6] month, day.
[Possession][7] shall be exercised, pursuant to precedent, in accordance
with that document. By this command, it is so decreed.[8]

1st year of Shōka [1257], 7th month, 6th day

> Musashi no kami, Taira ason
> (monogram)
> Sagami no kami, Taira ason
> (monogram)

81

That Koshirō Fujiwara Hideie shall forthwith possess 3 *chō* of
myō paddy and 2 service households from within Iitsuka *gō*,
Ōharaki Tribute Estate, Kōzuke Province—land specifications
and other details appear in Ietoki's quitclaim (*sarijō*).[9]

Because the late father, Hiroie, [died] intestate, a compromise was agreed to by the brothers.[10] Let possession be exercised pursuant to this agreement, free of any disturbance. By this command, it is so decreed.

1st year of Shōgen [1259], 12th month, 23d day

> Musashi no kami, Taira ason
> (monogram)
> Sagami no kami, Taira ason
> (monogram)

82

That Ōhata Motokane shall forthwith possess the Ushikuso district headship of Satsuma Province as well as the *myōshu shiki* for 11 villages.

Owing to the departed father Kunimoto's sudden severe illness he granted no testament. Nevertheless, as his only son, you shall possess his inheritance (*ato*), with no questions about it. Forthwith, possession shall be exercised pursuant to precedent. By this command, it is so decreed.

2d year of Bun'ei [1265], 12th month, 27th day[11]

> Sagami no kami, Taira ason seal
> sakyō, gon no daibu, Taira ason
> seal

83

That the nun—the widow of Sōma Magogorō *saemon no jō* Tanemura—shall forthwith possess Masuo[12] village in [Sōma][13] Tribute Estate (*mikuriya*), Shimōsa Province; and [Banzaki] and Otaka villages, in Namekata District, Mutsu Province.

Inasmuch as no disposition was made by the late husband Tanemura of his estate, it has now been [parceled].[14] Possession shall be exercised forthwith pursuant to precedent. By [this command], it is so [decreed].

9th year of Bun'ei [1272], 10th month, 29th day[15]

> Sagami no kami, Taira [ason]
> sakyō, gon no daibu, Taira [ason]

SOURCES: Document 80: *Kobayakawa ke monjo*, 1257/7/6 Kantō gechijō, *DNK, iewake 11*, 1: 71, doc. 95 (*KI*, 11: 232, doc. 8126). Document 81: *Chōrakuji monjo*, 1259/12/23 Kantō gechijō, *Gunma kenshi, shiryō hen 5, chūsei*, 1: 47, doc. 3 (*KI*, 11: 375, doc. 8452).

Document 82: *Sōgi monjo*, 1265/12/27 Kantō gechijō an, *Sappan kyūki zatsuroku, zenpen*, 5: 13, doc. 375 (*KI*, 13: 139, doc. 9477). Document 83: *Sōma monjo*, 1272/10/29 Kantō gechijō, *Sōma monjo*, pp. 1–2, doc. 2 (*KI*, 15: 34–35, doc. 11135).

1. Several characters missing here.

2. Nuta (or Numata) *shin-shō*.

3. I.e., of the locales or land units concerned.

4. The register itself is not extant, but the Kobayakawa genealogy lists three sons of whom Ryōen was the youngest; see *Kobayakawa keizu*, in *DNK, iewake 11*, 2: 394–99. For details on the Kobayakawa, see Documents 84–85.

5. Kunihira was a nephew of the clan chieftain, Kobayakawa Shigehira.

6. Several characters missing here.

7. More characters missing.

8. It is noteworthy that the present confirmation (unlike Documents 76–79) is issued as a *gechijō*. The same is true for Documents 81–83, all treating unbequeathed lands.

9. Ietoki was obviously a brother of the confirmee here, Hideie. The document in question is not extant.

10. I.e., Hiroie's elder and younger sons.

11. There is a discrepancy here on the date. *Sappan kyūki zatsuroku, zenpen* (5: 13) has it 1265/12/29, as does *Kyūshū chihō chūsei hennen monjo mokuroku* (1: 68). Two more recent volumes, however, have it 12/27: *KI* (13: 139) and *Kagoshima ken shiryō, Kyūki zatsuroku zenpen* (1: 256).

12. A later release in *kana* shows the correct pronunciation; see *Sōma monjo*, 1285/6/5 Tanemura goke yuzurijō, *Sōma monjo*, pp. 2–3, doc. 4.

13. Whole and partial words appearing in brackets in this document are interpolations; original characters have been lost.

14. On the same day, the Bakufu granted allocations to two of Tanemura's sons; see *Sōma monjo*, 1272/9/29 Kantō gechijō, *Sōma monjo*, pp. 1–2, docs. 1, 3. To one son the grant was two villages in Sōma Tribute Estate and one village in Namekata District. To the other son the award was limited to Namekata. There may in fact have been additional Bakufu allotments, since a document of 1294 lists nine sons of Tanemura with their respective land shares; see *ibid.*, 1294 gohaibun keizu, *Sōma monjo*, pp. 4–5, doc. 7.

15. In 1285, the widow deeded Masuo Village to the principal heir (*chakushi*), Morotane; see the document cited in n. 12.

DOCUMENTS 84–85

A Secondary Line Within a Prominent Jitō House Receives and Transmits Property, 1258, 1289

The branching of families was an inevitable consequence of the partible inheritance system, of a Bakufu policy not opposed to such branching, of a distribution of landholdings that clearly favored it, and of a family system that accorded but limited powers to the chieftain. Aware of all these circumstances, the donor in our first document, a release to a secondary heir, took steps to block excessive fragmentation even as his conveyance, involving rights in three disparate areas, was promoting it. Specifically, he called on his son to obey the vassal-service requisitionings of the principal heir, to provide support for his sister by way of an annual stipend, to choose a male relative as heir in the absence of male offspring of his own, and to be prepared to surrender his inheritance as the consequence of his own misbehavior. A generation later, on the occasion of the earlier recipient's transmission to his own heir, we note that some additional holdings had been received from Kamakura, that the strictures laid down earlier were mostly repeated, and that an elder sister, obviously left out of the inheritance, was now preparing a challenge.

84

Conveyed: holdings constituting the share of my son, Masakage.[1]
    In total:
    The *jitō*, *kumon*, and *kendan* [authorities] for the Tsuu-Takehara double estate, Aki Province; and the *sō[ken]gyō* title of Takehara Estate.[2]
    Five *chō* of *jitō* residence land (*monden*) within Nashiba *gō*, Nuta Estate, same province.[3]
    The *jitō*, *kumon*, *anzu*, *tadokoro*, *zushi*, *sōkengyō*, and *kendan* titles[4] of Yoda *gō*, Sanuki Province.[5]
    One service household (*zaike*) site within Kamakura's Komemachi [District]—the residence site left by Sōji *nyūdō*.[6]

The aforesaid holdings shall be possessed in accordance with this conveyance. As for the service obligations (*onkuji*) to the Kamakura lord, these shall be discharged without negligence, pursuant to the regulations (*rippō*) laid down by Honbutsu,[7] and in accordance with the requisitioning (*saisoku*) of the [house] administrator (*sōbugyō*), Masahira.[8] Also, 50 out of the 100 *koku*—standard measure—of income (*tokubun*) from Yoda *gō* shall, without fail, be earmarked on a permanent basis for the six priests of the Ji sect who perform continuous Nenbutsu on the holy mountain, and for sacred lamp oil expenses. The other 50 *koku* shall, without fail, be conveyed every year to Masakage's younger sister, Matsuya, for as long as she shall live.[9] In the event there is any negligence in upholding this [income] provision, Masahira is to administer the requisitioning. As concerns the present landholdings, should there be no male offspring, release shall be to a mutually agreeable person chosen from within the kindred (*ichimon*). Conveyance may not be to outsiders (*tanin*) or to external kindred (*tamon*).[10] However, if in spite of this release [Masakage] violates Hon-

butsu's orders during [the latter's] lifetime, [his inheritance] will be re-scinded.[11] As the basis for future authority, our conveyance is thus.[12]
2d year of Shōka [1258], 7th month, 19th day

shami

85

Conveyed: holdings constituting the share of my true son (*jisshi*), the youth (*kanja*) Iyajō.[13]
In total:
The *jitō shiki* and other rights (*shoshiki*) in Tsuu Estate, Aki Province.[14]
The *jitō shiki* and other rights once held by Ogasawara Jūrō Yasukiyo in Lower Banzai Estate, Awa Province.[15]
The *jitō shiki* and other rights in Mokake Estate, Bizen Province.[16]
One service household site within Kamakura's Komemachi [District].

The aforesaid holdings shall be possessed in accordance with this conveyance. As for the service obligations to the Kamakura lord, these shall be discharged without negligence, pursuant to the regulations laid down by your grandfather—Buddhist name, Honbutsu. However, if in spite of this release [Iyajō] violates Jōshin's orders during [the latter's] lifetime, [his inheritance] will be rescinded.[17] As the basis for future authority, our conveyance is thus.
2d year of Shōō [1289], 2d month, 16th day

shami (monogram)

Because Nagatsuna, the representative of Kakushō,[18] has claimed that this document is a forgery, the two commissioners hereby affix their seals.
4th year of Einin [1296], 10th month, 24th day

Fujiwara (monogram)
Hyōgo no jō Sugawara (monogram)[19]

SOURCES: Document 84: *Kobayakawa ke monjo*, 1258/7/19 Kobayakawa Honbutsu (Shigehira) yuzurijō an, *DNK, iewake 11*, 1: 35–56, doc. 52 (*KI*, 11: 290, doc. 8268). Document 85: ibid., 1289/2/16 Kobayakawa Jōshin (Masakage) yuzurijō, *DNK, iewake 11*, 1: 37–38, doc. 54 (*KI*, 22: 186–87, doc. 16881).
    1. A secondary heir of the donor, Kobayakawa Shigehira. The primary heir, Masahira, received *jitō* rights for one of the family's other major bases in Aki Province, Old Nuta Estate (*honshō*). There emerged in this way two distinct branches issuing from Shigehira. (A third branch issued from a brother of Shigehira.) The father of Shige-

hira, Kobayakawa Kagehira, was evidently the adopted son and heir of Doi Tōhira, himself a son of the illustrious Yoritomo-era vassal, Doi Sanehira. For details, see *Kobayakawa keizu*, in *DNK*, *iewake 11*, 2: 393–94; and *Kokushi jiten*, 4: 168. Peter Arnesen has provided a summary history of this family; "The Provincial Vassals of the Muromachi Shoguns," in Jeffrey P. Mass and William B. Hauser, eds., *The Bakufu in Japanese History* (Stanford, 1985), pp. 106–7.

2. The Kobayakawa had received the *jitō shiki* for Tsuu-Takehara as a Jōkyū War reward. This fact and the references to the *kumon* (tax) and *kendan* (policing) authorities (*kendan* = *sōtsuibushi shiki*) are noted in *Kobayakawa ke monjo*, 1240/int.10/11 Kantō gechijō, *DNK*, *iewake 11*, 1: 548–54, doc. 5 (*DKR*, doc. 41). The *sōkengyō shiki*, an administrative post, was within the *jitō* orbit of influence by 1240 (*ibid.*) and obviously came to be fully absorbed at some point.

3. Thus Masakage, a secondary heir, was deeded a residence area within a sector of Nuta Estate that had been passed as a life bequest to his sister, Jōren: see the references in *Gakuonji monjo*, 1288/4/12 Kantō gechijō, *KBSS*, 1: 231–32, doc. 169 (*KB*, doc. 72); and *Kobayakawa keizu*, in *DNK*, *iewake 11*, 2: 396. As we have noted, moreover, the *jitō shiki* for the full estate was granted to the principal heir, Masahira.

4. For all of these *shiki* titles (except *zushi*), see the Glossary in *KB*. *Zushi* was a kind· of *shōen* registrar, cartographer, and census-taker.

5. It is not known when the Kobayakawa originally received these rights in Sanuki.

6. Identity unknown.

7. Honbutsu is the present donor, Kobayakawa Shigehira. The house rules referred to here do not survive.

8. Masahira, as we have seen, was the principal heir; he had had two elder brothers who died young. See *Kobayakawa keizu*, in *DNK*, *iewake 11*, 2: 394–95.

9. This was thus a life bequest under her brother's administration. For the treatment accorded the other sister, Jōren, see n. 3.

10. As we note in the first line of Document 85, the admonition here was intended to prohibit adoption from outside the Kobayakawa.

11. The donor, Honbutsu (Shigehira), was thus to retain ultimate authority until his death.

12. The Bakufu confirmed this inheritance in 1264 following Honbutsu's death; *Kobayakawa ke monjo*, 1264/3/12 shōgun ke mandokoro kudashibumi, *DNK*, *iewake 11*, 1: 36–37, doc. 53.

13. Kobayakawa Masamune (Kagemune), principal heir of the donor, Masakage (Jōshin). The reference to a true son is obviously in answer to the stricture imposed a generation earlier (Document 84).

14. The absence of any reference here to Takehara Estate is not explained.

15. The Ogasawara were *shugo* of Awa (Shikoku) from 1221 to 1333. Evidently, Yasukiyo, of a secondary line, had incurred the displeasure of the Bakufu, leading to his dispossession in favor of an unrelated family. For details, see Okino Shunji, *Awa no kuni shōen kō*, p. 22.

16. The donor Masakage had received this *jitō shiki* from the Bakufu just three months earlier; *Kobayakawa ke monjo*, 1288/11/21 shōgun ke mandokoro kudashibumi, *DNK*, *iewake 11*, 1: 18, doc. 29. This shows (among other things) that Kamakura was granting new *jitō* titles to branch heads; Masakage, we recall, had been only a secondary heir.

17. Note the identical language in Document 84.

18. An elder sister of the present recipient, Masamune (Kagemune); a marginal note in *KI* mistakenly has it as younger sister. This section, with the date line and two monograms, was added to the reverse side of the document in 1296.

19. Kakushō's challenge to her younger brother would continue and be centered on her charge that he was not a true son; see *Kobayakawa ke monjo*, 1320/9/25 Kantō gechijō, *DNK*, *iewake 11*, 2: 160–63, doc. 285.

DOCUMENTS 86–87

A Donor Changes the Status of His Wife's Bequest and the Bakufu Confirms the New Arrangement, 1260, 1261

In this interesting episode a donor canceled the life bequest earmarked for his wife and substituted a smaller grant made now in perpetuity. This shift probably had nothing to do with a change in feelings toward the wife but rather resulted from expressions of unhappiness by the couple's children, who wanted their inheritance shares immediately. The father evidently took the course of least resistance, but to ensure that his widow's interests were not violated he obliged the children to countersign his deed of release to her. The Bakufu approved the arrangement, noting the presence on the conveyance of the additional signatures.

86

(monogram)[1]

Conveyed: a residence plot (*yashiki*) and *myō* paddy in Hirai *gō*.
   The widow's share[2]—a cherry grove[3] and one *chō* of *myō* paddy—itemized by unit in the master log (*sō-nikkijō*).

The aforesaid paddy and upland are the hereditary possessions of Minamoto Yorinaga. Accordingly, the share to my widow is herewith conveyed in perpetuity. Originally, [the allotment] to my children was [granted] as a widow's portion in a release of the 2d year of Shōka [1258], 8th month,   day. On that occasion, it was recorded in the release that the widow's portion was limited to her lifetime.[4] This is now revoked, and the said paddy and upland is conveyed in perpetuity this 2d year of Shōgen [1260], 3d month, 15th day.[5] As concerns obligations (*shoyaku*), the imperial guard service (*ōbanyaku*) in Kyoto is [levied at] one *kan*, 500 *mon*, cash; the upland levies total 387 *mon*; the quadrennial land survey levy (*kenchūyaku*) is to be as before; and the guard service (*ōban*) in Kamakura is excused.[6] Should any of Yorinaga's children go against this accord and create disturbances, they shall not be granted the paddy and upland recorded in their respective conveyances. As proof for posterity, this revised deed of release (*gohan no yuzurijō*) is thus.[7]

2d year of Shōgen [1260], 3d month, 15th day

Minamoto Yorinaga[8]
Naganaga
Minamoto Arinaga
principal heir, Minamoto Takanaga[9]

87

That Minamoto *no uji*[10]—the wife of Hirai Jirō[11]—shall forthwith possess *myō* paddy and upland within Hirai *gō*, Kai Province—the names, sizes, and boundaries [of fields] appear in the conveyance.[12]

Possession shall be exercised in accordance with the release of the husband Yori—naga, character omitted[13]—of the 2d year of Shōgen [1260], 3d month, 15th day—details recorded therein, along with countersignatures by the principal heir Takanaga and his brothers. By this command, it is so decreed.[14]

1st year of Kōchō (1261), 8th month, 29th day

Musashi no kami, Taira ason[15]
Sagami no kami, Taira ason[16]

sources: Document 86: *Shoke monjo san*, 1260/3/15 Minamoto Yorinaga yuzurijō, *Shinpen Kōshū komonjo*, 2: 363, doc. 1859 (*KI*, 11: 390, doc. 8488). Document 87: *ibid.*, 1261/8/29 Kantō gechijō an, *Shinpen Kōshū komonjo*, 2: 363, doc. 1860 (*KI*, 12: 97, doc. 8713).

1. The *KI* version contains the monogram, marking it as the document original.

2. The reference to a "widow's share" (*goke bun*) is anticipating the donor's death.

3. Or (if "sakura" is a place name), "one plot of Sakura upland" (*Sakura-batake issho*).

4. In other words, the widow would serve as executrix for what was essentially an entailed estate to the donor's children.

5. Under this new arrangement, the widow received a permanent (but obviously smaller) share, while the children received their shares immediately.

6. The references to cash dues constitute the widow's share; payment would have been through the son chosen as the new house head. The widow received a commuted levy for the imperial guard service, but was excused altogether from its Kamakura counterpart.

7. The original release of 1258 is thus rendered null and void.

8. The present donor.

9. We note the signatures here of Yorinaga's sons, connoting their assent.

10. Yorinaga's wife.

11. I.e., Yorinaga.

12. According to the conveyance itself (Document 86), this information was in the accompanying log (*sō-nikkijō*).

13. Phrase from "naga" in half-size characters. This was a common technique in documents, involving superstition and taboo (see, e.g., *DKR*, doc. 144).

14. The use of a *gechijō* format here is noteworthy. Four days later the *mandokoro*, as was standard, confirmed the share of a daughter from another vassal family; see Document 89.

15. In the *KI* version, the name Nagatoki is placed alongside in smaller letters. The *Kōshū komonjo* version omits this.

16. Same as above with the name Masamura.

DOCUMENTS 88–91

A Daughter Receives and Releases a Permanent Tenure, 1260, 1261, 1263, 1269

We have already encountered "ability" as a criterion for the selection of house heads. During the thirteenth century donors increasingly cited this quality as a basis for making decisions. At the same time, the importance of making good choices was enhanced as the main heir took on new duties. In the present sequence an inheriting daughter moved quickly to choose her own heir—a son—and to call for the selection of an able brother in the event of that son's dying without male heirs. We later learn (Documents 144–46) that inheritance in the male line had been secured, but also that secondary shares, on a life basis, continued to be made.

88

Conveyed: Naruta *gō*, within Gōdo [Estate], Mino Province.

Regarding the above, conveyance is made herewith to my daughter, the Lady Nagoe. Specifications on service allotments (*onkuji haibun*) are [recorded] separately.[1] Let [authority] be discharged pursuant to the present document. It is thus.

1st year of Bun'ō [1260], 8th month, 27th day

Chikakazu (monogram)

89

The chancellery of the shogun's house directs: to the residents of Naruta *gō*, Gōdo Estate (*ryō*), Mino Province.

That the custodial (*azukari dokoro*) and *jitō* titles shall forthwith be held by Nakahara *no uji*—the Lady Nagoe.[2]

Pursuant to precedent, authority (*sata*) shall be exercised under these *shiki*, in accordance with the conveyance of the late father, the former governor of Ōsumi, Chikakazu,[3] dated the 1st year of Bun'ō [1260], 8th month, 27th day—details recorded therein.[4] By this command, it is thus. Wherefore, this order.

    1st year of Kōchō [1261], 9th month, 3d day

anzu, Sugano

chikeji, Kiyohara

ryō, saemon no jō, Fujiwara

bettō, Sagami no kami, Taira ason (monogram)

Musashi no kami, Taira ason (monogram)

90

Conveyed: Naruta *gō*, within Gōdo [Estate], Mino Province.

Regarding the above, conveyance is made herewith to my principal heir, Tsukishine-maru. Both the release of our late lord, the governor of Ōsumi,[5] as well as the [Kantō's] edict of confirmation, [are conveyed]. In the event that something should happen to Tsukishine, possession (*chigyō*) shall be [assigned] according to ability (*kiryō*) from among his younger brothers. Specifications on service allotments are [recorded] separately. Let [authority] be exercised pursuant to the present document. It is thus.

    3d year of Kōchō [1263], 2d month, 17th day

Nakahara no uji (monogram)

91

That the *azukari dokoro* and *jitō* titles of Naruta *gō*, Gōdo Estate (*shō*), Mino Province, shall forthwith be held by Tsukishine-maru.

Possession (*ryōshō*) shall be exercised in accordance with the conveyance of the late mother, Nakahara *no uji*, dated the 3d year of Kōchō [1263], 2d month, 17th day. By command of the Kamakura lord, it is so decreed.[6]

    6th year of Bun'ei [1269], 12th month, 19th day[7]

Sagami no kami, Taira ason (monogram)

sakyō, gon no daibu, Taira ason

(monogram)

sources: Document 88: *Ikeda monjo*, 1260/8/27 Chikakazu yuzurijō, *Gifu kenshi, kodai-chūsei shiryō*, 4: 1059, doc. 1 (not in *KI*). Document 89: *ibid.*, 1261/9/3 shōgun ke man-dokoro kudashibumi, *Gifu kenshi, kodai-chūsei shiryō*, 4: 1059–60, doc. 2 (*KI*, 12: 97, doc. 8714). Document 90: *ibid.*, 1263/2/17 Nakahara no uji Nagoe nyōbo yuzurijō, *Gifu ken-shi, kodai-chūsei shiryō*, 4: 1060, doc. 3 (not in *KI*). Document 91: *ibid.*, 1269/12/19 Kantō gechijō, *Gifu kenshi, kodai-chūsei shiryō*, 4: 1060, doc. 4 (*KI*, 14: 107, doc. 10549).

1. No allotment register (*haibunjō*) is extant. As we have seen, service obligations would have been owed from each recipient of an inheritance share.

2. From the release itself we would not have known the specific *shiki* involved or the clan name of the Lady Nagoe. When the document was sent to the Bakufu for approval, it was probably accompanied by the *haibunjō* and a cover letter.

3. At almost the same time, *AK* identifies "the former governor of Ōsumi, Chikakazu," as Shimazu Tadatoki (1202–72), second scion of the great Shimazu house; see *Azuma kagami jinmei sakuin*, p. 263. Yet the present Chikakazu is almost certainly not that person but rather a member of the Kamakura bureaucratic house of Nakahara: in 1250, the *jitō* of Gōdo Estate is identified as Nakahara Morokazu. See *Kujō ke monjo*, 1250/11 Kujō Michiie shobunjō, *KI*, 10: 199–201, doc. 7251.

4. The *KI* version has it "details" (*shisai*) and this is probably correct (even though no details actually appear; they must have been included in the *haibunjō*). The *Gifu ken-shi* has an indecipherable term in place of *shisai*.

5. I.e., the present donor's father.

6. The present confirmation is in the *gechijō* style, whereas the earlier confirmation (Document 89) was a *kudashibumi*.

7. The next surviving document in the Ikeda collection comes half a century later; see Document 144.

DOCUMENT 92

A Vassal Warns Against Passage of His Inheritance to an Adopted Son, 1264

As we have seen, a growing tendency was for heirless property holders to release their legacies to unrelated persons under the guise of their being adopted. This was because adopted sons, being of the "next" generation, would have seemed more manageable and attractive than same-generation collaterals. Thus, despite the increase of paternal exhortations in favor of lateral inheritance, receiving sons only rarely viewed this option favorably. For them, an adopted stranger was normally preferable to a brother.

Conveyed: the administrator's title (*kengyō shiki*) of Himisaki Shrine, Izumo Province, and the *jitō shiki* of three bay areas—Uryō, Saki, and Hauda—which are holdings of the shrine.

[To:] Hioki Masayoshi.

The aforesaid *shiki* [have been administered] without neglect down through the generations. However, with the onset now of old age and in anticipation of death, I deed them to Saburōjirō Masayoshi and his descendants, pursuant to the principle of heredity (*sōden no ri*) and accompanied by the Kantō edict[s] and sequence of hereditary proof records.[1] Should Masayoshi have no surviving sons, the bequest after his lifetime shall go to Saburōshirō Masamura.[2] For even if there are no descendants, must there not still be devotion to the deity Myōjin? Yet, release shall not be to an outsider (*tanin*) under the claim that he is an adopted son (*yōshi*). In respect to shrine affairs, these are to be carried out without negligence and in accordance with precedent; prayers shall be said with full devotion, with no one neglecting this. Accordingly, for the future, petition shall be made for an edict of confirmation (*ando no onkudashibumi*).[3] By this conveyance, it is thus.

> 1st year of Bun'ei [1264], 10th month, 3d day

> > san-i, Hioki Masaie seal

SOURCE: *Himisaki jinja monjo*, 1264/10/3 Hioki Masaie yuzurijō an, *Shinshū Shimane kenshi, shiryō hen*, 1: 276 (*KI*, 12: 371, doc. 9164).

  1. The only surviving record bearing on this inheritance is the Bakufu's confirmation eleven years earlier of the present donor Masaie's possession; *Himisaki jinja monjo*, 1253/3/12 Kantō kudashibumi, *Shinshū Shimane kenshi, shiryō hen*, 1: 275–76.

  2. Obviously, a brother of Masayoshi.

  3. This was granted; *Himisaki jinja monjo*, 1265/4/12 Kantō gechijō, *Shinshū Shimane kenshi, shiryō hen*, 1: 276.

DOCUMENTS 93–94

A Jitō Passes His Inheritance to a Grandson, 1264, 1270

In light of what we have just seen, the dispensation here—release to a grandson in lieu of a son now dead—makes sense. Apparently, a daughter was being passed over in favor of a grandson. This neglect of female offspring remained qualified, however: the donee was to transmit to a female, possibly his own sister (the donor's granddaughter), in the event he should have no sons. In other words, a son or grandson was to be given precedence; lacking these the closest female was to be made principal heir. As we note in the Bakufu's confirmation, the least attractive prospect was the adoption of an outside successor.

93

Conveyed: the *jitō* and *kumon shiki* for 5 *gō* within Niho Estate, Suō Province.

The aforesaid *shiki*, as hereditary private holdings for past generations,[1] are deeded herewith to Taira Shigechika.[2] A dispensation (*goseibai*) from the house of the shogun should be petitioned for. As the basis for future administration, our conveyance is thus.

    1st year of Bun'ei [1264], 2d month, 18th day

                        jitō, Taira Shigesuke seal

94

That Taira Shigechika shall forthwith possess the 5 *gō* within Niho Estate, Suō Province: the *jitō* and *kumon shiki*.

Pursuant to precedent, authority shall be exercised under these *shiki*, in accordance with a conveyance of the grandfather, *saemon no jō* Shigesuke *hosshi*—Buddhist name, Nen'a—dated the 2d year of Kōchō [1262], 11th month, 17th day:[3] it is recorded therein that in the absence of a true son, release shall be to the female Senju;[4] moreover, that no disturbance shall befall the share of Horikawa, a daughter.[5] By this command, it is so decreed.

    7th year of Bun'ei [1270], 8th month, 28th day[6]

                        Sagami no kami, Taira ason seal

                        sakyō, gon no daibu, [Taira] ason

SOURCES: Document 93: *Miura ke monjo*, 1264/2/18 Taira Shigesuke yuzurijō an, *DNK, iewake 14*, pp. 287–88, doc. 1.8 (*KI*, 12: 319, doc. 9057). Document 94: *ibid.*, 1270/8/28 Kantō gechijō an, *DNK, iewake 14*, p. 287, doc. 1.7 (*KI*, 14: 168, doc. 10682).

    1. The present donor, Shigesuke, received the *jitō shiki* for the full estate in 1223–24; see Documents 29–31. Clearly, the five-*gō* portion now represented the main heir's share. (For the same dispensation in the next generation, see *Miura ke monjo*, 1293/7/25 Taira Shigechika yuzurijō an, *DNK, iewake 14*, p. 288, doc. 1.9.)

    2. Shigechika was the grandson of the present donor (see Document 94). The fate of Shigechika's father, Shigesada, is unknown; though listed in the Miura genealogy as principal heir (*Miura shi keizu*, in *DNK, iewake 14*, p. 477), there is no indication that he ever received his inheritance. Probably he predeceased his father, Shigesuke, thus necessitating the present release to a grandson (the donor had no other sons: *Miura shi keizu*, pp. 471–77).

    3. This release is not extant. It is curious, moreover, that the Bakufu was confirming an earlier conveyance, in light of the 1264 document, presented here. The earlier release was clearly more detailed.

    4. The identity of this person is unknown. Could it be a granddaughter of the

present donor (hence a sister of the present donee)? In other words, in the absence of a great-grandson, the chieftain's inheritance should go to the donee's sister rather than his daughter. The donee, of course, did have a son, so the point was moot (see the conveyance of 1293 cited in n. 1).

5. The identity of this person is unknown, though it seems most likely that she was a daughter of the present donor (i.e., the donee's aunt). Only one daughter of Shigesuke, unidentified, appears in the house genealogy; *Miura shi keizu*, in *DNK, iewake 14*, p. 477.

6. For a later dispute between Shigechika's heir and a cousin with interests in Niho Estate, see Document 139.

DOCUMENT 95

The Bakufu Confirms an Ex-Husband in His Wife's Inheritance, 1264

A topic thus far untreated is the effect divorce had on the disposition of property. We have seen in a number of contexts the right of parents to recall bequests; the Bakufu consistently underwrote this. The privilege, however, did not extend to ex-spouses—by definition no longer related. In the present case, an extremely important one, a distinction was apparently made between conditional grants to blood relatives and absolute releases to non-kin—including ex-husbands. A release to an ex-husband was thus no different from a sale to an outsider or a commendation to a religious institution. Perhaps the major question remaining is whether in a marriage that was still intact a spouse might reclaim what he had already released. In a previous case (Document 86) we saw a husband reducing the size of a wife's portion but making it now freely alienable. Had the lady contested this new arrangement it might have become a matter for the courts to decide.

Items in dispute between the nun-widow of Miyagi *uemon no jō* Hironari, represented by her son Kagehiro, and Nasu Hizenjirō *saemon no jō* Sukenaga.

Item: concerning one plot of land in Kamakura.
On the basis of plaintiff and defense statements, the two sides were summoned and interrogated before the *hikitsuke*.[1]
According to Kagehiro: "Taira *no uji*, the daughter of Mutsu *no suke* Kagehira, is the wife of Sukenaga. The aforesaid land was released by Kagehira to his daughter, and by the daughter to the nun. Nevertheless, Sukenaga has seized it."[2] According to Sukenaga: "The daughter is the former wife (*kyūsai*) of Sukenaga.[3] Nevertheless, she released

[her property] to Sukenaga in the 7th month of the 2d year of Kenchō [1250]. How on the basis of a document (*jō*) of the 8th month held by the nun could [that release] be overturned (*kuikaesu*)?"[4] Kagehiro stated: "The release held by Sukenaga concerns the entire estate (*ka no chi no sōryō*), of which the nun's share is but two service households (*zaike*).[5] Sukenaga is the former husband of the daughter, [whereas] the nun is an unrelated person (*tanin*) with a different surname (*ishō*). Why cannot this circumstance be recognized? Since Sukenaga has received in heredity (*sōden*) the daughter's entire portfolio of property (*shoryō*),[6] her land site in Kamakura, as well as her servants and other wealth, it seems difficult to consider him an unrelated person (*tanin*)."[7] Sukenaga stated: "A former wife is [like] a stranger (*gainin*). How can Sukenaga have a portion of the release to him overturned?"[8]

According to the release by the daughter of the 2d year of Kenchō [1250], 8th month,   day,[9] submitted by Kagehiro, it is clear that the Shirō *nyūdō* and Araya [service household] sites were deeded to the nun [effective] after the daughter's lifetime.[10] According to Kagehira's release to his daughter of the 2d year of En'ō [1240], 8th month,   day,[11] submitted by Sukenaga: "Our southern property, [located as follows] . . .,[12] is deeded to Tsuruishi—our daughter."[13] According to the daughter's release to Sukenaga of the 2d year of Kenchō [1250], 7th month,   day:[14] "Our southern property . . . is deeded [to him]." Even though Kagehiro has requested a judgment (*saikyo*) on the basis of the daughter's release,[15] it seems clear in both law (*hōi*) and custom (*bōrei*) that property deeded to a husband is not revocable.[16] Accordingly, it is hard to credit a partitioning and bequest to the nun coming after the daughter's release of the land in question to Sukenaga. Therefore, the nun's suit cannot be acted upon.

. . .[17]

By command of the shogun's house, the foregoing matters are so decreed.

　　　1st year of Bun'ei [1264], 10th month, 10th day

　　　　　　　　　　　　sama gon no kami, Taira ason
　　　　　　　　　　　　(monogram)
　　　　　　　　　　　　Sagami no kami, Taira ason (monogram)

SOURCE: *Yūki monjo*, 1264/10/10 Kantō gechijō, *KBSS*, 1: 145–47, doc. 112 (*KI*, 12: 372–73, doc. 9166).

　　1. The *hikitsuke* (board of coadjutors) was established in 1249. The present reference to it is the earliest in any extant document.

　　2. The argument by the plaintiff, then, is that the inheritance went from Kagehira

to his daughter (Taira *no uji*), and from the daughter to Miyagi Hironari's widow (relationship unknown). Despite this, Sukenaga, the husband of Taira *no uji*, had illegally seized it.

3. Sukenaga's need to clarify that he was a former husband is at first puzzling. As we will see, however, it was necessary for him to establish the independence of his claim; the property he had received (much as in a land-sale transaction) could not be retrieved.

4. Normally, conveyances bearing later signatures would be credited, but not, as we shall see, in the present instance. This was because the release here was not from a parent, but rather from an "unrelated" person: Sukenaga's possession, as in a sale, could not be rescinded without his consent.

5. We note the dramatic shift in Kagehiro's position away from his initial statement.

6. These holdings were in Mutsu Province; see *Akita han shūshū monjo*, 1272/4/5 Kantō gechijō, *KBSS*, 1: 165, doc. 126.

7. Both sides, then, were stressing their unrelatedness by blood to the donor.

8. See n. 3.

9. Not extant.

10. The possession of this document (of 1250/8) explains why the nun's son, Kagehiro, was bringing the present suit: the daughter (Taira *no uji*) had seemingly deeded a portion of her inheritance to the nun. But of course she had also deeded the entire inheritance to Sukenaga a month earlier, as we see below.

11. Not extant.

12. I.e., the site in Kamakura. We recall that the family's homelands were in Mutsu Province far to the north; see n. 6.

13. The same person as Taira *no uji*.

14. Not extant.

15. I.e., the conveyance of 1250/8 to the nun.

16. According to Bakufu law, a parent could revoke a release to a child at any time (*Goseibai Shikimoku*, art. 20). But evidently a conveyance once made to an "unrelated person" could not be withdrawn. See p. 103, n. 50.

17. An unrelated second item follows. Unfortunately, no documents are extant that might shed additional light on the present episode.

DOCUMENT 96

The Bakufu Confirms Proprietor-Level Shiki, 1265

It was highly unusual for the Bakufu to become involved in the confirmation of custodial-level land rights save for those in which the proprietorships lay with the shogun. Yet there were clear exceptions—in particular, those for which a precedent of confirmation dated back to the start of the period. Even at that, the Bakufu was careful not to claim for itself too great an authority in a matter which, after all, involved courtiers. The confirmation here can probably best be understood as a courtesy extended by Kamakura to friendly aristocrats.

Concerning the custodial titles (*azukari dokoro shiki*) of Yuge Estate in Mimasaka Province, Saeki Estate in Bizen Province, and Kaitō Upper and Middle Estates in Owari Province. Possession (*chigyō*) shall be without challenge, in accordance with the deed of release by Lady Sanjō.[1] Proprietary rights (*ryōke shiki*) shall similarly follow that dispensation. As for residence land (*yachi*) within the capital, let it be announced that the Kantō exercises no jurisdiction (*gokunyū*). Respectfully.[2]

2d year of Bun'ei [1265],[3] intercalated 4th month, 29th day

Sagami no kami seal

sakyō, gon no daibu seal

SOURCE: *Koga ke monjo*, 1265/int. 4/29 Kantō migyōsho an, in "Koga ke monjo," *Kokugakuin zasshi* 60: 12 (1959), pp. 100–101, doc. 209.10 (*KI*, 13: 22, doc. 9289).

1. For this conveyance, see *Koga ke monjo*, 1257/9/19 Sanjō-no-tsubone yuzurijō an, *KI*, 11: 243, doc. 8150. Lady Sanjō was one of seven daughters who received an inheritance consisting of *shōen* proprietorships or custodianships in the 1220s; *ibid.*, 1229/6 Taira Mitsumori shobunjō, *KI*, 6: 131–32, doc. 3841.

2. The Bakufu's confirmation here followed a precedent on behalf of this noble house dating back to the era of Yoritomo; *ibid.*, ?/11/19 Minamoto Yoritomo shojō an, "Koga ke monjo," *Kokugakuin zasshi* 60: 12 (1959), p. 98, doc. 299.7. The *shobunjō* of 1229/6 (n. 1) was similarly confirmed by Kamakura; *ibid.*, 1229/7/18 Kantō migyōsho an, *KI*, 6: 134, doc. 3846.

3. In half-size characters; added later.

DOCUMENTS 97–98

The Bakufu Omits Confirmation of a Cash Bequest, 1265, 1268

Cash and movables were not normally given much space in Kamakura-era release documents, and they were given virtually no attention by the Bakufu in its confirmations. The grant that is dealt with here is interesting on two counts. First, a father-donor made a permanent settlement of a *jitō shiki* on a fourth daughter but limited a cash bequest to her lifetime, after which it was to fall to her brother, the principal heir. And second, the Bakufu, in its approval of the transaction in question, said nothing whatever about the money, which in fact is not heard of again. A further point of note is the profusion of names used to refer to the daughter.

97

Conveyed: the *jitō shiki* of Itagasaki *gō*, within the Ichinohasama [region] of Kurihara [Estate], Mutsu Province; and 30 *kanmon* of the annual tax (*nengu*) in cash from Fuse Estate, Mimasaka Province.[1]

The aforesaid holdings (*shoryō*) are deeded herewith to our fourth daughter, Lady Sasaki—called Monju.[2] However, after her lifetime the said cash will become part of the share of Saburō *saemon no jō* Tamenari.[3] Let there be no challenge to this. As proof for the future, our deed of release is thus.

2d year of Bun'ei [1265], 9th month, 23d day

shami, Iren (monogram)

98

That Fujiwara *no uji*[4]—called Monju—shall forthwith possess the *jitō shiki* for Itagasaki *gō*, within the Ichinohasama [region] of Kurihara Estate, Mutsu Province.

Regarding the aforesaid, possession shall be exercised in accordance with the deed of release of the late father, the former governor of Kai, Tametoki *hosshi*—Buddhist name, Iren—dated the 2d year of Bun'ei [1265], 9th month, 23d day. By command of the Kamakura lord, it is so decreed.[5]

5th year of Bun'ei [1268], 9th month, 19th day

Sagami no kami, Taira ason (monogram)
sakyō, gon no daibu, Taira ason
(monogram)

SOURCES: Document 97: *Kuchiki monjo*, 1265/9/23 shami Iren yuzurijō, *Kuchiki monjo*, 1: 56, doc. 105 (*KI*, 13: 47, doc. 9354). Document 98: *ibid.*, 1268/9/10 Kantō gechijō, *Kuchiki monjo*, 1: 56–57, doc. 106 (*KI*, 13: 423, doc. 10301).

1. The prior history of these two interests is unknown.
2. The donor here is referring to his daughter by her married and her given names. See n. 4.
3. Probably the donor's principal heir.
4. The Bakufu refers to the female recipient by her clan name.
5. A generation later a nun named Kakui (= Lady Sasaki, Fujiwara *no uji*, Monju?) deeded the Itagasaki *gō jitō shiki* to her son. No mention was made of the cash share from Fuse Estate, since presumably this had lapsed to her brother's line. See *Kuchiki monjo*, 1294/8/20 ama Kakui yuzurijō, *Kuchiki monjo*, 1: 58–59, doc. 108. The Bakufu's confirmation came five years later; *ibid.*, 1299/6/26 Kantō gechijō, *Kuchiki monjo*, 1: 20, doc. 40.

DOCUMENT 99

An Alleged Profusion of Conveyance Deeds Helps Muddle an Inheritance Dispute, 1267

Here we have a sibling dispute—typical of the age—in which the issues (and their solutions) were buried in a plethora of release documents. The negative side to a parent's freedom to write and rewrite such conveyances was that these records presented contradictory visions of the future. It was almost an invitation to misunderstanding, which often included the charge of forgery. In the present case, four siblings—three against one—were involved in the kind of intragenerational rivalry that the Bakufu could never put to rest, only temporarily disarm. The great achievement of its justice was to keep most of this discord from inflaming whole areas. Nevertheless, it can scarcely be doubted that rivalries of the type described here were among the most intractable of the age.

Items in dispute between Yamanouchi *ukon no shōgen* Toshi [ie— character omitted] and his younger siblings, *hyōe* Saburō Tokimichi, Shirō Kiyotoshi, and Fujiwara *no uji*.[1]

Item: four locales within Jibi Estate, Bingo Province—Hon *gō*, Kawakita *gō*, Iyo-higashi Village, Eki residence land (*monden*). The plaintiff and defense statements contained numerous details.[2] In essence, however, it seems difficult to call [the estate] a separate award (*bekkyū*) to Shinnen—father of Toshi[ie] et al.—in view of the [Kantō] edict (*ongechi*) of the Jōkyū era [1219–21] and the [Kantō] directive (*migyōsho*) from the Jōō age [1222–24].[3] Yet it [also] seems difficult to invalidate Saimyō's conveyance to Shinnen of the intercalated 1st month, same [year],[4] [merely] on the basis of a private letter (*shojō*) from Saimyō—Shinnen's father—submitted by Toshi[ie].[5]

Next, concerning the conveyance of Shinnen dated the 11th month, 12th day, same [year],[6] and that of Saimyō dated the 3d year of Ninji [1242],[7] there seems no lack of reason in Tokimichi's labeling them as forgeries (*bōsho*). Accordingly, Toshi[ie's] false suit (*ranso*) is dismissed in regard to Hon *gō*, Kawakita, Iyo-higashi Village, and the Eki residence land. The individual possessions there shall be exercised free of challenge, in accordance with Shinnen's Kenchō-period [1249–56] conveyance[s] and the Shōka-era [1257–59] [confirmatory] edict (*onkudashibumi*).[8]

Next, concerning Toshi[ie's use of] forged documents, such offense will be dealt with in accordance with regulations.

Next, concerning Kamibara Village within the same estate,[9] Toshi[ie] has stated that no proof records (*shōmon*) exist save for the Kangi [1229–31] and Ninji [1240–43] releases of Shinnen and Saimyō.[10] To the contrary, Tokimichi et al. have asserted that other releases were hidden away. Yet since neither Toshi[ie] nor Tokimichi et al. dispute the long possession (*tanen chigyō*) of Toshi[ie] [there], further details seem unnecessary.[11] In the matter of despoilments (*rōzeki*), Tokimichi et al. have claimed that Toshi[ie] sent an agent into the estate who cut down timber and seized authority over foodstuffs (*kuriya*). However, not only has Toshi[ie] defended this point, but many side issues have emerged. Thus no decision will be rendered. . . .[12]

By this command, the foregoing points are so decreed.

4th year of Bun'ei [1267], 10th month, 27th day[13]

> Sagami no kami, Taira ason (monogram)
> sakyō, gon no daibu, Taira ason
> (monogram)

SOURCE: *Yamanouchi Sudō ke monjo,* 1267/10/27 Kantō gechijō, *DNK, iewake 15,* pp. 7–8, doc. 7 (*KI,* 13: 292, doc. 9788).

1. Tokimichi, though younger than Toshiie, had been selected as principal heir. For details, see Documents 43 and 44 (at that time, Tokimichi was called Tokitoshi). Fujiwara *no uji* was of course a sister.

2. The plaintiff here was Toshiie.

3. The only surviving Jōkyū-era edict credited Shinnen (Munetoshi) with fighting loyally for Kamakura in 1221, but confirmed his father (Shigetoshi = Saimyō) in the Jibi Estate *jitō shiki*; 1221/7/26 Kantō gechijō, *DNK, iewake 15,* p. 1, doc. 1 (*KB,* doc. 21). No Jōō-era documents are extant. The argument here seems to be part of the presentation of the three defendants. As they may have seen it, if Jibi went directly to Shinnen (who then parceled it among themselves), no prior promise by Saimyō to Toshiie could have been valid (see n. 5).

4. Which year? The only surviving release from Saimyō (Shigetoshi) to Shinnen (Munetoshi) is that of 1230/int.1/14—Document 42. However, this conveyance deals exclusively with the family's base area in Sagami; Jibi Estate is not mentioned. Moreover, a document of 1236 makes clear that, even beyond 1230, Shigetoshi was still the *jitō* for (at least) the Hon *gō* portion of Jibi Estate; *Yamanouchi Sudō ke monjo,* 1236/9/4 Kantō gechijō, *DNK, iewake 15,* pp. 1–2, doc. 2 (*DKR,* doc. 91). Some portion of the puzzle is obviously missing, since details are lacking on the mainline disposition of Jibi Estate (for a fragment, see Document 45).

5. Though this is speculative, it would seem that Toshiie's hope lay in gaining official recognition for a private letter dealing with Jibi that he had received from his grandfather Saimyō. Such an acceptance might mean the invalidation of Saimyō's deed to Shinnen, which in turn might invalidate Shinnen's releases to his sons and daughter.

6. We know only that this release was from the Kangi era (1229–31). At all events, as we shall see, it was denounced as a forgery.

7. According to *Yamanouchi shi keizu* (*DNK*, *iewake 15*, p. 538), Saimyō (Shigetoshi) died in 1242. This would have made his supposed conveyance of that year truly a "final will." It also suggests that releases from a father might postdate (supersede?) those of a son. However, this document too was judged a forgery. This left Toshiie without a documentary basis for his claim, save for the private letter from his grandfather discussed in n. 5.

8. The only extant Kenchō-era deed by Shinnen is one of 1249 to Tokimichi (Document 44), though it does not deal with Jibi Estate. Obviously, there were others. Similarly, the only Bakufu confirmation from the Shōka era is one to Tokinari (Document 45), who was not a litigant in the present case; see n. 9.

9. For adjacent Shimobara Village (confirmed by the Bakufu to a cousin of the present disputants), see Document 45.

10. These, of course, were judged to be forgeries; see notes 6 and 7.

11. The Bakufu, in other words, was letting this matter stand. Kamibara Village may in fact have been Toshiie's rightful share; see the name "Kamibara" next to Toshiie's name in the house genealogy: *Yamanouchi shi keizu*, *DNK*, *iewake 15*, p. 538. The other areas in dispute were judged to belong to his brothers and sister.

12. An unrelated second "item" follows here.

13. In 1295, Yamanouchi Tokimochi, the victor here, deeded the family's main holdings to his own heir. See Document 121.

DOCUMENT 100

A Donor with True Sons Deeds a Jitō Shiki to an Adopted Son, 1268

Logic suggests that men and women who were heirless would make the most extensive use of the period's free adoption practices, and so it likely was. Yet there were always instances in which landholders who were rich in children but relatively poor in property nevertheless added to their offspring by artificial means. The present document illustrates this. With no hint of any animus toward the donor's natural sons, one of whom was obviously named principal heir, the donor here was even so releasing a portion of his estate—and a *jitō shiki* at that—to someone who had been adopted. In the same year the Bakufu routinely confirmed the passage citing the release by the recipient's foster father.

For the future, written in our own hand.[1]

Conveyed: to *sa hyōe no jō*, Fujiwara Tsunekiyo.[2]

The *jitō shiki* of Hisamatsu[3] *myō*, within Asahi *gō*, Asai District, Ōmi Province—provincial headquarters (*kokuga*) rice to be paid to the house chieftain (*sōryō*).[4]

As a hereditary holding for many generations, I herewith deed it to my adopted son (*yōshi*), Tsunekiyo. Management and possession (*shintai ryōshō*) shall forthwith be exercised [by him]. Let there be no discord (*fuwagi*) on the part of his brothers. It is thus.

5th year of Bun'ei [1268], intercalated 1st month, 28th day

saemon no jō[5] seal

SOURCE: *Gion shaki zassan*, 1268/int.1/28 saemon no jō Kiyotoki yuzurijo an, *Higashi Asai gunshi*, 4: 529 (*KI*, 13: 329–30, doc. 9854).

1. In half-size characters; hence a form of prescript added, perhaps, to give the present transcribed copy (*an*) more force.

2. The *Higashi Asai gunshi* version places the name of this recipient in the prescript; *KI* corrects this error.

3. *Higashi Asai gunshi* has it "Hisakome."

4. I.e., through the house chieftain. Taxes from this *kokugaryō* (public land) unit were to be collected and paid by the house head.

5. The Bakufu confirmed this release nine months later, referring to *saemon no jō* Kiyotoki as the recipient's foster father (*yōfu*); *Gion shaki zassan*, 1268/10/29 Kantō gechijō an, *Higashi Asai gunshi*, 4: 529 (not in *KI*).

DOCUMENT 101

A Jitō Shiki Is Deeded to a Sister After Four Generations in the Male Line, 1269

If proof were needed that historical trends need to be "tolerant" of counter-examples or developments that may seem anomalous, the present episode should be noted. A tradition of main heir inheritance within the male line was upset in 1269 when the current holder, following the wishes of his late father, deeded the family's *jitō shiki* to his younger sister. Apparently neither the son nor the father was aware that he was bucking the tide by settling (or hoping to settle) so valuable a property on a sister and daughter, respectively. Equally important is that no "harm" was done, since the recipient here revived the male tradition of *jitō*-holding by transmitting it to her own son.

Conveyed: the *jitō shiki* for Haruke *ho*, Oki District, Hizen Province.
　　To: Fuji[wara][1] *no uji*—child's name, Senju; now called Lady Munakata.

The aforesaid estate (*shō*) was granted, for cause, by the late Kamakura *utaishō* house[2] to Takaakira's great-grandfather, Owari *no shōshō* Takayori.[3] In turn, Takayori passed it to his son, Narisuke,[4] who then released it to his son, Akitsugu,[5] who finally released it to his son,

Takaakira—child's name, Iyatsuru[6]—a total of four generations. It is clear from the sequence of Kantō edicts that possession has been exercised without disruption. Nevertheless, Fujiwara *no uji*, as our younger sister born of the same father and mother,[7] and in accordance with the final wishes (*yuigon*) of our late father,[8] is herewith made this conveyance in perpetuity, along with the sequence of proof records. It is thus.[9]

 6th year of Bun'ei [1269], 8th month, 21st day

gon no risshi, Takaakira (monogram)

SOURCE: *Munakata jinja monjo*, 1269/8/21 Fujiwara Takaakira yuzurijō, *Munakata gunshi*, 2: 181 (*KI*, 14: 61, doc. 10478).
 1. Character omitted in the original, a common device when writing the name Fujiwara.
 2. I.e., by Yoritomo.
 3. This grant to Takayori occurred on 1185/8/5. See the reference to this date in *Munakata jinja monjo*, 1221/7/21 Fujiwara Takayori yuzurijō, *Munakata gunshi*, 2: 150. An actual Yoritomo document survives, but only the date and signature are left; the entire content has been lost (*ibid.*, 1185/8/5 Minamoto Yoritomo kudashibumi, *Munakata gunshi*, 2: 140).
 4. See the 1221 document cited in n. 3.
 5. *Munakata jinja monjo*, 1237/2/12 Fujiwara Narisuke (Shobutsu) yuzurijō, *Munakata gunshi*, 2: 158–59.
 6. I.e., to the present donor. In fact, this is not entirely accurate: Akitsugu deeded the *jitō shiki* to his wife, Ōe *no uji*, under the stipulation that his son, Iyatsuru, receive the inheritance when he came of age; *Munakata jinja monjo*, 1241/6/21 Fujiwara Akitsugu yuzurijō, *Munakata gunshi*, 2: 159–61. The Bakufu quickly confirmed this; *ibid.*, 2: 161–62. Thirteen years later Ōe *no uji* fulfilled the terms of this agreement; *ibid.*, 1254/6 Ōe no uji yuzurijō, *Munakata gunshi*, 2: 166–67.
 7. The phrase appearing here is *dōfu ippuku no imoto*, implying a full sister, born of Akitsugu and Ōe *no uji*.
 8. The conveyance left by the father, Akitsugu, makes no mention of a release in future to Iyatsuru's (Takaakira's) sister; see n. 6.
 9. Eight years later the recipient here, Fujiwara *no uji*, deeded the *jitō shiki* to her own son; *Munakata jinja monjo*, 1277/6/15 Fujiwara no uji yuzurijō, *Munakata gunshi*, 2: 196–97.

DOCUMENTS 102–5

A Father Issues Four Conveyances on the Same Day, 1270

That partible inheritance remained operational for typical families of modest means is shown in these four releases. Nor was the donor here merely adopting the simplest solution. Among other things, he passed over his eldest son in the matter of the house headship, and he granted an independent *jitō shiki* to a demonstrably junior heir. On the other hand, he deeded a share to a grandson (the son of the principal heir), and he called on the secondary heirs to obey the requisitioning orders of the head-designate. It can thus be said that the disposition of this family's property rights adhered to two principles—the tradition of partible inheritance, but also an increasing emphasis on the powers of the chieftain.

102

Conveyed: the *jitō shiki* of Irobe-jō within Koizumi Estate, Echigo Province.

Regarding the above, our son Saburō Taira Tadanaga, now designated as house chieftain (*sōryō*), is given this release along with the full sequence of hereditary proof records.[1] Let authority be exercised by him in accordance with precedent and free of disturbance. It is thus.

7th year of Bun'ei [1270], 8th month, 25th day[2]

shami, Gyōnin[3] (monogram)

103

Conveyed: the *jitō shiki* for the area to the west of the roadway in Ushiya-jō, Koizumi Estate, Echigo Province—minus Jōshin *ho*. Boundaries: the roadway to the east, the stone wall along the dry streambed to the south, the mountains to the west, and Irobe-jō to the north; the *jitō shiki* of Iinashi Estate, Izumo Province.[4]

Regarding the aforesaid, conveyance is made to our son Shichirō *saemon no jō* Taira Nagashige. Let possession (*ryōchi*) be exercised by him free of disturbance. However, concerning the regular and emergency [shogunal] services, these shall be discharged in accordance with allocations set by the *sōryō* Tadanaga. Wherefore, our conveyance is thus.

7th year of Bun'ei [1270], 8th month, 25th day[5]

shami, Gyōnin seal

104

Conveyed: the *jitō shiki* for the area to the east of the roadway within Ushiya-jō, Koizumi Estate, Echigo Province—minus the new paddy (*shinden*) of Matsuzawa.
Boundaries: the mountains to the east, the stone wall along the dry streambed to the south, the roadway to the west, Irobe-jō to the north.[6]

Regarding the aforesaid, conveyance is made to our son Gorō *saemon no jō* Taira Ujinaga. Let possession be exercised by him free of disturbance and in accordance with precedent. However, concerning the regular and emergency [shogunal] services, these shall be discharged in accordance with allocations set by the *sōryō* Tadanaga. Wherefore, our conveyance is thus.

7th year of Bun'ei [1270], 8th month, 25th day[7]

shami, Gyōnin seal

105

Conveyed: the *jitō shiki* of Awashima within Koizumi Estate, Echigo Province.

Regarding the aforesaid, conveyance is made to our grandson Saburō Taira Naganobu.[8] Let possession be exercised by him free of disturbance. Concerning the regular and emergency [shogunal] services, these shall be discharged without negligence and in accordance with precedent.[9] It is thus.[10]

7th year of Bun'ei [1270], 8th month, 25th day[11]

shami, Gyōnin

SOURCES: Document 102: *Irobe monjo*, 1270/8/25 shami Gyōnin (Irobe Kiminaga) *yuzurijō*, *Irobe shiryō*, p. 9 (*KI*, 14: 166–67, doc. 10,677). Documents 103–5: *ibid.*, 1270/8/25 shami Gyōnin *yuzurijō an*, *Irobe shiryō*, pp. 4, 5, 14 (*KI*, 14: 167, docs. 10,678–80).

1. A document of nine years later makes clear that Tadanaga's elder brother, Kiyonaga, was deliberately passed over for the house headship owing to unfilial behavior. Kiyonaga contested this with his brother but was defeated in the suit: *Irobe monjo*, 1279/10/26 Kantō gechijō an, *Irobe shiryō*, pp. 9–10.

2. For the Bakufu's immediate confirmation, see *ibid.*, 1270/12/14 Kantō gechijō an, *Irobe shiryō*, p. 9.

3. Gyōnin himself (Irobe Kiminaga) received his father's inheritance in 1227; for the Bakufu's confirmation (conveyance not extant), see *ibid.*, 1227/4/9 shōgun sodehan kudashibumi, *Irobe shiryō*, p. 2. A second confirmation of Kiminaga based on an updated release by his father came in 1255; *ibid.*, 1255/3/27 shōgun ke mandokoro kudashibumi, *Irobe shiryō*, p. 2.

4. In addition to rights in the family's base area, the present recipient (a younger son) was thus deeded a *jitō shiki* in a distant region. It is noteworthy that this release did not go to the new house chieftain. The *sōryō*, however, may have acquired a second family-held *jitō shiki*—in equally remote Sanuki Province. For Gyōnin's confirmation in this title, see the 1255 document cited in n. 3. For the new *sōryō* Tadanaga's interest in it (no actual deed is extant), see the 1279 document cited in n. 1. The Sanuki title, however, disappears from view, and the Irobe family may indeed have lost it.

5. The Bakufu's confirmation came on the same day as that for the other heirs: *Irobe monjo*, 1270/12/14 Kantō gechijō an, *Irobe shiryō*, p. 4.

6. This grant area was immediately adjacent to that for Nagashige in Document 103.

7. For the Bakufu's confirmation, see *Irobe monjo*, 1270/12/14 Kantō gechijō an, *Irobe shiryō*, p. 5.

8. This grandson was the son of the new chieftain, Tadanaga. The present conveyance updated a similar one of two years earlier; *ibid.*, 1268/4/28 Irobe Kiminaga yuzurijō, *Irobe shiryō*, pp. 13–14. Evidently, all of this was a way of strengthening the line of the designated heir; see n. 11.

9. We note that no admonition to obey the allocations of the *sōryō*—the recipient's father—is included.

10. Compare the formats of Documents 102 and 105 (for the *sōryō* line) with those of Documents 103 and 104 (for secondary heirs).

11. For the Bakufu's confirmation, see *Irobe monjo*, 1270/12/14 Kantō gechijō an, *Irobe shiryō*, p. 14. A bare six years later the recipient here was himself named *sōryō* and granted a deed by his father for the Irobe-jō *jitō shiki*; *ibid.*, 1276/6/19 Irobe Tadanaga yuzurijō, *Irobe shiryō*, p. 14. It seems likely, however, that Tadanaga himself retained authority, since it was he who was defendant against his older brother in 1279 (n. 1) and he (rather than his son Naganobu) who deeded the chieftain's inheritance to Naganobu's son (i.e., Tadanaga's grandson) in 1299; *ibid.*, 1299/3/7 Irobe Tadanaga yuzurijō an, *Irobe shiryō*, p. 15. A Bakufu confirmation for the 1299 conveyance is extant, but not one for the 1276 inheritance (*ibid.*, 1299/5/12 Kantō gechijō, *Irobe shiryō*, p. 16).

DOCUMENT 106

A Sequence of Bakufu Confirmations Determines the Winning Side in an Inheritance Dispute, 1271

Time and again we have seen that the standard pattern of devolution was from father to son but that exceptions were common. In the present case the one pattern we do not find is the standard one. The inheritance here passed to an adopted son and then to his younger brother, was subsequently sold to a priest who deeded it to his younger brother, and then was divided between the latter's two sons in an unusual 50–50 settlement. At this juncture, a descendant of the "original holder" from nearly a century earlier came forward and challenged the present arrangement, but his suit was dismissed on the basis of the Bakufu's confirmations of the opposing side as well as on the statute of limitations. The case is interesting, then, for its atypicality, which, upon reflection, seems not so unusual after all.

Concerning a dispute over the Urafuku area of Nagano Village, Isahaya Estate, Hizen Province, between Funatsu Jirō Ieshige, and Munakata Rokurō Ujinari *hosshi*[1]—Buddhist name, Jōkei— and Nagano Kotarō Ujisato.[2]

Regarding the above, plaintiff and defense arguments contained many details. In brief, however,[3] the said Urafuku area was deeded by E *no* Tarō *daibu* Takamune to his adopted son (*yōshi*) Genzō *kenjō* Osamu on the 4th day of the 12th month of the 2d year of Shōji [1200].[4] Accordingly, a [confirmatory] edict (*onkudashibumi*) was granted on the 6th day, 2d month, 2d year of Genkyū [1205]. By virtue of Osamu's release to his younger brother Minamoto *sakon no shōgen* Tōru in the 4th month of the 2d year of Jōgen [1208], Tōru was similarly granted a [confirmatory] edict on the 13th day, 12th month, 3d year of [Jōgen]. However, Tōru sold [this holding] to Munakata head priest (*daigūji*) Ujikuni in the intercalated 9th month, 3d year of Kenryaku [1213], and Ujikuni was granted a [confirmatory] edict on the 13th day, 7th month, 1st year of Jōō [1222].[5] Release was then made to his younger brother *hyōe no jō* Ujitsune—forebear (*fuso*) of Jōkei and [Ujisato]—in the intercalated 3d month of the 3d year of Karoku [1227], and as a result of a divided conveyance from Ujitsune, Jōkei and [Ujisato] came to exercise possession.

At present, Ieshige is arguing that the possession is his since the original holder (*honshu*) E *no daibu* Sukemune deeded it, with his son Takamune's signature, to Takaie, Ieshige's grandfather, in the 3d year of Jishō [1179],[6] and that furthermore he knows nothing of Osamu's receiving a conveyance from Takamune during the Shōji era [1200]. Notwithstanding,[7] it is clear from Osamu's and Tōru's [confirmatory] edicts of Genkyū [1205] and Jōgen [1209] that these were issued [after] the summoning to trial of Takaie and Osamu.[8] Most important of all, Jōkei and [Ujisato] have asserted that the statute of limitations (*nenjo*) has been exceeded since the possessions of Osamu and Tōru. [Indeed,] Ieshige has acknowledged that more than 20 years have passed since Takaie and Iemasa—Ieshige's father—were [allegedly] dispossessed (*ōryō*) by Tōru. Accordingly, Ieshige's false suit (*ranso*) concerning the Urafuku area is dismissed, and the possession of Jōkei and [Ujisato] shall continue without disturbance.

Next, although Ieshige charged that Jōkei and Ujisato were non-vassals (*higokenin*), generations of [confirmatory] edicts have been granted since the time of Munakata head priest Ujizane, Ujikuni's father;[9] and vassal services (*gokeninyaku*) have evidently been performed. Hence Ieshige's suit cannot be acted upon. By command of the Kamakura lord, it is so decreed.[10]

8th year of Bun'ei [1271], 11th month, 19th day

Sagami no kami, Taira ason seal
sakyō, gon no daibu, Taira ason
seal

SOURCE: *Munakata jinja monjo*, 1271/11/19 Kantō gechijō an, *Munakata gunshi*, 2: 183 (*KI*, 14: 323, doc. 10918).

1. Ujinari was the winning defendant here. For two earlier cases in which he was the plaintiff, see *Munakata jinja monjo*, 1257/3/5 Kantō migyōsho an, 1257/int.3/20 Kantō migyōsho an, *Munakata gunshi*, 2: 170 (*DKR*, docs. 106–7).

2. Seven years earlier the two defendants here had opposed one another in a dispute that led to a division (*shitaji chūbun*) between them of a neighboring village. See *ibid.*, 1264/5/10 Kantō gechijō an, *Munakata gunshi*, 2: 175. Now they were on the same side against an external challenger.

3. What follows here is the defendants' argument.

4. None of the documents referred to here and later is extant.

5. This document is not extant, but one of two weeks later does survive confirming Ujikuni's *daigūji* post; *Munakata jinja monjo* 1222/7/27 Kantō gechijō, *Munakata gunshi*, 2: 151 (*DKR*, doc. 12). Noteworthy in the present instance is Kamakura's apparent confirmation of a land right transferred by sale.

6. The connecting link here is Takamune, as we see in the clause that follows. Ieshige's allegation of a cosignature is partly contradicted by Takamune's conveyance of 1200.

7. The Bakufu's interpolation begins here.

8. We have no background information here, but evidently Osamu and Takaie had contested the inheritance, leading to Osamu's confirmation.

9. For the initial confirmation of Ujizane, see *Munakata jinja monjo* 1187/8/7 Minamoto Yoritomo shojō an, *Munakata gunshi*, 2: 141.

10. A summary of this case appears in *Munakata jinja shi*, 2: 682.

DOCUMENT 107

The Bakufu Hears an Appeal-Level Inheritance Suit, 1272

The case presented here has a certain poignancy to it—centering around the lifelong struggle of a second son to regain the small inheritance granted him by his father but then withdrawn. A full thirty years after this loss, the current holder, a nephew of the earlier victim, granted his uncle a subauthority within the disputed region, in return for which the uncle promised not to challenge his benefactor's *jitō shiki* there. And so it continued until in the next generation a dispute over income shares erupted, which led in turn to a judgment and then to an appeal of that judgment, i.e., the present suit. The Bakufu's verdict, a reaffirmation of its earlier verdict, was that the two levels of authority should stand. Thus, quite unlike most partible arrangements, which involved parallel tenures over different areas, this one involved concentric interests in the same area. On the other hand, the division was the result not of a release but rather of an accord: we find no conveyances in which concentric authorities were transmitted.

Concerning the petition of Mine Matagorō Tatō regarding the
jitō shiki of Urabejima, Ojika Island, Hizen Province.[1]

Numerous details were presented in the appeal-level suit (*osso*).[2]
In summary, on the occasion of the release of this island by Jinkaku,
original holder (*honshu*) of Ojika Island, to his first-born (*chaku-nan*) Michitaka—revised name, Michizumi—in the 2d year of Jōgen
[1208],[3] Urabejima, the allotment of the second son Aokata Genji
Ietaka *hosshi*—Buddhist name, Sainen—was recalled and released to
Michizumi.[4] When Michizumi, moreover, deeded this in the 1st year
of Jōkyū [1219] to Mine Genji Tamotsu[5]—Tatō's grandfather—a confirmatory edict (*ando no onkudashibumi*) came to be granted in the 3d
year [1221].[6] In turn, when Yamashiro Saburō Katashi brought his
false suit (*ranso*), Tamotsu was granted a [judgment] edict (*ongechi*) in
the 2d year of Antei [1228].[7] After that, when Tatō was given his inheritance,[8] a confirmatory edict (*ando no onkudashibumi*) was granted
in the 1st year of Shōgen [1256].[9] In that document, the words "minus
Urabejima" do not appear, and indeed a [judgment] edict (*ongechi*)
of the 1st year of Shōgen contains the phrase "Urabejima is within
Ojika Island."[10] Thus, even though Sainen—revised name, Kakuen—
claimed to possess a revised document (*gohan no jō*) of Jinkaku, he was
not granted a [confirmatory] edict (*onkudashibumi*).[11] As for the subauthority (*shita-no-sata*) for Urabejima, Tamotsu relinquished that to
Sainen in the 1st year of Ryakunin [1238].[12] Moreover, Tatō issued a
similar quitclaim (*sarijō*) in the 7th year of Kenchō [1255].[13] As for the
jitō shiki, Kakuen issued documents during Ryakunin and Kenchō to
the effect that there would be no challenge to Tamotsu's and Tatō's
authority (*chigyō*).[14]

A dispute over income shares (*tokubun*) between Yoshitaka, [Ka-
kuen's][15] son, and Tatō was resolved in the 5th year of Bun'ei [1268],[16]
though at present Tatō argues against any tenure (*ryō*) of Sainen, calling it no more than an income share. This is a petition (*mōshijō*) obviously filled with exaggeration (*henhen kyōshoku*). [Tatō] argues furthermore that whereas Sainen possessed hereditary proof records
(*shidai shōmon*),[17] he was never granted a confirmation. A confiscation
(*kessho*) was thus in order since the compromise (*wayo*) was agreed to
by others,[18] and since neither side enjoyed sufficient authority.[19]

By virtue of Sainen's possession of the subauthority stemming from
Tamotsu's and Tatō's quitclaims (*sarijō*), any such confiscation seems
most unwarranted. Therefore, in accordance with the agreement
records (*wayojō*) of Ryakunin [1238] and Kenchō [1255], both Tatō

and Yoshitaka shall exercise possession free of disturbance.[20] By command of the Kamakura lord, it is so decreed.[21]

9th year of Bun'ei [1272], 5th month, 10th day

> Sagami no kami, Taira ason seal
> sakyō, gon no daibu, Taira ason
> seal

SOURCE: *Aokata monjo*, 1272/5/10 Kantō gechijō an, *Aokata monjo*, 1: 26–27, doc. 30 (*KI*, 14: 385, doc. 11129).

1. For Ojika Island in the period to 1228, see *DKR*, pp. 95–101.

2. The original dispute came in 1268 (see below), though the judgment edict is not extant.

3. See Document 17: 1208/7 Jinkaku yuzurijō an.

4. *Ibid.* Sainen, as we note, spent the rest of his life trying to retrieve this lost holding.

5. *Aokata monjo*, 1219/11 Fujiwara Michizumi yuzurijō an, *Aokata monjo*, 1: 10, doc. 10. Tamotsu (referred to in error as "Mochi" in *DKR*, pp. 98–100, 275) was a cousin who became an adopted son of Michizumi.

6. *Ibid.*, 1221/5/26 Kantō gechijō an, *Aokata monjo*, 1: 10–11, doc. 11.

7. *Ibid.*, 1228/3/13 Kantō gechijō an, *Aokata monjo*, 1: 11–14, doc. 12. For an extended treatment of this suit, see *DKR*, pp. 95–101.

8. Conveyance not extant, but the date (1254/3/27) is cited in a later confirmation; *Aokata monjo*, 1271/11/25 shōgun ke mandokoro kudashibumi an, *Aokata monjo*, 1: 25–26, doc. 29. Tatō received his inheritance directly from his grandfather, Tamotsu.

9. Not extant.

10. *Aokata monjo*, 1256/7/16 Kantō gechijō an, *Aokata monjo*, 1: 17–18, doc. 16. This edict made clear, in other words, that Sainen (Ietaka) possessed no separate confirmation for Urabejima.

11. In fact, there was a later-sealed conveyance by Jinkaku (from 1209), which did provide Ietaka with a portion of the Urabejima inheritance he had lost a year earlier (n. 3). According to this newer release, Michitaka (Michizumi) and Ietaka would share authority there; *Aokata monjo*, 1209/2 Jinkaku yuzurijō an, *Aokata monjo*, 1: 7–8, doc. 8. Yet it must be noted that this conveyance was never cited in a subsequent record; only the deed of 1208 (Document 17) is referred to. This suggests that the 1209 release may never have been recognized or made effective, or that its validity (or authenticity) was in doubt.

12. *Aokata monjo*, 1238/12/25 Mine Tamotsu—Aokata Ietaka wayojō an, *Aokata monjo*, 1: 15, doc. 13. The background to this agreement was evidently a desire on the part of Tamotsu to quiet Sainen's dissatisfaction.

13. Not extant. This quitclaim came in the year following Tatō's receipt of his inheritance; see n. 8.

14. In other words, each side had agreed not to interfere with the authority sphere of the other. This was the situation until 1268.

15. The name Kakuen appears in a copy of the same document; *Aokata monjo*, 1272/5/10 Kantō gechijō an, *Aokata monjo*, 1: 27–28, doc. 31 (see also *KBSS*, 1: 168–69, doc. 127).

16. This was the suit on which the present appeal-level action by Tatō is based. The 1268 settlement is not extant, though obviously Tatō had come away dissatisfied. He

lodged his appeal, moreover, despite the Bakufu's confirmation of his *jitō shiki* in 1271; see n. 8.

17. What are these? The documents we find referred to are (1) Sainen's pre-1208 deed from his father (rendered invalid in 1208); (2) the 1209 release (n. 11) that was never recognized; (3) Tamotsu's quitclaim of 1238 (n. 12); and (4) Tatō's quitclaim of 1255 (not extant).

18. In other words, the *wayo* of 1238 (n. 12) had been agreed to by Tamotsu (the grandfather of Tatō) and by Sainen (the father of Yoshitaka). A new generation required a new dispensation.

19. Tatō was arguing, then, that Yoshitaka should be dispossessed and full authority granted to himself.

20. In effect, then, Kamakura was rejecting the appeal and continuing the dual possession.

21. Yoshitaka wasted little time before passing his inheritance to his own son; *Aokata monjo*, 1274/4 Aokata Yoshitaka yuzurijō an, *Aokata monjo*, 1: 31–32, doc. 36.

DOCUMENT 108

The Bakufu Adds a Long-Delayed "Marginal Confirmation" to an Inheritance Deriving from Two Sources, 1273

Here we see one of those interesting cases in which a donor, himself an adoptive son, had received his inheritances from two sources, his foster mother and (seemingly) the latter's husband. (The language of the document seems to indicate that the adoption relationship was with the mother, not the father.) The other point of note regarding this release is that it was confirmed by the Bakufu on the same piece of paper. In other words, the practice of issuing edicts of confirmation now gave way to granting "marginal" confirmations in the blank spaces of conveyances. The delay of 45 years here is probably explainable by the donor's having lived to a great age. The release, functioning as a testament, was not submitted until after his death.

Release of land holdings by the priest Kakujitsu to his son Banmanmaru.
> In total:
> One locale: the Hirata [holding] in Terahara Estate, along with Miya Estate, Aki Province[1]—details appear in the release from our foster mother (*yōbo*), Oshi.[2]
> One locale: one *chō* of *jitō* stipend land (*kyū shitaji*) in Fukumitsu *myō*, same estate[3]—details [appear in][4] the release by Rokurō Takanobu.[5]

Among the aforesaid holdings, Miya Estate was deeded to Kaku-jitsu—at that time Seitakamaru[6]—by his foster mother, Lady Hirata, or Oshi. The *jitō* stipend [fields] of Fukumitsu *myō* were deeded to Ka-kujitsu by Hirata Rokurō Takanobu.[7] Details appear in the respective [conveyances. Now, however,][8] with the onset of illness and because it is difficult to know when I might die, I herewith deed these holdings to my son, Banmanmaru. As stated herein, he shall exercise posses-sion henceforth, free of disturbance. However, as concerns the Kyoto imperial guard duty and the irregular services (*rinji no onkuji*) owed the Kantō, these should be discharged on a *tan*-unit basis.[9] Thus, as proof (*kikei*) for the future, our release is so recorded, and is accom-panied by [prior] releases and other documents.[10] Wherefore, this pe-tition (*ge*).[11]

10th year of Bun'ei [1273], 10th month, 5th day

local lord (*ryōshu*), the priest (*sō*)
Kakujitsu seal

Possession shall be exercised in accordance with this document. By this command, [it is so decreed].[12]

2d year of Bunpō [1318], 4th month, 29th day

Sagami no kami seal
Musashi no kami seal[13]

SOURCE: *Kikkawa ke monjo*, 1273/10/5 sō Kakujitsu yuzurijō an, *DNK, iewake* 9, 2: 302–4, doc. 1138 (*KI*, 15: 175–76, doc. 11427).

1. The language of the document makes it appear as if Miya Estate is within Terahara Estate (*Aki no kuni Terahara no shō nai Hirata Miya no shō*). But Terahara and Miya are in fact in separate districts; see Takeuchi Rizō, ed., *Shōen bunpu zu*, 2: 238, 242, and the identification in *KI*. Thus the meaning seems to be Miya Estate plus Hirata (= Fukumitsu *myō*; see n. 2) in Terahara Estate.

2. *Kikkawa ke monjo*, 1243/12/7 Oshi no onna yuzurijō an, *DNK, iewake* 9, 2: 301–2, doc. 1137. Both Miya Estate and Fukumitsu *myō* (= Hirata, i.e., a property of the Hirata family) are cited here.

3. I.e., Terahara Estate. This would make Fukumitsu *myō* the Hirata holding men-tioned above.

4. Several characters lost.

5. Relationship unknown, though later we see that Takanobu's surname was Hirata and that the adoptive mother, Oshi, is referred to as Lady Hirata. Perhaps Takanobu was the husband of Oshi. The conveyance deed itself is not extant.

6. I.e., his name as a child.

7. Thus the present donor had received his inheritance from two sources: from his adoptive mother and from Hirata Takanobu.

8. Characters lost.

9. I.e., the size of the burden will be a multiple of the total number of *tan* of land.

10. The only extant document is that cited in n. 2.

11. Use of the term *ge* here suggests that this release deed was to be submitted to the Bakufu for confirmation. As we see, a "marginal confirmation" (*gedai ando*) was eventually granted.

12. Characters lost.

13. The entire postscript (from "Possession") appears on the reverse side of the release. For unexplained reasons, the confirmation and the conveyance were separated by 45 years.

DOCUMENT 109

A Childless Woman Adopts a Son and Deeds Him Her Constable's Title, 1274

In the same way that women might hold the putative military title of *jitō*, they might also hold other military offices, for example, that of constable—*sō-tsuibushi*. In the present instance a female constable who was heirless adopted a son and made him her legatee. Interestingly, the only constabulary position that women could not occupy was that of *shugo*—and in that regard this highly politicized office was like most governmental positions within the Bakufu, i.e., closed to women.

Conveyed: the constableship (*sōtsuibushi shiki*) of Kehara *gō*.[1]

The aforesaid *shiki* is the hereditary possession of Inukai *no uji*—named Ken.[2] Owing to the fact that she has no natural son (*jisshi*), she has taken Gyōken—Jōshunbō—as her adopted son (*yōshi*) and now makes permanent conveyance to him.[3] The release is so made, along with the [relevant] documents, in the interest of future administration.

11th year of Bun'ei [1274], 3d month, 21st day

Inukai Ken (monogram)[4]

SOURCE: *Naka ke monjo*, 1274/3/21 Inukai Ken yuzurijō, *Kōyasan monjo (kyū Kōya ryōnai monjo)*, 11: 438, doc. 425 (*KI*, 15: 267, doc. 11617).

1. In Kii Province.

2. We can trace this constableship back to 1231 when a certain Fujiwara Tametoshi was appointed to the post by the area's custodian (*azukari dokoro*); see *Naka ke monjo*, 1231/2/14 Kehara gō sōtsuibushi shiki buninjō, *Kōyasan monjo*, 11: 434–35, doc. 411. Though only a surmise, it is possible that Inukai *no uji* was Tametoshi's widow and heir in the absence of children.

3. Gyōken's identity is unknown, though we are informed that he received a second inheritance two years later in a neighboring district. The donor in that instance was a priest named Kenyo, and the release was cosigned by Kenyo's principal heir, Ryūken;

ibid., 1276/5 sō Kenyo yuzurijō, *Kōyasan monjo*, 11: 438–39, doc. 416. Perhaps Ryūken and Gyōken were older and younger sons of this second donor, Kenyo. A younger son, not in line to succeed his father, would thus have been adopted by Inukai *no uji* as her heir.

4. The fate of the constableship is unknown.

DOCUMENT 110

A Scion of the Hōjō House Allows an Inheritance Portion to Pass to His Wife, 1275

The Hōjō, like the rest of warrior society, were influenced by changes in the inheritance system. In the present document, a wife was given a life portion as part of her inheritance, but was given a permanent grant as the other part. Many years later she took the alienable portion and commended it to a local temple.

Conveyed: various landholdings.[1]

Ōkura and Ishimura *gō*, in Ōta Estate, Shinano Province; Mae-bayashi and Kōzuma *gō*, plus Hirano Village (*mura*), in Shimo-kabe Estate, Shimōsa Province.

The aforesaid places are deeded to Fujiwara *no uji*.[2] Nevertheless, the *gō* and *mura* in Shimokabe shall be assigned to the chieftain (*sōryō*)[3] after [Fujiwara *no uji*'s] lifetime.[4] It is thus.

12th year of Bun'ei [1275], 4th month, 27th day

Echigo no kami, Taira (monogram)

SOURCE: *Kanazawa Shōmyōji monjo*, 1275/4/27 Hōjō (Kanazawa) Sanetoki yuzurijō, *Shinano shiryō*, 4: 300–301 (*KI*, 16: 18, doc. 11877).

1. The donor here was Hōjō Sanetoki (1224–76), a grandson of one Bakufu regent (Yoshitoki) and the grandfather of another (Sadaaki). Sanetoki himself was the founder of Shōmyōji Temple and the famous Kanazawa Library (*bunko*).

2. Almost certainly the wife of the donor.

3. I.e., the donor's main heir, Hōjō Akitoki.

4. Thus only the Ōta Estate portion was made a free inheritance to the testator's widow. At the end of her life she commended one (and probably both) of her two *gō* in Ōta Estate to Shōmyōji, the temple established by her late husband; see *Kanazawa bunko monjo*, 1310/1/22 Kantō kishinjō, *Shinano shiryō*, 4: 543; and *ibid.*, (no date) bō kishinjō an, *Shinano shiryō*, 4: 301. It seems likely that the widow's rights in the two *gō* were at the level of *jitō*, since in 1295 a dispute arose between the proprietor (*ryōke*) and the estate deputy (*zasshō*) over taxes (*onnengu*) owed from the two units; she is not mentioned. See

Waseda daigaku shozō monjo, 1295/3/25 Shinano no kuni Ōta no shō zasshō Dōnen wa-yojō, *Waseda daigaku shozō monjo,* 1: 230–31, doc. 434.

DOCUMENT 111

The Bakufu Affirms a Brother's Acknowledgment of His Sister's Inheritance Share, 1277

During the second half of the Kamakura period sibling disputes were often resolved, under threat of a court trial, by the rivals themselves. In this case, a younger brother relinquished claims that he had against certain holdings of his elder sister. Within days the Bakufu confirmed the arrangement.

Concerning a dispute between Suruga Hikoshirō Arimasa and his elder sister, Taira *no uji*—named Iyatsuru—over paddy and service households within their late father Tokiyoshi's landed legacy (*iryō*) of Ishizaka *gō*, southern Hiki District, Musashi Province.

Adjudication was sought in response to plaintiff and defense briefs (*sochinjō*) regarding the above. However, according to a quitclaim (*sarijō*) by Arimasa dated the 12th month, 26th day of last year:[1] "I relinquish my claim pursuant to the conveyances held by the daughter and others." As cited in the conveyances submitted by the daughter dated the 6th year of Kenchō [1254], 8th month, 24th day, and the 8th year of Bun'ei [1271], 9th month, 10th day:[2] "within Ishizaka *gō*, the Egasa Jirō service household plus one *chō* five *tan* of paddy; the *uemon* Tarō service household plus one *chō* of paddy." Let possession be exercised free of future disturbance, in accordance with the said document.[3] By command of the Kamakura lord, it is so decreed.

3d year of Kenji [1277], 1st month,   day

> Musashi no kami, Taira ason
> Sagami no kami, Taira ason
> (monogram)

SOURCE: *Kuchiki monjo,* 1277/1 Kantō gechijō, *KBSS,* 1: 186, doc. 140 (*KI,* 17: 8, doc. 12660).

1. Not extant.
2. Neither of these is extant. We note the 17-year separation between the two.
3. Presumably the reference is to Arimasa's quitclaim.

DOCUMENT 112

A Kyushu Vassal Petitions Kamakura for Confirmation of a Myōshu Shiki, 1282

Here we have one of the earliest references to a written release involving a minor administrative headship—a *myōshu shiki*. The release, dating from 1247, was from a grandmother to a grandson, but it was not until much later—when conditions were receptive to such action—that the recipient petitioned the Bakufu for a confirmation. The holding of *myōshu shiki* by Kamakura vassals was especially common in Kyushu, site of the present possession.

Hashiguchi Jirō *daizō* Ietada, a vassal of Satsuma Province, respectfully petitions:

> That in accordance with the deed of release of my grandmother, Dō-Amidabutsu, the headship (*myōshu shiki*) of Kawakami *myō*, Ichiki-in, might be confirmed to me by formal edict.[1]
>
> Appended: a transcribed copy (*anmon*) of the release.

The aforesaid *myōshu shiki* was deeded to Ietada by his grandmother Dō-Amidabutsu on the 5th day, 5th month, of the 1st year of Hōji [1247].[2] Therefore, in accordance with that release, we respectfully petition for a confirmatory edict, to serve as proof for the future.[3]

5th [year][4] of Kōan [1282], 3d [month], 11th day

SOURCE: *Sappan kyūki zatsuroku*, 1282/3/11 Hashiguchi Ietada mōshijō, *Kagoshima ken shiryō, kyūki zatsuroku zenpen*, 1: 312, doc. 838 (*KI*, 19: 309–10, doc. 14590).

1. We note the formal petition to Kamakura for confirmation of a *myōshu shiki*. This appeal may have anticipated a policy decision of 1284 to honor such requests from vassals who had participated in the defense effort against the Mongols.

2. Document not extant. The 35-year delay suggests that the likelihood of Kamakura's granting a confirmation of a *myōshu shiki* was now enhanced; see n. 1. This same grandmother deeded the Ichiki-in district headship (*gunji shiki*) to a brother of the present petitioner in 1244; that release was immediately confirmed by Kamakura. *Kawakami monjo*, 1244/8/18 Kantō kudashibumi an, *Kagoshima ken shiryō, kyūki zatsuroku zenpen*, 1: 186, doc. 424.

3. Whether or not this petition was honored is unknown.

4. The characters for "year" and "month" have been omitted in the document. Also, there is no signature.

DOCUMENT 113

The Bakufu Confirms a Widow's Allocation of Her Late Husband's Legacy, 1282

It occasionally happened that a father did not quite get around to preparing deeds of release for his offspring but did prepare an outline of how such a division should work. In the present case, a widow, following the allocations proposed by her late husband, proceeded to release the property on that basis. The actual partition of holdings is of interest: to the son and four daughters went shares in the family's *jitō shiki* in remote Iyo Province, whereas to the widow went the homelands in adjacent Musashi Province. At the same time, the son was clearly the beneficiary of the future. He had already been granted the bulk of the Iyo perquisites, and the Musashi base area would be his eventually.

The chancellery of the shogun's house directs: to Taira Yorihiro.
  That [the following] shall forthwith be held: the *jitō shiki* for Nii *gō*, Iyo Province—minus set shares for the four daughters; the residence plot(s), paddy, and upland of Kaneko-Kumazumi *gō*, Musashi Province—though as recorded in the widow's release, possession [of the latter][1] to begin only after the widow's lifetime.[2]

In response to the late father *saemon no jō* Hirotsuna's letter of intent, allocations (*haibun*) were made by the nun-mother Myōkaku on the 4th month, 13th day, of the 3d year of Kōan [1280].[3] In conformity with that document,[4] authority shall be exercised, pursuant to precedent. The command is thus. Wherefore, this order.
  5th year of Kōan [1282], 7th month, 16th day[5]

          anzu, Sugano
          chikeji
ryō, saemon no jō, Fujiwara
bettō, Sagami no kami, Taira ason

SOURCE: *Kaneko Ieyoshi shi shozō monjo*, 1282/7/16 shōgun ke mandokoro kudashibumi an, *Ehime ken hennen shi*, 2: 365 (*KI*, 19: 331, doc. 14644).
 1. I.e., Kaneko-Kumazumi; this was the Kaneko family's eastern homeland. The Kaneko house itself had joined the Minamoto at the start of the Genpei War; see *AK*, 1180/8/26.
 2. In other words, the homeland area was to remain in the widow's hands until her death, whereas the family's Iyo Province holding was to pass immediately to her son. (It

is noteworthy that the daughters' shares were established in Iyo, rather than in the family's home area of Musashi.) The date and circumstances of the original award of Nii *gō* to the Kaneko are unknown, though it is possible that the appointment came in the wake of the Jōkyū War. Various members of the family were recorded as having fought valorously at the Battle of Ujigawa; see *AK*, 1221/6/18, and Tanaka, "Iyo," pp. 248–49.

3. This is presumably the date of the widow's release, referred to in the introductory portion of our document.

4. Presumably the widow's release.

5. There appear to be no other Kamakura-period documents relating to the Kaneko family or Nii *gō*. However, *AK* has numerous entries describing the activities of that house.

DOCUMENT 114

A Major Vassal Clarifies Rights and Obligations for a Female Legatee, 1283

In the document presented here, we encounter again what daughters were always hoping for—*jitō shiki* bequests that were not entailed to their brothers. Moreover, the obligations and perquisites are unusually clear in this conveyance, for the father-donor took pains to educate his daughter about what was hers to keep and do with as she pleased.

Conveyed: The *jitō shiki* for Saruta Village and for Jirōmaru[1] in Nurugawa-jō, Shirakawa Estate, Echigo Province.[2]

The aforesaid places are herewith deeded to my daughter—named Shinju.[3] However, whereas two *chō* shall be stipend land (*kyūden*),[4] the remainder shall be obligated to pay the regular annual tax (*onnengu*) to the patron (*honke*),[5] in accordance with precedent. As for mountain and plain areas . . .[6] the boundaries are as stipulated. The taking of animal life is prohibited. As concerns the boundaries for paddy and upland, details appear in the release held by the house head-designate (*sōke*).[7] Wherefore, this instrument (*jō*) is thus.

6th year of Kōan [1283], 4th month, 5th day

Taira ason (monogram)[8]

SOURCE: *Yasuda monjo*, 1283/4/5 Ōmi Yukisada yuzurijō, *Hokuetsu chūsei monjo*, p. 5, doc. 2 (*KI*, 20: 27–28, doc. 14836).

1. A place name.

2. Our information concerning the Ōmi family's rights in Shirakawa Estate begins in 1229 with a deed of release by Ōmi Sanekage to his son, Yukisada, the present

donor; see *Ōmi Nagahara monjo*, 1229/8/11 Ōmi Sanekage yuzurijō an, *Hokuetsu chūsei monjo*, p. 36, doc. 1. Obviously, the rights predated 1229, and in fact the Ōmi family's association with the Bakufu dates all the way back to 1180. Sanekage's father (Yukisada's grandfather), Ōmi Iehide, was a warrior from Izu Province who joined Yoritomo's movement at the start of the Genpei War; *AK* 1180/8/20, 1180/10/23. See also n. 8.

3. On the same day, the donor here granted other portions of Shirakawa Estate, along with holdings in other provinces, to different children: see *Nakajō ke monjo*, 1283/4/5 Ōmi Yukisada yuzurijō, *KI*, 20: 27, doc. 14835; *Ōmi Nagahara monjo*, 1283/4/5 Ōmi Yukisada yuzurijō, *KI*, 20: 28, doc. 14837; and *Nakajō ke monjo*, 1283/4/5 Ōmi Yukisada yuzurijō, *KI*, 20: 28, doc. 14838.

4. I.e., land that is tax-free.

5. In 1186, Shirakawa Estate was identified as a Fujiwara holding (*denka goryō*); see *AK* 1186/3/12. In 1204, Fujiwara (Kujō) Kanezane deeded it to his grandson, Michiie (*Kujō ke monjo*, 1204/4/23 Kujō Kanezane okibumi, *KI*, 3: 136–40, doc. 1448), who in turn deeded it to a daughter (*ibid.*, 1250/11 Kujō Michiie sō shobunjō, *KI*, 10: 183–99, doc. 7250). At the same time, a daughter of Kanezane (an aunt of Michiie) appointed a custodian (*azukari dokoro*) to Shirakawa Estate in 1228 (*ibid.*, 1228/6 Gishumon'in-no-chō kudashibumi, *Kujō ke monjo*, 5: 108, doc. 1450; not in *KI*).

6. The actual boundaries follow here in half-size characters.

7. The reference here is to Ōmi Iemasa; for his holdings, see the first document cited in n. 3 and *Ōmi Nagahara monjo*, 1287/10/8 shōgun ke mandokoro kudashibumi, *KI*, 21: 308, doc. 16355.

8. The donor here, Ōmi Yukisada, was a prominent vassal whose activities are described in more than two dozen entries in *AK* beginning in 1243. An earlier published transcription of the present document identifies the signature here (Taira *ason*) as that of Hōjō Tokimune, Bakufu regent and chieftain of the Hōjō! This is obviously an error; see *Essa shiryō*, 2: 108–9.

DOCUMENT 115

The Bakufu Approves a Release Written in the Donor's Own Hand, 1286

A *yuzurijō* was the proper instrument for bequeathing land rights. When a dispute arose between siblings, the issue often came down to a "conflict of wills," which itself was resolvable only by submitting the wills for scrutiny. In the present case, one document was judged to be a legal testament of the claimant's grandmother, while the other document, held by his opponent, was not. The criteria used by the Bakufu to make this discrimination are of special note.

Concerning a dispute over a fractional (*ichibu*) *jitō shiki* in Osa *gō*, Tajima Province, between Date Gorōshichirō Suketomo and [Date] Gorōsaburō Munetomo.

Plaintiff and defense statements contained numerous details. In brief, however, this *gō* has been the holding of Myōhō—Suketomo's and [Munetomo's] grandmother[1]—the widow-nun of Date *shuri no suke* Tokitsuna. Accordingly, Suketomo has argued that the document in his possession by Myōhō dated the 5th year of Kōan [1282], 6th month, 14th day, is a testament (*yuzurijō*) and that the document of the 16th day held by Munetomo is a forgery (*bōsho*).[2] [Indeed,][3] the document of the 16th day contains no year period (*nengo*) and is also written in a different hand (*tahitsu*); the name (*myōji*) on it is not that of Myōhō. Consequently, it is inadequate as a proof record (*shōmon*). A marginal notation (*hashigaki*) to this document (*jō*), indicating that it was not an instrument of Myōhō, makes clear that it is [not][4] a testament. Furthermore, in Munetomo's reply (*ukebumi*) of the 11th month, 22d day,[5] he does not state that he holds a testament. Also, he has acknowledged that the testament possessed by Suketomo is in Myōhō's own hand (*jihitsu*). He asserts, however, that the seal (*hangyō*) [on that document] was not affixed by Myōhō and that, because Suketomo contrived to have a forged seal (*bōhan*) added, the ink impression (*sumitsuki*) was irregular (*sōi*). Nevertheless,[6] the fact that Myōhō failed to add her seal (*han*) is not in itself specific proof. Also, since [Suketomo's document] was actually written in her hand (*jihitsu*), there seems no need for further details. Consequently, the *shiki* in question shall be held by Suketomo, in accordance with Myōhō's testament of the 5th year of Kōan [1282], 6th month, 14th day.[7] By command of the Kamakura lord, it is so decreed.

9th year of Kōan [1286], 5th month, 3d day

Sagami no [kami], Taira ason
(monogram)
Mutsu no kami, Taira ason
(monogram)

SOURCE: *Kōda Naritomo shi shozō monjo*, 1286/5/3 Kantō gechijō, *KBSS*, 1: 209–10, doc. 158 (*KI*, 21: 99, doc. 15888).

1. This dispute, then, is between two grandsons, who might or might not have been brothers. For the grandmother's own confirmation by the Bakufu, see Document 71.

2. Note the potential importance of a "later" document—even by two days. To win the case, Suketomo would have to discredit this later document. Neither of these records is extant.

3. The Bakufu interpolates.

4. Character lost, but added by the translator.

5. A reply to the court, presumably.

6. The Bakufu interpolates.

7. This verdict in Suketomo's favor seems to overturn the existing condition: a year earlier it was Munetomo ("Date Gorōsaburō") who was listed in the Tajima provincial register as *jitō* of a portion of Osa *gō*; Suketomo's name does not appear. *Tajima no kuni ōtabumi, KI*, 21: 38, doc. 15774.

DOCUMENT 116

The Bakufu Checks with the Branch Lines of a Family Before Replacing a Lost Investiture Edict, 1287

The destruction of documents in fires often necessitated a special petition such as the one referred to here. Of particular interest is the need to corroborate the accuracy of the claim with other family members. Without such verification the Bakufu might inadvertently confirm an authority that no longer (or never) existed.

That *saemon no jō* Munenobu shall forthwith possess the *jitō shiki* for Yama Village, Miyagi District, Mutsu Province, and [the *jitō shiki*] for Tsunematsu *myō*, Iyo Province.

A petition regarding the above has stated: "In response to our appeal that a [Kantō] edict (*onkudashibumi*) and other proof records (*shōmon*) were destroyed in a fire at our residence in the 3d year of Kōan [1280], 11th month, 28th day, inquiries were made to Takayanagi Magoshirō Naoyuki and to Kiyohisa Iyajirō *nyūdō* Jōshin, both of our clan (*ichimon*).[1] According to their reply (*ukebumi*), no discrepancies existed in what had been reported."[2] Forthwith, authority shall be exercised pursuant to precedent. By this command, it is so decreed.

10th year of Kōan [1287],[3] 2d month,[4] 13th day

> Sagami no kami, Taira ason
> (monogram)
> Mutsu no kami, Taira ason
> (monogram)

SOURCE: *Hōzawa monjo*, 1287/2/13 Kantō gechijō, *Miyagi kenshi shiryōshū*, 1: 164, doc. 57 (*KI*, 21: 231, doc. 16186).
1. Their precise relationship to the petitioner Munenobu is unknown, though Munenobu's surname is identified as Takayanagi in *Kaisetsu chūsei Rusu ke monjo*, p. 12. The "inquiries" referred to were evidently made by the Bakufu.

2. Munenobu had come to receive the two areas in question by a deed from his father. This document (dated 1265/5/7) was one of those destroyed in the fire, though it is referred to and summarized (obviously using a transcribed copy—an *anmon*) in a Bakufu settlement edict of 1295; see *Hōzawa monjo* 1295/3/28 Kantō gechijō, *KBSS*, 1: 260–62, doc. 198. The Kantō edict (*onkudashibumi*) that was lost may have been the original appointment decree, a subsequent confirmation, or the confirmation of Munenobu's 1265 deed from his father.

3. The delay of seven years between the fire and the present Bakufu edict is not explained.

4. The *Miyagi kenshi* version has it "3d month," though this is clearly in error; see *KI*, a transcription in *Ehime ken hennen shi* (2: 376), the 1295 document cited above (n. 2), and *Kaisetsu chūsei Rusu ke monjo*, pp. 11–12, doc. 5.

DOCUMENT 117

A House Chieftain Is Obliged to Seek an External Judgment in Order to Reclaim a Relative's Land Share, 1287

It is highly revealing that the trunk lines of provincial families could be vulnerable to the violations of branches. Not only did *sōryō* exercise weak horizontal powers over collaterals; they might even be victimized by them. At any rate, violations of land rights were not normally put right by counterviolence; someone appealed instead. It was government that resolved disputes— whether the Bakufu, an estate proprietor, or, as in the present instance, the civil governor and his provincial headquarters.

[The absentee headquarters][1] directs:
> That in accordance with the import of the governor's edict (*go-chōsen*), the chieftain (*sōryō*) Saisho [Chikamiki . . .][2] shall forthwith [exercise][3] management and possession (*shintai ryōchi*) over paddy and upland [confiscated from][4] Mikawa-no-bō En'a.

The governor's edict states: "'The[5] said paddy and upland lie within personally held areas originally hereditary with the Saisho. Accordingly, during the time of En'a's grandfather, the land was parceled [and distributed].[6] At present, owing to En'a's crimes, the paddy and upland in question have been confiscated.[7] Therefore, in accordance with customary procedure (*bōrei*), it should be assigned as before to the chieftain.'[8] Because En'a can hardly escape [responsibility for] his crimes, there is no [lack of][9] reason in what Chikamiki, as chieftain, has claimed.[10] Forthwith, [the land in question] is restored as before to the chieftain, Chikamiki. Let the fixed Buddhist and shrine dues, as well as provincial obligations, be discharged. Our edict is thus."[11] In accordance with this governor's edict, the chieftain Chikamiki shall exercise management and possession free of disturbance. The province[12] shall know this and not be remiss. Wherefore, this order.

10th year of Kōan [1287], 7th month,   day

mokudai, san-i, Fujiwara ason

(monogram)

SOURCE: *Saisho monjo*, 1287/7 Hitachi no kuni rusudokoro kudashibumi, *Saisho monjo*, p. 34, doc. 5 (*KI*, 21: 289, doc. 16308).

1. I.e., the *rusudokoro*; characters lost but interpolated from context.
2. Characters lost, but interpolated.
3. *Ibid.*
4. *Ibid.*
5. Note the interior quotation here; see n. 8.
6. Characters lost. En'a's grandfather evidently had divided the family legacy among several heirs.
7. Presumably by the provincial authorities; see n. 8. The crimes themselves are never described.
8. The interior quotation here is clearly that of the complainant, Chikamiki, who is asking to have lands earlier detached from the main line now legally restored. It is noteworthy that in Hitachi Province, appeals of this kind were still being directed to the governor's office (for a second example, see *DKR*, doc. 82), and that custom evidently favored a retrocession of such lands to the main line.
9. Characters lost.
10. As noted by the compiler of *Saisho monjo* (pp. 3–4), there is a discrepancy here with the Saisho genealogy, which separates En'a and Chikamiki by four generations. The En'a of the present case is probably a cousin of the chieftain, Chikamiki.
11. The governor's edict (itself not extant) ends here.
12. I.e., its residents.

DOCUMENT 118

A Donor Bypasses His Daughter in Favor of Grandsons, 1287

It is hardly surprising that daughters left out of an inheritance pool should have been unhappy. It was bad enough when they lost out to brothers; but when the recipients of a father's legacy were his grandsons, the anger of daughters (aunts of the legatees) is understandable. In the present case, a daughter brought suit on these grounds but had no basis for her claim beyond the charge—proved false—of forgery. That she had no basis is significant. For her troubles, the unfortunate daughter was convicted of bringing an unfounded accusation—and then punished.

> Concerning a dispute between Ia, the daughter-nun of Takai Saburō Tokimochi *hosshi*—Buddhist name, Dōen—and her nephew Wada Saburō Mochitsura[1] (original name Yoshiyori), his younger brother Shirō Nagatsura (original name Mochinaga), and Wada Jirō *uemon no jō* Yoshimoto (original name Yoshinaga) over Dōen's legacy (*iryō*):[2] Okuyama Estate in Echigo Province;[3] Tsunemaki *gō* in Dewa Province; Mano Imperial Estate in Sanuki Province;[4] Katsurayama in Awa Province;[5] paddy and service households in Tsu Village, Sagami Province; and residence land (*yachi*) in Kamakura.[6]

Plaintiff and defense statements contained numerous details. In brief, however, [Mochitsura et al.] argued as follows: "In response to Ia's objection that the releases of the 3d year of Kenji [1277], 11th month, 5th day were forgeries because they did not contain Dōen's handwritten seal (*shuseki hangyō*), a comparison of the seals was made but no discrepancies whatever were found on the four documents.[7] In addition, confirmatory edicts were granted to Mochitsura et al. in response to those releases,[8] followed by the passage of eight years."[9] Had there been knowledge of a forgery, a complaint should have been lodged then. Instead, years passed, making the thrust of [Ia's] false suit (*ranso*) difficult to credit. Moreover, inasmuch as no daughter's share (*joshibun*) is included in Dōen's handwritten earlier draft of the disposition plan for his holdings (*sennen shoryō haibun jihitsu sōan*),[10] it is hard to claim that the portion received by Ia is too small. Accordingly, there is no specific proof of a forgery. In consequence, each [heir] shall exercise possession in accordance with the releases of the [3d][11] year of Kenji [1277].

Next, as concerns the punishment for labeling a valid document a forgery, repairs shall be contributed to [local] shrines and temples,[12] pursuant to [the Kantō's] regulations. By command of the Kamakura lord, it is so decreed.

> 10th year of Kōan [1287], 9th month, 1st day[13]

>> saki no Musashi no kami, Taira
>> ason seal
>> Sagami no kami, Taira ason seal

SOURCE: *Nakajō ke monjo*, 1287/9/1 Kantō gechijō an, *Okuyama-no-shō shiryōshū*, p. 103, doc. 23 (*KBSS*, 1: 217–18, doc. 163).

1. The *KBSS* transcription has it "Tokitsuna," which is incorrect.

2. Yoshiyori, the nephew of Ia, was thus a grandson of the donor, Dōen. The same was true of Yoshiyori's younger brother, Mochinaga. The third defendant, Yoshinaga, was a cousin of the two brothers and also a nephew of Ia and grandson of Dōen. As we shall see, Dōen granted conveyances to each of his grandsons—but failed to release anything to his daughter Ia. Dōen (Tokimochi) himself was confirmed by the Bakufu almost half a century earlier; see Document 23.

3. The family's interest in Okuyama Estate dated back to 1192; see *KB*, doc. 12, and *supra*, Documents 20–23.

4. Mano-*no-chokushi-gō* makes its initial appearance in our documents in a conveyance of Dōen dating from 1264: *Nakajō ke monjo*, 1264/3/11 shami Dōen yuzurijō, *Okuyama-no-shō shiryōshū*, p. 100, doc. 12. When or how it came into Dōen's hands is unknown.

5. See n. 4 and also Dōen's deed to Yoshiyori of 1277 (cited in n. 7).

6. The house patrimony had obviously expanded since Dōen's own confirmation in 1241; see Document 23.

7. The original releases to Yoshiyori and Mochinaga (two of the three defendants) survive: *Nakajō ke monjo*, 1277/11/5 shami Dōen yuzurijō, *Okuyama-no-shō shiryōshū*, p. 101, doc. 15; *Miura Wada shi monjo*, 1277/11/5 shami Dōen yuzurijō, *ibid*., p. 2, doc. 5. Several transcribed copies without monograms also survive. The only extant deed to Yoshinaga (the third defendant) is dated seven months earlier; *Nakajō ke monjo*, 1277/4/28 shami Dōen yuzurijō an, *ibid*., p. 188, doc. 3.

8. For the confirmation of Mochitsura (Yoshiyori) and Nagatsura (Mochinaga), see *Nakajō ke monjo*, 1278/5/18 shōgun ke mandokoro kudashibumi, *Okuyama-no-shō shiryōshū*, p. 102, doc. 17; and *Miura Wada shi monjo*, 1278/5/18 shōgun ke mandokoro kudashibumi an, *ibid*., p. 4, doc. 12.1.

9. It is actually nine years (1278–87), although the suit may have been brought in 1286.

10. The *KBSS* version has it "*sennen shoryōbun* . . . ," but this is probably in error.

11. Character lost but interpolated.

12. I.e., by Ia. Here, then, is a rare instance in which a judgment edict cited a punitive action. For a discussion of this, see *DKR*, pp. 143–44.

13. Ten years later Ia was still seeking to obtain a portion of Dōen's estate. She lodged an appeal (*osso*), only to have her suit thrown out; see *Miura Wada shi monjo*, 1297/2/20 Kantō migyōsho an, *Okuyama-no-shō shiryōshū*, p. 4, doc. 12.2.

DOCUMENT 119

The Holder of a Life Bequest Is Deemed Ineligible to Issue a Conveyance, 1290

In this extremely important case, several key principles bearing on changes in the inheritance system were enunciated. The father-donor selected his principal heir but stipulated that the son would not take actual possession until his mother, the interim legatee, had died. Here, in other words, was an example of a standard life bequest to a widow. But the son died before his mother did, though not so suddenly that he had failed to arrange a transfer to his own heir. The problem was that he was bequeathing what he had never held— only been promised. Even so, the Bakufu confirmed the inheritance—to take effect after the death of the widow. Yet the real difficulty arose when a challenger charged that the dead son had been unfilial to his mother, leading her to release the inheritance to this interloper. The Bakufu's verdict is significant: not only was there no proof of unfiliality, but the widow, the holder of a life bequest, had no authority to issue a conveyance. Clearly, the rights of alienation lay with an ultimate heir, not with an interim legatee.

> Concerning a dispute over the *jitō shiki* of Kashiro *gō*, Shinano Province, between Ryōi, agent for Shimazu Shimotsuke Hikosaburō Tadanaga, and Mitsutaka, agent for Echigo Hikosaburō Masakuni.

Plaintiff and defense statements contained numerous details. In brief, however, [this *shiki*] was a holding of the former governor of Ōsumi, Tadatoki.[1] Upon its release to his son, Hisatsune[2]—the father of Tadanaga—it was recorded that possession should lie with the widow-nun Sainin for the duration of her lifetime.[3] Nevertheless, Tadanaga claimed that when Hisatsune predeceased Sainin,[4] Tadanaga was awarded a confirmatory edict stemming from the deed to him [by Hisatsune].[5] Mitsutaka[6] counterargued that while Sainin was alive, Tadanaga, not waiting for her death, acted against her bringing the matter to a suit. As a result, [he continued, Sainin] deeded [the post] to Masakuni. Though Mitsutaka has claimed[7] that [Tadanaga] acted against Sainin while she was still alive,[8] there is no actual proof of this. Not only that, but Sainin was holder only for her lifetime (*ichigo chigyō ryōshu*). It would be difficult to credit any conveyance by her as evidence.[9] As for Tadanaga, we see from the release of the original holder (*honshu*)[10] that there was no departure from the principle of hereditary succession. In consequence thereof, Tadanaga shall exercise possession.[11] By command of the Kamakura lord, it is so decreed.

  3d year of Shōō [1290], 5th month, 12th day

                                      Mutsu no kami, Taira ason
                                      (monogram)
                                      Sagami no kami, Taira ason
                                      (monogram)

SOURCE: *Shimazu ke monjo*, 1290/5/12 Kantō gechijō, *DNK, iewake 16*, 1: 189–90, doc. 196 (*KBSS*, 1: 245–46, doc. 181).
    1. Shimazu Tadatoki (1202–72) received it from his father Tadahisa (progenitor of

the great Shimazu house) in 1227; see Document 36. The *jitō shiki* itself dated from 1221; *ibid.*, n. 10.

2. Hisatsune (1225–84) was the third chieftain of the Shimazu.

3. Sainin was Tadatoki's widow; see *Shimazu ke monjo*, 1267/12/3 Shimazu Tadatoki yuzurijō, *DNK, iewake 16*, 1: 84–87, doc. 141.

4. Hisatsune died on 1284/int. 4/21 at the age of 60; *Shimazu shi keizu*, in *Kagoshima ken shiryō, kyūki zatsuroku zenpen*, 1: 307. Sainin, his mother, did not die until 1289; see the reference to this in *Shimazu ke monjo*, 1292/4/12 Kantō gechijō, *DNK, iewake 16*, 1: 190–91, doc. 197.

5. For Hisatsune's release, see *ibid.*, 1281/4/16 Shimazu Hisatsune yuzurijō, *DNK, iewake 16*, 1: 489–90, doc. 494. For the Bakufu's confirmation (which also recognized Sainin's life tenure), see *ibid.*, 1285/7/3 shōgun ke mandokoro kudashibumi, *DNK, iewake 16*, 1: 188, doc. 194. This left conditions in some confusion.

6. Mitsutaka, we recall, was the agent for Masakuni, plaintiff in the case. Unfortunately, we are lacking Masakuni's identity. What was his relationship to Sainin, whose conveyance he now claimed to have received?

7. The Bakufu interpolates from here.

8. As we have noted, Sainin died sometime in 1289.

9. The possessor of a life (*ichigo*) bequest, in other words, was ineligible to issue a release.

10. The reference here is to either Tadahisa or Tadatoki (see n. 1), who contemplated a lineal succession.

11. This was not the end of Tadanaga's troubles, however. Two years later he was embroiled in another suit over Kashiro *gō*, this time with his father's sister; see the 1292 document cited in n. 4. Once again Tadanaga emerged the victor.

DOCUMENT 120

A Brother and Sister Reach an Accord After an Inheritance Dispute, 1294

When an uncontested will was submitted to Kamakura for probate, the Bakufu issued a standard confirmation. By contrast, when the disposition of an estate was established not by a testament but by an accord reached between contesting siblings, the confirmation was by judgment edict. In between, intestate cases had solutions that were guided mostly by practicality. In the present instance, involving a dispute between a sister and a brother, the former sought an accord and an accompanying Bakufu judgment edict as the most effective means to safeguard a life tenure awarded her by her grandfather. Though the tenure was eventually earmarked for her brother, she wished to be assured that he would not attempt to obtain it prematurely. For her part, this careful daughter was willing to relinquish a small parcel immediately in return for her brother's acknowledgment regarding the rest—all duly certified by Kamakura.

Regarding a dispute between Minamoto *no uji*, daughter of
Fukazawa Aritsune *hosshi*—Buddhist name, Zenshin—of Kai
Province, and her younger brother Akimachi Gorōjirō Nobutsune, over paddy, residence areas, and mountains and forests
within Fukazawa Village.[1]

Adjudication was sought in response to plaintiff and defense [state-
ments] regarding the above. However, on the 6th day of the 5th
month of the present year compromise statements (*wayojō*) were mutually issued.[2] According to the daughter's document: "The aforesaid
holdings were received by release from my grandfather Fukazawa
Tarō Takatsune *hosshi*—Buddhist name, Zen'en—on the 10th day of
the 2d month of the 3d year of Kōchō [1263].[3] Because their passage
is to go to Nobutsune after my lifetime, the Kōchō-era deed will be
transferred to him after an affirmation of our compromise (*wayo no
ongechi*) is awarded [by the Kantō].[4] However, concerning one *tan* of
paddy and five *tan* of upland along with Saburōtarō *nyūdō*'s residence
area—minus specified fields long in cultivation—a request has been
made to relinquish them now. Accordingly, a release is made to Nobutsune in the daughter's own hand, with area specifications appended.[5] In the event that this compromise document should be violated, not even the most minuscule land unit will be conveyed [to
Nobutsune] and the daughter will exercise total possession (*ichien
shintai*)." The details in Nobutsune's document were the same. Beyond
this mutual accord no differences remain. Forthwith, each side shall
exercise possession in accordance with that document. By command
of the Kamakura lord, it is so decreed.

2d year of Einin [1294], 12th month, 2d day

Mutsu no kami, Taira ason
(monogram)
Sagami no kami, Taira ason
(monogram)

SOURCE: *Kobayakawa ke monjo*, 1294/12/2 Kantō gechijō, *DNK, iewake 11*, 2: 346, doc.
556 (*KBSS*, 1: 259–60, doc. 197).
    1. Five weeks earlier Nobutsune was confirmed by the Bakufu in an inheritance of
landholdings in Shinano and Aki provinces; Fukazawa Village was not mentioned. See
Kobayakawa ke monjo, 1294/10/27 Kantō gechijō, *DNK, iewake 11*, 2: 345, doc. 555. As
we shall see, its exclusion was tied to a compromise between the present disputants,
which required a judgment edict (i.e., the present document), not merely an edict of
confirmation. Nobutsune's inheritance was deeded to him in 1288; *ibid.*, 1288/12/5
Fukazawa Zenshin yuzurijō, *DNK, iewake 11*, 2: 343–45, doc. 554.
    2. Not extant.

3. The source of the dispute, then, would seem to lie in the daughter's fear that her grandfather's release to her might be undercut by her father's deed to her brother. As we see here, she is merely seeking protection for her own life tenure. The 1263 conveyance is not extant.

4. Here we see the clear value to disputants of the Bakufu's authority to guarantee compromise agreements.

5. In other words, the daughter was willing to make this concession to her brother in return for his written promise not to make further claims.

DOCUMENTS 121–22

A Father Arranges for an Orderly Succession to His Son and Grandson, 1295, 1303

Here we encounter (Document 121) another in the sequence of very carefully prepared wills by scions of the Yamanouchi house. Though partible inheritance would not be abandoned until 1330 (Document 150), the donor here was clearly thinking of ways to foster greater cooperation among his offspring. Thus he selected his eldest son as principal heir, but he granted considerable recognition to the next eldest son; the two were enjoined to work together. Yet the donor did not designate this second son as successor following the elder brother. The person nominated as future head was the principal heir's own son, i.e., the donor's grandson. Lineality was to be maintained. On the other hand, if the grandson died young or was deemed unacceptable by the kindred, the current heir—his father—would choose a substitute successor. In the actual event, the headship was passed, without apparent incident, according to the present donor's wishes (Document 122).

121

Conveyed: landholdings—a total of four places, to my principal heir, Iyasaburō Michitsuna.[1]

One locale: Hon *gō*, within Jibi Estate, Bingo Province, plus the [latter's] *kumon shiki*; also the *jitō shiki* for the Takayama residence fields (*monden*).[2]

One locale: the *jitō shiki* of Tomishima Estate, Settsu Province,[3] plus the *jitō shiki* for the *gesu* and *kumon* private lands (*myō*).[4] However, during the lifetime of the nun-lady,[5] 10 *koku* of rice—as determined by the estate's measuring instrument—shall be conveyed to her annually from this place. In the event that even one grain of rice should be short, Nokano *myō* shall be made the permanent possession of the nun-lady.

One locale: a *jitō shiki* over 5 of the 8 *chō* of taxable paddy (*kōden*) within Lower Hirata *gō*, Kyū *fu*,⁶ Shinano Province. Despite the smallness of this place, it was awarded [by the Kantō] to Jizen.⁷ Accordingly, the *jitō shiki* for the [remaining] 3 *chō* is deeded to Gorō Michiuji.⁸ Also, tax-exempt fields that are not fixed (*uki-menden*), as well as service households, will be held in accordance with the size of these [land] shares. The division shall be made by Iyasaburō, with selection by Gorō.⁹

One locale: the paddy, service households, and residence areas belonging to Jizen within Ittoku *myō*, Hayakawa Estate, Sagami Province,¹⁰ are deeded to Michitsuna. However, 6 *tan* therein, as well as the Ōyanagi service household, are deeded to my wife (*nyōbō*). Let there be no intrusions whatever. As for the boundaries involved, they are evident from the conveyance of our grandfather *nakatsukasa nyūdō dono*,¹¹ as well as from subsequent proof records.

The aforesaid places are the generations-old hereditary holdings of Jizen. In consequence, release is made to our principal heir, along with the [Kantō's] confirmatory edicts and the succession of proof records. After Michitsuna's lifetime, conveyance shall be to our grandson, Chōjumaru.¹² In the event Chōjumaru should prove unfit and the members of the kindred (*ichimon no tomogara*) should reject him, or if he should predecease his father, discretion will then lie with Michitsuna.¹³ In the event none of this occurs, let there be no departure from his (Chōjumaru's) grandfather's will. Likewise, regarding the lands divided among our children, let there be no disturbances. In regard to the [Kantō] dues obligations (*onkuji*), individual responsibilities shall follow basic paddy shares, in accordance with the stipulations set down by the late *nyūdō dono*.¹⁴ Also, concerning the annual tax owed the proprietor (*ryōke*), there shall be no negligence [in paying it], in conformity once again with those basic paddy shares. In sum, Iyasaburō is to consider Gorō as he would Jizen, and Gorō shall rely on Iyasaburō as he would Jizen; neither is to commit any breach.¹⁵ Moreover, the various shares deeded to [our other] sons and daughters [shall suffer] not the slightest disruption, pursuant to the present document. Wherefore, our conveyance to Michitsuna is thus.

3d year of Einin [1295], 3d month, 29th day

Jizen (monogram)

122

Conveyed: landholdings.

Release is hereby made to our son Sudō Saburō Michisuke—child's name, Chōjumaru—accompanied by the conveyance of Jizen, dated the 3d year of Einin [1295], 3d month, 29th day.[16] Because the list of holdings as well as the [relevant] documents are noted in that deed, there is no need to record them here. Not a single holding is omitted in the present release. Let there be no difficulty regarding their possessions in perpetuity. It is thus.

2d year of Kengen [1303], 3d month, 3d day

Kukaku (monogram)[17]

SOURCES: Document 121: *Yamanouchi Sudō ke monjo*, 1295/3/29 Yamanouchi Jizen (Tokimichi) yuzurijō, *DNK, iewake 15*, pp. 9–11, doc. 10 (*KI*, 24: 258–59, doc. 18790). Document 122: *ibid.*, 1303/3/3 Yamanouchi Kukaku (Michitsuna) yuzurijō, *DNK, iewake 15*, p. 12, doc. 12 (not in *KI?*).

1. This release is from the Yamanouchi chieftain Tokimichi (cf. Document 99) to his primary heir Michitsuna.

2. Later, these fields would be commended to a local temple, whereas Hon *gō* itself (that is, its *jitō shiki*) would remain a possession of the Yamanouchi house; see Document 150. The Hon *gō jitō shiki* dated from before 1221; see *KB*, doc. 21; *DKR*, doc. 91; and *supra*, Documents 46, 99.

3. This *jitō shiki* was a Jōkyū War reward; see Document 43.

4. This unusual reference suggests that a portion of the perquisites attached to these two traditional estate offices was now under the authority of the *jitō*.

5. Presumably the reference is to a daughter of the donor Tokimichi, yet no such person appears in the house genealogy. As we note, at any rate, her share was merely a stipend from an area administered by the main legatee.

6. Meaning unclear.

7. I.e., to the present donor Tokimichi. Once again, therefore, we see that prominent families seemed to receive new lands with each generation.

8. In other words, 5 *chō* were granted to the principal heir Michitsuna, and 3 *chō* to his younger brother Michiuji. See n. 15.

9. The reference here must be to the exempt fields and service households, not to the unequal 5- and 3-*chō* main shares.

10. For Hayakawa Estate, see Document 42.

11. The conveyance referred to (Document 42) is Yamanouchi Shigetoshi's deed of 1230 to his son Munetoshi (the present donor's father).

12. This was actually done; see Document 122.

13. In fact, this leaves relatively little discretion to the present donee Michitsuna, Chōjumaru's father. Only in the event of untoward circumstances was Michitsuna to be allowed to determine his own successor.

14. The reference is to the present donor's father Munetoshi. In the latter's release to his son (actually, one of several releases: see Document 44), the principal heir's right to apportion the dues obligation among house members is carefully noted.

15. The two printed versions of our document (*DNK* and *KI*) have this sentence separated by a comma in different places; the *KI* transcription makes better sense. At any rate, the admonition was well-founded. In 1317, a major dispute occurred between Gorō Michiuji and the son of Iyasaburō, Michisuke; see *Yamanouchi Sudō ke monjo*, 1317/5/26 Yamanouchi Sukemichi—dō Michitada (Michiuji) rensho wayojō an, *DNK*, *iewake 15*, pp. 16–18, doc. 15.

16. I.e., Document 121.

17. Yamanouchi Michitsuna, the recipient of his father's inheritance in 1295 (Document 121). For the next generation's inheritance (in 1330), see Document 150.

A Deed of Conveyance with a Later Seal Is Deemed Valid by a Local Court, 1298

In Japan's premodern society the oldest documents were not sacrosanct; in some cases, the newest ones were. Nowhere was this more important than in disputes involving multiple wills. The operating principle at all levels of society was that the most recent release was the will of record. Here we see the principle in its most explicit expression.

Ordered:

(monogram)

Concerning the administrative headship (*mandokoro shiki*) for the dance ritual (*kagura*) at the tutelary junior shrine (*chinju no wakamiya*) in Ajisaka Estate.[1]

Appointed: Yakushi *hosshi*.

The aforesaid *shiki* is the generations-old hereditary possession of Birei *hosshi* of Mizuma Estate.[2] Recently, on the occasion of its being deeded to a younger brother (*chakutei*), Yakushi *hosshi*, Tokuō *hosshi* contested this.[3] When particulars on both sides were solicited, the release with the later seal held by Yakushi *hosshi* was clear. Generations of proprietors' edicts (*ryōke daidai no onkudashibumi*) were also explicit.[4] In accordance, therefore, with generations of proprietors' edicts, as well as with the later-sealed release of Birei *hosshi*, this appointment is hereby made. Let there be no further disturbances in future. Wherefore, this appointment is thus.

6th year of Einin [1298], 2d month, [   ][5] day

deputy jitō-in-chief (sōjitōdai), saemon no jō[6]

SOURCE: *Umezu monjo*, 1298/2 Ajisaka no shō kagura mandokoro shiki buninjō, *Chikugo no kuni Mizuma no shō shiryō*, pp. 43–44, doc. 15 (*KI*, 26: 101, doc. 19615).

1. In Mii District, Chikugo Province.

2. In Mizuma District, Chikugo. Mizuma and Ajisaka estates were actually quite distant from one another; see *Shōen bunpu zu*, 2: 301.

3. A *chakutei* is a younger brother who is the offspring of a primary wife. Thus the donor, Birei *hosshi*, may have been transferring this *shiki* to a true brother and excluding a half brother. Other interpretations are possible.

4. Unfortunately, none extant.

5. Character lost.

6. This arbiter's role in a local inheritance dispute obviously did not foreclose the absentee proprietor's regular confirmatory authority. But it does indicate how an on-the-spot title holder might come in time to appear as a more logical mediator.

DOCUMENTS 124–31

A Vassal House Allows Portions of Its Patrimony to Be Sold Off and the Bakufu Confirms This, 1300, 1304, 1310, 1317, 1318

As noted in so many of our documents, the devolution of property could proceed in curious ways. In this fascinating sequence, the conveyance of a *jitō shiki* to a grandson was followed by his release of a portion of it to his own younger brother. The latter, however, deciding that he wished to sell it, requested of his brother a confirmation of his possession and a promise of no interference with the ownership rights of the prospective buyer. This done, the sale—to the wife of a Kamakura vassal—went forward, to be followed by another sale to the same woman, this time by the original elder brother–donor. Throughout these transactions the tone of the various documents was one of providing assurances for the respective sales; no one could come forward in future with a counterclaim. Equally interesting is a petition by the buyer for a Bakufu confirmation of the transfer. That this was granted shows that Kamakura, despite its public position against the sale of *jitō* portions, was nevertheless approving them. Even so, the Bakufu was probably not prepared for the ultimate transfer—a commendation to a local temple by the woman who had purchased the lands and been confirmed in them. This kind of passage into nonvassal hands both diluted the meaning of *jitō shiki* and undermined the Bakufu's authority over an identifiable corps of retainers.

124

That *saemon no jō* Fujiwara Toshitada shall forthwith possess the *jitō shiki* for Sakai *ho*, Noto Province.[1]

Regarding the above, possession shall be exercised pursuant to precedent, in accordance with the release of the 6th year of Bun'ei [1269], 9th month, 10th day, of the late grandfather Sakai Jurō Norinaga *hosshi*—Buddhist name Saigan.² By this command, it is so decreed.

    2d year of Shōan [1300], 12th month, 22d day

Mutsu no kami, Taira ason seal
Sagami no kami, Taira ason seal

125

Conveyed: a residence area, private paddy, etc., within Sakai *ho*, Noto Province.

    In total: one residence area and one *chō* of paddy in Nakamura.
    One paddy area, 150 sheaves. . . .³
    Two upland areas. . . .⁴
    Mountain fields. . . .⁵

The aforesaid residence area, private paddy, and mountain fields are the generations-old hereditary private holdings (*shiryō*) of Toshitada. As a consequence, they are deeded in perpetuity to my younger brother Norikane. Notwithstanding, taxes (*shotō*) to the provincial headquarters (*kokuga*) shall be at the rate of . . .⁶ per *tan*. Our descendants shall be free entirely from disturbance. And there shall be no fishing in local waters. Thus, for the future, our conveyance is as above.

    2d year of Kagen [1304], 9th month, 6th day

saemon no jō, Toshitada

126

I hereby affirm no change in my conveyance of the 2d year of Kagen [1304], 9th month, 6th day, in which mountain fields within Sakai *ho*, Noto Province, were deeded to my younger brother Norikane.⁷ The said portion (*ka no bun*) shall not be subject to any interference whatever by the house chieftain (*sōryō*).⁸ Also, a transcribed copy (*anmon*) of this release, duly endorsed on the reverse side,⁹ is being forwarded. There can thus be no objection to Norikane's selling [of this land]. When confirmation (*ando*) [of such a transaction] is requested,¹⁰ these facts shall be made known. Respectfully.

    3d year of Enkei [1310], 7th month, 28th day

saemon no jō, Toshitada seal

To: Umino Saburō dono¹¹

127

Forwarded: 3 copies of the sale deed.

Sale and transfer: of mountain fields within Sakai *ho*, Noto Province.
Boundaries: . . .[12]

The aforesaid mountain fields are the generations-old hereditary private holdings of Norikane. Nevertheless, by reason of pressing need, [land] within the specified boundaries is sold in perpetuity to Taira *no uji* for the price of 17 *kanmon* cash. Let there be no disturbances. Moreover, as proof for the future, transcribed copies of the sequence of evidence papers, duly endorsed on the reverse side, are passed on as well. Inasmuch as document originals (*shōmon*) refer to unrelated residence areas and private fields and are on a continuous sheet, it is transcriptions (*anmon*) that have been given. In the event that originals need to be perused, neither Norikane nor his descendants shall begrudge their inspection. Wherefore, this deed of sale (*kokenjō*) is thus.

3d year of Enkei [1310], 8th month, 3d day[13]

Fujiwara Norikane seal

128

Sale and transfer: mountain fields plus new paddy and upland [attached to] the *jitō shiki* for Sakai *ho*, Noto Province.[14]
Boundaries: . . .[15]

The aforesaid mountain fields plus paddy and upland are the generations-old hereditary vassal holdings (*gokenin ryō*)[16] of Toshitada. Nevertheless, by reason of pressing need, [land] within the specified boundaries is sold in perpetuity to Taira *no uji* for the price of 15 *kanmon* cash. Let there be no disturbances. As proof for the future, the sequence of evidence papers, confirmatory edicts, and other documents is passed on as well, duly endorsed on the reverse side.[17] In the event that originals need to be perused, neither Toshitada nor his descendants shall raise any objection (*igi*) to their being inspected. In the event that Toshitada or his descendants should create disturbances to these mountain fields, etc. in violation of this bill of sale, an equivalent portion shall be possessed (*chigyō*)[18] from the mountain fields, paddy and upland, belonging [to the seller]. Wherefore, this bill of sale is thus.

3d year of Enkei [1310], 8th month, 28th day

saemon no jō, Fujiwara Toshitada
seal

129

Alienated: [mountain fields plus new][19] paddy and upland [attached to] the *jitō shiki* for Sakai *ho*, Noto Province.

Boundaries: . . .[20]

The aforesaid mountain fields plus new paddy and upland are the generations-old [hereditary *goke*]*nin* holdings of Toshitada. Nevertheless, by justification of succession (*yuisho*) to them, [alienation is now made] in perpetuity to [Taira] *no uji*. Let there be no disturbances. In the event Toshitada [or his descendants] should create any disturbances to these mountain fields, etc., an equivalent portion shall be pared (*wari-wake*) from the [mountain fields, paddy and upland] belonging [to the seller], and these shall be possessed. [Wherefore, this deed of alienation is thus.]

    3d year of Enkei [1310], 8th month, 28th day[21]

                        saemon no jō, Fujiwara Toshi-
                        tada seal

130

Concerning the mountain fields and new paddy and upland— boundaries recorded in the deed of alienation (*hōken*)—within Sakai *ho*, Noto Province, as petitioned by Sakawa Hachirō Yorichika's daughter, Taira *no uji*—the wife of Umino Saburō Nobunao.[22]

The aforementioned mountain fields and new paddy and upland were purchased by deed of alienation from Sakai Jurō *saemon* Toshitada on the 28th day, 8th month, of the 3d year of Enkei [1310]. In response to the lady's request that a [confirmatory] edict be granted, a warrant (*meshifu*) was issued to help clarify the facts (*jippi*). According to the reply (*ukebumi*) of the 1st year of Ōchō [1311], 10th month, 18th day,[23] there were no [special circumstances][24] concerning the sale. Also, previous dispensations (*sata*) have referred to this *ho* as a private holding (*shiryō*). In consequence, the lady shall possess the mountain fields and new paddy and upland, in accordance with the bill of sale (*koken*) by Toshitada. By command of the Kamakura lord, it is so decreed.

    1st year of Bunpō [1317], 3d month, 23d day[25]

                        Sagami no kami, Taira ason seal
                        Musashi no kami, Taira ason seal

131

Commended: mountain fields and upland within Sakai *ho*, Noto Province.
Boundaries appear in the deeds of alienation (*hōken*) of Toshitada and Norikane.

Taira *no uji*, the daughter of Sakawa Hachirō Yorichika, petitioned for and was granted edicts of confirmation[26] over the said mountain fields and paddy and upland, in accordance with the deeds of alienation by Sakai Jurō *saemon* Toshitada and by Sakai Yozō Norikane. She possesses [these holdings] as private lands (*shiryō*).[27] Nevertheless, in order to promote the wisdom of Buddha (*mujō-bodai*), Taira *no uji* bestows them in perpetuity to the priest (*oshō*) Jōkin,[28] along with the two edicts of confirmation, the two alienation deeds, and copies of the original holder's sequence of documents. Let our descendants create no disturbances. For the future, this instrument of commendation is thus.

2d year of Bunpō [1318], 10th month, 15th day

Taira no ujime seal

SOURCES: Document 124: *Eikōji monjo*, 1300/12/22 Kantō gechijō an, *Zōtei Kano komonjo*, p. 83, doc. 137 (*KI*, 27: 261, doc. 20692). Document 125: *ibid.*, 1304/9/6 Sakai Toshitada yuzurijō an, *Zōtei Kano komonjo*, p. 85, doc. 141 (*KI*, 29: 31, doc. 21988). Document 126: *ibid.*, 1310/7/28 Sakai Toshitada shōmon an, *Zōtei Kano komonjo*, p. 91, doc. 152. Document 127: *ibid.*, 1310/8/3 Sakai Norikane baiken an, *Zōtei Kano komonjo*, p. 92, doc. 154. Document 128: *ibid.*, 1310/8/28 Sakai Toshitada baiken an, *Zōtei Kano komonjo*, pp. 93–94, doc. 157. Document 129: *ibid.*, 1310/8/28 Sakai Toshitada saribumi an, *Zōtei Kano komonjo*, p. 94, doc. 158. Document 130: *ibid.*, 1317/3/23 Kantō gechijō an, *Zōtei Kano komonjo*, p. 97, doc. 165. Document 131: *ibid.*, 1318/10/25 Taira no uji kishinjō an, *Zōtei Kano komonjo*, pp. 98–99, doc. 169.

1. The origins of this *jitō shiki* are unknown. In a conveyance of 1269 (n. 2) it is referred to as "the hereditary private holding of [the donor's] ancestors."

2. *Eikōji monjo*, 1269/9/10 shami Saigan yuzurijō an, *Zōtei Kano komonjo*, p. 65, doc. 100. This is the earliest document relating to the house of Sakai and is the only extant record before 1300. The delay of 31 years (1269–1300) before the Bakufu issued its confirmation is puzzling, especially since the 1269 release makes clear that the family's documents were being given directly to Toshitada, Saigan's grandson. There are no references to Toshitada's father.

3. Specifications appear here for yield figures drawn from eight parcels of paddy making up one *chō* of land.

4. Their locations are given here.

5. *Ibid.*

6. The text is corrupt here.

7. As we shall see, the present document is an acknowledgment by a donor of a donee's right to sell his share.

8. Toshitada is referring here to himself and to future house heads.
9. I.e., by Toshitada.
10. Of the Bakufu, as we shall see.
11. The husband of the prospective buyer and a Kamakura vassal. A nearly identical document of one day later by Toshitada to the same addressee makes it explicit that Norikane is about to alienate his land to Umino's wife, Taira *no uji*; *Eikōji monjo* 1310/7/29 Sakai Toshitada andojō an, *Zōtei Kano komonjo*, p. 92, doc. 153. See also n. 21.
12. Exact specifications (west-north-east-south) follow here.
13. Norikane issued a second document on the same day promising permanent alienation of the sold areas. Should he or his descendants interfere in any way with the locales just disposed of, his own remaining share would be forfeited; *Eikōji monjo*, 1310/8/3 Sakai Norikane saribumi an, *Zōtei Kano komonjo*, pp. 92–93, doc. 155.
14. The seller in this instance is Toshitada, the donor to his brother in 1304 (Document 125). Clearly, then, Toshitada had retained a portion of the estate confirmed to him by the Bakufu in 1300 (Document 124).
15. These are not the same, obviously, as those for the land disposed of 25 days earlier by Norikane.
16. This reference to *gokenin ryō* is unusual, especially since the Bakufu normally forbade such sales. But see n. 27.
17. Though not designated as such, these were transcribed copies, as we see in the next sentence.
18. I.e., by the buyer or her descendants. This was to be in addition to the areas sold.
19. Characters lost, but interpolated by the translator. The bracketed words and phrases in this document have all been interpolated.
20. These are identical to those in Document 128.
21. The need here for complementary sale and alienation documents is noteworthy. Norikane's sale of 8/3 (Document 127) was similarly paralleled by a relinquishment record, as we saw in n. 13.
22. As we are about to see, the purchaser of the area in question, Taira *no uji*, was now seeking Bakufu confirmation of that transaction.
23. Not extant. Who was the author of this document? The seller?
24. Characters lost but interpolated.
25. Why six years should have elapsed (1311–17) between petition and confirmation is not clear. On the same day, the Bakufu issued an identical confirmation for the other land sale involving Norikane, Toshitada's brother; see *Eikōji monjo*, 1317/3/23 Kantō gechijō an, *Zōtei Kano komonjo*, p. 97, doc. 166. In both cases the format of the document is very similar to that of a *saikyojō*—a judicial edict.
26. I.e., the Bakufu confirmations of 1317/3/23; see n. 25.
27. Earlier they were called *gokenin ryō* in order to increase the chance of their being confirmed by the Bakufu. Now they are being labeled *shiryō* in anticipation of their alienation to a local temple.
28. Jōkin was obviously a priest of Eikōji, a local temple of Noto Province.

DOCUMENT 132

A Clan Head Calls for Unitary Inheritances, 1301

As we enter the fourteenth century, calls for direct inheritance begin to appear. In the present early example, we note that youngest sons, women, and outsiders were henceforth to be excluded, a limitation that was repeated in the next generation when the current recipient made his own bequest.

Conveyed: landholdings of Kashima Shrine, Hitachi Province.
Tachibana *gō* of [Namekata] District, with these boundaries: . . . ;[1]
plus Ōga village of Namekata District—[Kantō] edict appended.[2]
Private paddy and upland within the precincts of Kashima Shrine, including two parcels of purchased land—to the left and right of the gate.

The said Tachibana *gō*, a land [originally] commended by the *utaishō* house,[3] is a generations-old hereditary holding of Tomochika.[4] Nevertheless, in accordance with the admonition (*imashime*) of the original holder (*honshu*) Masachika,[5] the present conveyance does not apportion *tan* and *bu*.[6] Exclusive and permanent release is hereby made to my principal heir Yoshichika, along with the full sequence of proof records.[7] As for holdings of this shrine, for now and ever more let no release take place—for as much as a *tan* or *bu*—to a youngest son, a daughter, a widow, or to any different-surnamed outsider (*ishō tanin*).[8] Obligations to the shrine (*shayaku*) shall be discharged pursuant to precedent. Thus, as proof for the future, our conveyance is as above.
3d year of Shōan [1301], 4th month, 22d day[9]

> saki no ōnegi, san-i Nakatomi Tomochika (monogram)

SOURCE: *Hanawa Fujimaru shi shozō monjo*, 1301/4/22 saki no ōnegi Nakatomi Tomochika yuzurijō, *Ibaragi ken shiryō, chūsei hen*, 1: 298, doc. 20 (*KI*, 27: 291, doc. 20868).
1. The boundaries—east, south, west, north—follow here.
2. Probably the Bakufu's confirmation of the present donor's receipt by inheritance of Ōga Village.
3. This commendation by Minamoto Yoritomo occurred in 1181; see the reference in *Kashima jingū monjo*, 1205/8/23 Minamoto Sanetomo kudashibumi, *Ibaragi ken shiryō, chūsei hen*, 1: 167, doc. 121 (*KB*, doc. 35).
4. The present donor.
5. In fact, Masachika was the successor to the first Kamakura holder, Chikahiro;

Kashima jingū monjo, 1185/8/21 Minamoto Yoritomo kudashibumi, *Ibaragi ken shiryō, chūsei hen*, 1: 168, doc. 124 (*KB*, doc. 10); see also Document 11 above.

6. I.e., tiny portions. Masachika received Tachibana *gō* and other holdings from his father in 1200 (Document 11 above). His deed to his heir, Yorichika, is dated 1227/ 10/12, but unfortunately is not extant (it is referred to in *Kashima jingū monjo*, 1240/ 12/7 shōgun ke mandokoro kudashibumi, *Ibaragi ken shiryō, chūsei hen*, 1: 222, doc. 318).

7. Moreover, on the same day as the present conveyance, Tomochika issued a second release to his heir, which included other holdings as well as the family's traditional shrine post of *ōnegi*; *Hanawa Fujimaru shi shozō monjo*, 1301/4/22 saki no ōnegi Nakatomi Tomochika yuzurijō, *Ibaragi ken shiryō, chūsei hen*, 1: 298, doc. 19.

8. The present recipient repeated a version of this stricture to his own heir in 1326: in the event the principal heir had no sons, an able person from within the clan (*ichimon*) should be chosen as successor. Under no circumstances was a release to be made to "a daughter or to an outsider." *Ibid.*, 1326/3/17 ōnegi Nakatomi Yoshichika yuzurijō an, *Ibaragi ken shiryō, chūsei hen*, 1: 303, doc. 28.

9. The Bakufu issued its confirmation a year later; *ibid.*, 1302/2/3 shōgun ke mandokoro kudashibumi an, *Ibaragi ken shiryō, chūsei hen*, 1: 237, doc. 362. Interestingly, the confirmation is based on a somewhat later conveyance (dated 1301/10/25, but not extant) than the one presented here.

DOCUMENT 133

Rival Branches of a Family Stand Together Against an Estate Proprietor, 1302

The trend toward unitary inheritance could only affect the present and future; it could not draw back together families that had already branched. Only when the enemy was common to rival branches could there be joint action. During the Kamakura age, a proprietor's challenge might meet that criterion, since branches with separate interests might still be beholden to a single estate holder. In the case presented here, lineages that had spent most of the century fighting one another were able to come together in the face of a common threat.

The terms of a dispute between *hokkyō* Raishū, estate deputy (*zasshō*) for Kutsuna Island, Iyo Province, a Chōkōdō holding,[1] and Magojirō Shigeyoshi, the eastern inlet *jitō*;[2] *saemon* Jirō Tōshige, the western inlet *jitō*;[3] and Saburō Yasuhisa.[4]

Item. Concerning the land (*shitaji*).
Numerous details have come out in this appeal-level suit (*osso*).[5] In essence, however, [the appeal argues that] Matsuyoshi *myō* and Mutō *myō* of this island constitute the *jitō*'s share (*jitō bun*);[6] all other land (*shitaji*) is under the jurisdiction of the proprietor (*honjo no shinshi*). In

response to a suit alleging incursions (*ōryō*) by *jitō* Saigan[7]—Shigeyo-shi's grandfather—and by [*jitō*] Tōshige,[8] the matter was heard by the fourth unit of the board of coadjutors (*hikitsuke*)[9]—Echigo *nyūdō's* section—with Shimada Magoroku Yukishige as magistrate (*bugyō*). [However,] the resulting edict of the 3d year of Einin [1295], 5th month, 23d day, calling for joint administration (*ryōhō no shomu*), con-travened the facts. According to a [Kantō] edict of the 2d year of Gen-kyū [1205], 5th month, 6th day,[10] in the *jitō's* possession, authority (*sata*) over Mutō *myō* on the eastern side of this island, a [one-time] holding (*shoryō*) of Shigeyoshi's ancestor, Toshihira, was to be exer-cised by Iehira—the younger brother of Kanehira.[11] Thus although Raishū has argued the clarity (*bunmei*) of the admonition against [*jitō*] involvement beyond the two *myō*, the issuance of that document was owing to incursions (*ranbō*) by Kane[hira] against Matsuyoshi *myō* in violation of Toshihira's release.[12] Summary of main points.[13]

4th year of Shōan (1302), 7th month, 7th day

> Sagami no kami, Taira ason seal
> Musashi no kami, Taira ason seal

SOURCE: *Chōryūji monjo*, 1302/7/7 Kantō gechijō an, *Ehime ken hennen shi*, 2: 441–42 (*KBSS*, 1: 305–6, doc. 235).

1. According to the Kutsuna house genealogy, Kutsuna Island was commended to Chōkōdō (a newly constructed temple of the imperial family) in 1182; see *Kutsuna ke monjo* (*Iyo shiryō shūsei*, 1), p. 22. For a documentary reference to this commendation, see *Chōryūji monjo*, 1233/12/10 Kantō gechijō an, *Ehime ken hennen shi*, 2: 263 (*KB*, doc. 106).

2. I.e., Kutsuna Shigeyoshi, chief (*sōryō*) of the family and the *jitō* of the eastern inlet (*higashi no ura*). What follows is a scaled-down genealogy of the Kutsuna house, contain-ing the names that appear in the several Kutsuna records translated in this book (see Documents 73–75); it is drawn from *Kutsuna ke monjo* (*Iyo shiryō shūsei*, 1), pp. 36–38.

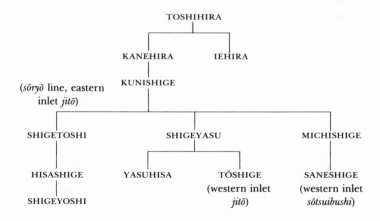

3. I.e., the nephew of Shigetoshi and son of Shigeyasu (Shigetoshi's brother). Clearly, the inheritance within the western inlet *jitō* line was one generation "behind" its main line counterpart.

4. I.e., the nephew of Shigetoshi and brother of Tōshige. Thus the three defendants were two brothers and a cousin, representing the Kutsuna family's interests in both halves of the island. This division into eastern and western sectors dated back to 1205; see n. 11.

5. The original suit was judged in 1295, as we see below. The edict itself is not extant.

6. Matsuyoshi *myō* was the profit-yielding share of the western inlet *jitō shiki*, while Muto *myō* was its counterpart for the eastern inlet.

7. Shigetoshi, the former eastern inlet *jitō*.

8. The western inlet *jitō*.

9. By this time, the main investigatory organ of the Bakufu; see *DKR*, pp. 115–16.

10. *Kutsuna ke monjo*, 1205/5/6 Kantō gechijō an, *Ehime ken hennen shi*, 2: 200 (*KB*, doc. 100).

11. This account of the 1205 document contains a remarkable error—it gets everything backwards! According to the original of that document (see n. 10), it was Matsuyoshi *myō* (not Mutō *myō*) that was to be held by Iehira; Mutō *myō* was to be held by Kanehira. The background to this inversion cannot be explained, but it did not affect the main arguments in 1302.

12. In other words, Raishū had attempted to use a century-old record dealing with an inheritance dispute over Matsuyoshi and Mutō *myō* between two brothers. But this was insufficient to establish that the authority of the Kutsuna house was limited to those two *myō*. In fact, the family's interests were considerably broader than that; see Document 75.

13. The original (*shōmon*) of the present document copy (*anmon*) doubtless concluded with the standard formulaic expressions. The original is not extant.

DOCUMENT 134

An Eldest Son Loses a Dispute over Intestate Property, 1304

Intrigue within families is graphically revealed in this tale of murder, ambition, and forgery. Following the violent deaths of their parents, an eldest son and a third son submitted a forged document claiming it to be a testament. A second son, however, brought suit and was rewarded with the unbequeathed estate. A unitary inheritance was thus the result, though the road to this end was anything but normal.

Concerning the petition of Oniyanagi *saemon* Shirō Noriyoshi, represented by Shinben, regarding Oniyanagi Village, Waka District, Mutsu Province, the legacy of [Mitsuyoshi,][1] his late father.

Regarding the above, Shinben has brought suit claiming that Mitsu-yoshi, before disposing of his property, was murdered in a night raid on the 10th day of the 10th month in the 5th year of Einin [1297]. [Subsequently, Noriyoshi's] elder brother Saburō Mitsukage and his younger brother Gorō Ieyuki—child's name, Kan'on—concocted a forged document, claiming it to be a testament, and obtained shares (*bunryō*) in the legacy (*iryō*), wholly without justification.² In response thereto, an effort was made to examine the testament for authenticity (*shingi*), but neither Mitsukage nor Ieyuki responded to the summons (*meshibumi*). In consequence, and because the act of forgery is a crimi-nal offense, a decision (*hyōjō*) of the 23d day of this past month desig-nated the legacy unbequeathed land (*mishobun no chi*) and called for a parceling out (*shihai*) of income shares (*tokubun*) to family members, excluding Mitsukage and Ieyuki. At this point Shinben stated that the eldest son (*chakushi*)³ Mitsukage and the third son Ieyuki among Mitsuyoshi's four sons were accordingly so excluded, but that the fourth son, Tsurumatsumaru, as well as the mother were both killed along with Mitsuyoshi. This leaves no family member for an income share from Mitsuyoshi's estate (*ato*) apart from Noriyoshi.⁴ In conse-quence, Noriyoshi shall possess the villages⁵ in question. By command of the Kamakura lord, it is so decreed.

2d year of Kagen [1304], 4th month, 24th day⁶

> Sagami no kami, Taira ason seal
> sakyō, gon no daibu, Taira ason
> seal

SOURCE: *Oniyanagi monjo*, 1304/4/24 Kantō gechijō an, *Miyagi kenshi, shiryōshū*, 1: 182, doc. 102 (*KBSS*, 1: 311, doc. 242).

1. Characters lost but interpolated.

2. Shinben's petition ends here.

3. If *chakushi* here also implied "principal heir," it would suggest that that status, without an accompanying testament, did not guarantee rights to property.

4. Note the assumption here that intestate property would normally be divided among a widow and immediate progeny. It cannot be determined whether the absence of any reference to daughters was owing to a lack of female children or to some exclu-sion practice.

5. The plural (*mura-mura*) here does not accord with the earlier reference to a single village.

6. No related documents survive.

DOCUMENT 135

A Father Places Primary Authority in the Hands of His Chosen Heir, 1306

When a Kamakura vassal had fifteen children, a wife, at least one grandson, and a principal heir who was not his eldest son, his blueprint for harmony was bound to be tested. As we see in the present instance, the father did what he could, which was to grant tiny portions to each of his flock and implore them all to cooperate. In addition, he stipulated the limit of dues payable to the chieftain-designate, inveighed against shares to women and adoptees, and called on his successor to choose a brother in the event he had no sons. He concluded with a threat—a failure of filiality would lead to a takeover of portions by the principal heir. In fact, the eight secondary sons adopted new surnames and apparently went their own ways. It is significant, perhaps, that we hear nothing further of the donor's daughters—all six of them.

It is hereby decreed that possession be exercised in accordance with the present document.

3d year of Shōwa [1314], 12th month, 20th day

Sagami no kami (monogram)[1]

Conveyed: The *jitō shiki* of Kōsokabe *gō*, Kagami District, Tosa Province.

Boundaries: . . .[2]

The aforesaid *gō* has been held as a reward for merit since its receipt (*hairyō*) by our ancestors Akiie and Akimichi.[3] As for Shigemichi, now in the sixth generation,[4] his hereditary possession has continued without change. On the basis of ability (*kiryō*), Shirō Hideyori is to be considered principal heir, and release is made to him, along with generations of Kantō orders (*onkudashibumi*) and edicts (*ongechi*) as well as other proof records. Also, concerning the income shares (*tokubun*) for our 15 sons and daughters[5]—plus shares for my widow and grandson, Senyojumaru—paddy and upland within the *gō* have been allocated. Copies (*anmon*) of the various releases (*menmen no yuzurijō*) as well as a register (*mokuroku*) [of holdings] are appended.[6] In accordance with these documents, authority shall be observed (*zonchi*). Moreover, when the house chieftain (*sōryō*) travels on Kantō or Rokuhara business, expenses (*yōto*) of 40 *mon* for each *tan* of land possessed will be levied on the secondary shares (*shoshi bun*). There will be no other miscellaneous obligations (*manzō kuji*). Also, in the event that Hideyori should have no sons, conveyance shall be to the person selected as the most able among his brothers.[7] The inheritance shall not fall to daughters or adopted sons (*yōshi*). Wherefore, as proof for the future, our conveyance is thus.

4th year of Kagen [1306], 4th month, 16th day

Nakahara Shigemichi (monogram)

I herewith add a postscript (*okugaki*) for the future.[8] Should anyone disobey our intent by even a single particular, the *sōryō* will assume control (*shinshi*) [of his lands] on the basis of unfiliality (*fukō*). Wherefore, our postscript is thus.

SOURCE: *Kōsokabe kaden shōmon*, 1306/4/16 Nakahara Shigemichi yuzurijō, *Kōsokabe shiryō*, pp. 147–48 (*Kōchi kenshi, kodai-chūsei hen*, p. 299).

1. This is the Bakufu's formal confirmation of the present conveyance, in the *gedai ando* format.

2. The boundaries—east, south, west, north—follow here.

3. The *jitō shiki* was originally granted to Nakahara (Kōsokabe) Akiie in 1193; see *Kōsokabe kaden shōmon*, 1193/6/9 shōgun ke mandokoro kudashibumi, *Kōsokabe shiryō*, pp. 143–44 (*KI*, 2: 74, doc. 671). For Akiie's early service in Kamakura, see *AK* 1184/ 6/18, 10/6, 1185/4/13, 9/5 (the family was originally from Kai Province in the east). Akimichi was Akiie's principal heir; *Kōsokabe kaden shōmon*, 1223/7/16 Kantō ando gechijō, *Kōsokabe shiryō*, p. 146 (*KI*, 5: 215, doc. 3137).

4. For a Kōsokabe genealogy, see *Kōchi kenshi, kodai-chūsei hen*, p. 1062. A document relating to Munemichi, successor to Akimichi, is translated in *KB*, doc. 164. There are no extant inheritance materials for the remainder of the thirteenth century.

5. The genealogy in *Kōchi kenshi, kodai-chūsei hen* (p. 1062) lists a total of nine sons including Hideyori. The eight brothers of Hideyori all became heads of branch lines bearing new surnames.

6. Two interpretations are possible here: that copies of these secondary releases are appended to the chieftain's release; or that copies of past and present chieftains' releases were appended to the secondary releases; *Kōchi kenshi, kodai-chūsei hen* (pp. 299–300) favors the latter, though this seems unlikely to me.

7. This stipulation proved to be unnecessary; a son, Tokihide, succeeded his father. The reference to a conveyance here must relate to the main *jitō shiki* and accompanying family headship.

8. This postscript is in *kana*, suggesting that it was personally written by the donor; the conveyance proper is in standard *kanbun*. The reason for the postscript is merely to strengthen the force of the document.

DOCUMENT 136

A Father Designates His Wife as Peacemaker Between His Sons, 1308

The author of the present conveyance seems to be aware of the fragility of relations between his two inheriting sons. He thus interposes their mother by making her legatee in the event either son predeceases her and is without issue. Moreover, if either son instigates trouble the mother is to take over his share. Some fifteen years later, the two brothers did come to blows, but it is not known whether the mother interceded.

Concerning the portion of land possessed by [Wada] Kanetsura within the northern sector of Okuyama Estate, Echigo Province.

The aforesaid holdings are being deeded in perpetuity to our sons, Iyafuku and Inuwakamaru.[1] The legacy of [either son] who predeceases his mother without sons of his own shall be possessed by her for the duration of her lifetime. After that, release should be made to the survivor, whether to Iyafuku or to Inuwaka. If, however, our conveyances (*yuzurijō*) should be contravened and our legacy despoiled, or if the interests of the mother are violated, the holdings of the [guilty] person will be made subject to the mother, and release shall be made to the more peacable (*onbin*) son.[2] Wherefore, for the future, this statement of intention (*okibumi*) is thus.[3]

3d year of Tokuji [1308], 8th month, 13th day

Kanetsura (monogram)

SOURCE: *Miura Wada shi monjo*, 1308/8/13 Wada Kanetsura okibumi, *Okuyama-no-shō shiryōshū*, p. 8, doc. 2 (*Essa shiryō*, 2: 167–68).

1. I.e., Wada Shigezane and Wada Noritsura. According to the house genealogy, Shigezane became house chieftain; see *Miura Wada keizu*, in *Essa shiryō*, 2: 168.

2. In 1323, Inuwaka (Noritsura), the younger son, brought suit against his brother, charging "despoilments" (*ranbō*). He submitted a copy (*anmon*) of the present document ("his late father Kanetsura's release") and then quoted it almost in full as part of his brief; *Miura Wada shi monjo*, 1323/10 Wada Noritsura sojō an, *Okuyama-no-shō shiryōshū*, p. 9, doc. 5. The outcome of the suit is unknown, although a year earlier Inuwaka was upheld in a related suit against his aunt; *ibid.*, 1322/7/7 Kantō gechijō, *ibid.*, p. 9, doc. 4.

3. It is probable that individual *yuzurijō* (not extant) were issued at this time, with the Bakufu evidently confirming them in 1320; see the references to an *ongedai* of 1320/6/16 in *ibid*. The documents of 1322 and 1323 also refer to *yuzurijō*.

DOCUMENTS 137–38

The Ashikaga House Head Confirms a Private Vassal's Deeds of Release to a Younger Brother and Adopted Son, 1309

As mentioned earlier, the Ashikaga house head regularly issued edicts of confirmation on behalf of members of his own vassal band. Here we see examples that validated transfers to a younger brother and an adopted son. Presumably the vassal had no natural sons. It is noteworthy, moreover, that the major share seems clearly to have gone to the adoptee—land rights in some four provinces. Thus a vassal of a Kamakura vassal is shown to have possessed heritable interests in widely dispersed areas.

137

(Ashikaga Sadauji's monogram)[1]

Directed: to Kuramochi *saemon* Saburō Morotada.
    That he shall possess forthwith one residential area plus one *chō* of paddy within Kido *gō* of Ashikaga Estate.[2]

In accordance with the release of the 3d year of Tokuji [1308], 8th month, 8th day,[3] by his elder brother Kuramochi *saemon* Jirō Morotsune,[4] this possession is confirmed.[5] Our command is thus.
    2d year of Enkei [1309], 6th month, 16th day[6]

138

Directed: to Kuramochi Otsuwakamaru.
    That he shall possess forthwith Numabukuro-naka *gō* in Kami District[7] plus Kamakura residence land (*yachi*); the Kozutsumi paddy and residence area (*yashiki*) in Katsuma *gō* of Shisai District, Kazusa Province (not, however, until after the lifetime of his grandmother);[8] and the residence area and grant fields (*kyū-den*) of Shō Temple in Nukata District, Mikawa Province—same conditions as above.[9]

In accordance with the release of this past year—the 3d of Tokuji [1308]—8th month, 8th day, by his foster father (*yōfu*) Kuramochi *saemon* Jirō Morotsune,[10] these possessions are confirmed. Our command is thus.[11]
    2d year of Enkei [1309], 6th month, 16th day

SOURCES: Document 137: *Kuramochi monjo*, 1309/6/16 Ashikaga Sadauji kudashibumi, *Tochigi kenshi, shiryō hen, chūsei*, 3: 12, doc. 8 (*Miyagi kenshi, shiryōshū*, 1: 188, doc. 116). Document 138: *ibid.*, 1309/6/16 Ashikaga Sadauji kudashibumi an, *Tochigi kenshi, shiryō hen, chūsei*, 3: 10, doc. 4 (*Miyagi kenshi, shiryōshū*, 1: 188, doc. 117).

1. Sadauji was the father of Ashikaga Takauji, founder of the Muromachi Bakufu. Confirmatory edicts (*ando no kudashibumi*) of the type presented here (emulating the format of Kamakura's own edicts) have been discovered for only two warrior families— the Hōjō and the Ashikaga. For the Hōjō, see Documents 51–52.

2. Ashikaga Estate in Shimotsuke Province was the Ashikaga family's ancestral homeland, with an association dating back to the late Heian period; *WG*, pp. 43, 46.

3. Not extant.

4. Morotsune himself was confirmed by Sadauji in this and other holdings only six years earlier, pursuant to conveyances of 1292 and 1300 by Morotsune's grandfather and father respectively; *Kuramochi monjo*, 1303/int.4/12 Ashikaga Sadauji kudashibumi an, *Tochigi kenshi, shiryō hen, chūsei*, 3: 10, doc. 3.

5. Morotada, the recipient here, was also deeded rights in land by his (and Morotsune's) father Ieyuki in 1300; Ashikaga Sadauji confirmed this transfer on the same day as that for Morotsune (see n. 4); *ibid.*, 1303/int.4/12 Ashikaga Sadauji kudashibumi, 3: 11, doc. 6. Morotada thus received bequests from his father and his older brothers.

6. Morotada's own release to a son took place in 1331 and was confirmed in 1348; *ibid.*, 1348/11/7 Ashikaga Tadayoshi kudashibumi, 3: 13, doc. 11.

7. In Mutsu Province.

8. This grandmother is probably the mother of Morotsune, the donor here; the recipient, as we will see, is Morotsune's adopted son.

9. I.e., after the grandmother's lifetime.

10. Not extant, but we note that Morotsune had prepared conveyances for his younger brother (see Document 137) and adopted son on the same day. All of the lands deeded to this son had been confirmed to the donor in 1303; see the document cited in n. 4.

11. From these two confirmations, then, we see that the Kamakura Ashikaga house enjoyed interests in at least five provinces—Shimotsuke, Mutsu, Sagami, Kazusa, and Mikawa.

DOCUMENT 139

The Bakufu Approves an Accord Between a House Head and a Branch Line, 1312

When branches of a family shared the *jitō* authority over an estate divided into two sectors, it was as if neighbors who were rivals were facing one another waiting for trouble to occur. In the present instance, a senior branch got its way by obliging its rival, under threat of a lawsuit, to surrender an important communications link. Though not specified, the trunk line probably had the stronger claim, since Kamakura would not have favored it solely on the basis of seniority. Noteworthy as usual is the willingness of vassals to submit their family's disputes to arbitration (or to private compromise) rather than to attempt to resolve them by force of arms.

Concerning a dispute over Mount Ita's main road—called Mount Nami by Shigeari—between Taira-no-ko *uemon* Rokurō Shige-yori,[1] the *jitō* of Fukano *gō*, Niho Lower Estate,[2] Suō Province, and [Taira-no-ko] Hikorokurō Shigeari,[3] *jitō* of the upper estate.[4]

According to a writ of compromise (*wayojō*) by Shigeyori dated the 3d year of Tokuji [1308], 4th month, 25th day,[5] and forwarded by the *shugo*, the former Ōmi governor Tokinaka:[6] "Although plaintiff and defense [statements] were exchanged, the suit is dissolved now under a compromise. Henceforth the said mountain will not be an object of contention (*kyōmō*)." According to Shigeari's corresponding writ of the same day: "Since it is recorded in his compromise writ that Shigeyori's contention is terminated, a [Kantō] edict (*gechijō*) should be granted." Shigeari is to exercise possession.[7] By command of the Kamakura lord, it is so decreed.

2d year of Ōchō [1312], 3d month, 2d day

Sagami no kami, Taira ason (monogram)

Mutsu no kami, Taira ason (monogram)

SOURCE: *Miura ke monjo*, 1312/3/2 Kantō gechijō, *DNK*, *iewake 14*, pp. 303–4, doc. 8 (*KBSS*, 1: 333, doc. 260).

1. Shigeyori was the head of a branch line that had separated from the Taira-no-ko trunk during the 1220s. The Taira-no-ko itself had branched from the Miura during late Heian times; *Miura shi keizu*, in *DNK*, *iewake 14*, pp. 470–72.

2. Fukano was deeded to Shigeyori's father (Shigetsuna) in the 1220s; see the reference in Document 31.

3. The Taira-no-ko family chieftain who was formally named principal heir by his father in 1293; *Miura ke monjo*, 1293/7/25 Taira-no-ko Shigechika yuzurijō an, *DNK*, *iewake 14*, p. 288. For the father's own investiture in the 1260s, see Documents 93–94.

4. The family link between the two disputants here went back several generations: Shigeyori's grandfather and Shigeari's great-grandfather were brothers; *Miura shi keizu*, in *DNK*, *iewake 14*, pp. 470–77. Though only a guess, the mountain pass being fought over may have connected Fukano *gō* with Shigeari's much larger territorial interests.

5. *Miura ke monjo*, 1308/4/25 Taira-no-ko Shigeyori wayojō, *DNK*, *iewake 14*, pp. 302–3, doc. 7.

6. A member of the Hōjō clan. The Suō *shugo* post had been taken over by the Bakufu's leading family in 1276; Satō, *Zōtei-Shugo*, pp. 176–79.

7. Earlier, Shigeari had struggled against his own elder brother, who had been passed over for the house chieftainship; *Miura ke monjo*, 1303/4/26 Taira-no-ko Shigeari wayojō, *DNK*, *iewake 14*, pp. 298–99, doc. 4.

DOCUMENT 140

A Wealthy Scion Releases a Land Share to a Secondary Heir, 1312

In cases where there were only two sons (or two favored sons) a father-donor might attempt some balance between them. This was designed to soften the blow of one brother's being chosen as principal heir. In the release presented here, a second son was granted a rich legacy and was also made the brother's successor should the latter die without male issue. At the same time, however, the recipient was warned to be appreciative of his father's generosity. Disobedience would lead to disinheritance, a threat that the Kamakura Bakufu would certainly uphold.

> Possession shall be exercised in accordance with the present document. By this command, it is so decreed.
> 1st year of Shōwa [1312], 4th month, 22d day
>> Sagami no kami seal
>> Mutsu no kami seal[1]

Conveyed: to Matagorō Fujiwara Munezane.[2]
> The *jitō shiki* of Narabara *gō*, within Nagae Estate, Mutsu Province—this legacy (*ato*) of Ken no Tōta[3] to be held only after Jōnin's lifetime.[4]
> The *jitō shiki* of Isō *gō*, Mino Province.[5]
> A one-half *jitō shiki* over Kamo *gō*, Awaji Province.[6]

The aforementioned holdings are deeded to Munezane. In the event he should commit any disturbance (*iran*), in violation of this release, Munezane's holding should be bestowed upon the chieftain (*sōryō*) Mitsuru *hosshi*.[7] If Mitsuru *hosshi* should die without sons, Munezane is to take possession of his lands and should become the chieftain.[8] Wherefore, this instrument is thus.
> 1st year of Shōwa [1312], 4th month, 14th day
>> saki no Awaji no kami, Munehide seal[9]

SOURCE: *Naganuma monjo*, 1312/4/14 Naganuma Munehide yuzurijō an, *Fukushima kenshi, kodai-chūsei shiryō*, p. 776, doc. 105.2 (*Aizu-Wakamatsu shi, shiryō hen*, 1: 76).

1. This is the Bakufu's confirmation (*gedai ando*) of the present document. Note that it came only eight days after the issuance of the release itself.
2. Munezane was a secondary heir of the donor, Naganuma Munehide.

3. Identity unknown.

4. Jōnin was the wife of Munehide, the present donor; *Fukushima kenshi*, 1: 450. Hence this was a delayed bequest.

5. Isō *gō* first appears as a Naganuma possession in the earliest surviving deed of release of that house; *Naganuma monjo*, 1230/8/13 Naganuma Munemasa yuzurijō, *Fukushima kenshi, kodai-chūsei shiryō*, p. 776, doc. 105.1 (Munemasa was the great-grand-father of Munehide).

6. Kamo *gō* first appears in a Bakufu confirmation of Munehide's inheritance from his own father, Muneyasu (the release itself is not extant); *Onjōji monjo*, 1299/12/6 shōgun ke mandokoro kudashibumi, *Fukushima kenshi, kodai-chūsei shiryō*, pp. 903–4, doc. 158.1. The Naganuma family's interests in Awaji Province dated from Munemasa's appointment to the *shugo* post and to two *jitō shiki* in 1221; *Minagawa monjo*, 1221/7/20 Kantō gechijō, *KI*, 5: 26, doc. 2779.

7. I.e., to Naganuma Hideyuki, the present donor's principal heir. This suggests an effort on the part of Munehide to concentrate considerable authority in his chosen successor. The conveyance to that successor is not extant.

8. None of this came to pass, since Mitsuru *hosshi* (Hideyuki) was able to transmit the family headship without incident to his son, Hidenao; *Fukushima kenshi*, 1: 450–51, 1060. Similarly, Munezane (the present recipient) was able to pass along his inheritance (*Naganuma monjo*, 1331/9/15 Naganuma Munezane yuzurijō an, *Fukushima kenshi, kodai-chūsei shiryō*, pp. 776–77, doc. 105.3), though the Bakufu's collapse intervened before a confirmation could be granted. This obliged Munezane to petition the new government in Kyoto for such a confirmation; *ibid.*, 1333/9 Naganuma Munezane mōshijō, *ibid.*, p. 777, doc. 105.4. The request was granted; *Date monjo*, 1334/6/13 Go-Daigo tennō rinji, *Aizu-Wakamatsu shi, shiryō hen*, 1: 79.

9. A reference in Munezane's petition of 1333 (n. 8) makes clear that Kamakura granted two marginal confirmations to the present release—one dated 1312/4/22 (see n. 1) and the other dated 1322/5/25. Presumably, both were added to the original (*shōmon*) of the present transcribed copy (*anmon*).

DOCUMENT 141

The Bakufu Confirms a Release That Seems to Leave the Disposal of Secondary Shares to the Heir-Designate, 1313

In this interesting release a father authorizes his successor to (seemingly) provide for his siblings by granting them life tenures. Previously, parents made such awards, not same-generation house heads. Indeed, donors often warned their principal heirs not to interfere with their siblings. Here, however, a father-donor seems clearly intent on enhancing the powers of his successor. It is all the more curious, therefore, that this inheritance should have been diluted, as it was, by a major grant to someone outside the donor's line. Of all persons, a niece was deeded a permanent portion beyond the reach of the heir-designate.

Possession shall be exercised in accordance with the present document. By this command, [it is so decreed].[1]

2d year of Shōchū [1325], 5th month, 4th day

> Sagami no kami seal
> shuri, gon no daibu seal

Conveyed: to Magotarō Norinaga.[2]

In total:

Item: the *jitō shiki* of Shigefuji *myō*, Yano Estate, Harima Province, plus paddy, upland, mountains, [and forests];[3] the *kumon shiki* of the *rei myō*;[4] and the *bettō, kannushi,* and *shukushi shiki* of Daiheki Shrine.[5]

Item: the *ji*[*tō shiki*][6] for two *tan*[7] of upland within Tsutsumi-Kizu Village in the inlet portion of Sagoshi Estate, same province.[8]

Item: the Okawara residence area, plus paddy and upland, which are part of the *jitō shiki* of Kami Village, Higashi *ho*, Fukui Estate, same province.[9]

Item: the Shiro upland area—unit measures recorded separately—and a residence plot within Mitsunobe and Kunitomi *myō*, Bizen Province.

Item: Tomosada and Shirō *myō*, which are part of the *jitō shiki* of Zuda Temple, Settsu Province.

> Five places, as above.

The aforesaid holdings are the undisputed hereditary landed possessions of Norikane. Now, a one-third share of the *jitō shiki* of Shigefuji *myō*, of the *kumon* [*shiki*] of the *rei myō*, and of the other *shiki*, is released at our pleasure to our niece, Minamoto *no uji*—named Chiyo.[10] The remainder,[11] plus our other possessions, is deeded in perpetuity to Norinaga, the [next] house head (*katoku*),[12] along with Kantō and Rokuhara edicts and orders (*ongechi onkudashibumi*) and the full sequence of proof records. Let there be no challenges to this. As for the release (*yuzuru*) of small parcels (*tsubo-tsubo*) to [Norinaga's] younger brothers Norinatsu and Yoshikane as well as to his sisters (*joshi*), transfer (*watasu*) is to be at the discretion of Norinaga.[13] However, the daughters' shares (*joshi bun*), after a life tenure, are to become part of the chieftain's share (*sōryōbun*).[14] Service obligations (*onkuji*) and taxes (*onnengu*) will be paid without objection.[15] Wherefore, for the future, our conveyance is thus.

2d year of Shōwa [1313], 9th month, 12th day

> uhyōe no jō seal

SOURCE: *Tōji hyakugō monjo,* 1313/9/12 uhyōe no jō Norikane yuzurijō an, *DNK, iewake 10,* 2: 720–22 (*Himeji shishi, shiryō hen,* 1: 416).

1. Characters lost but interpolated.

2. The present conveyance is by Terada Norikane, son of Terada Hōnen, the leader of a famous "criminal band" (*akutō*) based in Yano Estate, Harima Province. The Terada were longtime residents of Yano and alternated between opposing the estate proprietor and a Kamakura-appointed *jitō* (the Ebina). *Gokenin* themselves, the Terada were well-situated to increase their influence locally. For details, see Miyagawa Mitsuru, "Harima-no-kuni Yano-no-shō," in Shibata Minoru, ed., *Shōen sonraku no kōzō,* pp. 71–80.

3. Characters lost but interpolated.

4. *Rei myō* were a category of local taxation units as distinguished from *betsumyō,* which contained paddy areas earmarked expressly for a proprietor's use; Shibata Minoru, ed., *Shōen sonraku no kōzō,* p. 39. The Terada family's authority in Yano centered in this generations-old *kumon shiki* for the *rei myō,* of which Shigefuji *myō* was an example.

5. These latter three are all priestly officerships common in medieval shrines. The separation of the various elements in this "item" remains speculative, since they appear in the original as a sequence with no breaks.

6. Again, characters lost but interpolated.

7. In the margin next to the word *tan* is written *chō*; perhaps this is a correction.

8. Sagoshi Estate directly bordered Yano Estate.

9. According to a judgment edict of 1232, a *jitō shiki* in Nishi *ho* of Fukui Estate dated from the time of the second Kamakura lord, Yoriie (r. 1199–1203). The settlement itself called for the precedents of Higashi *ho* to be followed; *Jingoji monjo,* 1232/9/24 Kantō gechijō, *KBSS,* 1: 47–48, doc. 51.

10. Was she a favorite of the donor, or was this the fulfillment of an obligation to the donor's brother (i.e., the niece's father)? Later we see that the donor had daughters of his own who did not fare so well.

11. I.e., the other two-thirds share.

12. Later in our document the more usual term (*sōryō*) is used.

13. Two meanings are possible here: that the father designated actual parcels but allowed Norinaga the right to allocate them; or that the father was merely stating his desire that Norinaga should provide for his siblings.

14. Thus the legacy made to the donor's niece becomes even more striking, especially if she was exempted (not clear here) from the present reversion stipulation. It is noteworthy, at any rate, that the shares given to brothers were to be permanent.

15. Presumably through the *sōryō*.

DOCUMENT 142

The Bakufu Awards the Formal Symbols of Family Headship to the House's New Chieftain, 1314

So prominent was headship becoming in the early fourteenth century that brothers might engage one another over possession of its physical symbols. In the case described here, a father died intestate, leaving it to the Bakufu to confirm one son over the other as the new house head. The loser responded by seizing the family's "hereditary armor, banners, and documents," citing as his pretext that he was a son of his father's legitimate wife and that the father wished him to be chieftain. The second part of this claim was the critical one, and since it could not be proved, the Bakufu reaffirmed its earlier decision. This suggests, as we know from other evidence, that the conditions of one's birth could be overridden by other considerations. Legitimacy was a factor for wives (determining whether they were primary or secondary), but there was no absolute conception of bastardy affecting children. Even at that, we are struck by the desperate strategy of the losing son: a father's (or mother's) deed of release, or a decision by Kamakura, was the only way to be recognized as a house head. In a legalistic society, symbolism, such as that represented by armor and banners, meant little. But perhaps this was now changing.

> Concerning a dispute between Edo Jirōtarō Shigemichi and [Edo] Magotarō Masashige over hereditary armor (*yoroi*), banners (*hata*), and documents (*monjo*).[1]

Regarding the above, the legacy (*ato*) of the grandfather Shigemasu was allocated (*haibun*) to Shigemichi as the principal heir of his father Tarōjirō Yukishige on the 17th day of the 3d month of the 6th year of Einin [1298].[2] Now once again because Yukishige's legacy was not bequeathed by him, a dispute has arisen between primary and secondary heirs (*chakusho*), leading to a judgment (*saikyo*) of this past 12th month, 5th day, that Shigemichi should be house head (*katoku*).[3] Notwithstanding, Shigemichi has petitioned that Masashige had seized the hereditary armor, banners, and documents on the pretext that he was born of the legal wife (*tōfuku*).[4] Although [Masashige] claims his takeover to be in response to the original lord's wish (*honshu no soi*),[5] there is no clear proof of this since Yukishige's legacy was not bequeathed.[6] Moreover, the recent judgment (*seibai*) cites Shigemichi as principal heir (*chakushi*). In consequence, the armor, banners, and documents from Shigemasu's legacy shall be transferred to Shigemichi.[7] By command of the Kamakura lord, it is so decreed.

> 3d year of Shōwa [1314], 5th month, 12th day[8]

> Sagami no kami, Taira ason (monogram)

SOURCE: *Tōkyō kokuritsu hakubutsukan shozō monjo*, 1314/5/12 Kantō gechijō, *Edo shi kankei monjo shū*, p. 5, doc. 7 (*KBSS*, 1: 341, doc. 266).

1. From the context here it is evident that this was a dispute between a house head (Shigemichi) and one of his brothers. (However, there exists at least one family genealogy that lists Masashige as Shigemichi's uncle, not his brother; cf. *Edo shi kankei monjo shū*, p. 5.)

2. Clearly, this occurred by judgment of the Bakufu, not by release of Shigemichi's father, who had died intestate two years earlier; see *ibid.*, p. 5. Thus the Bakufu awarded the family headship to the heir-designate—even without a will from his father. The Bakufu's edict is not extant.

3. In fact, Shigemichi had been house head since 1298; the decision of 1313/12/5 (not extant) was a reaffirmation of this.

4. The loser in two regular lawsuits (1296–98 and 1313), Masashige had now evidently changed strategy: he seized the physical symbols of family headship from his brother upon the pretext that he (Masashige) was a legitimate son. Presumably he meant to suggest that Shigemichi was not.

5. The reference is to Yukishige, Masashige's father.

6. I.e., there is no deed of release.

7. I.e., by Masashige, who had seized them.

8. There are no related documents that survive.

DOCUMENT 143

A Sōryō Shiki Is Passed to an Heir, 1316

A further step in the advance of the concept of house headship was the appearance of a new title—*sōryō shiki*. Previously, it was fathers who selected their principal heirs—*chakushi*—who then, upon the death of that parent, became *sōryō*. In the face of a challenge such as the one being experienced here, a father might attempt to make this equation explicit. In his deed of conveyance, a revision of an earlier deed, he handed down the *sōryō* title itself. The rest of the release is typical of the period and included the standard checks and balances between primary and secondary heirs. Notwithstanding, in less than a century the term *sōryō* had advanced from a status deriving from principal heirship to a title of headship that was itself transmittable.

Conveyed: offices (*shotai*) plus private paddy and upland.
  [To:] Saburōjirō Morouji.
Item: the headship (*kannushi shiki*) of Sōsha Shrine, Hitachi Province; the *monomōshi shiki*[1] [of that shrine]; and attached residence land, private paddy, and upland. . . .[2]
Item: a provincial government officership (*zaichō shiki*), along with the paddy and upland of Komeyoshi *myō*.

The aforesaid offices (*shoshiki*) and private paddy and upland have been hereditary over many generations within [the line of] Moroyuki. By virtue thereof, release of these offices and private paddy and upland is made [in perpetuity][3] to Morouji. However, because of our awareness of . . . on the part of Iyajirō Yukichika,[4] release of the family's headship (*sōryō shiki*) is [also] made to Morouji.[5] Portions of private paddy [and upland . . .][6] from within [this legacy] are deeded to my various secondary heirs (*menmen shoshi*). As for shrine obligations (*onshinjiyaku*) and services (*onkuji*) [to the province],[7] [shares shall be][8] in accordance with the size of allotments. Should there be any who raise objections or create disturbances in violation of this conveyance, such disloyal persons (*fukō no jin*) [shall not][9] hold [any part of] our estate (*ato*), and the possession shares (*chigyō bun*) of disrupters (*iran no jin*) will be held [instead] by chieftain Morouji. [Even so,][10] let no trouble (*wazurai*) be caused to our secondary heirs (*shoshi*) upon some pretext.[11] When obligations are owed to the provincial capital (*kokufu*) and to Kashima Shrine, let performance be done jointly by the secondary heirs of [this house].[12] Pursuant to the present convey[ance . . .],[13] let possession be exercised mutually by the siblings, free of disruption. Now, although release was previously made to our secondary heirs under the handwriting (*shuseki*) of Ryūshin *ajari*, an instrument of recall (*kuikaeshijō*) [has been issued],[14] and this conveyance is made anew.[15] Wherefore, as proof for the future, our release is thus.

　　5th year of Shōwa [1316], 7th month, 7th day

　　　　　　　　　　　　　san-i, Kiyohara Moroyuki . . .[16]

SOURCE: *Sōsha jinja monjo*, 1316/7/7 Kiyohara Moroyuki yuzurijō, *Sōsha jinja monjo*, pp. 32–33, doc. 16 (*Ibaragi ken shiryō, chūsei hen*, 1: 393, doc. 16).

　　1. Apparently a warden's or usher's authority.

　　2. Several characters lost here. The two transcriptions used in this translation differ in various places in the number of characters thought to be lost. Generally speaking, the *Ibaragi ken shiryō* version seems to be more accurate in this regard.

　　3. Characters lost; interpolation by the translator.

　　4. Several characters lost here. Years earlier, Moroyuki, the present donor, had sold certain parcels to Yukichika, a transaction that was invalidated by the invocation of a Kamakura cancellation order (*tokusei*); see the references in *Sōsha jinja monjo*, 1297/4/1 rusudokoro kudashibumi, *Sōsha jinja monjo*, p. 27, doc. 8. Possibly, Yukichika had never accepted that decision.

　　5. This is one of the earliest references to a *sōryō shiki*, though the precise implications here are uncertain. Passage of the headship (rather than merely landed perquisites—the future connotation of some *sōryō shiki*) was obviously considered important owing to the threat from Yukichika.

　　6. See n. 3.

　　7. Later in our document we see a reference in this context to the provincial capital.

　　8. See n. 3.

　　9. *Ibid.*

　　10. *Ibid.*

　　11. The chieftain, in other words, should not impinge without cause on the land shares of his siblings.

12. See n. 3.
13. Characters lost.
14. See n. 3.
15. The difference between the two releases was presumably the strengthened authority awarded to the *sōryō* in the later deed.
16. A monogram was probably present but has been lost through paper deterioration.

DOCUMENTS 144–46

An Inheritance Transaction Extends into the Post-Kamakura Age, 1318, 1332, 1345

In the early fourteenth century no one knew that the Kamakura Bakufu would shortly be overthrown. Petitions for confirmation of inheritances continued—indeed, continued up until the end. After the end, warrior houses simply looked to the successor authorities for confirmations, though probably (since conditions were volatile) with greater urgency. In the case described here, a father-donor deeded his *jitō shiki* to his chosen heir, but granted lifetime shares to his wife and other children, including an adopted son, and also including someone who was probably a brother. Interestingly, the brother's share was granted in perpetuity as long as his own release went to a true son—an unusual arrangement. An opposite note was the admonition against life holders' attempting to pass on their inheritances to their children. At any rate, the major heir transmitted the *jitō shiki* to his own heir, who was confirmed by the Ashikaga Bakufu.

144
Conveyed: the *jitō shiki* of Naruta *gō*, Gōdo Estate, Mino Province.

The aforesaid place is the hereditary landholding (*sōden no chi*) of Ennin.[1] Accordingly, it is deeded to Iyasaburō Shigechika as my principal heir (*chakushi*), along with [Kantō] orders from generations past and the sequence of hereditary instruments (*tetsugi no jō*).[2] The portions to my secondary heirs (*shoshibun*) are excluded from this. However, the portions of the widow-nun Komano, and of Tonkyō, Tōgomaru, Midaōmaru, and our adopted son (*yōshi*) Hannyo[3] shall be held by the chieftain (*sōryō*) after their lifetimes. Also, if Chikakane should have no true sons, his portion shall similarly be held by the chieftain after his lifetime.[4] Should there be any who, in violation of this purport, oppose the chieftain, they, as unfilial persons (*fukō no jin*), will have their portions taken over. In addition, if any should make a petition claiming to have sons or daughters, this is not to be recognized.[5] As concerns service obligations (*onkuji*) and taxable paddy and upland (*kōdenpata*), there is a separate record.[6] Wherefore, our conveyance is thus.[7]

2d year of Bunpō [1318], 4th month, 3d day

shami, Ennin (monogram)

145

Conveyed: the *jitō shiki* of Naruta *gō*, Gōdo Estate, Mino Province.

The aforesaid place is the hereditary holding (*sōden no shoryō*) of Shigechika. Accordingly, it is deeded in perpetuity to my principal heir Iyaōmaru as chieftain[-designate] (*sōryō*),[8] along with the sequence of hereditary proof records (*tetsugi no shōmon*). Let no one disturb this. Wherefore, for the future, our conveyance is thus.

1st year of Shōkei [1332], 12th month, 14th day[9]

Fujiwara Shigechika (monogram)

146

(Ashikaga Tadayoshi's monogram)

Directed: to Mizutani *kurōdo* Tarō Chikasada—child's name Iyaōmaru. That he shall forthwith possess the *jitō shiki* for Naruta *gō*, Gōdo Estate, Mino Province—minus two-fifths of the barrens area (*arano*).

Regarding the above, possession shall be exercised in accordance with the release of the late father Shigechika[10] dated the 1st year of Shōkei [1332], 12th month, 14th day.[11] It is thus.

4th year of Kōei [1345], 5th month, 27th day

SOURCES: Document 144: *Ikeda monjo*, 1318/4/3 shami Ennin yuzurijō, *Gifu kenshi, shiryō hen, kodai-chūsei*, 4: 1061, doc. 5. Document 145: *ibid.*, 1332/12/14 Fujiwara Shigechika yuzurijō, *ibid.*, 4: 1061, doc. 6. Document 146: *ibid.*, 1345/5/27 Ashikaga Tadayoshi sodehan kudashibumi, *ibid.*, 4: 1063, doc. 12.

1. In Documents 88–91 we saw the passage and confirmation of Naruta *gō* (both its *jitō* and *azukari dokoro shiki*) to forebears of Ennin. There are no intervening records between that sequence (dating from 1260–69) and the present release of 1318. The fate of the *azukari dokoro* title is unknown.

2. Presumably, Documents 88–91 were among these.

3. The final four names are obviously those of brothers of the recipient here, i.e., the *shoshi* referred to in the previous sentence.

4. Chikakane is not identified, but perhaps he is a younger brother of the donor.

5. In other words, the secondary heirs were to have no rights of alienation.

6. I.e., a separate document itemizing various monetary responsibilities.

7. No Bakufu confirmation is extant, and the next surviving record is Document 145—the present recipient's release to his heir.

8. It is clear from the recipient's name that he is a child (see also the reference in Document 146). Thus Shigechika would continue to exercise actual authority. As the country fell into civil war, Shigechika sought other means to secure his family's lands and status, as is shown in two documents (not reproduced here) in which he enumerates his battle exploits and receives the acknowledgment of Ashikaga Takauji; *Ikeda monjo*, 1336/9 Fujiwara Shigechika gunchūjō, *Gifu kenshi, shiryō hen, kodai-chūsei*, 4: 1062, doc. 9; *ibid.*, 1336/9/5 Ashikaga Takauji sodehan kanjō, *ibid.*, 4: 1062, doc. 8.

9. Coming as it did just before the collapse of the Kamakura Bakufu, this conveyance would have to await confirmation from the successor regime; see Document 146.

10. Shigechika died in battle on 1338/3/15; see this reference in *Ikeda monjo*, 1338/3 Fujiwara Iyaōmaru gunchūjō, *Gifu kenshi, shiryō hen, kodai-chūsei*, 4: 1063, doc. 11.

11. I.e., Document 145.

DOCUMENT 147

A Warrior Deeds His Property to a Daughter, 1323

Just at the point when we might have expected female inheritances to disappear, we encounter the present release. In fact this is only logical: in a family with all daughters, the choice was to adopt or to deed to a natural child. We gain no sense here of any reservation on the part of the father-donor. Similarly, we see no indication (here or elsewhere) of dissatisfaction with a wife who failed to provide sons.

Conveyed: Tamura Village in Hitachi Province; the deputyship (*daikan shiki*) of Katayama Village, Kanabara *ho*, Igu Estate, Mutsu Province;[1] and land near the western gate in Kamakura.

The aforesaid places are deeded to my daughter, the Lady Kaisu. Let there be no disturbances about this. Should something untoward arise, judgment shall lie with her mother (*haha no hakarai*). Should there be no children, release will be made to her younger sisters.[2] Wherefore, this instrument is thus.

3d year of Genkyō [1323], 11th month, 3d day[3]

uemon no jō, Sadayuki

SOURCE: *Nanbu ke monjo*, 1323/11/3 Kudō Sadayuki yuzurijō, *Nanbu ke monjo*, p. 1, doc. 1 (*Iwate ken chūsei monjo*, 1: 29, doc. 79).

1. Expressed as *Michi-no-kuni*—standard in *kana* documents of this period.
2. Obviously there are no sons here.
3. There appear to be no related documents. The Kudō family was a private retainer house (*miuchi*) of the Hōjō (Satō, *Soshō seido*, p. 113). Thus the deputyship being devised may well have been a *jitōdai* title under Hōjō superintendence; see, e.g., Documents 51–52 above.

DOCUMENT 148

An Inheritance Dispute Leads to a Division of All Property, 1323

The ultimate estrangement among family members involved an irrevocable splitting of property. Here we see a widow and son arrayed against another pairing of house members in a dispute involving unbequeathed property. In the accord reached by the warring factions, everything was divided—real property and movables—just as in a modern divorce settlement. Thus the armor and long swords were exchanged for the family's main residence and traditional banners. Here was one warrior house that was not coalescing out of a sense of increasing social unrest; the predators in this case were themselves.

> Concerning a dispute between Jōnin and Hikoshichi Yori—tada, character omitted—the widow-nun and son of Hara Magosaburō Sadayori, and [Hara] *saemon no jō hosshi*—Buddhist name, Jōnin[1]—and his son *saemon no jō* Tokitada, over the landed legacy (*iryō*) and other property (*ika*) left by Sadayori and [another] son Kosaburō Yasusada.[2]

Owing to the dispute there was a desire for judgment (*sata*); however, according to a cosigned document of Jōnin and Tokitada[3] representing a compromise (*wahei*) of the 5th day of this month: "In response to Jōnin's and Yori[tada's] suit,[4] plaintiff and defense statements were investigated. However, through compromise (*wayo no gi*), the places in question have been divided (*setchū*).[5] As for the main residence compound (*hon yashiki*) and banners from generations past (*jūdai no hata*), these are relinquished to Yori[tada and Jōnin], in exchange for the [family] armor (*yoroi*) and long swords (*tachi*). Similarly, when the life-tenure shares (*ichigo ryōshu bun*) come to be returned, these too shall be divided."[6] The document [cosigned] by the nun Jōnin and by Yori[tada] is the same as that above and thus no further particulars are needed. In mutual pursuance of these documents, possession shall be exercised free of future disturbance. By command of the Kamakura lord, it is so decreed.

3d year of Genkyō [1323], 12th month, 12th day

> Sagami no kami, Taira ason (monogram)
> shuri, gon no daibu, Taira ason (monogram)

SOURCE: *Isogawa Kiyoshi shi shozō monjo*, 1323/12/12 Kantō gechijō, *KBSS*, 1: 372, doc. 398.

1. There are two persons named Jōnin here, a male and a female.

2. We can only speculate on the lineup of interests here, since no related documents appear to survive. It is possible that the widow and one son were pitted against another son and his son (or possibly against the late father's brother and his son). The spoils were the unbequeathed holdings of the late Sadayori and a portion granted by him to Yasusada, a son now dead. Later we see that there were also female shares.

3. That is, the side of Jōnin and Tokitada.

4. The widow and her son, then, lodged the suit, which explains why the statement of their rivals is quoted here.

5. Most land division settlements (*shitaji chūbun*) occurred between *jitō* and central proprietors (see my "Jitō Land Possession in the Thirteenth Century"). Here is a case, however, of a division within the same family.

6. The reference here is presumably to female shares, which would revert upon the deaths of their holders to the chieftain. In the present case, however, the family was breaking irretrievably into two lines.

DOCUMENT 149

A Father Reacquires Property Deeded to a Son and Allots It Instead to a Daughter, 1329

As we have seen in countless examples, a father's plans for his property could be ruined by a premature death. Here a secondary share to a son now dead was returned to the father, who released it to a daughter on a lifetime basis. After her death the property was to go to the main line. Of note here is that the father did not simply assign the returned holdings to his principal heir; he deeded them instead to his daughter.

> Possession shall be exercised [in accordance][1] with the present document. By this command, [it is so decreed].
>
> 2d year of Gentoku [1330], 2d month, 25th day
>
> > Sagami no kami[2]

Concerning hereditary private holdings (*sōden shiryō*).
[To:] our daughter, Kami *no uji*—the widow of Ōkaya Kotarō *nyūdō*.
Two *tan* of paddy within the northern sector of Imamizo Estate, Minochi District, Shinano Province—units originally cultivated by Minamoto Tōzō *nyūdō*.

The [aforesaid] are the generations-old hereditary private holdings of Jūa. Yet because Nagatomo has pre[deceased] Jūa, they have been re-called and are now re-deeded.[3] Thus, our daughter Kami *no uji* shall [possess them] for the duration of her lifetime. After her lifetime they will be returned to the chieftain (*sōryō*) of the *gō*, Chikatomo. Next, regarding service obligations (*onkuji*), these have been set out in a separate record. If any persons should commit intrusions, their portions shall be bestowed upon Chikatomo. Wherefore, our conveyance is thus.

 1st year of Gentoku [1329], 12th month, 10th day

        shami, Jū[a (monogram)]

SOURCE: *Yahiko jinja monjo*, 1329/12/10 shami Jūa yuzurijō, *Shinano shiryō*, 5: 109–10.
 1. All words and phrases appearing in brackets are interpolations of the translator; the characters have been lost.
 2. A monogram, now lost, may have followed this *gedai* confirmation.
 3. Nagatomo was a secondary heir of the present donor. Since the release to Naga-tomo is not extant, we do not know whether his portion was a life bequest or a permanent inheritance. At all events, it was not transmitted to any heirs he might have had.

DOCUMENT 150

A Father Ends a Family Tradition of Divided Inheritances, 1330

The present conveyance represents a fitting conclusion to an era. A father, heir to a tradition of inheritance shares to all children, turned his back on that tradition and created a new one. Henceforth, unitary inheritances were to prevail, since otherwise the shares "would be of very small size." It is noteworthy that the Yamanouchi were actually in a better position to maintain the partible system than were many poorer families. Yet when houses such as this one chose a new direction, the influence of their action must have been compelling. Families of lesser wealth must have found it difficult—on several counts—to continue the older practices.

Conveyed: land holdings.[1]

In total:

One locale: the *jitō shiki* for Hon *gō*, within Jibi Estate, Bingo Province—minus the Takayama residence fields, etc. (*monden ika*).[2]

One locale: the partial (*ichibu*) *jitō shiki* for Taga Village, same estate.[3]

One locale: the *jitō shiki* for Tomishima Estate, Settsu Province.[4]

One locale: the *jitō shiki* for Lower Hirata *gō*, Shinano Province.[5]

One locale: peasants (*tago*), paddy and upland, service households (*zaike*), and residence compounds (*yashiki*) in Ittoku *myō*, Hayakawa Estate, Sagami Province.[6]

One locale: land within Kamakura's Amanawa [District].[7]

The aforesaid places are the hereditary possessions of Chōkai—lay name, Michisuke; child's name, Chōjumaru. Accordingly, they are conveyed to my principal heir Hikosaburō Michitoki, along with the succession of proof records. Although portions ought to be allocated to my other children (*shoshi*), these would be of very small size, and thus the release is to Michitoki alone because of the need to avoid a crisis involving allotments. Although the future is unending, Chōkai's estate (*ato*) shall be succeeded to by one person among his descendants [in each generation].[8] However, as concerns the Takayama residence fields, etc., within Hon *gō*, Jibi Estate, Bingo Province, these have been commended in perpetuity to that locale's Kan'onji Temple. Exact specifications are recorded in a separate document.[9] Moreover, because the present conveyance was prepared by someone else (*tahitsu*), a statement in our own hand (*jihitsu*)—in Japanese letters (*wa no ji*)—will be added to the reverse side as proof for the future. Forthwith, possession shall be exercised pursuant to this document. Wherefore, our conveyance is thus.

2d year of Gentoku [1330], 3d month, 18th day

shami, Chōkai (monogram)

For the future I add this statement in my own hand to the reverse side of this deed of release.[10]

2d year of Gentoku [1330], 3d month, 18th day[11]

Chōkai (monogram)

SOURCE: *Yamanouchi Sudō ke monjo*, 1330/3/18 Yamanouchi Chōkai (Michisuke) yuzurijō, *DNK, iewake 15*, pp. 19–20, doc. 16 (*Shinano shiryō*, 5: 115–16).

1. The present conveyance is from Yamanouchi Michisuke to his principal heir, Michitoki. For Michisuke's own inheritance in 1303, see Document 122.

2. For the history of Hon *gō*, see the references in Document 122, n. 2.

3. We see no prior reference to Taga Village in earlier Yamanouchi documents (cf. Documents 42–46, 99, 121–22).

4. See Documents 43 and 121.

5. See Document 121.

6. See Documents 42, 44, 46, 121.

7. Was this a new acquisition? The full list here should be compared with that deeded to the present donor and his father; see Documents 121–22.

8. The present recipient followed this stricture and incorporated the same admonition in the conveyance to his son; *Yamanouchi Sudō ke monjo,* 1347/12/3 Yamanouchi Michitoki yuzurijō, *DNK, iewake 15,* pp. 23–24, doc. 22.

9. Not extant.

10. This sentence, the date, and the signature appear in *kana* script on the reverse side.

11. There is no indication that a confirmation by the Bakufu was ever issued. In 1346, the Ashikaga regime awarded a confirmation of the present release, though only two of the six areas transmitted were included (Hon *gō* and Tomishima Estate); see *Yamanouchi Sudō ke monjo,* 1346/3/29 Ashikaga Tadayoshi sodehan kudashibumi, *DNK, iewake 15,* p. 23, doc. 21. Nevertheless, in the year following, Michitoki deeded all six properties to his own principal heir (see n. 8).

REFERENCE MATTER

CHRONOLOGICAL INDEX OF DOCUMENTS TRANSLATED

The list is offered for quick identification. The actual year periods—eras—appear in the translations themselves. In a few instances, years have been determined from context and then inserted. The user should bear in mind that the labeling of documents is often imprecise. For example, there are numerous records that are *gechijō* (decrees) in style but *saikyojō* (judicial edicts) in content. Which designation should we use, then? Even within single volumes compilers regularly switch from one form to the other. There are also the many instances in which documents are not clearly of *any* style. There are some conveyances, for instance, that exhibit the qualities of both *yuzurijō* and *shobunjō*.

DOCUMENT COLLECTIONS
REPRESENTED IN THE TRANSLATIONS

As with the labeling of documents, there is no uniformly acceptable way to list collections. A recent trend (in *KI*) has been to place the province name ahead of the collection. But this would have made alphabetization meaningless. Another uncertain area involves documents traditionally associated with some well-known collection but now in private hands. Many editors give credit to both sources. A third difficulty occurs when a document's ownership has changed recently or is simply attributed differently in different books. Scholars have yet to agree on a single system of identification. Finally, there are the many instances in which documents survive only in chronicles or diaries or on the reverse sides of such sources. Complicated classification schema abound. The present listing follows a somewhat abbreviated method, concentrating on main or "core" sources. The numbers cited here refer to documents, not pages.

BIBLIOGRAPHY

Japanese characters for virtually all primary source titles appearing here can be found in the Bibliography of my earlier book *The Kamakura Bakufu* (Stanford, Calif., 1976), which also contains a full title index and an index of compilers and publishers (the latter again includes Japanese characters).

PRIMARY SOURCES IN JAPANESE

Aichi kenshi, bekkan. Compiled by Aichi ken. Tokyo, 1939.

Aizuwakamatsu shi 8, shiryō hen 1. Compiled by Takahashi Tomio et al. Aizuwakamatsu, 1967.

Aokata monjo. Compiled by Seno Seiichirō (Zoku Gunsho ruijū kanseikai, *Shiryō sanshū—komonjo hen*). 2 vols. Tokyo, 1975–76.

Asō monjo. Compiled by Shinjō Tsunezō (*Kyūshū shiryō sōsho* 17). Fukuoka, 1966.

Azuma kagami. Edited by Nagahara Keiji and Kishi Shōzō. 5 vols. Tokyo, 1976–77.

Chikugo-no-kuni Mizuma-no-shō shiryō. Compiled by Seno Seiichirō (*Kyūshū shōen shiryō sōsho* 14). Tokyo, 1966.

Chūsei hōsei shiryōshū. Compiled by Satō Shin'ichi and Ikeuchi Yoshisuke. 4 vols. Tokyo, 1955–78.

Dai Nihon komonjo, iewake 1: Kōyasan monjo. Compiled by Tōkyō daigaku shiryō hensanjo. 8 vols. Tokyo, 1904–7.

———, *iewake 5: Sagara ke monjo.* 2 vols. Tokyo, 1917–18.

———, *iewake 9: Kikkawa ke monjo.* 3 vols. Tokyo, 1925–32.

———, *iewake 11: Kobayakawa ke monjo.* 2 vols. Tokyo, 1927.

———, *iewake 14: Kumagai ke monjo—Miura ke monjo—Hiraga ke monjo.* Tokyo, 1937.

———, *iewake 15: Yamanouchi Sudō ke monjo.* Tokyo, 1940.

———, *iewake 16: Shimazu ke monjo.* 3 vols. to date. Tokyo, 1942–.

Dai Nihon shiryō, series 4 and 5. Compiled by Tōkyō daigaku shiryō hensanjo. 17 and 24 vols. to date. Tokyo, 1902–.

Dazaifu—Dazaifu Tenmangū shiryō. Compiled by Takeuchi Rizō. 11 vols. to date. Dazaifu, 1964–.

Echigo monjo hōkanshū. Compiled by Satō Shin'ichi and Miya Eiji (Niigata ken kyōiku iinkai). Niigata, 1954.

Edo shi kankei monjo shū. Compiled by Tōkyō to Chiyoda kushi hensan iinkai. Tokyo, 1957.

Ehime ken hennenshi. Compiled by Ehime ken hensan iinkai. 9 vols. to date. Matsuyama, 1963–.

Essa shiryō. Compiled by Takahashi Yoshihiko. 7 vols. Niigata, 1925–31.

Fukushima kenshi 7, kodai-chūsei shiryō. Compiled by Fukushima ken. Fukushima, 1966.

Gifu kenshi, kodai-chūsei shiryō. Compiled by Gifu ken. 4 vols. Gifu, 1969–72.

Gunma kenshi, shiryō hen 5, chūsei 1. Compiled by Gunma kenshi hensan iinkai. Maebashi, 1978.

Hagi han batsuetsu roku. Compiled by Yamaguchi ken monjokan. 5 vols. Yamaguchi, 1967–71.

Heian ibun. Compiled by Takeuchi Rizō. 15 vols. Tokyo, 1947–80.

Hennen Ōtomo shiryō. Compiled by Takita Manabu. 2 vols. Kyoto, 1942–46.

Higashiasai gunshi 4. Compiled by Higashiasai kyōikukai. Higashiasai gun, 1927.

Higo-no-kuni Kanokogi—Hitoyoshi-no-shō shiryō. Compiled by Sugimoto Hisao (*Kyūshū shōen shiryō sōsho 3*). Tokyo, 1963.

Himeji shishi, shiryō hen 1. Compiled by Himeji shishi henshū iinkai. Himeji, 1974.

Hirado Matsuura ke shiryō. Compiled by Kyōto daigaku bungakubu kokushi kenkyūshitsu. Kyoto, 1951.

Hiroshima kenshi, kodai-chūsei shiryō hen. Compiled by Hiroshima ken. 5 vols. Hiroshima, 1974–80.

Hokuetsu chūsei monjo. Compiled by Satō Shin'ichi et al. Tokyo, 1975.

Ibaragi ken shiryō, chūsei hen. Compiled by Ibaragi kenshi hensan chūsei shi bukai. 2 vols. to date. Mito, 1970–.

Ichikawa shishi 5, kodai-chūsei shiryō. Compiled by Ichikawa shishi hensan iinkai. Tokyo, 1973.

Iga-no-kuni Kuroda-no-shō shiryō. Compiled by Takeuchi Rizō (*Shōen shiryō sōsho*). Tokyo, 1975.

Irobe shiryōshū. Compiled by Inoue Toshio. Niigata, 1968.

Iwami Kuri monjo no kenkyū. Compiled by Kinugasa Yasuki (*Ritsumeikan daigaku jinbun kagaku kenkyūjo kiyō 16*). Kyoto, 1967.

Iwate ken chūsei monjo. Compiled by Iwate ken kyōiku iinkai. 3 vols. Morioka, 1960–68.

Kagoshima ken shiryō, kyūki zatsuroku zenpen. Compiled by Kagoshima ken ishin shiryō hensanjo. 2 vols. Tokyo, 1979–80.

Kaisetsu chūsei Rusu ke monjo. Compiled by Mizusawa shiritsu toshokan. Mizusawa, 1979.

Kamakura bakufu saikyojō shū. Compiled by Seno Seiichirō. 2 vols. Tokyo, 1970–71.

Kamakura ibun. Compiled by Takeuchi Rizō. 37 vols. to date. Tokyo, 1971–.

Kanagawa kenshi, shiryō hen, kodai-chūsei. Compiled by Kanagawa ken kikaku chōsabu kenshi henshūshitsu. 4 vols. Yokohama, 1971–79.

Kashima jingū monjo. Compiled by Kashima jingū shamusho. Kashima, 1942.

Katsuodera monjo. Compiled by Ōsaka-fu shiseki meishō tennen kinenbutsu chōsakai. Osaka, 1931.

Koga ke monjo. Compiled by Kokugakuin daigaku toshokan. *Kokugakuin zasshi*; serialized monthly beginning May 1957.

Koji ruien. Compiled by Koji ruien kankōkai (reprint). 60 vols. Tokyo, 1931.

Kōsokabe shiryō. Compiled by Maeda Kazuo. Kōchi, 1964.

Kōyasan monjo. Compiled by Kōyasan shi hensanjo. 7 vols. Kyoto, 1936–41.

Kuchiki monjo. Compiled by Okuno Takahiro and Katō Tetsu. (Zoku Gunsho ruijū kanseikai, *Shiryō sanshū, komonjo hen*). 3 vols. to date. Tokyo, 1978–.

Kujō ke monjo. Compiled by Kunaichō shoryōbu. 7 vols. Tokyo, 1971–76.

Kumagai ke monjo. Compiled by Saitama kenritsu toshokan. Urawa, 1970.

Kutsuna ke monjo. Compiled by Kageura Tsutomu (*Iyo shiryō shūsei* 1). Matsuyama, 1964.

Masaki komonjo. Compiled by Jōmō kyōdoshi kenkyūkai. Maebara, 1938.

Minoo shishi, shiryō hen 1–2. Compiled by Minoo shishi hensan iinkai. Minoo, 1968–73.

Miyagi kenshi 30, shiryōshū 1. Compiled by Miyagi kenshi hensan iinkai. Sendai, 1965.

Munakata gunshi 2. Compiled by Itō Bishirō. Wakamatsu, 1932.

Nanbu ke monjo. Compiled by Washio Yorikata. Tokyo, 1939.

Nejime monjo. Compiled by Kawazoe Shōji (*Kyūshū shiryō sōsho* 14). 3 vols. Fukuoka, 1955–58.

Nitta shi konpon shiryō. Compiled by Chijiwa Minoru (revised edition). Tokyo, 1974.

Ogashima monjo—Ōkawa monjo—Madarashima monjo. Compiled by Seno Seiichirō (*Kyūshū shiryō sōsho* 11). Fukuoka, 1960.

Ōita ken shiryō. Compiled by Ōita ken shiryō kankōkai. 32 vols. to date. Ōita, 1960–.

Okayama ken komonjo shū. Compiled by Fujii Shun and Mizuno Kyōichirō. 3 vols. Okayama, 1953–56.

Okuyama-no-shō shiryōshū. Compiled by Inoue Toshio. Niigata, 1965.

Ōshū Hiraizumi monjo. Compiled by Iwate ken kyōiku iinkai. Morioka, 1958.

Ōta ku no komonjo, chūsei hen. Compiled by Ōta ku kyōiku iinkai. Tokyo, 1968.

Oyama shishi, shiryō hen, chūsei. Compiled by Oyama shishi hensan iinkai. Oyama, 1980.

Saga ken shiryō shūsei. Compiled by Saga kenshi hensan iinkai. 21 vols. to date. Saga, 1955–.

Saisho monjo. Compiled by Miyata Toshihiko (*Ibaragi komonjo shūsei* 2). Mito, 1962.

Sappan kyūki zatsuroku, zenpen. Compiled by Takeuchi Rizō (*Kyūshū shiryō sōsho* 1). 10 vols. Fukuoka, 1955–66.

Satsuma-no-kuni Isaku-no-shō shiryō. Compiled by Kōriyama Yoshimitsu (*Kyūshū shōen shiryō sōsho* 5). Tokyo, 1963.

Shinano shiryō. Compiled by Shinano shiryō kankōkai. 30 vols. Nagano, 1956–67.

Shinpen Kōshū komonjo. Compiled by Ogino Minahiko and Saitō Shunroku. 3 vols. Tokyo, 1966.

Shinpen Shinano shiryō sōsho 3. Compiled by Shinano shiryō kankōkai (reprint). Nagano, 1971.

Shinshū Shimane kenshi, shiryō hen 1. Compiled by Shimane ken. Hirata, 1966.

Shizuoka ken shiryō. Compiled by Shizuoka ken. 5 vols. Shizuoka, 1932–41.

Shōen shiryō. Compiled by Shimizu Masatake. 2 vols. Tokyo, 1933.

Shunjōbō Chōgen shiryō shūsei. Compiled by Kobayashi Takeshi. Tokyo, 1965.

Sōma monjo. Compiled by Toyoda Takeshi and Tashiro Osamu (Zoku Gunsho ruijū kanseikai, *Shiryō sanshū, komonjo hen*). Tokyo, 1979.

Sonpi bunmyaku. In *Shintei zōho kokushi taikei*. 5 vols. Tokyo, 1957–64.

Sōsha jinja monjo. Compiled by Miyata Toshihiko (*Ibaragi ken komonjo shūsei* 1). Mito, 1962.

Tochigi kenshi, shiryō hen, chūsei. Compiled by Tochigi kenshi hensan iinkai. 4 vols. Tochigi, 1973–79.

Tosa monjo kaisetsu. Compiled by Kimura Tokue. Tokyo, 1935.

Waseda daigaku shozō Ogino kenkyūshitsu shūshū monjo. Compiled by Waseda daigaku toshokan. 2 vols. Tokyo, 1978–80.

Zoku Gunsho ruijū 5–7, keizu bu. Compiled by Hanawa Hokiichi. 3 vols. Tokyo, 1904.

Zōtei Kano komonjo. Compiled by Heki Ken. Addendum compiled by Matsumoto Mitsumasa. Tokyo, 1972.

SECONDARY SOURCES IN JAPANESE

Aida Nirō. *Mōko shūrai no kenkyū*. Tokyo, 1958.

———. *Nihon no komonjo*. 2 vols. Tokyo, 1968 ed.

Endō Motoo. *Josei shi nōto*. Tokyo, 1976.

Fukuda Toyohiko. "Dainiji hōken kankei no keisei katei—Bungo no kuni Ōtomo shi no shujūsei o chūshin ni shite." In Yasuda Motohisa, ed., *Shoki hōkensei no kenkyū* (Tokyo, 1964): 1–64.

Fukuo Takeichirō. *Nihon kazoku shi seido gaisetsu*. Tokyo, 1972.

Gokeninsei kenkyūkai, comp. *Azuma kagami jinmei sakuin*. Tokyo, 1971.

Gomi Yoshio. "Chūsei shakai to gokenin—sōryōsei to gokeninsei." *Rekishi kyōiku* 8.7 (1960): 45–54.

———. "Kamakura bakufu no gokenin taisei—Kyōto ōbanyaku no tōsei o chūshin ni." *Rekishi kyōiku* 11.7 (1963): 12–19.

———. "Kamakura gokenin no banyaku kinshi ni tsuite." *Shigaku zasshi* 63.9 (1954); 28–45.
———. "Ōsumi gokenin ni tsuite." *Nihon rekishi* 130–31 (1959): 34–45, 21–32.
———. "Tōgoku bushi saisen no keiki—Satsuma no kuni no baai." *Rekishi kyōiku* 16.12 (1968): 20–26.
Haga Norihiko. *Sōryōsei.* Tokyo, 1966.
Hirayama Kōzō. *Wayo no kenkyū.* Tokyo, 1964.
Hosomi Sueo. *Tanba no shōen.* Tokyo, 1980.
Ishii Ryōsuke. "Chōshi sōzokusei." *Hōritsugaku taikai hōgaku riron* 84 (1939).
———. *Chūsei buke fudōsan soshō hō no kenkyū.* Tokyo, 1938.
———. "Chūsei kon'in hō." *Hōgaku kyōkai zasshi* 60.12 (1942).
Kawai Masaharu. "Chūsei bushidan no ujigami ujidera." In Ōkura Toyobumi, ed., *Chiiki shakai to shūkyō no shiteki kenkyū* (Tokyo, 1963): 4–28.
———. "Kamakura bakufu no seiritsu to saigoku no dōkō." *Rekishi kyōiku* 8.7 (1960): 30–36.
———. "Kamakura bushidan no kōzō." *Rekishi kyōiku* 16.12 (1968): 1–8.
Kawazoe Shōji. "Chinzei dangijo." *Kyūshū bunkashi kenkyūjo kiyō* 18 (1973): 1–49.
———. *Mōko shūrai kenkyū shiron.* Tokyo, 1977.
Kobayashi Hiroshi. "Iwami no kuni Masuda shi no ryōshusei ni tsuite." In Yasuda Motohisa, ed., *Shoki hōkensei no kenkyū* (Tokyo, 1964): 119–80.
Kōchi ken, comp. *Kōchi kenshi, kodai-chūsei hen.* Kōchi, 1971.
Matsumoto Shinpachirō. *Chūsei shakai no kenkyū.* Tokyo, 1956.
Megura Hiroshi. "Kamakura ki Kyūshū ni okeru gokenin oyobi zaichi ryōshu kenkyū." *Kyūshū shigaku* 30 (1965): 7–13.
Miyagawa Mitsuru. "Harima-no-kuni Yano-no-shō." In Shibata Minoru, ed., *Shōen sonraku no kōzō* (Tokyo, 1955): 11–196.
Munakata jinja fukkō kiseikai, comp. *Munakata jinja shi.* 3 vols. Tokyo, 1961–71.
Nagahara Keiji. "Tōgoku ni okeru sōryōsei no kaitai katei." In *idem, Nihon hōkensei seiritsu katei no kenkyū.* Tokyo, 1961.
Nakada Kaoru. "Chūsei no katoku sōzoku hō." In *idem, Hōseishi ronshū* 1. Tokyo, 1926.
Nishioka Toranosuke. *Shōen shi no kenkyū.* 3 vols. Tokyo, 1953–56.
Nitta Hideharu. "Aki no kuni Kobayakawa shi no sōryōsei ni tsuite." *Rekishigaku kenkyū* 153 (1951).
———. "Kamakura bakufu no gokenin seido." In Rekishigaku kenkyūkai and Nihonshi kenkyūkai, eds., *Nihon rekishi kōza* (Tokyo, 1968 edition), 2: 229–55.
Okino Shunji. *Awa no kuni shōen kō.* Tokyo, 1962.
Satō Shin'ichi. "Bakufuron." *Shin Nihon shi kōza* 4. Tokyo, 1949.
———. *Kamakura bakufu soshō seido no kenkyū.* Tokyo, 1943.
———. *Komonjogaku nyūmon.* Tokyo, 1971.
———. *Zōtei—Kamakura bakufu shugo seido no kenkyū.* Tokyo, 1971.

Seno Seiichirō. "Chinzei ni okeru Rokuhara tandai no kengen." In Takeuchi Rizō, ed., *Kyūshū shi kenkyū* (Tokyo, 1968): 155–74.

——. "Chinzei ni okeru tō—Matsuura tō no baai." *Rekishi kyōiku* 7.8 (1959): 66–72.

——. "Chinzei ni okeru Tōgoku gokenin." *Nihon rekishi* 168 (1962): 32–42.

——. "Hizen no kuni ni okeru Kamakura gokenin." *Nihon rekishi* 117 (1958): 30–40.

——. "Kamakura bakufu metsubō no rekishiteki zentei—Chinzei tandai saikyojō no bunseki." *Shien* 75 (1958): 75–105.

——. "Kamakura bakufu no seiritsu to Kyūshū chihō no dōkō." *Rekishi kyōiku* 8.7 (1960): 37–44.

Shimode Sekiyo. *Ishikawa ken no rekishi.* Tokyo, 1970.

Suzuki Hideo. "Katoku to sōryō no kan suru oboegaki." In Yasuda Motohisa, ed. *Shoki hōkensei no kenkyū* (Tokyo, 1964): 281–310.

Suzuki Kunihiro. "Zaichi ryōshusei no keisei zokuen genri ni tsuite." In Toyoda Takeshi hakushi koki kinenkai, comp. *Nihon chūsei no seiji to bunka* (Tokyo, 1980).

Takeuchi Rizō. *Shōen bunpu zu.* 2 vols. Tokyo, 1980–81.

Tanaka Minoru. "Kamakura shoki no seiji katei—Kenkyū nenkan o chūshin ni shite." *Rekishi kyōiku* 11.6 (1963): 19–26.

——. "Sanuki no kuni jitō gokenin ni tsuite." In Hōgetsu Keigo sensei kanreki kinenkai, comp. *Nihon shakai keizai shi kenkyū, kodai-chūsei hen* (Tokyo, 1968): 355–82.

Toyama Mikio, "Kamakura ki ni okeru Ōtomo shi no dōkō," *Rekishi kyōiku* 16.12 (1968): 61–67.

Toyoda Takeshi. *Bushidan to sonraku.* Tokyo, 1963.

Uwayokote Masataka. "Shiryō no tokushitsu." In Ishimoda Shō and Satō Shin'ichi, eds. *Chūsei no hō to kokka* (Tokyo, 1960): 295–327.

——. "Sōryōsei josetsu." *Jinbun* 8 (1962): 74–97.

SOURCES IN ENGLISH

Arnesen, Peter Judd. *The Medieval Japanese Daimyo.* New Haven, Conn., 1979.

——. "The Struggle for Lordship in Late Heian Japan: The Case of Aki." *The Journal of Japanese Studies* 10.1 (Winter 1984): 101–41.

Asakawa, Kan'ichi. *The Documents of Iriki.* Tokyo, 1955.

Bloch, Marc. *Feudal Society.* 2 vols. Chicago, 1964.

Bolitho, Harold. *Treasures Among Men.* New Haven, Conn., 1974.

Butler, Kenneth D. "Woman of Power Behind the Kamakura Bakufu." In Murakami Hyoe and Thomas J. Harper, eds., *Great Historical Figures of Japan* (Tokyo, 1978): 91–101.

Gay, Suzanne. "The Kawashima: Warrior-Peasants of Medieval Japan." *Harvard Journal of Asiatic Studies* 46.1 (1986): 81–119.

Goble, Andrew. "Go-Daigo and the Kemmu Restoration." Ph.D. dissertation, Stanford University, 1987.

Goody, Jack. "Inheritance, Property, and Women." In *idem,* Joan Thirsk, and E. P. Thompson, eds., *Family and Inheritance: Rural Society in Western Europe, 1200–1800* (Cambridge, Eng., 1976).

———. *Production and Reproduction.* Cambridge, Eng., 1976.

———. *The Development of the Family and Marriage in Europe.* Cambridge, Eng., 1983.

Grossberg, Kenneth Alan. *Japan's Renaissance: The Politics of the Muromachi Bakufu.* Cambridge, Mass., 1981.

Hall, John Whitney. *Government and Local Power in Japan, 500–1700.* Princeton, N.J., 1966.

———. "Reflections on Murakami Yasusuke's '*Ie* Society as a Pattern of Civilization.'" *Journal of Japanese Studies* 11.1 (1985): 47–55.

Harrington, Lorraine F. "Social Control and the Significance of *Akutō*." In Jeffrey P. Mass, ed., *Court and Bakufu in Japan* (New Haven, Conn., 1982): 221–50.

Herlihy, David. *Medieval Households.* Cambridge, Mass., 1985.

Hori, Kyotsu. "The Economic and Political Effects of the Mongol Wars." In John W. Hall and Jeffrey P. Mass, eds., *Medieval Japan* (New Haven, Conn., 1974): 184–98.

Hurst, G. Cameron. "An Emperor Who Ruled as Well as Reigned: Temmu Tennō." In Murakami Hyoe and Thomas J. Harper, eds., *Great Historical Figures of Japan* (Tokyo, 1978): 16–27.

———. *Insei: Abdicated Sovereigns in the Politics of Late Heian Japan: 1086–1185.* New York, 1976.

Kanda, James. "Methods of Land Transfer in Medieval Japan." *Monumenta Nipponica* 33.4 (1978): 379–405.

Kiley, Cornelius J. "Estate and Property in the Late Heian Period." In John W. Hall and Jeffrey P. Mass, eds., *Medieval Japan* (New Haven, Conn., 1974): 109–24.

———. "Property and Political Authority in Early Medieval Japan." Ph.D. dissertation, Harvard University, 1970.

———. "The Imperial Court as a Legal Authority in the Kamakura Age." In Jeffrey P. Mass, ed., *Court and Bakufu in Japan* (New Haven, Conn., 1982): 29–44.

Mass, Jeffrey P. "*Jitō* Land Possession in the Thirteenth Century: The Case of Shitaji Chūbun." In John W. Hall and Jeffrey P. Mass, eds., *Medieval Japan* (New Haven, Conn., 1974): 157–83.

———. "Patterns of Provincial Inheritance in Late Heian Japan." *The Journal of Japanese Studies* 9.1 (1983); 57–95.

———. *The Development of Kamakura Rule, 1180–1250: A History with Documents.* Stanford, Calif., 1979.

———. "The Early Bakufu and Feudalism." In *idem,* ed., *Court and Bakufu in Japan* (New Haven, Conn., 1982): 123–42.

———. *The Kamakura Bakufu: A Study in Documents.* Stanford, Calif., 1976.

————. *Warrior Government in Early Medieval Japan: A Study of the Kamakura Bakufu, Shugo, and Jitō.* New Haven, Conn., 1974.

McCullough, William. "Japanese Marriage Institutions in the Heian Period." *Harvard Journal of Asiatic Studies* 27 (1967): 103–67.

Miller, Richard J. *Japan's First Bureaucracy: A Study of Eighth Century Government.* Ithaca, N.Y., 1978.

Miyagawa, Mitsuru. "From Shōen to Chigyō: Proprietary Lordship and the Structure of Local Power." In John Whitney Hall and Toyoda Takeshi, eds., *Japan in the Muromachi Age* (Berkeley, Calif., 1977): 89–105.

Murakami, Yasusuke. "*Ie* Society as a Pattern of Civilization." *Journal of Japanese Studies* 10.2 (Summer 1984): 281–363.

Sansom, George B. *A History of Japan to 1334.* Stanford, Calif., 1958.

Sheehan, Michael M. *The Will in Medieval England.* Toronto, 1963.

Shinoda, Minoru. *The Founding of the Kamakura Shogunate, 1180–85.* New York, 1960.

Steenstrup, Carl. *Hōjō Shigetoki (1198–1261) and his Role in the History of Political and Ethical Ideas in Japan.* London, 1979.

————. "Sata Mirensho: A Fourteenth Century Law Primer." *Monumenta Nipponica* 35.4 (1980): 405–35.

Toby, Ronald P. "Why Leave Nara? Kammu and the Transfer of the Capital." *Monumenta Nipponica,* 40.3 (1985): 331–47.

Tonomura, Hitomi. "Women and Property in a Warrior Society: Patterns of Inheritance and Socio-Political Change in Early Medieval Japan." M.A. thesis, University of Oregon, 1979.

Totman, Conrad. *Politics in the Tokugawa Bakufu.* Cambridge, Mass., 1967.

Varley, H. Paul. "The Hōjō Family and Succession to Power." In Jeffrey P. Mass, ed., *Court and Bakufu in Japan* (New Haven, Conn., 1982): 143–67.

————. *The Ōnin War.* New York, 1967.

Wakita, Haruko. "Marriage and Property in Premodern Japan from the Perspective of Women's History." *The Journal of Japanese Studies* 10.1 (Winter 1984): 73–99.

Whitelock, Dorothy, ed. *Anglo-Saxon Wills.* Cambridge, Eng., 1930.

INDEX

In this index an "f" after a number indicates a separate reference on the next page, and an "ff" indicates separate references on the next two pages. A continuous discussion over two or more pages is indicated by a span of page numbers, e.g., "pp. 57–58." *Passim* is used for a cluster of references in close but not consecutive sequence.

Library of Congress Cataloging-in-Publication Data

Mass, Jeffrey P.
  Lordship and inheritance in Early Medieval Japan : a study of
the Kamakura Soryō system / Jeffrey P. Mass.
     p.   cm.
  Bibliography : p.
  Includes indexes.
  ISBN 0-8047-1540-8 (alk. paper)
     1. Japan—Politics and government—1185–1333.
2. Primogeniture—Japan—History.   3. Inheritance and
succession—Japan—History.   4. Land tenure—Japan—History.
5. Power (Social sciences)
I. Title.
DS859.M245 1989
952'.021—dc19   88-31214
                                                      CIP